Crucible of American Democracy

American Political Thought
edited by
Wilson Carey McWilliams and Lance Banning

Crucible of American Democracy

The Struggle to Fuse Egalitarianism & Capitalism in Jeffersonian Pennsylvania

Andrew Shankman

 UNIVERSITY PRESS OF KANSAS

Published by the University Press of Kansas (Lawrence, Kansas 66049), which was organized by the Kansas Board of Regents and is operated and funded by Emporia State University, Fort Hays State University, Kansas State University, Pittsburg State University, the University of Kansas, and Wichita State University

Library of Congress Cataloging-in-Publication Data

Shankman, Andrew, 1970–
    Crucible of American democracy : the struggle to fuse egalitarianism and capitalism in Jeffersonian Pennsylvania / Andrew Shankman.
        p.   cm. — (American political thought)
    Includes bibliographical references and index.
        ISBN 0-7006-1304-8 (cloth : alk. paper)
    1. Republican Party (Pa. : 1792–1828   2. Political parties—Pennsylvania—History.   3. Pennsylvania—Politics and government—1775–1865.   I. Title. II. Series.
        JK2318.P5S43   2004
        324.2732´6´09748—dc22   2003020238

British Library Cataloguing in Publication Data is available.

Printed in the United States of America

10 9 8 7 6 5 4 3 2 1

The paper used in this publication meets the minimum requirements of the American National Standard for Permanence of Paper for Printed Library Materials Z39.48-1984.

Contents

Preface and Acknowledgments

I began the thinking that resulted in *Crucible of American Democracy* during the middle 1990s. The cold war had recently ended, and many in the West were talking blithely about the last impediments to democracy being swept away. It struck me then (and it strikes me now, as the second week of the second war with Iraq begins) that democracy is not such an easy thing to establish. Perhaps Americans expect it to be so because we have paid insufficient attention to the difficulties and complexities involved in our nation's initial experience with it. I wrote this book because I wanted to know whether the experience with democracy during the nation's formative years was as smooth and straightforward as many early twenty-first-century policy makers expect it to be throughout the world.

From the broad to the specific, I also wrote this book to answer a second question: Why did Pennsylvania Jeffersonians argue so bitterly with each other? Answering this narrower question helped me explore my broader one. I knew as I began my research that Pennsylvania had experimented with democracy during and after the American Revolution. I knew that Pennsylvania had among the most complex economic and social relations of any of the colonies turned states. And I knew that it had a rich newspaper culture and tradition of popular politics. Pennsylvania, I believed, was an ideal place to watch people building democracy, and the sustained arguments among Pennsylvania Jeffersonians, I suspected, reflected the social, economic, and political challenges of trying to do it.

In this book I explored the emergence of democracy by examining the struggles among Pennsylvania Jeffersonians. I was quite conscious when conceiving and writing it that discussing these issues allowed me to consider some of the most significant questions that historians of the early national period had been asking. The scholars whose work most interested me sought the intellectual and ideological traditions and developments that shaped Jeffersonian political thought and the reasons that democracy and capitalism were fused during this era. It was the Jeffersonian achievement in effecting this fusion that made the nation what it became, which in our time (among other things) is one that believes it can rather easily spread this merging of political and economic practices to the rest of the world.

In writing this book my view was confirmed that Pennsylvania provided rich material for considering these issues. With regard to the advent of democracy, its fusion with capitalism, the anticipated and unanticipated consequences, and the many benefits and causes for regret, Pennsylvania's Jeffersonians had a tale to tell. Democracy was difficult then, and it remains so today. Unprecedented wealth and military might little short of infinite, in this regard, change nothing.

I have been profoundly aware in writing this book how much care has been taken in educating me. I was privileged to earn a B.A. at Northern Illinois University when its history department housed an unequaled assemblage of scholars of early America. Alfred F. Young, Alan Kulikoff, and above all Stephen Foster showed me that early America was fascinating. Dr. Foster made me realize how careful and scrupulous one needs to be when studying the ideas of the past. From him I learned it is imperative to remember that they were at least as smart and just as complex as are we. Finally, Dr. Foster, in his endearing and laconic way, left no room for doubt when as a nervous junior I bravely ventured to his office and explained that I planned to go to graduate school to study early American history. Foster nodded impatiently, as if this had all been settled long ago, and responded, "Yes, yes, of course, very sensible."

At NIU it was first made clear to me how connected early America was to Britain and the wider Western world. I was lucky enough to study early modern England with C. H. George, France with William H. Beik and Harvey Smith, and German central Europe with Elaine Spencer. From them, and especially from Bill Beik, I learned that those who study ideas and political economy ignore social history at their peril.

I do not know of a more exciting place to study the early modern anglophone world than Princeton University in the early and middle 1990s. From my arrival, I was expected to read more than I had ever thought possible (I soon learned otherwise). I was challenged, encouraged, argued with, and quite simply included. I learned about early modern England from the wonderful late Lawrence Stone and the equally wonderful Peter Lake. Peter Lake in particular wrote brilliantly the kind of history that I appreciate most. Through discussion and example he taught me that scholars must earn the right to think big and that they do so by allowing the most careful, meticulous, and, when necessary, plodding research to lead them step by step from myopia. Also at Princeton I benefited enormously from the wisdom and friendship (often blended together) of William Chester Jordan, Paul Cohen, Jerry Podair, Stephen Aron, Brad Verter, Johannes Wolfhart, and Evan Haefeli. In addition, Sean Wilentz and Dirk Hartog helped me to shape my ideas and advised me well through the writing of my dissertation. Toward the end of my time at Princeton, Gordon S. Wood of Brown University, quite graciously to a stranger, agreed to sit on my committee as the outside reader.

While at Princeton I benefited enormously from my friendship with David Como, and it was a wonderful circumstance that brought us both to Chicago for the years 1998 and 1999. Dave is one of the most intellectually able people I have known. His eagerness to answer my questions about Stuart England and his insistence that I explain my period to him have forced me to confront what I do not know and to keep learning.

One of the happiest results of coming to Princeton was becoming a friend of Ignacio and Anjali Gallup-Diaz. I doubt any of us expected to end up thinking as we do or to agree with each other about so many of the things that we have experienced. But their friendship has provided me precisely what I hoped to find when I went in search of a broader and more satisfying world.

By the happiest coincidence Elspeth Carruthers and Cliff Doerksen have also made the move from Princeton to Chicago. From my first graduate seminar Elspeth has been the kindest and most reliable friend. Her unerring judgment and humor were essential to me throughout the process of writing this book, and I am lucky that she lived and lives about a fifteen-minute walk from my living room. Cliff Doerksen has been a friend almost from the moment we met. From explaining to Carlo Ginzburg that Aristotle was a Greek philosopher, to discussing the complexities of fragging poststructuralist sergeants in Nam, to leading forced marches to some of the worst hole-in-the-wall eateries on Chicago's north side, Cliff is the funniest and wittiest person I know. He is also a brilliant critic and has read different drafts of much of what became this book.

The day after I arrived in Princeton I met Jacob Cogan and soon after that Sarah Lytle. None of my peers has been a closer friend or helped me more than Jacob. Jacob and I share most of the same intellectual interests. I have been back and forth with him about my ideas since 1992. He has always seemed just a bit ahead of me and is forever willing to help me with what he has already learned how to do. By showing me how to survive in the Ivy League, by suggesting which newspapers and archives to begin with, and by providing a bed week after week in Philadelphia, Jacob made this book immeasurably less difficult to write. I have taken advantage of Jacob's and Sarah's hospitality from Philadelphia to Boston, and now that they live in the same city as the Library of Congress, they will never be rid of me.

When I moved from Princeton to Chicago in 1998, I began an odd half-life that ended two years ago and about which the less said the better. But during a difficult time I made two wonderful friends who helped keep me in the proper frame of mind to remain productive. Doug Montagna is one of the world's true eccentrics and also a deeply curious and engaged intellectual. He was full of questions about my work and my views on early American history. His humor, hospitality, and general view of things kept me laughing and will continue to do so.

In 1999 I met Paul Murphy, and for reasons that he and I know well, I don't see how I would have managed for half of each week (not counting summers) for the next three years without him. There is none more generous, more devoted to the life of the mind, or more eager to talk about history, politics, and culture than my good friend Paul. My conviction that small-group work is the refuge of charlatans is proved beyond a doubt since this wise man agrees.

In 2002 it was my privilege to join the history department of Northeastern Illinois University in Chicago, and I completed the final revisions of this book in that congenial setting. My colleagues Greg Singleton, Susan Rosa, Chuck Steinwedel, Mike Tuck, Zack Schiffman, June Sochen, Patrick Miller, Steve Riess, and Andy Eisenberg are a wonderful and vital group, as are the members of our department staff, Margie Greif and Erin Postilion-Dony. Impressive and accomplished scholars, the members of my department understand that good teaching is only possible alongside the commitment to scholarship, that city air makes you free, and that PowerPoint is the work of the devil. I belong where I am and am happy to be there. I have my fine colleagues to thank for it.

One of the many reasons to write and publish is the opportunity it brings to meet other scholars. In two different versions, Herb Sloan read and helped me to improve this book. Lance Banning has been as good a friend as this book has had and as important a mentor as its author will ever get. From a conference paper of mine that he read to his encouragement and welcome when I sent him my manuscript to read and consider, he has been committed to making this book as good as it could be and to seeing it published. Equally generous has been John Lauritz Larson. He read every page of this book in manuscript and gave freely of his powerful critical abilities and deep learning. Throughout the process of revising, Lance Banning and John L. Larson have been precisely what every junior scholar hopes leading figures in his field will be. By pushing me to push myself, by prodding me to think through my ideas one final time, they have helped me to make my argument as complete as I am able to make it.

During this process Fred Woodward and his staff at the University Press of Kansas have been encouraging, patient, professional, and kind. Fred Woodward has always understood the anxiety of a young scholar in the final stages of producing a first book. I never understood how essential a compassionate and committed editor was until I needed one.

My mother, Kathleen Shankman, has always supported and valued my efforts and the world of scholarship in general. In addition to always wanting to know what I was thinking and writing, in her capacity as a professional editor with over thirty years' experience, she read my manuscript and did much to help make it seaworthy.

I began to revise this book when I moved to Chicago in 1998. Because I had returned to Illinois, I was able to renew two very dear friendships with Leo Bacino and Carl Parrini. Leo was my very first college teaching assistant and more than any other person introduced me to serious students of history. My first efforts to think like a scholar happened with Leo, and more than anyone he showed me that people like us, young men from the Midwest attending a not particularly prestigious university, belonged in the world of the life of the mind. A French Catholic priest once said in answer to a question about what he had learned in forty years of pursuing his calling that "fundamentally there are no adults." Since I first met Leo, I have come to know an exception to that rule.

When I returned to Illinois in 1998, Leo and I made sure to begin visiting Dr. Carl Parrini. If Leo showed me that I should become serious, Dr. Parrini showed me what I should do with this new resolve. He is one of the three people without whom this book would not exist. Dr. Parrini digs deep, he taught me the meaning of political economy, and he introduced me to this fascinating subject for the early national period. After studying with him for my entire junior year, I was able to go to Stephen Foster to tell him my plans and hear how sensible my decision was. My scholarly life is a significant part of what brings me joy, and Carl Parrini introduced me to it.

I could not have begun to perceive what became this book without John Murrin. I first met John in 1992, and from that lunch in a Chicago coffee shop until yesterday he has never stopped doing whatever he could to teach and assist me. Virtually every page of this book was written with some comment or query of his in mind. His ability to draw connections, to see what was important and interesting in my findings when I could not, and to say precisely the right thing at the right time comes from a generosity and erudition that I have never found so completely fused in such heaping quantities in anyone else. I cannot imagine whom I would have rather studied with, been advised by, first gone with my ideas to, batted behind, asked advice of, or depended on. For reasons that one cannot understand without knowing him, John always reminds me of the story told by Dylan Thomas about the Welsh shepherd who, when asked why from within fairy rings he slaughtered his finest sheep to the full moon to protect his flocks, replied, "I'd be a damn fool if I didn't." From the moment we met, I realized that here was a teacher, and I'd be a damn fool if I hadn't.

Finally I would like to thank my wife, Cathy Comrie. Cathy knows the person that no one else does. Every single day that this book has been with me, Cathy's care and love have led me to it or away from it depending on what I needed at the time. I am so lucky to have such a beautiful and lifelong friend. Because of her I have known calm and peace and strength and home. And without them all, I could not write. I was so young when we first met and on the edge of such a broader and more fulfilling world. And none of it, not one thing in it, would mean anything without her.

Introduction

The Crucible of Conflict

On March 28, 1803, a concerned Thomas Jefferson wrote to his secretary of the Treasury, the Pennsylvanian Albert Gallatin, that he had "for some time been satisfied a schism was taking place in Pennsylvania between moderates and high flyers." President Jefferson was not describing the still acrimonious Federalist and Republican political conflict of the 1790s, for he feared that "the same [split that he perceived in Pennsylvania] will take place in Congress . . . and we must expect a division of some kind in other states as soon as the Republicans shall be so strong as to fear no other enemy."[1]

That there were moderates and high flyers and bitter conflict among Pennsylvania Jeffersonians by 1803 was a serious problem, for after 1800 Jeffersonians had expected conflict to rapidly disappear. The Jeffersonian opposition had cohered during the 1790s, in Pennsylvania as elsewhere, around the assumption that a self-interested, antirepublican faction had hijacked political power for the purpose of destroying liberty.[2] The vicious behavior of the Federalists did provoke complex results, it was true. These results were so complex that at times even members of the Jeffersonian opposition might not agree about how best to respond to them. But it was not to be doubted that the fundamental source of conflict and discord was Federalist tyranny. Once the people—the many—defeated the efforts of the interested few, the Republic would return to its natural state. In this natural state the Republic would be at peace, it would promote a uniformity of interests among the people, and it would pursue a straightforward and easily comprehended common good that citizens could collectively move toward and in which they could all mutually share. If there were moderates and high flyers among the people in Pennsylvania, indeed if there was conflict of any kind, then something had gone seriously wrong.

The conflict that Jefferson noted in 1803 began in Pennsylvania almost

1

immediately after Jeffersonian triumph and continued to influence the contours of political thought and behavior in Pennsylvania well into the 1830s. Though conflict among Jeffersonians demonstrated a grave problem, that conflict was not going away. Debates among those who conceived and articulated Jeffersonian political thought in Pennsylvania quickly revolved around the slippery concept of democracy. By 1803 (profoundly precociously), all Pennsylvania Jeffersonians believed that Jeffersonian victory meant, somehow and in some way, that the state and the nation both needed to be democracies. But this apparent consensus produced deep conflicts. For it quickly became apparent that Pennsylvania Jeffersonians had a variety of competing, even mutually exclusive, definitions of democracy. They agreed they wanted it. But they disagreed about how it was best structured, what it was supposed to do, and in which ways the fundamental principles of a democratic people intersected with the daily fluctuating needs and desires of temporary majorities of that people.

After 1803, Pennsylvania Jeffersonians discovered that they could not even agree about who should decide legal disputes and to what degree (or whether) individuals and private property rights should be accountable to community and majority desires. Indeed, it became a matter for debate whether it was acceptable to make constitutional fundamental law in a society where popular sovereignty suggested that majorities ruled. Though once the Federalists were defeated there was no longer supposed to be conflict, the struggles among Pennsylvania Jeffersonians dealt with the most substantive and fundamental legal, political, and economic issues that they could imagine.

That after Jeffersonian victory everything suddenly seemed subject to debate and liable to be rethought and restructured surprised Pennsylvania Jeffersonians as much as it did their president. For during the 1790s the Jeffersonians of Pennsylvania had become just as committed as Jefferson himself to the explanatory power of the category "the people." All Pennsylvania Jeffersonians agreed that "the people" (or the citizenry) was that homogeneous group invested with the right to vote and possess property. It was the needs of this group that republics existed to protect and foster. These needs could certainly be threatened. Indeed, given the Jeffersonian understanding of the nature of power inherited from commonwealth thought, it was likely that a republic's ability to protect the people's needs would be in constant danger.[3] But Pennsylvania Jeffersonians agreed with their fellows that threats to the people could not come from within that category; the idea itself was nonsense.

Rather, threats to the people came from the great and powerful few who sought to set themselves above the people and who pursued political power because it provided the artificial means to create and then consolidate unnatural distinctions. Once the people seized power and established democracy, these artificial avenues to political (and so eventually economic and social) inequality would be closed. Thus democracy, by definition, was the end of conflict and the beginning of the natural condition of the homogeneous people. Without the interference of an interested few wielding decision-making power, none would be able to acquire wealth and power beyond their own natural abilities to labor, accumulate, and influence. Regardless of how talented a citizen was, Pennsylvania Jeffersonians assumed that talent could never produce the sorts of distinctions that could upset the fundamental independence of each citizen — what Pennsylvania Jeffersonians referred to as "that happy mediocrity of condition."[4] Inequities in wealth and power exposed the absence of democracy. Once each citizen was forced to rely solely on his own talents, those distinctions that remained would be negligible. The rough equality of condition, and the fundamental material independence that was the natural state of democracy, would therefore reinforce that "the people" was a homogeneous category whose needs and interests could always be simultaneously met with a uniform pursuit of the public good.

A fine way to investigate the assumptions about democracy that came to shape the political thought of Pennsylvania Jeffersonians after 1790 is to examine a fairly well-known exchange, the 1786 debate between William Findley and Robert Morris concerning whether the Pennsylvania legislature should recharter the Bank of North America.[5] Findley, a western Pennsylvanian, became a key Jeffersonian leader during the 1790s and served as a senator after the Jeffersonian triumph. In his 1786 remarks he revealed many of the assumptions that those who eventually became Pennsylvania Jeffersonians made about "the people" as a category, and the source of the threats these Jeffersonians perceived to the needs of those they included in that category.

Findley's remarks also revealed a fatal flaw in his and fellow Jeffersonians' political thought. Even as Findley spoke, the people included within the category "the people" were rapidly creating and participating in processes that caused them to experience increasingly diverse social and economic conditions. These processes of accumulation, profit-seeking, and increasingly unequal distribution of the benefits that came with development of the domestic economy showed that those within the category "the people" were quite capable of producing the social distinctions Jeffersonian thinkers said that their actions would never cause. Jeffersonian thinkers in Pennsylvania, then, struggled to maintain egalitarianism even as the assumptions they held about what made it possible were exposed as fallacious. Long after it made any sense to do so, Jeffersonian thinkers in Pennsylvania would generalize about the homogeneous category "the people" while actual people's pursuit of capitalism was rendering the conditions that citizens experienced ever more heterogeneous. As various factions of Jeffersonians struggled to conceive ways to pursue the needs of "the people," the efforts of each faction could increasingly appeal only to a portion of what was no longer a homogeneous category. The result was democratically induced conflict, something that Pennsylvania's Jeffersonians continued to maintain was impossible.

In his debate with Robert Morris, the future Jeffersonian Findley unwittingly revealed virtually all the assumptions that would shape, and eventually expose the flaws of, Pennsylvania Jeffersonian political thought. Findley's primary objective in 1786 was to ensure that Pennsylvania remained what he identified as a democracy. For reasons that he sought to explain, Findley had concluded by 1786 that permitting the Bank of North America to remain in business would hinder this all-important goal of maintaining democracy. Thus Findley insisted, "The government of Pennsylvania being a democracy, the bank is inconsistent with the bill of rights thereof, which says the government is not instituted for the emolument of any man, family, or set of men. Therefore, the institution being a monopoly, and having a natural tendency, by affording the means, to promote a spirit of monopolizing, is inconsistent not only with the frame but the spirit of our government."[6]

But what was the spirit of this government that Findley called democracy? What did democracy require in order for this spirit to survive? First, Findley made clear that it would be difficult to guarantee the survival of democracy as it was understood by the ancients, for "we are too unequal in wealth to render a perfect democracy suitable to our circumstances."[7] Perfect democracy required perfect equality, not just before the law but also in wealth, in property. Pennsylvanians were not perfectly equal. But the Bank of North America was an immense concentration of wealth. This concentration was more dangerous to democratic Pennsylvania than it would have been to a nondemocratic polity because Pennsylvanians were "so equal in wealth, power, etc. that we have no counterpoise sufficient to check or control an institution of such vast influence and magnitude."[8] Perfect democracy required perfect equality in all things, which did not exist in Pennsylvania. But in Pennsylvania in 1786, according to Findley, there was a great deal of equality when compared with other societies in the past and the present. Property was widely distributed, Findley argued, and though "enormous wealth possessed by individuals, has always had its influence and danger in free states," in Pennsylvania there was independence and equality enough that citizens were rarely threatened by enormous wealth. In 1786 no men or group of men possessed the enormous wealth that allowed them to undermine equality and shape society to serve their private needs. Property and wealth were so important, Findley suggested, that every citizen had to possess some, and the closer the size of each citizen's holdings was to the size of others, the better.

All citizens had to be free to pursue wealth for the sake of democracy, which remained healthy only if it remained as close to the perfect equality of perfect democracy as was humanly possible. Thus, "wealth in many hands operates as many checks: for in numberless instances, one wealthy man has control over another."[9] What commitments motivated the citizen who was free of the dependence and inequality inevitable when a few possessed great wealth? The independent citizen, Findley insisted, was motivated by the desire to preserve the conditions that allowed all citizens to remain independent. He pursued his modest wealth so that he could remain the independent, engaged, and useful citizen who could participate in a democracy that forever perpetuated the social and economic conditions of independence and near equality. In the context of continued near equality, it was necessary to defend private property and the pursuit of wealth. But the spirit of democracy could be preserved only if this near equality survived. Thus one pursued one's interests precisely to the point where one could independently contribute to a politics that worked to ensure that none became too wealthy or mighty.

When wealth in many hands operated as many checks, Findley explained, "every man in the disposal of his own wealth, will act upon his own principles. His virtue, his honour, his sympathy, and generosity, will influence his disposals and designs, and he is in a state of personal responsibility."[10] Findley did not eschew commitment to a commonweal larger than his personal interests. Rather, he imagined a future of widespread property ownership and independence. Widespread independence inculcated in each citizen the desire to work to guarantee that none were denied the social and economic conditions that allowed for true democratic citizenship.

For Findley, the primary components of this democratic citizenship were the pursuit of virtue and devotion to needs larger than the self. But in his debate with Robert Morris, Findley did reject the idea that powerful and wealthy gentlemen could be the source of that virtue and devotion. Wealth in many hands checked avarice and encouraged quiet living, sober commitment to the community, generosity, and sympathy for fellow citizens. But

> when such an unlimited institution [as the Bank of North America] is erected with such a capital, for the sole purpose of increasing wealth, it must operate according to its principle; and being in the hands of many, having only one point of view, and being put in trust, the personal responsibility arising from the principles of honor, generosity, etc., can have no place. The special temper of the institution pervades all its operations, and thus like a snowball perpetually rolled, it must continually increase its dimensions and influence.[11]

At this point Findley denounced the bank as only a devoted democrat could. The Pennsylvania legislature had to prevent recharter because "this institution having no principle but that of avarice, which dries and shrivels up all the manly — all the generous feelings of the human soul will never be varied in its object."[12]

Democracy could survive, then, only in a particular social and economic context. The vast majority of citizens had to live in near equality, productive property had to be widely distributed, and those conditions would instill in all citizens the virtue and responsibility that encouraged them to preserve the widespread ownership of productive property and near equality. Democracy could exist only in the social and economic context of this near equality. But that context, since it allowed for democracy, created a politics that gave citizens the power to preserve the social and economic near equality that made democracy possible. This was what Findley was doing that day in 1786: wielding democratic power to preserve as near a social and economic equality as Pennsylvania could manage.

Democrats such as Findley understood that the easiest way to preserve democracy was to mandate perfect equality. Enforced equality was desirable in the abstract, since "our wealth is less equal than our kind of government seems to require." But mandating perfect equality would destroy respect for private property, and private property, when widely held, was the foundation of independence and justice. Findley acknowledged, therefore, that "agrarian laws are unjust in our present situation."[13] How, then, would democracy be preserved? It would be preserved by understanding that though Pennsylvania did not, and never would, enjoy perfect equality, it was closer to that state in 1786 than most societies ever were or could be. The conditions for a very good, if not a perfect, democracy currently existed. The responsibility of democrats, happily, was not to create the conditions for a very good democracy, but to prevent new developments that in the future could undermine those conditions.

The development that threatened to do so in 1786 was Morris's bank. If the legislature agreed to charter "away portions of either the privileges or power of the state — if they may incorporate bodies for the sole purpose of gain with the power of making bye-laws, — and cannot disannul their own deed, and restore to the citizens their right of equal protection, power, privilege, and influence, — the consequence is, that some foolish and wanton assembly may parcel out the commonwealth into little aristocracies, and so overturn the nature of our government without remedy."[14] Chartering the bank would allow a few the special, artificial, and privileged means to acquire wealth. They could amass wealth beyond the capacity of their fellow citizens to equal or even approximate their holdings. Any who cared for democracy had to oppose such artificial advantage. It was, in Findley's view, "absurd" for the legislature "to lend its special aid in so partial a manner, to wealth, to give it that additional force and spring, which it must derive from an almost unlimited charter. Can any gentleman avoid seeing this to be eventually and effectually overturning our government? Democracy must fall before it. Wealth is its foundation, and gain its object and design."[15]

But what if the legislature withheld the artificial aids and privileges that allowed a few to amass more wealth than their fellow citizens could? Findley suggested that the natural state in Pennsylvania was the near equality that existed in 1786, and that allowed for a very good democracy. What could upset this very good democracy was interested, antidemocratic use of political power. If a few artificially manipulated political power, they could use it to acquire wealth beyond their own capacity to produce it. If the state's political power continued to be wielded democratically, then all citizens would remain confined within their own talents and industry. But, crucially, they would be forced to rely on their own talents and industry in the democratic context of Pennsylvania. In this context of available resources, and general respect for ensuring their widespread availability, citizens would be able to earn their independence. By achieving it themselves, they would continue to learn and perpetuate the values that prized independence: personal responsibility for the commonwealth, equality, generosity, and thus justice and democracy. The ways in which Pennsylvania's citizens amassed wealth would instill the beliefs that taught them to despise great wealth.

Forcing each individual to rely on his own industry in a social and economic context where industriousness was likely to produce independence, a rough equality of condition, and no more than that, would, in salutary fashion, stigmatize the desire to possess great wealth. That was why Findley sought to discredit Morris. Rendering the desire to possess great wealth culturally obnoxious was essential for democracy. For, Findley noted, "great wealth seems, even with individuals, to have a tendency to monopolizing. It was the saying of a wise writer, when riches increase, they are increased that have them — increased in the appetite for riches and in their endeavors to procure them."[16] Celebrating independence and holding the desire for great wealth in contempt stimulated citizens to seek a democratic politics that prevented the conditions that could upset near equality and widespread independence. These values, and the conditions they produced, allowed for a very good democracy. Fortunately, agrarian laws were unnecessary. Pennsylvanians did not have to establish the conditions for a very good democracy; they merely had to preserve them. And the most important way to do that was to understand that the gravest threat to the social and economic conditions necessary for a very good democracy was the undemocratic use of political power, the only source of great and dangerously unequal possession of wealth. Findley called for the pursuit of modest wealth because he distinguished the citizens' interest in preserving democratic independence from the desire of an individual citizen to be acquisitive. Acquiring wealth was not a positive good, nor was it an end in itself. Indeed, wealth was to be scorned as sordid and undignified except in a very particular context of equality and democracy, a context where the possibility of accumulating much wealth was sharply limited.

The problem with this argument for the ability of the homogeneous democratic people to naturally perpetuate a rough equality of condition was that all around Findley in Pennsylvania, reality showed that it was not true. During the 1780s and 1790s in Philadelphia, in its hinterland, and even in Findley's West, social and economic complexity and inequality increasingly characterized Pennsylvania.[17] By the late 1790s and early 1800s, far too many of those citizens included within the Jeffersonian category "the people" experienced conditions that Findley's democratic theories held would destroy democracy. Jeffersonians such as Findley believed that they understood why. Robert Morris threatened "the people" in Pennsylvania in 1786 with a bank. His Federalist Party threatened "the people" throughout the nation during the 1790s by wielding power.

The problem for Jeffersonians, and it was most acute in Pennsylvania, the state with the most developed economy and most complex social relations in the new nation, was that this analysis made just enough sense to discourage Jeffersonians from looking further or thinking harder.[18] Federalist policies were never the sole (or even the most critical) source of economic differentiation and social complexity in early national Pennsylvania or the rest of the United States. Far more significant were the myriad actions, aspirations, efforts, impulses, and dreams of the very diverse people about whom the makers of Jeffersonian political thought generalized.[19] Rapidly after 1800, Pennsylvania Jeffersonians could no longer cite Federalist policy as the reason that William Findley's democracy was not emerging naturally. Since it was not, the methods for building democracy had to be rethought. During this process, Pennsylvania Jeffersonians found themselves having the disagreements about democracy discussed previously. The desire to maintain egalitarianism in the presence of capitalism led to sustained and increasingly bitter struggles over precisely what kind of democracy would (if indeed it could) nurture both.

As "the people" increasingly confounded the generalizations Pennsylvania's Jeffersonians made about them, all Pennsylvania Jeffersonians continued to have one thing in common. None of the various factions that emerged during these debates wanted to rethink the category "the people." Instead, all the various competing groups sought to articulate ever more precise definitions of democracy that could, at long last, fit the needs of "the people," which remained for a considerable time in Pennsylvania Jeffersonian political thought a homogeneous category.

Debating the proper definition of democracy became a process by itself that drove the articulation of Jeffersonian political thought — a process that I call the crucible of conflict. The need to triumph in debate and to defeat opponents' ideas led all the Pennsylvania Jeffersonians participating in these debates in directions they did not foresee and toward conclusions that produced outcomes they did not desire. This process of ideological formation — the crucible of conflict — forced particular Pennsylvania Jeffersonians to respond to ideas that threatened deeply held principles. As they articulated responses, their opponents had no choice but to counter with new challenges. The crucible of conflict created a volatile and fluid situation where ideas were constantly rethought and where, at times in the space of mere months, those within it could find themselves swearing to positions they had never initially expected to take. This vital process of ideological formation drove a frantic conceptualizing and reconceptualizing of (what it became clear were) profoundly dubious initial assumptions and slippery first principles. The crucible of conflict ensured that the period of debate among Pennsylvania Jeffersonians amounted to an era of intense ideological fluctuation and creativity.

Recognizing this period as such an era (and for me that recognition came only slowly) led me to rethink how the process of articulating Jeffersonian political thought in Pennsylvania occurred and what the content of that thought was. In *Crucible of American Democracy*, I explore why democracy became so important to Jeffersonians in Pennsylvania. I wanted to find out what the Jeffersonians who pursued democracy thought it was. And I wanted to discover why, though they could all agree that democracy was a good thing, their pursuit of it led to bitter conflict. As I studied the discussions of those Pennsylvanians who talked in a sustained way about what democracy was and why it was important, I developed two insights. First, the process of defining democracy was driven by different Pennsylvania Jeffersonians' competing conceptions of it. Second, this process of definition revealed a broader world of actors who participated in the formation and articulation of Jeffersonian political thought than studies of Jeffersonian political ideas have suggested.

My research revealed that, as Jeffersonian ideas were being worked out by Jeffersonians, figures other than those who were nationally prominent (and well studied), many at the local level, often not holders of formal offices, played significant roles in conceiving the content of Jeffersonian political thought. My goal was to understand this content of Jeffersonian political thought, and why it was so preoccupied with questions regarding the meaning of democracy and the causes of inequality among citizens. As I explored these questions, I let the sources where the debates took place lead me to other relevant sources that helped shed light on how the content of Jeffersonian political thought came to be what it was. The newspapers, pamphlets, and private letters produced by Pennsylvania Jeffersonian activists led me to texts such as the transcript of *Commonwealth v. Pullis*, the first labor conspiracy trial in the nation's history, and *Modern Chivalry*, a novel by the Pennsylvania Jeffersonian Hugh Henry Brackenridge. Previous scholars had granted these sources much attention, but my understanding of how Jeffersonian political ideas were being formed in Pennsylvania allowed me to realize their significance for the shaping of the content of Jeffersonian political thought.

In studying the process by which Pennsylvania Jeffersonians shaped their political thought, I began to see that I was witnessing a more popular process of articulating this thought than the scholars of Jeffersonian political ideas generally describe. I believe that explaining this more popular process builds in a salutary and respectful fashion on the methods for studying Jeffersonian political ideas that rely primarily on the examination of long-standing ideological traditions and the contributions to them of the most famous Jeffersonians.[20]

Crucible of American Democracy is not a study of popular politics generally. As I researched the content and change over time of Jeffersonian thought in Pennsylvania, I realized that the story was so complex that it was essential to focus on the Pennsylvania Jeffersonians articulating these ideas. As I did so, it became necessary to look at sources and conditions other than the ones traditionally studied by scholars of Jeffersonian political figures. I examined these sources and considered these conditions because as Pennsylvania Jeffersonians articulated their political thought, they were more preoccupied with current social and economic developments and popular concerns than studies of Jeffersonian political thought generally show.

I did not originally expect a history of political ideology to require so much attention to contemporary social processes. But my research revealed that as Pennsylvania Jeffersonians conceived the content of their political thought, they reacted to certain contemporary developments and popular concerns. These developments brought the experiences of certain groups of ordinary Pennsylvanians into the thought process of Jeffersonian political figures. I examined these more popular experiences (such as conflicts within the Philadelphia crafts and the real possibility during the 1790s and afterward of losing one's land) in order to investigate the thought process of these political figures. I discussed the conditions of certain groups of ordinary people to the extent that I did because they influenced the political thinking of the Jeffersonians I was studying. I examined only those more popular conditions and experiences that were of interest to the articulators of Pennsylvania Jeffersonian political thought, conditions that became caught up in the process of Pennsylvania Jeffersonians conceiving and arguing about the content of that thought.

Crucible of American Democracy, then, is very much a political history and a history of political ideology, not a study of popular political culture. A history of political culture with politics broadly defined as the interaction of ordinary people (the poorest white men, blacks of both genders, and white women) with the public sphere in the Jeffersonian era would have been much more interested in looking at such ordinary people for their own sakes. Such a study (and there are such studies with increasing frequency) would tell us much.[21] But it would not provide the careful understanding of why Pennsylvania Jeffersonians demanded democracy, what they meant by it, why they disagreed about it, and how their differing visions of democracy and efforts to promote egalitarianism merged or did not merge with the nascent political economy of liberal capitalism. That is what *Crucible of American Democracy* seeks to do.

All the Pennsylvania Jeffersonians who argued with each other about democracy agreed with William Findley. They understood that democracy could work only if virtually all citizens were free of dependence on resources controlled by their fellow citizens. But they disagreed about how best to ensure that happy condition. Their conflict was shaped by thoughtful and deeply engaged political commitment that concerned itself with almost everything except accumulation for its own sake. From within the crucible of conflict Pennsylvania Jeffersonians eventually produced a body of thought that became the core of what later nineteenth-century Americans understood to be mainstream liberal and capitalist values and ideals. Yet the democratic, liberal, capitalist belief system that emerged from the debates among the Pennsylvania Jeffersonians often provided far less than what they had originally wanted for their fellow citizens.

Crucially, however, these ideas offered far more than what these Jeffersonians' initial opponents, the Federalist Party of Alexander Hamilton, John Jay, Fisher Ames, William Duer, and the rest, felt that ordinary Americans could manage or benefit from. In forming their Jeffersonian party, triumphing, and then descending into bitter conflict, Pennsylvania Jeffersonians helped lead the way toward the deep democratization of every aspect of American society. The world they built was far more egalitarian than it would otherwise have been, and it was also far more brutal, narrow-minded, and limited than Pennsylvania Jeffersonians had hoped or imagined it would be.[22]

To tell this story it is essential to pay careful attention to the same political, economic, and social developments that preoccupied the makers of Jeffersonian political thought in Pennsylvania. *Crucible of American Democracy* begins with a chapter that explains the efforts of the Federalist Party to contain and direct the fluid and raucous society produced by the American Revolution. Chapter 1 explains how and why these Federalist efforts had a particular influence in Pennsylvania beyond the general impact that Federalist policy had in the new nation. In this chapter I show why a very diverse Jeffersonian opposition formed in Pennsylvania in response to the Federalists, an opposition unlikely to reach a consensus after its victory.

The remainder of the book explores how and why the Pennsylvania Jeffersonian party began to argue about egalitarianism and capitalism and the relationship between them. Chapters 2 and 3 explain how urban and rural radicals, the Philadelphia Democrats and the Snyderites, began to push for a sweeping democratization of Pennsylvania's politics and legal system. The influences on these two groups ranged from local conditions to the hopes for a worldwide democratic revolution, a development that appeared possible to them in the early nineteenth century. In chapters 2 and 3, I show how radical demands were intended to forge an equality of condition based in commerce and wealth similar to the vision of William Findley. Finally, chapter 3 begins to explain how radical, potentially anarchic, demands for majority rule led moderate Pennsylvania Jeffersonians to seek an alternative definition of democracy. These moderates, the Tertium Quids, feared, often for good reason, that radicals threatened private property and Pennsylvania's (and the nation's) constitutional order. The Quids struggled to articulate a belief system that could preserve both Findley's society of widely distributed productive property and a commitment to fundamental law that would limit the power of particular, temporary majorities to act rashly and dangerously.

Chapter 4 brings the three groups together during the long year 1805. It begins with the effort to impeach the Pennsylvania Supreme Court in December 1804 and closes with the conflict surrounding *Commonwealth v. Pullis*, which occurred in January 1806. In between these two events, Pennsylvania Jeffersonians divided in a bitter gubernatorial election. Chapter 4 shows the three groups sharpening their beliefs in the crucible of conflict. Polemic and argument forced Pennsylvania Jeffersonians to pursue ideas to their logical (and at times their illogical) conclusions. In particular, during 1805, in response to fierce and effective challenge, the Philadelphia Democrats voiced their most extreme ideas to date. Although they did not intend to in March, by May they had renounced the American constitutional orthodoxy that emerged from the pen of John Adams in 1780 and that was enshrined at Philadelphia in 1787. The year 1805 was one of grave crisis in Pennsylvania, and this crisis among Pennsylvania Jeffersonians profoundly influenced the ways in which ideas about democracy, egalitarianism, and capitalism came to be linked in Pennsylvania and the United States. After 1805 the option to qualify, to acknowledge nuance and complexity, indeed to compromise at all, narrowed considerably. Pennsylvania Jeffersonians grew shrill and uncompromising. After 1805 the belief system that triumphed in Pennsylvania would possess those unfortunate characteristics.

The final chapter shows how after 1805 the Quids and the Snyderites managed to push the Philadelphia Democrats to the margins. Between 1806 and 1830 the Quids, and especially the Snyderites, forged a belief system of liberal democratic capitalism. For reasons that *Crucible of American Democracy* explores, the Quids became strong nationalists, and the Snyderites became equally committed advocates of states' rights. In the aftermath of the panic of 1819, surviving Philadelphia Democrats revived the challenge to the Quids' and Snyderites' commitment to capitalism. In response, the two groups moved in the directions that produced the National Republican movement (and eventually the American Whig Party) and the procapitalist ideals of the moderate wing of Andrew Jackson's Democratic Party. When the Philadelphia Democrats tried to revive the ideals of 1805, they could not penetrate the new, democratic, capitalist, and liberal consensus that now shaped Pennsylvania's mainstream. The radicals' only option was to swim outside of it. They did so by helping to form the nation's first workingmen's parties.

The debates that occurred within Pennsylvania's Jeffersonian party produced ideas that did much to shape the boundaries of permissible thought in the Jacksonian era concerning political economy and the extent of popular democratic power. Pennsylvania was deeply influential because its Jeffersonian politics produced a tested body of ideas that could respond to radical and potentially anticapitalist demands. But Pennsylvania did not merely influence by example. As *Crucible of American Democracy* explains, when, after 1820, the nation began to deal with the nagging questions concerning egalitarianism, capitalism, and democracy that Pennsylvania Jeffersonians had long addressed, it was often Pennsylvanians who made the key decisions or advised those who did. This influence would be particularly apparent in the National Republican movement and the American Whig Party. These Pennsylvanians drew on their Pennsylvania experiences, and so produced a vision of democracy that was ultimately quite distinct from William Findley's.

I studied Pennsylvania, then, because it provided the richest material to explain how democracy arose, how it came to accommodate capitalism, and why nineteenth-century American liberalism found it increasingly difficult to nurture many of the original democratic egalitarian assumptions. *Crucible of American Democracy* explores ideas; it discusses how those ideas cohered to form ideologies. The ideas that bound democracy and capitalism together, and that produced this nineteenth-century liberalism, were rooted in the concrete conflicts of the Pennsylvania Jeffersonians who conceived and spoke them. To recover something approaching the complexity of this American political thought, I found it necessary to try to capture the bursts of intense ideological creativity that characterized Pennsylvania's Jeffersonian era. In

Pennsylvania, Jeffersonians did not merely imbibe long-established ideological traditions. In the end *Crucible of American Democracy* remains a history of political ideas, but with the piques, aspirations, fears, hatreds, dreams, generous impulses, noble strivings, selfish cant, and enormous capacity to imagine possessed by the makers of Pennsylvania's Jeffersonian political thought left in.

Chapter One

Background to the Struggle: The Federalist Challenge and the Origins of Pennsylvania's Jeffersonian Conflict

In 1810 John Jay, revolutionary leader, contributor to the *Federalist Papers*, and former Supreme Court chief justice, suggested that "those who own the country are the most fit persons to participate in the government of it."[1] To our twenty-first-century ears, Jay's notion sounds profoundly cynical and perhaps distressingly prescient. In fact Jay expressed a high-minded eighteenth-century ideal, one inspired by a devotion to what his generation considered the noble legacy of the classical world. Jay meant that the wealthiest, the most comfortable, those whom God favored should be active in their nation's public affairs. The more one enjoyed of the world, the greater one's responsibility to it. The elites of the United States were duty-bound to engage in more than their private concerns. They had to accept the burden of public service and devote themselves to the needs and affairs of the community. Indeed, if they were honest about their oft-stated goal of carrying on the legacy of the republican statesmen of the classical world, they would often have to sacrifice private concerns should the commonweal, the public good of the Republic, require it.[2]

Republics depended on this public-spirited engagement of the wealthy and wellborn. Gentlemen such as Jay understood that as an axiom. Discerning what course of policy the Republic needed to pursue was difficult and time-consuming. The happiness of smaller property holders and other laboring men was intimately connected to pursuing that proper course, but their ability to contribute to discovering it was limited. Gentlemen such as Jay firmly believed that those citizens of the United States who labored were industrious, sound, and capable of productive citizenship. They had understood the nature of British tyranny and resisted it. But those who labored had, of necessity, to concern themselves primarily with private affairs. They could not frequently leave their farms and forges to deliberate and govern.

16

They did not enjoy the intimate knowledge of past republics, and the threats to them, that statesmen had to possess.

This last quality, knowledge of the past, was essential. Gentlemen such as Jay knew that the history of republican experiments was grim, one of failure. All past republics — the city-states of Greece, Rome, England, the Netherlands, recently France, and (Jay might have added) Haiti — had been destroyed by either conquest or coup. The failure of republics seemed to follow a distressing but clear pattern. The republics began as noble experiments. Boldly and bravely, the people declared a commitment to liberty and justice and an end to the mistreatment of the citizenry and the selfish pursuit of private privilege. Yet over time this love of liberty became intoxicating and proved licentious. Citizens began to pursue liberty for their own ends, creating faction and discord. Turmoil and division replaced order and harmony. Eventually the times became so chaotic that an enervated people accepted a Caesar, Cromwell, or Napoleon who imposed chilling order. The lesson was clear. Republics needed liberty, but their survival depended on its careful direction and control. When the United States declared its republican experiment, no past republic seemed to have succeeded for very long. Modern republican statesmen understood this sad history. They had constantly to remind each other how difficult their duty was.[3]

The wealthy and wellborn were most capable of fulfilling the duty of statesmen — that gentlemen such as Jay fully understood. They were secure in their fortunes and so would not be interested in or dependent on a particular course of policy. They were men of leisure, with the time and education to grapple with the weighty complexities of republican governance. They were men of substance who had proved their capacities and worth by achieving the respectable positions they occupied. Those who owned the country, gentlemen such as Jay believed, had a duty to govern it.

Yet how could this new Republic, the United States, ensure that they would? The British thought they had constructed the perfect system for ensuring that the wise and wellborn sat high in the public councils. Their eighteenth-century mixed and balanced constitution brought together the one, the few, and the many in the king, Lords, and Commons. Public initiatives required the agreement of all three. The devotion to liberty intrinsic to the many could be checked or guided by the wisdom of the few. Voltaire considered the British constitution the best humanity had ever conceived, and prior to 1763 the British in North America agreed with him.[4]

But the American Revolution seemed to prove that hereditary power was inherently dangerous and, given time, would encroach upon and eventually overawe the people. English critics had long warned that the king enjoyed far too may methods for seducing, corrupting, and controlling those representatives the people sent to speak for them.[5] Gradually after 1763, American colonists concluded that the British constitution had ceased to be a source of liberty. Hereditary privilege had proved too powerful for the republican part of British government. The lesson was clear. Republics might have little chance of securing liberty for very long, but nations with kings and aristocrats had no chance at all.[6]

The American revolutionaries united around this conviction and embraced the bold and radical belief that no man, regardless of what he accomplished in his life, was born to rule.[7] But in eschewing hereditary governance, the revolutionaries created the challenge faced by all republics. Republics required liberty, and hereditary governance destroyed it. Yet republics depended on stability, order, and deference toward those best qualified to govern, those among the citizens who were true statesmen. Monarchy and aristocracy were time-tested agents of stability, indeed, the only institutions in the history the revolutionaries knew that had guaranteed it for very long. If a nation courageously dispensed with them for the sake of liberty, how did it ensure that liberty did not become the license that caused the people to long for order and the direction of hereditary rulers? Those who owned the country could certainly be of service here. But without hereditary guarantees, how would they be assured of power? The republic would survive only if gentlemen governed it. But those gentlemen were among the first to insist that if they did not perpetually earn the right to govern, then they would become entrenched and unaccountable and so a source of tyranny.

The solution emerging after 1776 was to ask the republican citizenry regularly to discern the statesmen among them. The people would then elect these men to office and obey their republican betters unless they began to violate their sacred trust and pursue private interest at the expense of the public good.[8] The problem, gentlemen such as Jay sadly concluded, was that almost from the beginning this bold, even utopian, vision began to go seriously wrong.

To explain why the republican experiment almost from the beginning threatened to destroy itself, all American gentlemen had to do was look back on the Revolution they had recently led. The American Revolution was a tremendously complex affair primarily because of its unanticipated consequences. Over the course of the eighteenth century, an increasingly identifiable gentry class had evolved in each colony. The social and economic structure of British North America was anglicizing, and this process was readily discernible in the colonies' politics and culture. During the eighteenth century in virtually every colony, identifiable ruling classes emerged that modeled themselves after different aspects of British culture. The prevailing attitudes among elites in Virginia, for example, differed from those in Massachusetts. But in both colonies royal governors increasingly could look to a stable and identifiable coterie that was acknowledged as the legitimate governing class. In most colonies possession of offices grew more heavily concentrated, and economic stratification became more apparent, as did one's place in a culture of hierarchy and deference.[9]

The methods used by royal governors to forge stable and working relationships with their colonial ruling classes differed. In the South, governors came to understand the importance planters placed on the values of the English country opposition. They learned how to treat southern colonial elites as the country gentlemen they believed themselves to be and so produced unprecedented harmony in Virginia, South Carolina, and Georgia. In the North, especially in New England, governors increasingly presided over diverse societies that, in a limited way, replicated the economic, social, and cultural complexity of England. They were therefore able to employ the methods of court Whig management perfected by Robert Walpole. Though the methods were different, the result in the North was the same as in the South. As colonial ruling classes cohered and asserted themselves, colonial governors, particularly in royal colonies, discovered how to build harmonious relations with them.[10]

After 1763, as elite colonists grew alarmed about the seeming onslaught of British tyranny, they did not want to disorganize their own societies. But as gentlemen began to appeal to those below them to resist, they necessarily invited their inferiors into politics. As vague words such as "liberty," "equality," and the "public good" became the common currency of everyday discussion, they proved tremendously slippery, capable of engendering multiple definitions and of being attached to a variety of ideals and aspirations. In the eighteenth century, British colonial America's growing social, political, and economic inequality had provoked its own organic conflicts. But the ideologically charged atmosphere of revolutionary tumult brought to internal cleavages a new depth and scope. Gouverneur Morris was terrified as "the mob began to think and reason." As revolutionary crowds and committees began to engage in the day-to-day labors of resisting the British, they also began to demand a great deal more equality among Americans.[11]

This radical development took place in every colony. From New England to the Chesapeake, gentlemen began to fear for their liberty and property.[12]

More Americans could vote than could any other population in the world, and more still were enfranchised in the new Republic. From the beginning they applied these republican rights differently from the way gentlemen had hoped they would. During the 1780s Americans elected to their lower houses men farther down the social ladder than ever before. Some even made obscure men executives, such as the New Yorkers who elected George Clinton their governor. In Maryland gentlemen managed to retain their positions, but only by agreeing to legislation that wiped away one-third of their wealth.[13]

Radical developments occurred generally, but they were starkest in Pennsylvania. Pennsylvania was a peculiar colony. By 1720 most colonies were royal, but Pennsylvania remained proprietary until the Revolution. Between 1720 and 1760, as we have seen, most royal colonies grew more politically stable and harmonious as resident, Crown-appointed royal governors figured out ways to lead effectively with the cooperation of the gentlemen in their colonial assemblies. Pennsylvania remained notably disharmonious.[14] The thoroughly anglicized proprietor and former Quaker Thomas Penn had little sympathy for the Quaker-dominated colonial assembly. His governors were instructed to be obstructionist. The French and Indian War also created tremendous tensions. Western Pennsylvania was a war zone, and the pacifist Quaker assembly often refused to vote war supply. In the east, governor and assembly were fractious, and the west had little use for either faction. In 1763 westerners known as the Paxton Boys marched on Philadelphia. They came as far as Germantown before Benjamin Franklin convinced them to disperse.[15] Prior to 1763 the trend in most colonies was greater internal stability and harmony, especially among elites. Pennsylvania was a constant exception.[16]

Politics was not the only source of conflict. Pennsylvania's economy was one of the most dynamic in British North America. In the southeast the German and Scotch-Irish immigrants lived better than almost any other farmers in the Western world, but elsewhere economic dynamism was beginning to breed inequality and discontent.[17] The proprietor's holdings were considerable, and during the eighteenth century Pennsylvania's population grew, land values rose, and proprietary lands became more valuable than ever before. Penn's holdings were only the most obvious example of rural inequality. After 1750, even in the West, a process of accumulation began that would make the unequal distribution of property an acute concern by the 1780s and 1790s.[18]

After 1750 economic development in Philadelphia also became a source of conflict. Philadelphia's manufacturing capacities developed rapidly, starting the process that would keep the region the leading industrial center of the nation for the next one hundred years.[19] Over the next two decades this development had a profound impact on the social relations of production. The restructuring of the crafts, such a common theme of the early nineteenth century, happened much earlier in Philadelphia. By the 1760s and 1770s the trends were discernible. By the 1780s and 1790s masters and journeymen lived quite different lives and feared that they might not possess common interests.[20]

Political and economic fractiousness added up to a very radical internal revolution. The sources of this radicalism were not all long-term or structural. By 1760, as non-Quakers such as Franklin and Joseph Galloway began to lead the Quaker Party in the assembly, they were better able to defend the colony and appease the west. Through Franklin the Quaker or Anti-Proprietary Party also drew on the support of Philadelphia artisans. In the 1760s the artisans were much less divided than they eventually became, and they could all agree that Franklin was their friend and worthy representative. Franklin and Galloway made the Quaker Party a truly popular party by the late 1750s. With the conclusion of the French and Indian War, it seemed the right time finally to do something about the proprietor. Thus in the early 1760s the popular Anti-Proprietary Party began an active campaign for a royal takeover of Pennsylvania.[21]

Franklin brought to this movement the same energy and innovation that characterized all his endeavors. He organized a popular campaign and led a vocal opposition in the assembly. In the early 1760s he even conceived one of the first political slogans used on American soil, the aphoristic and winning "From proprietary slavery to royal liberty." Franklin then left for Britain to lobby for the royal takeover. However sensible the idea, it was colossal bad timing. The popular Anti-Proprietary Party associated itself with the Crown and an expansion of the royal prerogative just as the Stamp Act crisis began. The campaign for royal government survived until the late 1760s. By the Townshend Acts crisis, Pennsylvanians were as suspicious of the Anti-Proprietary Party as they were of the proprietor. Franklin himself was absent for much of the 1760s and so was able to rebuild his reputation from a distance. He also experienced the arrogance and foppish luxury of the British court firsthand. One wonders what his fate would have been had he remained in Pennsylvania. Men like Franklin, who interested themselves in the health of the British Empire, and who came to value it while at a distance from London, were often disillusioned with Britain when they finally saw it up close. But for those who remained far away, things were different.

Galloway became a loyalist, as did Franklin's son William, the governor of New Jersey.

The campaign for royal government had significant consequences. The Proprietary Party had long been hated, but by 1770 the opposition leaders were too. Between 1774 and 1776 elites in most colonies accommodated themselves to Revolutionary times. John Jay in New York spoke of swimming with the stream in hopes of better controlling the tide. Charles Carol of Maryland explained to his father that the willow tree survived a gale when the oak did not because it bent with the wind.[22] But the governing class of Pennsylvania was the exception; it did not swim or bend. In 1776 virtually all the colony's governing elite became loyalists or remained neutral. Pennsylvania faced the revolution without experienced leaders, and men thrust up and radicalized by revolutionary ideals rushed to fill the vacancies.

The result was the most radical constitution and polity found in the thirteen new states. Pennsylvania embraced near-universal manhood suffrage along with a weak plural executive and a unicameral and annually elected legislature. Each legislature could propose bills, but they had to be printed and sent to the people for approval before a new legislature elected the next year could pass them.[23] There was also a great deal of radical political consciousness. The Pennsylvania militia, particularly the committee of privates, was a source of politicization and introduced many ordinary people to revolutionary politics. In Pennsylvania, as elsewhere, popular committees oversaw much of the day-to-day revolutionary activity and spread politics and participation in public life to places where they had rarely been.[24] In 1775 James Wilson, who even at that late date was uncertain about independence, feared that Pennsylvania would soon be "in a state of nature."[25]

Wilson was not the only concerned Pennsylvanian. By 1779 a coalition that included early critics and supporters of independence, and those who supported and opposed the constitution of 1776, formed to quell what it saw as the dangerous radicalism of the lower orders. In the famous confrontation at James Wilson's Philadelphia home, the radicals believed themselves betrayed by men they had considered allies.[26] During the 1780s there was a slow and steady reaction against the Pennsylvania constitution. It was at odds with the constitutional sensibility that formed between 1776 and 1780. Further, it had been written by the revolutionary committee that became the state legislature and not by a constitutional convention. For that reason it was vulnerable to criticism that it could not serve as fundamental law and violated the increasingly cherished ideal of popular sovereignty.[27]

The reaction in Pennsylvania against the state constitution was part of a general trend in the 1780s. Radical politics in states such as Massachusetts, New York, Pennsylvania, and Maryland convinced many — and not merely gentlemen — that the new nation was upsetting the balance so essential for any republic. Tyranny came from a powerful oligarchy to be sure, but as James Madison would soon argue in *Federalist* No. 10, the majority could also behave as a tyrannical faction. When republican states were organized so that the legislature dominated government, the likelihood grew that it would become unaccountable and tyrannical.

Those concerned with the overly democratic politics of the 1780s could make a compelling republican case. As John Adams explained, the people were sovereign, and government was constituted to preserve the first principles and noblest commitments of the people. Each branch of government was equally not the people, and if any one branch dominated the others, it would begin to overawe them. It could then interpose itself between the people and the purposes for which they had created their government. Perhaps this overmighty branch would concern itself with first principles. Probably it would not. But it was domination by one branch that left this republican commitment to chance.[28]

This ideal of popular sovereignty, republican balance, and sober checks on what the late eighteenth century understood as democratic license was deeply influential by the mid-1780s. It shaped the Constitution of 1787, which Pennsylvanians were among the first to ratify. By 1790, because the political critique of the 1780s was legitimately republican and genuinely concerned with the first principles of popular sovereignty, personal freedom, and individual liberty, Pennsylvanians were willing to recast their constitutional values. That year they ratified a new constitution modeled on the Constitution of 1787.

Thus by 1790 Pennsylvanians believed they would create a stable polity. Nevertheless, this polity had been transformed by the Revolution. New men who had emerged during the 1760s and 1770s had replaced traditional elites. Though this radical legacy animated Pennsylvania politics, a broad coalition of Pennsylvanians endorsed the constitutions of 1787 and 1790. Pennsylvania, it seemed, was prepared to practice a credible but less democratic and explosive republican politics.

But few in Pennsylvania or elsewhere were prepared for what some gentlemen had in mind for the nation under the new constitution. In 1790 the new government had to tread carefully. Anti-Federalists had raised compelling concerns about the new government. They argued that it was too distant and unaccountable. They feared that only the great would secure office. Anti-Federalist fears were strong among western Pennsylvanians, who had long disliked distant governments making decisions for the region. That the new national government would soon be located in Philadelphia seemed to westerners properly symbolic.[29]

Many middling supporters of the Constitution agreed in 1787 with the republican critique of politics in the 1780s. They were moved by denunciations of the nation's weakness, of its inability to protect its commerce, police its borders, or receive respect from the world's monarchies. They expected a more energetic national government to resolve these problems. But the Revolution had taught them that the best solution relied on the people's energies and spirit, that the nation grew stronger when its citizens were able to ensure their independence and political engagement. In 1790 most Pennsylvanians agreed with their fellow Americans that a republic was foolish to deny itself the sage leadership of gentlemen statesmen. But those statesmen would still have to swim and bend, for the Revolution had also taught the people that they, too, were virtuous, that they could participate usefully in the grand republican experiment.

The 1790s would produce bitter political conflict over this belief. Americans would divide over how extensive the involvement of ordinary people should be in determining the course of the Republic's grand affairs. The positions marked out were generally coherent and clear and almost always irreconcilable. And much of the time this conflict emanated from Pennsylvania. Often it centered in Philadelphia.

In 1790 Philadelphia was the center of the new Republic. The site where the new federal constitution was conceived, it was also the capital of a central and wealthy state and of the new nation itself. A manufacturing center and a vital seat of commerce, Philadelphia drew local and national politicians and public servants. It was a crowded, densely populated, boisterous city of about forty-five thousand. Dockworkers and artisans lived and worked near lawyers, merchants, and rulers. Philadelphia was a true test for the ideal of gentlemanly republican leadership. The citizens who would have to identify and respect their republican betters were perpetually on hand and could observe their leaders carefully.

Nevertheless, wealth and status organized Philadelphia's urban geography. Artisans and mariners tended to live in the suburbs of Southwark and the Northern Liberties or on the city's outskirts away from the waterfront. Philadelphia's elite generally lived in the central business district or in a region adjacent to it called Society Hill. Society Hill attracted many of the newcomers, those who would govern the republic. Alexander Hamilton,

President Washington's secretary of the Treasury, lived in Society Hill, as did the prominent locals Benjamin Chew and William Bingham. Edward Shippen, the respected jurist and Pennsylvania Supreme Court justice from 1791 to 1806, also resided there.[30]

During the first years of the 1790s this small part of the city, no more than a few blocks, sought to provide a model of republican leadership which its residents believed the events of the 1780s had shown the nation needed. That decade had threatened chaos, and the impressive collection of gentlemen now in Philadelphia planned to provide a distinct alternative. They hoped to establish the proper tone for a republican society so that the courageous rejection of monarchy and aristocracy would not prove disastrous.

For many in Society Hill, ratification of the Constitution was but the first step. Few believed that the structure of the new government alone could guarantee that proper men would occupy the places of authority and responsibility that the survival of republican liberty demanded. When the people decided who their leaders would be, the proper choices had to be obvious. The residents of Society Hill understood that it was their responsibility to demonstrate beyond any doubt who the nation's statesmen were. The people needed guidance, and so those who were supposed to rule, who were capable of governing in the interests of the nation as a whole, had to declare themselves.

During the first years of the 1790s the residents of Society Hill and their prominent neighbors sought to live and function as a true ruling class. They hoped to establish a culture and a web of social relations between their peers and inferiors that would begin to eradicate the conditions that encouraged more ordinary Americans to think that others besides the gentry might govern. The worldview of what would soon be known as the elite of the Federalist Party combined cultural values, social prestige, political ideals, and economic policy. Each aspect of this vision was equally important. Federalist leaders pursued a vision of the Republic where cultural leadership, social grandeur, and political and economic power combined to produce a class whose claim to govern was irresistible. Thus, for example, the ostentatious purchase of carriages and Alexander Hamilton's *Report on Manufactures* emanated from the same set of concerns and the same hopes for the future. Many within the nation's republican elite concluded by 1790 that only an all-encompassing effort to combine cultural, social, political, and economic leadership would place in positions of responsibility those who could save the nation from itself and protect it from its enemies. Federalists hoped that cultural display and a properly structured political economy would begin to remind republican citizens that generally they were most virtuous and useful when they trusted and respected their republican betters.

From the beginning of George Washington's first term, Philadelphia elites fashioned a cultural milieu designed to establish their credentials as a republican gentry. The combination of local leading financial and mercantile personalities as well as municipal, state, and national dignitaries allowed for a respectable polite society. Philadelphia's leading citizens regularly hosted tea and card parties, exclusive suppers and dances, and engaged in a carefully planned round of social calls. Added to these affairs were levees, government balls, and state dinners presided over by the president and Martha Washington, who lived in the mansion of Philadelphia's first citizen and the Revolution's unofficial minister of finance, Robert Morris. One member of this elevated society believed that "certainly there never was in our country a series of such distinguished reunions, brilliant balls, sumptuous dinners, and constant receptions."[31]

Federalist worthies, when they dined, danced, and gamed together, sought to forge a polite society of the aristocracy of talents. They hoped to establish a readily identifiable group of the prominent whose positions were so unassailable that their fellow citizens would never again go astray when choosing their republican rulers. The talent and achievement of this group would be palpable, and the citizenry would defer to it. The display of cultural grandeur at times bordered on the extreme. The Philadelphia Federalist merchant William Bingham built a home modeled on the duke of Manchester's London mansion, and many of the ubiquitous and luxurious four-wheeled carriages that clogged Philadelphia's crowded streets were emblazoned with fictional coats of arms.[32]

Indeed, at times Federalist elites appeared to protest too much, to assert their claims so vociferously they sounded shrill. They did so in part because their claims were not impregnable and their perch atop American society was precarious. When compared with that of Britain or the Continent, the social structure of the United States, as Gordon S. Wood has observed, was truncated.[33] Federalist elites were uncomfortably close to those they sought to rule, and the fortunes they so carefully cultivated often did not provide unassailable social positions. The Atlantic economy was quite unforgiving, with its myriad disasters and fluctuations. A merchant could never relax. The best example was Robert Morris. Few in 1790 disputed that Morris belonged among the cultivated statesmen of the Republic. Yet after disastrous land speculations, Morris died in 1806 in debtors prison.[34]

To be republican statesmen, gentlemen had to remain disinterested, above the struggle over particular courses of policy. The people's respect and deference had to be earned, and it could be only if a gentleman's position was so secure that suspicions of self-interest never arose. That was one reason gentlemen such as George Washington speculated so heavily in land. They hoped that the vast acres of the new Republic could become that source of independent income that would protect them from charges of partiality as they guided the nation.[35]

Thus the social and cultural display of the elites of the nation's capital could only be part of their attempt to lead. At the highest levels of government, Federalist leaders hoped to craft policies that would strengthen those citizens farsighted enough to pursue the fundamental needs of the people, regardless of what a temporary majority identified as its immediate interest. Between 1790 and 1795, Federalists sought to structure the state and articulate policies that would consolidate a virtuous elite and reestablish appropriate social and economic relations between statesman and citizen. Quickly these efforts began to center around the proposals of Alexander Hamilton.

Hamilton deplored what he identified as the chaos of the 1780s, a decade that threatened to destroy the republican experiment. A newcomer to the colonies, and an officer in the Continental army, he felt little loyalty to any region or state. Further, his spectacular rise from West Indian bastardy to membership in the first circles of New York society confirmed for him the legitimacy of republican hierarchy. He did not draw leveling conclusions from his own experience. Rather, his life confirmed that the polite, virtuous, and republican elites of the new nation were not an unaccountable oligarchy. The gentlemen and gentlewomen of the new nation embraced talent and welcomed virtue. Hamilton's rise seemed proof that industry and talent brought respect and deference. Hamilton's initial obscurity and eventual triumph confirmed for him the value and sound judgment of the republican elite. When Washington asked his former aide-de-camp to become secretary of the Treasury, Hamilton saw his chance to continue his public service. The best service he could conceive was assisting the fledgling Republic in building the social and political order it needed.[36]

Hamilton intended his financial and economic policies to provide to the elite he trusted the importance and grandeur they needed to be useful to the Republic. However, this republican elite believed that its achievements should already have earned it the social and political prestige the events of the 1780s showed it could claim only with difficulty. The people's past inability, or refusal, to identify their prerogative to rule provoked a crisis of confidence among elites about the virtue of their fellow citizens, the future of the

Republic, and even their own achievements. Hamilton designed his programs to enrich and empower a public-spirited elite that would use its wealth and influence to serve the Republic's interests. But the elites that he trusted often depended on his policies to bring them the stable prosperity that would make their positions unassailable and so bolster their claims to govern. Regardless of motive or belief, this balance was delicate. It would be easy for some to see self-interest where others sincerely claimed disinterest. Further, it could easily become impossible for those benefiting from Hamilton's programs to tell the difference. As committed as they were to republican ideals, at times they themselves were troubled by these circumstances. And so were those who quickly became their enemies.

Hamilton's initial efforts centered on the nation's public debt. The American Revolution had left the national and state governments roughly $80 million in debt, $13 million owed to foreign sources, $25 million owed by the states to domestic public creditors, and the rest owed by the national government to them as well. At first the domestic public creditors were a large, heterogeneous group. Many were veterans or artisans and farmers who had provided services and supplies to the Revolution at a time when the various American governments could not pay for them. During the 1780s, though some states had begun to pay their debts, many had not. Under the Articles of Confederation the national government had no power to coerce payment of the taxes it requested, and so it could not begin to repay its public creditors. During the 1780s the value of the debt plummeted. Its holders, fearing that the public debtors would never fulfill their obligations, became willing to sell their debt certificates for specie at a fraction of the face value. The value of the debt fell as low as fifteen cents on the dollar; in a few cases it sank to six cents.[37] Over the course of the 1780s, ownership of the debt became concentrated, and it grew even more so as news surfaced that a new national government would have the power to tax. Speculators in particular purchased the debt of the southern states, where the news surfaced last.[38]

By the time Hamilton joined Washington's cabinet, the process was complete, and it provided him his opportunity. The first Congress charged the secretary to provide a plan for ordering the nation's finances. In his first *Report on Public Credit,* which arrived at the House of Representatives on January 9, 1790, Hamilton proposed that the national government promise to make funding the debt its first revenue priority. To fund a debt meant that a government would pay the interest on its public debt each year before it did anything else. Hamilton's proposal called for both funding and assumption. By assumption the secretary meant that the national government would assume, or take over, the state debts, thus creating a single public creditor, the national government. Funding and assumption accomplished several things. First, the value of the debt immediately began to rise, moving close to par. Suddenly the debt certificates generated the stated interest, and the holder could again be confident of receiving the principal on the terms of the original loan. With Hamilton's proposal, the certificates became valuable commodities.

Since ownership of the debt was highly concentrated by 1790, funding and assumption also enriched and empowered those prosperous gentlemen who had been able to buy depreciated securities in the previous decade. Hamilton believed the purchasers had shown the proper public-spirited confidence in the nation's bonds and had assisted their struggling inferiors when their governments could not. Funding the debt in 1790 would forge a bond between the first citizens of the Republic and the new national government. It would also strengthen the economic position of the republican gentry and provide them a sounder foundation from which to launch their careers of public service.[39]

Funding and assumption also strengthened the nation's economy. With specie scarce, the value of paper currency fluctuated. By funding the debt, the national government provided a vast new source of paper currency that deserved public confidence. The debt certificates functioned as a circulating medium, and they bore interest, which made them a reliable source of income. Funding and assumption solidified the position of sober, dependable republican elites, brought those elites closer to the national government, discouraged them from identifying with the interests of a particular region, and provided a needed supply of money to improve the economy.

Hamilton's proposal immediately brought criticism. In the House of Representatives James Madison voiced a concern shared by many. Hamilton's program was inspired by the fiscal apparatus of public debt and the close relationship between the state and a moneyed elite that had emerged in Georgian England under Robert Walpole. The development of what the historian John Brewer calls the fiscal-military state provoked a cultural and intellectual movement of criticism and opposition.[40] This country ideology stressed the reliability of independent, landed proprietors and scorned those who depended on the state or on new, unsteady forms of wealth. This opposition language had resonated with many Americans, and nowhere more so than in Madison's Virginia.[41] After 1765, as Americans increasingly struggled to explain why the British state, long considered a source of liberty, had become an agent of tyranny, country assumptions had gained widespread credibility. Public debt and the dubious wealth it created had been sources of tyranny in Britain. The citizenry had accepted the republican critique of the 1780s and ratified the Constitution. But many members of the House of Representatives agreed with Madison that they had not done so to allow public servants to imitate Great Britain. Americans such as Madison and Thomas Jefferson understood that republics relied on natural aristocrats accepting the burdens of public service.[42] But what, they queried, was natural about funding the debt under the present circumstances? How could one claim that the advantage funding brought to the current holders had been earned, or that the wealth and power the policy provided was the product of talent and industry? Madison proposed what he called discrimination. The nation should fund the debt at par, but current holders would receive only the highest market price available before the debate on funding began. The difference would go to the original holders.[43]

Madison's concerns were compelling, especially since veterans had initially owned approximately $17 million of the debt. But the position of those who supported funding and assumption was equally so. Madison did not dispute the premise of the proposal's backers. No one understood better than he the dangers of a weak national government or what he termed the "tyranny of the majority faction."[44] Hamilton suggested a workable program to empower the proper sort and direct their energies toward the national government and national concerns. Funding and assumption would help the best sort, those most capable of accepting the burdens of public service, to fulfill their obligations to the Republic. The conflict grew so violent in the next few years because both sides sought the best interests of the Republic and had irreconcilable beliefs about how best to pursue them. President Washington supported funding and assumption, and the policies passed both the House and the Senate. The funded debt became the instrument Federalist policy makers used to rebuild necessary and appropriate social, cultural, political, and economic relations between republican citizens.

With passage of funding and assumption, the House of Representatives directed Hamilton to write a second report discussing further provisions necessary for establishing public credit. On December 14, 1790, the report arrived at the House and further delineated the secretary's plan for building a stable republican social order. In this second report Hamilton proposed the formation of a national bank. The bank would be capitalized at $10 million, and 80 percent of the money would come from private subscription. The remaining 20 percent of the stock would be purchased by the national government. The structure of the bank would connect the investors to the new national state and further focus their energies on national concerns. Of the 80 percent owned privately, 75 percent (or 60 percent of the entire $10 million) could be purchased with public debt. This provision meant that most of the bank stock would be owned by the credible and trustworthy gentlemen recently empowered by the funding plan. The structure of the bank allowed them to direct the institution and encouraged them to work closely with republican statesmen. The bank, Hamilton hoped, would blur the distinction between public republican statesman and private republican gentleman. The bank's board of directors reflected this ideal. The government chose some of its directors, and the private investors appointed the rest. The bank was a largely private institution designed to remind republican gentlemen that they had public responsibilities.[45]

From our modern perspective, plans such as that for the first Bank of the United States appear self-serving. The bank created a demand for government debt certificates, which raised their value and rewarded the public creditors. Bank stock had to be purchased in block shares costing $400 each, which guaranteed that primarily the wealthy would invest. Further, the more shares one owned, the more votes one had. But Hamilton proposed the bank, and the Federalist Congress approved it with pure, if very eighteenth-century, motives and assumptions. The two principal tasks of the bank would be strengthening the republic's economy and, connected to that, providing credit. The latter was a grave responsibility. A stable and vital republic had to assess creditworthiness correctly. If men of bad character benefited from credit, they could become powerful enough to endanger the Republic. If men with dubious schemes were mistakenly encouraged, they would destroy themselves. Control of financial institutions was part of a public trust to bolster a desirable social order and reinforce those relationships and values of sobriety and dignified deference upon which the Republic rested. The bank would ensure that republican gentlemen determined creditworthiness and directed the energies of the citizenry. These were awesome tasks. At one and the same time, the bank helped guarantee that only proper gentlemen would complete them, and it reminded those gentlemen that accepting public responsibilities for the sake of the entire nation was their duty.

Hamilton assumed that the bank and its branches would dominate the nation's finance and credit networks. The bank and its branches, he hoped, would supplant the unplanned and uncontrolled lending by private and state-chartered institutions. The bank's heavy capitalization, the backing of public funds, and its unique relationship with the new national state made such dominance likely. These goals pleased many Federalists. The bank's likely dominance, for example, relieved Fisher Ames, who agreed with Hamilton that ideally the state banks would function as "subbanks" of the national bank. Ames advised Hamilton, who needed little urging, that all "the influence of the monied men ought to be wrapped up in the union and in one bank. The state banks may become the favorites of the states. They, the latter, will be proud to emulate the example of the union and show their sovereignty by a parade of institutions like those of the nation."[46] If the national bank worked as Ames hoped, then it could check this "parade of institutions" and "overpower the state banks by giving borrowers better terms." Once it established its domination of the nation's credit structures, the national bank could responsibly confine the status of creditworthiness to those Ames considered "safer people."[47] Enriching wealthy public creditors and giving them the direction of the Bank of the United States, then, was a means to the vital end of allowing the natural aristocracy to again accept the burdens of public service.

Increasingly, however, the national state appeared to be too powerful. Jefferson, Madison, and congressmen such as Pennsylvania's Albert Gallatin feared that the government was growing beyond the capacity of the citizenry to direct or control it. The interrelated political, economic, social, and cultural power of an elite at once public and private looked enough like a European-style aristocracy to make resonant the charge that Hamilton and other Federalists wanted one. The bank only deepened the conviction that Hamilton's model was Walpole's England. By 1791 inchoate fears of unaccountable and aloof national power, the corrupting tendencies of great wealth, and suspicion of methods and institutions associated with Britain were beginning to produce a sustained opposition.

Gentlemen such as Jefferson and Madison faced a real dilemma when they considered providing an alternative to Hamilton and the cosmopolitans of the nation's capital. For they were republican gentlemen, too, and they shared many assumptions with men such as Jay, Ames, and Hamilton. They believed in a natural aristocracy; they understood the importance and value of acknowledging and deferring to the clearly superior. They accepted that all men had an equal claim to liberty but that not all men were equally qualified to identify and protect it. Therefore, they faced a difficult challenge. How could they explain to the people that their current leaders had to be replaced with different gentlemen who claimed the same superior qualifications to rule? Such a request asked a great deal of republican citizens. They had to be engaged enough to scrutinize, criticize, and alter government. They also had to be deferential and respectful enough to obey

deserving superiors. By 1791 nascent opposition leaders had to find followers; they had to convince ordinary citizens that the national government was
essential but that the current national governors threatened liberty. But by
1791 the course of Federalist policy was beginning to concern many who
would never be considered republican gentlemen. Ordinary Americans also
became alarmed at the sudden growth of the national state. In addition, they
began to reject the implications of the Federalists' political economy. After
1791 many Americans concluded that the growth of the national government's power and the commitments underpinning Federalist political economy were connected.

Gentlemen in the 1780s understood that the source of the Republic's ills
was internal. Much of the initiative in the early 1790s had been to establish
a proper republican society and polity. Proper relations would bring stability and restore order. But internal problems had external consequences.
Chaos and democratic excess weakened the nation and allowed hostile monarchies to manipulate and threaten it. The best example was when Britain
denied access to the West Indies and, in violation of the Treaty of Paris, retained forts in the west. Internal implosion destroyed republican liberty from
within, and it prevented the nation from being able to protect that liberty
against threats from without. Hamilton hoped that by restoring proper
republican order internally, the nation could better focus its energies to protect itself from hostile monarchies. If the Republic righted itself, its public
life would become a place to win fame and glory. The nation would begin
to cut an impressive republican figure in a world of monarchies.[48]

Reestablishing a proper republican social order internally and creating
a nation able to defend republican institutions from liberty's external enemies were linked. Federalists, therefore, understood that building a republic required an energetic political economy. A republic had to mobilize the
energies of its citizens. The nation's economy had to stimulate productive,
industrious labor, which encouraged proper republican attributes and attitudes. The economy also had to provide the means of defense and possibly
even the power to spread republican institutions if the opportunity arose.
Federalist gentlemen such as Hamilton, Ames, and lesser known but important figures such as the merchant and speculator William Duer and the merchant and manufacturer John Nicholson were committed to developing the
nation's economy.[49]

Promoting economic development raised significant social and political
anxieties given the larger republican concerns that undergirded all Federalist efforts. If the Federalists used the newly energetic national government to

promote manufacturing and to foster internal improvements, they would improve the Republic's capacity to defend itself against its enemies. But those measures could also potentially enrich and empower dangerous elements within the citizenry.

The best example of this potential problem was the impact a vigorous commitment to manufacturing could have on the nation's craftsmen. At first glance they seemed to share many concerns with Federalist gentlemen. Craftsmen abhorred the nation's weakness under the Articles of Confederation and had long called for a commitment to manufacturing. Most craftsmen supported ratification because, among other reasons, it allowed the new government to pursue policies such as protective tariffs. Craftsmen assumed the Federalists would endorse such tariffs, since they, too, worried about the nation's vulnerability. A protective tariff was certainly the most logical and direct way to encourage American manufactures. But what impact would it have on social relations inside the nation? Protective tariffs made foreign manufactures undesirable, and so all of a sudden, they created great demand for craftsmen's wares. Such tariffs would increase the wealth and importance of craftsmen considerably.

For many gentlemen that prospect was alarming. Craftsmen had been responsible for many of the radical developments of the 1770s and 1780s that many gentry feared threatened to destabilize the nation. They had sat on revolutionary committees, radicalized militia companies, voted obscure men into public office, and shown disrespect for property. Promoting manufactures was a central conundrum for Federalist gentlemen. The Republic needed a stronger economy and a stable polity, and both could develop only with the return of deferential social relations. Yet it seemed that strengthening the economy by promoting manufactures could further disrupt those relations.

During 1791 and 1792 Hamilton articulated a series of policies designed to structure economic development so that growth and diversification would foster and strengthen appropriate social relations. These policies earned the support of the gentlemen Hamilton relied upon. In December 1791 Hamilton delivered to the House his *Report on Manufactures,* in which he imagined a nation with flourishing manufactures and a population of laborers who would purchase agricultural surpluses. Hamilton argued that the nation should create a viable internal market and forge closer commercial ties between the North and the South. Yet he opposed protective tariffs.[50] There were a variety of reasons for this opposition, some straightforward and others complex. First, protective tariffs, by design, limited foreign imports.

Absent reliable or very lucrative excises, imposts were the primary source of the new national government's revenue. Without that revenue it could not continue to service the debt and solidify its relationship with trusted gentlemen. Hamilton argued that protective tariffs created scarcity too quickly and so caused inflation and encouraged smuggling, but he also had an ideological opposition to such tariffs. In *Federalist* No. 35 Hamilton had argued that protective tariffs "render[ed] other classes of the community tributary in an improper degree to the manufacturing classes."[51] In particular they "oppress[ed] the merchant." To Hamilton such a policy undermined the desired republican social and political order, one where "mechanics and manufacturers [understood] . . . that the merchant [w]as their natural patron and friend" and so were "disposed to bestow their votes upon merchants and those whom they recommend."[52] The Revolutionary era had, with terrifying consequences for social stability and republican liberty, discouraged the craftsmen's natural inclination "to give their votes to merchants" and to acknowledge that their own "habits in life have not been such as to give them those acquired endowments, without which in a deliberative assembly the greatest natural abilities are for the most part useless." Developing manufactures was essential, but further empowering craftsmen and so (Hamilton assumed) encouraging in them a selfish and distorted sense of their proper role as republican citizens would undermine the purpose for improving the economy.

Hamilton and other Federalists pursued manufactures in ways that would reinforce proper social and political relations between established, truly independent republican gentlemen and their fellow citizens. They did so by promoting enterprises such as the Society for Establishing Useful Manufactures. Hamilton and the gentlemen who invested in the enterprise imagined it as a grand concern. It was chartered by New Jersey and authorized to issue $1 million in stock. The stock was sold in $100 blocks, guaranteeing that only the trustworthy and dependable would control substantial holdings.[53] Most important, the prospectus allowed the entire stock to be purchased with public debt certificates. That was the crucial feature, for it allowed the society a sound chance of success without the passage of protective tariffs. The $1 million in public debt, which bore the established interest rate of 4 percent, provided the society with an income of $40,000 per year before it began production. Though Hamilton had no intention of supporting protective tariffs, in the *Report on Manufactures* he endorsed other forms of government assistance, such as bounties and premiums. Bounties were government grants provided to manufacturers who promised to meet an agreed-upon production quota within an established period of time. Premiums were rewards bestowed by the state on those manufacturers who met a stated production quota. These forms of state assistance were far more compatible than were protective tariffs with the overarching concerns of Federalist gentlemen. Protective tariffs, as Hamilton understood, simply protected the domestic market for all manufacturers and invited any of them to meet new demand. In the absence of protective tariffs, receiving bounties and premiums was essential. But with British imports still arriving regularly, virtually no craftsman could be competitive enough to assume the gamble of accepting bounties and would be much less likely to produce enough to earn premiums. The exception would be those manufacturers with a substantial alternative source of income, and that was precisely what the Society for Establishing Useful Manufactures enjoyed.

The society was meant to resolve most of the concerns the gentlemen of the Republic had expressed since the Revolution. It would strengthen and diversify the nation's economy. It would help generate an independent income for its shareholders — many of them among the nation's first citizens — while also providing them with a position of responsibility and leadership in the nascent manufacturing sector of the economy. Without the essential assistance of protective tariffs, craftsmen — as Tench Coxe, Hamilton's assistant at Treasury, pointed out, so often "an intemperate and disorderly class of people" — would not be able to compete with foreign manufacturers.[54] They would have little choice but to seek employment from enterprises such as the Society for Establishing Useful Manufactures. Craftsmen would at first be profoundly dissatisfied. As early as July 1791, Fisher Ames informed Hamilton that some feared "domestic manufactures will be injured by the company." He then wondered whether Hamilton had "any objection to a similar incorporation in New England."[55] If manufacturing could be pursued through similar enterprises, then the gradual diversification of the Republic's economy would also re-create and then reinforce social and economic hierarchy and eventually deference. Hamilton's financial program led to this method of manufacturing and so reinforced a top-down or hierarchical sensibility. Promoting manufactures was useful, even essential, but this commitment was so only if such promotion could be structured to consolidate order and reinvigorate republican hierarchy.

Though Hamilton's plans were in keeping with broader Federalist sensibility and were logical, consistent, at times even brilliant in their complexity, they were deeply flawed. They guaranteed that the Federalists would alienate most craftsmen, the men with the intimate knowledge of their crafts essential to sustain successful development of American industry. Hamilton did not seek to raise or empower skilled artisans when he imagined a vibrant manufacturing future. To oversee the Society for Establishing Useful Manufactures he relied on men such as his assistant secretary of the Treasury, William Duer.

Duer's career provides an excellent example of how the well connected made money in the eighteenth-century Atlantic economy. A planter in his own right, Duer used his acumen and West Indian connections to become a wholesale supplier as well. In America he quickly plunged into large-scale land speculation. In addition, during the 1780s he gambled heavily in various forms of public debt and became one of the chief beneficiaries of funding and assumption. Duer used his connections to secure contracts to supply the Spanish navy with masts and spars, and he relied on his fellow New York Federalist and minister to Spain, John Jay, to smooth over misunderstandings that arose from the contract. Through his friendships with Hamilton's father-in-law, Philip Schuyler, Hamilton, and chief war financier, Robert Morris, Duer secured highly profitable military purveyance contracts. Assessing Duer's financial and commercial endeavors, his most thorough biographer comments, "Duer was never a pioneer, moving into fields other Americans hesitated to enter. Rather he was always a speculator, looking for quick returns in familiar pastures."[56]

Duer was not simply a conservative. He was willing to take wild risks on variants of what he knew and understood, particularly speculation in both stocks and land (i.e., assessments of future price differentials). But these practices did not prepare him to develop domestic manufacturing. Men such as Duer flourished in an already established economy where the rules were clear. Indeed, their profits stemmed from underdevelopment, or securing favorable price differentials by moving goods from where they were plentiful to where they were scarce. They were also willing to diversify into financial speculations, particularly when their connections provided information that lessened the risk. Men such as Duer were not likely candidates to lead a radical and risky transformation of an underdeveloped economy.

The Federalists' manufacturing program depended on merchants and merchant speculators becoming directly involved in manufacturing, a task for which they were ill equipped and had little experience. Merchant speculators possessed little knowledge of the actual workings of the various crafts. Skilled artisans, with their intimate knowledge of each step in the production process, were much more capable of subdividing tasks, discovering shortcuts, understanding what could be mechanized, and even devising labor-saving machines. Craftsmen, not merchant speculators, were far more capable of ushering in a vibrant manufacturing future.

Hamilton could recognize and discuss the importance of the division of labor and other qualitative changes in production, but he knew that he must depend on artisans to conceive and implement such changes in a practical and sensible way. Not even Hamilton could promote manufacturing without ultimately depending on the knowledge of manufacturers. But Hamilton and Duer hoped to surround their dependence on artisans' knowledge with such a grand, awe-inspiring manufacturing edifice that it would all but demand the subjection and deference of troublesome post-Revolutionary artisans.

Stock of the Society for Establishing Useful Manufactures was fully purchasable with public debt. Actual craftsmen, of course, owned few debt certificates. The initial investors who can be traced were, like Duer, principal holders of the debt. They purchased $157,000 of the society's stock with the debt, an average of $5,639.28 worth of stock per investor. The society's prospectus stipulated that investors received a vote for each share of stock that they held, and each share cost $100. As with the stock of the Bank of the United States, few besides substantial holders of the public debt could acquire stock in the Society for Establishing Useful Manufactures. The more they acquired, the more they dominated the one form of domestic manufacturing capable of gradually becoming competitive with foreign manufactures in the absence of protective tariffs. The additional income of $40,000 per year the society would enjoy from the transfer of $1 million in public debt once its entire stock was sold made it the model for the only sort of industrial enterprise that could hope to compete with British manufactures without protective tariffs.[57]

Because the principal investors were primarily merchant speculators, few of them had any practical knowledge of manufacturing, and they were strongly inclined to view it as one among a number of opportunities. Indeed, manufacturing in America was more risky and costly than most other investments, a real burden for men who had no reason to value manufacturing, as craftsmen did, over commercial or financial enterprises. The investors viewed the society as simply one of a number of speculations, indeed, the most dubious one. The sorry outcome was that most investors proved unwilling to concentrate on manufacturing when more traditional and lucrative opportunities arose. Duer at one point even raided the society's capital reserves to gamble on a land speculation, a business he understood far better than manufacturing.[58]

The Society for Establishing Useful Manufactures, indeed, this model for promoting industrial development in America, was a spectacular failure.

The Federalists who planned it misjudged their own abilities and the political resolve and commitment to personal independence possessed by most craftsmen. Few craftsmen by 1792 were content to watch their businesses fail from the absence of protective tariffs and then seek employment at factories owned by men who believed themselves to be the craftsmen's republican superiors. Ironically, a Briton understood these craftsmen better than their fellow republican citizens did. In 1791 Thomas Marshall, the superintendent of the society's textile mill, wrote a concerned letter to Hamilton. Marshall, a skilled master craftsman and recent émigré enticed to America by Hamilton, understood the nature of craft production and the attitudes of his fellow skilled artisans. Commenting on the society's size, Marshall wrote, "Would not the union of so many qualities, on which the success entirely depends, be an absolute miracle, and would it be prudent to depend upon it? . . . The more I think on the affair, the more I am persuaded that there is a great risk in pursuing it in the manner in which it is proposed, and its advantageous execution must depend on fortune, more than on reason." Next Marshall discussed the danger of employing skilled craftsmen the way the society's investors planned:

> I have seen in Europe individual manufacturers employ two or three hundred hands, but in the same branch. . . . [B]esides they were employed for their own profit, and not as hirelings, and after all were often cheated in the details. In the establishment proposed we must in the first place [have] as many faithful and enlightened directors as there are different branches; then a number of managers each capable of following the branch entrusted to him with the eye of a real and intelligent manufacturer, without which it will be necessary to depend absolutely on the head workmen, who, even if they should all be honest, can never be stimulated by that interest which animates those who work for themselves. . . . I repeat it sir, unless God should send us saints for workmen and angels to conduct them, there is the greatest reason to fear for the success of the plan.[59]

When planning the Society for Establishing Useful Manufactures, then, Hamilton misjudged the men he relied on and the men he feared. Regarding the former, as the society went bankrupt, he could only berate himself for depending so completely on "those characters in the direction [of the society] who were too much enveloped in speculation to pay proper attention to the trust."[60] But as the society emerged and collapsed between 1792 and 1794, craftsmen became determined to challenge the methods the Federalists used to promote manufacturing and the assumptions that underpinned those methods. They were determined that the Federalists would not get a second chance.

By 1792, then, elite Federalist gentlemen had moved decisively to address the political, social, cultural, and economic traumas they believed threatened republican liberty in the new nation. Alexander Hamilton's financial system and the political economy surrounding the Society for Establishing Useful Manufactures were the culmination of the Federalist effort to preserve republican liberty by ensuring that those who owned the country also governed it. Between the mid-1780s and 1792 their efforts had known only success, and there was every reason to believe that this very hierarchical and largely socially static republic could be constructed and consolidated.

As is well known, between 1792 and 1800 nearly the opposite happened. The collapse of the Society for Establishing Useful Manufactures foreshadowed the defeat of the Federalist Party. Federalist initiatives provoked the formation of the Jeffersonian opposition, and differing reactions to the French Revolution intensified this conflict. This story has been well researched and well told. But though the impacts of Hamilton's financial program, the French Revolution, the Jay Treaty, the Whiskey Rebellion, the Quasi War, and the Alien and Sedition Acts are well known, these critical developments had a particular, and for the most part unique, impact on those who became Jeffersonians in Pennsylvania.

Pennsylvania, quite simply, was not Virginia. Hamilton's program could not have been better calculated to convince Virginians that the Federalists were enemies of republican liberty.[61] By the 1790s Pennsylvania was well on its way to creating a dynamic, mixed economy. Philadelphia was already the nation's manufacturing center, and virtually all the Pennsylvanians who would later shape Jeffersonian political thought in the state looked forward to a political economy that encouraged extensive manufacturing and economic development.

By the early 1790s Pennsylvania's economic activity had already led to clear social and economic differentiation and diversity of experience in urban Philadelphia, the long-settled rural southeast, and even the more immature, more recently settled, and more distant rural west. Pennsylvania conditions suggested that the less elite about whom the Federalists generalized had less and less in common with each other. At first glance there was little reason to expect that they would act together or find reason to follow a distant southern planter leadership, particularly a leadership that often

drew conclusions about what republics should be based on the more uniform and more generally agrarian conditions and experience of Virginia.
Yet, increasingly after 1792, urban and rural Pennsylvanians of very different impulses and conditions chose to become Jeffersonian activists. Thus
they did act together, and they did follow such a leadership. This decision
created a diverse Jeffersonian opposition that was capable of producing a
variety of conflicting ideals. Why could activists with potentially different
ideals and reactions to the social and economic developments around them
nevertheless unite during the 1790s? Answering this question necessitates
examining the social and economic terrain of eighteenth-century Pennsylvania and looking at how the well-known events of the 1790s were experienced by the nascent Pennsylvania Jeffersonians who lived on it.

Since 1750 Philadelphia had developed as the colonies' and then the new
nation's manufacturing center.[62] During these years, and especially after
1770, Philadelphia craftsmen experienced conditions and conflicts that did
not develop elsewhere on as great a scale until after 1815. In Philadelphia
during the last quarter of the eighteenth century, the crafts shifted rapidly
from the use of unfree to free labor. In 1745 artisans made up 48 percent of
Philadelphia's population, but they purchased 66 percent of all indentured
servants. They produced almost exclusively for the city and its hinterland,
usually engaging in bespoke work only. At most they owned the labor of a
few hands who during their bondage were supplied room and board in the
master's house as part of the indenture. But from 1750 the number of indentured servants owned by artisans dwindled. In 1800 only one artisan owned
indentured servants, and he possessed but one. At the same time, merchants
began to purchase more indentured servants. Thus, the typical indentured
servant went from being a skilled artisan to an unskilled domestic. By 1800
there were more female than male indentured servants in Philadelphia.[63]

The transformation of indentured servitude was connected to a transformation among craftsmen who were not masters. By 1800 craft workers
were wage laborers working in increasingly larger and more impersonal
shops. They produced for a growing domestic market created by the non-
importation movements of the 1760s and 1770s and the cessation of British
exports before 1783. The rapid development of Philadelphia's manufacturing capacities, and the economic fluctuations brought on by the boom and
bust of the crisis period between 1765 and 1787, made a more flexible labor
system attractive to Philadelphia's master craftsmen. In addition, rapid population growth created a labor surplus that drove wages down, making free
wage labor more desirable.[64]

Beyond that, the American Revolution itself discredited human bondage in the North. In Pennsylvania slavery declined rapidly after the state passed a gradual emancipation law in 1780, and this process became especially conspicuous in Philadelphia. Furthermore, apprentices and indentured servants themselves appropriated the rhetoric of equality and used it to criticize their own condition. This appropriation was one of the largely unanticipated radical developments of the American Revolution.[65]

After 1770 relations between masters and journeymen, and even apprentices, grew tenser and more hostile. During the 1790s the real incomes of masters rose, whereas those of journeymen remained stagnant or declined. During the final quarter of the eighteenth century, autonomous journeymen's organizations arose in Philadelphia for the first time. During the 1790s journeymen printers and cabinetmakers both struck. In the latter strike the journeymen cordwainers contributed to the strike fund. The cordwainers themselves would face prosecution for their own labor organizing efforts in 1806.[66]

As participants transformed craft relations in Philadelphia, masters and journeymen began to articulate opposing beliefs. Both desired a growing economy and increased opportunities. But masters began to anger journeymen by insisting that masters should be free to use their productive property with just their own interests in mind. They formed organizations solely for masters and sought to impose work requirements and wage rates on journeymen. For example, master craftsmen decided to pay wages by a flat rate during the summer but by a piece rate during the shorter winter months, when less production was possible.[67]

Journeymen had their own ideas. Politicized during the American Revolution, they also drew on the memory of Leveller traditions to conceive a critique of the master craftsmen's behavior. They insisted on their importance to successful craft production and their fundamental equality with their fellow American citizens. Their status as full citizens gave them, they argued, the right to prevent actions that endangered the comfortable existence that permitted them to participate fully in the life of the Republic. Because they were productive citizens, nothing should legitimately or lawfully prevent their complete and just involvement in the economic and political life of the new nation. A just involvement included a reasonably quick rise into the ranks of the master craftsmen.[68]

Thus it seemed unlikely in 1792 that masters and journeymen in Philadelphia would join to form a political opposition. If anything they were growing further apart. Indeed, "the people" (at least that portion of them involved in the Philadelphia crafts) that William Findley had invoked in 1786 were already creating conditions that made it difficult to generalize about them as a monolithic category. Yet despite their differences, masters and journeymen desired a dynamic internal economy and a government that could help them to compete with Great Britain and develop American manufactures. Both groups were beginning to suspect that they did not have common interests within their crafts, but all agreed that the crafts had to be protected and encouraged. Craftsmen genuinely connected the furtherance of their own livelihoods with patriotic sentiment and commitment to republican values and institutions. Domestic manufactures had assisted the struggle against tyranny before 1783. Now rising manufactures would allow the new nation to withstand the malevolence of monarchies. For the Philadelphia craftsmen, who overwhelmingly supported the new Constitution in 1787, securing a strong national government allowed them to pursue their private needs and the public good simultaneously.

Yet by 1792 Philadelphia masters and journeymen were beginning to understand that they had, if not common interests, at least a common enemy. It was clear that the Federalists promoted manufacturing as part of a broader plan to re-create hierarchy. A few examples from the early 1790s of the reaction to the Federalists' policies helps to explain the masters' and journeymen's growing, if temporary, unity. As the prospectus of the Society for Establishing Useful Manufactures and the *Report on Manufactures* became public knowledge, the *Independent Gazetteer* of Philadelphia reminded "the mechanics and manufactures" that Hamilton promised "to bring before Congress some plan for your benefit and encouragement, [but] the information [received from mechanics] so acquired by the Secretary enabled him to bring forward a lengthy report on manufactures to be introduced as the National Manufactory: But will not this scheme ruin you?"[69] A member of the Pennsylvania House of Representatives charged that the close cooperation between the national government and the Society for Establishing Useful Manufactures "would enable the company to work to a greater advantage than any private manufacture in this state . . . and to undersell their competitors." The society worked, then, "to the detriment of private manufacturers and artificers."[70]

The *National Gazette*, a Philadelphia newspaper close to Jefferson and Madison, insisted that "these extraordinary privileges granted to [the society] and their workmen will enable them with their large capital to draw all the journeymen of whatever branch they please to follow, through the United States which will act fully up to monopoly, and will inevitably cause the ruin of thousands of families." Finally the *Philadelphia General Advertiser*, renamed in 1794 the *Aurora* and fast becoming the most prominent Jeffersonian political organ in the North, insisted that "it would be well for private manufacturers, especially in this city and its vicinity, who do not expect to do well in this happy circle to take alarm, and consider what will become of the various trades when the workmen are tempted from their services by the advantages held out to them by this enormous, political, speculating, manufacturing scheme."[71]

Looking back from the year 1804, the *Aurora* explained why craftsmen and their allies came to oppose the Federalist methods for promoting manufacturing. The *Aurora* distinguished between support for manufactures that helped to establish a powerful aloof national state connected to a moneyed elite, and policies intended to promote the standing and dignity of actual craftsmen. In making this distinction the paper recounted the conclusions many craftsmen had drawn during the 1790s, namely, that "Mr. Hamilton's funding system was founded on securing a great number of persons of wealth." The nascent opposition had concluded, the *Aurora* observed, that as "a financier Mr. Hamilton was of the old school, substituting stock jobbing, loans, and debt for the system which could be an honor to the nation, and oppressive to none of its citizens."[72] Craftsmen of all varieties demanded, in Thomas Marshall's words, a world where they were "stimulated by that interest which animates those who work for themselves."

Craftsmen's hostility toward Federalist political economy was strongest in Philadelphia for three reasons. First, Philadelphia was the nation's industrial center, the crafts were more developed there, and there were more artisans. Second, it was the nation's capital. The Federalists whom the artisans were coming to despise were on hand; the Society for Establishing Useful Manufactures was located at nearby Paterson, New Jersey. Third, the artisans' general concerns were more easily articulated in Philadelphia because the craftsmen were intimately connected to Pennsylvania's revolutionary legacy. They possessed the rudiments of a language and a worldview that taught them to be critical and wary of the great and that encouraged them to take matters into their own hands. The ways the Federalists pursued manufacturing alienated and politicized the city's artisans again. In doing so, the Federalists temporarily arrested hostilities and divisions emerging within the crafts. The events of 1792–93 drove Philadelphia masters and journeymen closer together and further radicalized them. In the process, they moved toward the southerners who were already, albeit for somewhat different reasons, embracing opposition.

Conditions were already heated in the nation's capital, but by 1793 international events intensified a growing crisis. In 1789 most Americans had breathed a sigh of relief, believing that the ratification of the Constitution and the unanimous election of President Washington proved that they had finally protected republican liberty from post-Revolutionary chaos and had therefore concluded Revolutionary debates. The French Revolution in 1789, and the establishment of a constitutional monarchy by 1791, gave Americans further reason to celebrate. Not only had republican liberty been consolidated in the United States, it was now spreading to Europe.[73]

By 1792 and 1793 many Americans had grown much less confident that the events of 1787 through 1789 in their own nation provided long-term protection for republican liberty. At the same time, first with the leadership of Danton and the Girondin and then that of Robespierre and the Jacobins, the French Revolution entered its more radical and violent phase. American reactions to this development differed. For most the divisions over the French Revolution reinforced the emerging rifts within the United States, providing combatants with a greater sense of what was at stake. The French Revolution increased the fear and suspicion the Federalists felt toward the nascent opposition. It also encouraged those beginning to fear the Federalists to become even more deeply convinced that the party of Washington was the enemy of republican liberty.[74]

This merging of internal conflicts with disagreements about international events had a particular impact on the formation and subsequent complexity of the Jeffersonian opposition in Pennsylvania. A good illustration of this point was the development between 1793 and 1795 of the Democratic Republican Societies in Philadelphia and the Pennsylvania interior. The Democratic Republican Societies were initially created mostly by urban figures excited by the French Revolution. The growing anti-French and anti-revolutionary fears of the ministry of William Pitt the Younger also encouraged the growth of pro–French Revolution political organizations inside the United States, and particularly Pennsylvania. After 1789 the French Revolution focused long-standing radical impulses within the British Isles, impulses that had been dormant since the 1760s and the high tide of the Wilkesite movement.[75] During the 1790s English Jacobins, Irish republicans, and, to a lesser extent, Scottish critics all demanded various degrees of reform that at times led to radical opposition to the British state. By 1793 the Pitt ministry was concerned enough to draft legislation designed to silence radical organizations such as the London Corresponding Society. Legislation such as the Seditious Meetings Bill and the Treasonable Practices Act made it difficult to meet or speak freely. After 1792 those suspected of

French revolutionary sympathies increasingly found life dangerous in the British Isles.[76]

During the middle years of the 1790s, as seasoned, highly politicized radicals fled Britain and Ireland, many went to France, but many others sailed to the United States. A good number of these men, such as John Binns, Thomas Cooper, William Duane, and James T. Callender, would soon become major figures in the formation of the Jeffersonian party, the Democratic Republican Societies, and in later internal arguments among Jeffersonians. They fled to America determined to protect the fragile republican experiment from all developments that reminded them of Pitt's Britain.

Most of the British and Irish radicals first disembarked and then spent some time in New York City and especially in Philadelphia. There they were reunited with like-minded émigrés such as the Philadelphians Matthew Carey and Blair McClenahan who had been in the United States for some time and could focus the newcomers' considerable energies on the Federalists and introduce them to natives who shared their concerns. Many of the transatlantic radicals stayed in the seaboard cities, though some, such as Binns, headed into the Pennsylvania interior, where he joined Thomas Cooper and Joseph Priestly in Northumberland County, Pennsylvania. During the years 1793 through 1796, then, a sizable group of highly articulate internationalist republicans arrived in the United States and settled, particularly in cities and especially in Philadelphia. They arrived just as the divisions inside the United States were becoming apparent.

The transatlantic radicals' arrival in Philadelphia merged with the growing concerns of many city figures, especially artisans, about the Federalists. By 1793 and 1794 excitement over the French Revolution had produced in Philadelphia two Democratic Republican Societies, the German Republican Society and the Democratic Society of Pennsylvania. The Democratic Republican Societies formed at first to support "the glorious efforts of France" to foment republican revolution throughout Europe.[77] But this solidarity quickly led them to criticize the Federalists for a variety of reasons. The societies were hostile to the seemingly pro-British policies of the Federalists, such as their willingness to depend on the revenue generated by tariffs on British manufactures to fund the financial program and their refusal to honor the 1778 alliance with France. France had aided the United States during its Revolution; now it seemed that the Federalists abandoned a sister republic to please tyrannical Britain. The increasingly politicized and radicalized groups coming together in Philadelphia were convinced that Great Britain was the gravest threat in the world to republican ideals and institutions. Thus the choice in 1793 to assist Britain instead of France had profound implications. Benjamin Franklin Bache, editor of the *Philadelphia General Advertiser*, insisted in 1793 that "upon the establishment or overthrow of liberty in France probably will depend the permanency of the Republic in the new world."[78]

Supporting Britain in its war with France weakened republicanism everywhere. Since the Federalists appeared to be pro-British, one had to suspect their republican commitments in general. The Democratic Society of Pennsylvania, for example, did not concentrate solely on international issues. Its members sought to link commitments to international republican revolution with a correct position on national politics, which in the case of Philadelphia was also local politics. Thus the society insisted that "the dangers arising from a foreign source [are not] the only causes at this time of apprehension and solicitude. The seeds of luxury appear to have taken root in our domestic soil; and the jealous eye of patriotism already regards the spirit of freedom and equality eclipsed by the pride of wealth and the arrogance of power."[79]

Increasingly between 1793 and 1796, politicized Philadelphians began to connect internationalist commitments to republican France with nagging concerns about the Federalists. In this context policies such as the Federalist excise taxes of 1791 and 1794 became political issues. For the worried, their own interests and international republican impulses could be linked to anger over internal taxes and the Federalists' emerging interconnected political, economic, social, and cultural hierarchy of rule by the wellborn and high-toned. This was a potent combination. In the mid-1790s the emerging Jeffersonians of Philadelphia genuinely believed that the highest aspirations for the political advancement of humanity and their own particular economic interests and concerns rose or fell together.

This merging of principle and interest was so complete that it makes little sense to try to separate the two, or to speculate about whether one set of concerns was more important than the other. A fine illustration is the behavior and belief during these years of the Philadelphia manufacturers Thomas Leiper and Frederick Muhlenberg. In 1791 and again in 1794, these two artisans denounced the Federalists' excise taxes. Most of the revenue needed to fund the debt and cover the yearly expenses of the nation came from imposts. But as the wars of the French Revolution heated up, international trade grew less reliable, and the Washington administration sought additional sources of revenue.[80]

The nation's craftsmen hated the excise taxes. The Federalists denied them protective tariffs, established a hierarchical model for promoting industrial development, and now planned to tax what domestic production independent craftsmen could actually manage. In 1794 the Federalists placed excises on the manufacture of whiskey, snuff, refined sugar, and carriages. An additional measure further infuriated American carriage manufacturers, for the duty on imported carriages and carriage parts was reduced from 15 percent to 4.5 percent ad valorem.[81] The excises held dramatic implications for Philadelphia's artisans, for they directly affected the producers of ale, beer, cider, hops, chocolate, paste, vinegar, candles, glass, soap, paper, pasteboards, starch, hair powder, leather and skins, iron, and carriages. And of course in the absence of protective tariffs, the excise also frightened the rest of the city's artisans. By 1794 they perceived a pattern of hostility and contempt in Federalist policy and a likely precedent for future taxation.[82]

Looking back on these years a decade later, the *Philadelphia Aurora* reflected on the conclusions men such as Leiper and Muhlenberg had drawn by 1794. Under the Federalists, a reprinted article in the *Aurora* explained, it had been impossible

> to protect the unmolested exercise of industry in channels chosen by itself, it is certainly of importance little short of infinite to resist the establishment of a system which gives to governments the control and direction of every branch of internal manufacture; enabling them thereby to depress or elevate; according to the measure of taxation applied, the condition of every class of citizens; a power so nearly approximate to despotism, as to have become hateful in every nation not degraded to the lowest condition.[83]

By 1794 Leiper and Muhlenberg, manufacturers of snuff and finished tobacco, respectively, commodities affected by the 1794 excise, had become enemies of the Federalists and vocal antiexcise men. But they were more than that; they were also leaders of the two Democratic Republican Societies. For Leiper and Muhlenberg republican commitments; hostility for Britain and British-inspired visions of politics, economy, and society; and opposition to the Federalists were indissoluble. Britain threatened republican ideals; the Federalists did not rush to defend another republican nation and imitated British institutions. At the same time, the party pursued policies that threatened Leiper and Muhlenberg. This behavior, Leiper and Muhlenberg concluded, stemmed from the same conviction — fear of a future where ordinary people could control the decisions that shaped their lives. Thus, when the Philadelphia Democratic Republican Societies praised France and demanded direct assistance for actual craftsmen, they believed that it made no sense to endorse one stance and not the other. Republican institutions and values grew stronger when the social, economic, and so eventually political positions of republican citizens did as well.[84]

This politicizing, with its inevitably egalitarian, even nascent democratic, character, helped to at least paper over, and even bridge for a time, the growing rift within the crafts between masters and journeymen. All could agree about the threat of Federalist political economy; most were excited by the possibility of further republican revolution. Whatever the artisans' concerns about each other, they paled next to the stories they heard of Pitt's Britain and the insistence of many radical émigrés that the Federalists would produce in America something similar to it. Thus, after 1793 trends that had encouraged conflict among craftsmen in Philadelphia were temporarily arrested. Masters such as Leiper and Muhlenberg truly shared a politicized language and sensibility of concern and republican aspiration with the journeymen of their community.

The temporary restoration in Philadelphia of firm and intimate connections between masters and journeymen was greatly assisted by the efforts of political activists such as Dr. Michael Leib, who worked closely with the laboring people of Philadelphia. The son of a tanner, Leib lived in the Northern Liberties, a suburban neighborhood dominated by artisans. Trained in medicine, Leib served the city's poor at the city dispensary, the almshouse, the prison, and the Philadelphia Hospital. Leib's reputation was bolstered when he risked his life and stayed in Philadelphia during the yellow fever epidemic of 1793. As the wealthy fled, Leib remained and ministered to the poor.

Leib was also a charter member of the German Republican Society and an officer of the Democratic Society of Pennsylvania. He was a true ideologue who even eschewed the ethnic appeals that many of his fellow German political activists were beginning to make. He was energized by international republican commitments and hostile toward the political, economic, and social hierarchies that undermined them. Leib was a crucial figure in the making of a broad democratic Jeffersonian movement in Philadelphia that brought together a variety of groups in the city, though they already glimpsed that they did not always have common interests. From the beginning, Leib sought to bring Jeffersonian politics to the city's laborers and poor. Equally important, he tried to make working people regular political actors. When more established Philadelphians appealed to working people to help them defeat the Federalists, men such as Leib lent real credibility to their assertions.[85]

At the height of Federalist power in 1794, Philadelphia's manufacturing population was divided. But this rift seemed far less significant than the threat that the Federalists posed for all artisans. James Madison's call for commercial discrimination against Britain, combined with the more favorable stance of Jefferson and his political allies on the French Revolution, solidified this multifarious political coalition. As of 1794 Philadelphia masters, with visions of greatness in their heads, and Philadelphia laborers, concerned about the masters' aspirations, willingly joined Virginia planters in opposition to the Federalists. Virginia gentlemen were troubled by the messy politics of the Democratic Republican Societies, mass outdoor antiexcise meetings, incendiary newspaper articles, and drunken political toasts. But they accepted this fresh and essential injection of energetic support. With victory, they reasoned, the farsighted elites who truly acted in the people's best interests could guide the nation and make such unseemly politics unnecessary.[86]

By 1793 and 1794 most Americans swept up in these deeply politicized and charged events were becoming convinced that the world was dividing into two hostile camps. Americans during the 1790s used names such as the Friends of Liberty and the Friends of Order to describe themselves, and each group identified the other as the chief threat to republican institutions and the pursuit of happiness.[87] This conception of the Friends of Liberty works well for Pennsylvania in the Jeffersonian era, for it can help to explain that very different sorts of people could fancy themselves liberty's friends. In the early and mid-1790s, liberty's enemy appeared to be the aggressive Federalist policies now linked to an international effort to thwart republican revolution. Those frightened by the Federalists, and so convinced of their own commitment to liberty, were diverse enough for the relatively vague concept, Friends of Liberty, to serve them well. For the time being they could concentrate on what threatened liberty and not what liberty actually was. This was an enormous benefit in Pennsylvania, where an already diverse opposition knew precisely what liberty was not but had not yet had to discuss how liberty under the Friends of Liberty would be structured or maintained.

As opposition reached an acute phase in 1793 and 1794, the Pennsylvania Friends of Liberty were still not as diverse as they would shortly be. But already they encompassed a broad group ranging from Frederick Muhlenberg to Michael Leib to virtually unknown figures such as the journeymen cordwainers Philip Dwyer and John Hays. Dwyer and Hays survive only in brief testimony they gave in the cordwainers conspiracy trial of 1806 in Philadelphia. They were engaged in political battles to bring more democracy to the crafts and the world around them in the late eighteenth and early nineteenth centuries.[88]

The Friends of Liberty agreed that the French Revolution was a good thing. They believed that the world was moving toward a future where citizens would be freed from the dependencies that had made them subjects in the ancien régime. They insisted that their direct intervention in the decision making that shaped their societies was essential if this new world was to triumph over the old. Within this broad consensus in Pennsylvania (and outside of it), there was great diversity regarding the most useful methods of intervention, the most appropriate goals for change, and even what areas of life needed to be purged of ancient inequalities and superstitions. Virginia gentlemen such as Jefferson could include in their sincere devotion to the ideals of the Friends of Liberty belief in a natural aristocracy better qualified than the citizens it ruled to hold at bay the inequalities, dependencies, and injustices that destroyed republican values and institutions. Friends of Liberty such as Michael Leib were moving closer to the idea that massed majorities empowering representatives were essential for the defeat of those examples of tyranny. Figures such as Frederick Muhlenberg could agree with Leib and help found an organization to assist this mobilization. Yet as belief came to be defined after 1794, and especially after 1800, men such as Muhlenberg could conclude that their understanding of what produced and constituted inequality sharply diverged from that of those Friends of Liberty who identified with citizens who labored for others and earned wages in return.

During the 1790s a broad coalition of people could share real ideological commitments and identify the forces hostile to them. This unity of purpose resulted from a deep ideological consensus shaped at a particular time when it made sense to identify commitments and concerns in particular ways. But this consensus should not obscure the great diversity among the Friends of Liberty or the variety of potentially competing and divisive ideas that were present from the beginning among Jeffersonians. When at a later date it made sense to identify commitments and concerns in different ways, the very ideological, political, economic, social, and cultural aspirations and imperatives that had brought Jeffersonians together drove them apart. Nowhere was this truer than in Philadelphia and Pennsylvania. Because of their precocious political and economic experiences and development, that city and state included a greater variety of Jeffersonians within a single polity than did any other place where the party quickly triumphed. In Pennsylvania, more than in any other state, the universal Jeffersonian goal of controlling state politics and local offices would become a perpetual argument about the differences among Jeffersonians. These differences were present from the beginning but only grew paramount after 1800 when it was time to reshape the Republic with Jeffersonian ideals.

One major reason the Friends of Liberty could identify each other so readily and see little reason at first to emphasize (or even notice) their own differences was that they could define themselves through their opposition to the Federalists. They could oppose the worldview of intertwined political, economic, social, and cultural values possessed by those who saw themselves as the Friends of Order. In the mid-1790s the Friends of Order believed that the world was fast going mad. French revolutionary armies looked capable of exporting the worst examples of the tyranny of majority mobs throughout Europe, and foreign agents and their destructive American allies seemed to welcome these values to the United States. The French Revolution exemplified the pattern of birth, embrace of freedom, explosion of license, onslaught of chaos, and restoration of despotism that the history of republican experiments amply demonstrated. From the conservative New England clergy to the secular, rationalist, and skeptical salons of Federalist Philadelphia, the Friends of Order were convinced that if chaos went unchecked, republican liberty would die.[89]

As this great division developed, the key assumption made by Friends of Order such as Alexander Hamilton was that if the course of events continued, the people would create such unlivable conditions that they themselves would finally welcome a despot to restore order. The Federalists would feel more than vindication when after 1797 Napoleon began his rise. For the Friends of Order, the divisions of the 1790s produced a profound battle in which they defended moral and personal responsibility. They came to identify those virtues with the ability to identify the liberty all citizens deserved, and the capacity to deny oneself the intoxicating, initially liberating, but ultimately destructive, opportunity to separate from every past attachment and duty that had previously connected people. From the mid-1790s the Federalists, the Friends of Order, sought to consolidate a republican experiment where they would reshape the citizenry so that it could possess a permanently clear understanding of what republican citizens should demand and what they should acknowledge they had no right to possess. Order, hierarchy, greatness of vision, and kindly paternal guidance — these things strengthened valued and fragile republican liberty. Such liberty had never survived for very long in the past, and as the Federalists desperately tried to preserve it in the United States, they believed that it was dying in Europe. The Federalists were republicans in a largely monarchical world and sought ways to teach citizens to control themselves. If republican citizens learned the lessons the Friends of Order could teach them, they could then play a crucial role in promoting salutary hierarchies, and so preserve liberties that it appeared no other people on earth would enjoy. The conflict of the 1790s was so bitter because both Federalists and Jeffersonians felt with equally deep conviction that they alone could preserve the Republic, and that the other would destroy it.

In 1793 and 1794 the Federalists felt that events were slipping beyond their control. By 1794 the world and the nation seemed divided between the Friends of Liberty and the Friends of Order. Thus the response, the Federalists concluded, required both an international and a domestic solution. In 1794 they sought to move the United States closer to Britain, the one nation capable of defeating France, the agent of anarchy disguised as a republic. That same year they moved to reassert an internal order that had been shaken by the events of 1792 and 1793. Their efforts of 1794 attracted new and essential supporters to the emerging Pennsylvania Jeffersonian opposition. This new support added to the complexity and diversity of their ideas and aspirations.

The complexities and conflicts of 1794 that allowed the growing divisions in the United States to cohere and produce a sustained formal political conflict at the national, state, and local levels all swirled around the actions of one man, Hamilton's and Madison's former collaborator, John Jay. By 1794 the Friends of Order had made their choice. With the fate of their Republic uncertain, they could not allow the French example to gain more influence. In 1794 the Washington administration sent Chief Justice Jay to London to negotiate an alliance with Great Britain.

Before Jay departed, his mission had already made him highly suspect and seemed to confirm the worst fears of the emerging Jeffersonian opposition in Pennsylvania. Before he returned with a weak treaty to defend, the very idea of seeking closer relations with Britain confirmed for the Friends of Liberty in Philadelphia that the Federalists had ceased to be republicans. On the day Jay sailed from Philadelphia, the Friends of Liberty in the city hung his effigy, guillotined it, and then blew it up with gunpowder. As he sailed from the quay, a crowd mobilized to jeer him.[90] By 1794 rapidly cohering worldviews, which everyone involved in the growing political conflict considered essential for understanding the behavior of their enemies, were the starting point for the assumptions and conclusions that most politicized Americans drew. The outcome of the Jay Treaty only confirmed what the enemies of the Federalists believed the day Jay sailed.

While Jay was in England seeking an ordered international response to world chaos, the Federalists began to pursue a domestic one. This effort added new numbers and greater diversity and complexity to the Friends of Liberty and the Jeffersonian opposition in Pennsylvania. In 1794 the Federalists passed the second series of excises that so frightened Philadelphia craftsmen. The Federalists had more than one reason to support the excise. Federalist policy makers had long realized that diverse sources of revenue were desirable. Though most of the national government's income came from imposts, excises were not to be scorned. Furthermore, as international conditions grew unstable and the oceans more dangerous, it was sensible to rely somewhat less completely on imports for revenue. Beyond that, by 1794 the Federalists considered it salutary to create opportunities to remind American citizens of the legitimacy, authority, and presence of the national state. As the perceptions intensified of a society steadily moving beyond the control of proper authorities, the Federalists hoped that a more energetic government would command respect by reminding Americans that it deserved and could compel their obedience.[91]

Philadelphians reacted predictably to the 1794 excise. They connected it to Jay's negotiations and the Federalists' broad embrace of seemingly anti-republican institutions and values. The 1794 excise also began to drive farmers to the opposition. This drift was clearest in western Pennsylvania. Westerners were already suspicious of the Washington administration's choice of Jay as negotiator. Jay was disliked in the west for agreeing to the treaty of 1785 with Spain, in which the United States gave up the right to navigate the Mississippi River until 1810 in exchange for greater access to Spain and its colonies. Westerners believed that Jay had protected the needs of eastern merchants at their expense by bargaining away the only realistic passage they had to market, the port of New Orleans.[92]

Jay was already a suspicious figure in the west in 1794, and so was the government that sponsored him. The doubt westerners had about Jay, his mission, and the Federalist Party intensified as they learned of the excise tax. The tax did much to discredit the Federalists in the west and seemed to confirm the vaguer doubts westerners had about Jay and the search for closer relations with Britain. The government that passed the excise was dangerous and tyrannical, and since that government sought closer relations with Britain, westerners needed to pay attention to the opposition's explanation for and analysis of this search.

The excise united western Pennsylvanians against the Federalists. The

Federalists drove together a population that, like the Philadelphia craftsmen, had been dividing and becoming increasingly fractious since 1770. Between 1770 and 1800 landownership in western Pennsylvania became heavily concentrated. In 1770 the population of the western counties was approximately thirty-five thousand. Thirty years later it had ballooned to ninety-five thousand, though the population of the rest of the state increased by only 40 percent during the same period. This rapid growth compressed into one generation demographic and developmental changes that often took over a century to complete. The earliest arrivals and large absentee speculators eagerly purchased vast tracts, knowing that settlers would soon follow. Speculation tended to drive up prices, and as early as the 1780s, 33 percent of western Pennsylvanians owned no land. In some townships 60 percent of the population was landless. Despite this consolidation, during that decade the top 10 percent of landowners controlled only 25 percent of the land. But a future of heavier concentration could be perceived, for the bottom 10 percent (which did not include the substantial number too poor to be assessed) controlled only 2 percent. During the 1780s, though, aside from those at the very bottom, some form of landownership was still a reasonable expectation in western Pennsylvania.[93]

The boom of the 1790s, sparked by increased mercantile profits and the Federalists' financial program, encouraged heavy, large-scale speculation in recently cleared and still uncleared land. The number of landless increased during the 1790s, as did the population whose cleared land was less than fifty acres, the amount deemed the minimum for a competence. The median taxpayer in most western Pennsylvania townships by the mid-1790s was a landless laborer. By 1795 the top 10 percent of western Pennsylvanians owned between 37 percent and 50 percent of the land, depending on the county. Though such concentrations were not as high as they would become, they were a great deal higher than they had been. Increasingly westerners feared that landlessness was a permanent condition, that a competence was beyond their reach.

Local western elites rapidly diversified into commercial agriculture, sawmills and gristmills, iron foundries, and investment in craft manufactures. Entrepreneurs such as Hugh Henry Brackenridge and Albert Gallatin purchased 1,386 acres and 7,000 acres, respectively. Gallatin started a glass manufactory and a sawmill on his land. The two were joined by other vigorous westerners such as William Findley, who was able to make a career out of puncturing the vanity of supposedly disinterested Federalist elites.[94]

By 1794 classes of wealthy landed men and landless poor emerged in western Pennsylvania. By many accounts the region had become a vicious and violent place where initially high expectations had fallen.[95]

Westerners were hurt most acutely by the Federalist excise on whiskey. Albert Gallatin pronounced the excise "dangerous to liberty" because it produced an army of excise men who would trespass on property.[96] But the excise on whiskey was much more than an intrusive nuisance. Westerners had reacted furiously when Great Britain attempted to levy indirect but internal taxes during the 1760s. Now another distant and impersonal government, located in the city that they believed had always denied them fair representation, sought to impose the same sorts of taxes.[97] Anti-Federalism had always been sharper in western than eastern Pennsylvania. Even local elites such as Gallatin had initially opposed the Constitution. Now it seemed as if western Anti-Federalists had been right all along.

The excise on whiskey also threatened to cripple the western Pennsylvania economy. Westerners constantly complained of the dearth of good roads from the west to the state's principal eastern markets. Difficulties of transport and denial of access to the Mississippi forced them to distill grain into whiskey, which was much easier to transport. In addition, whiskey, always in demand, often acted in place of more traditional forms of currency given the scarcity of specie. In effect the excise taxed the use of money.[98]

The excise focused preexisting tensions, but it also created real and significant new ones. Virtually all western Pennsylvanians owned a still, and one concern raised was the regressive nature of an excise that taxed personal and commercial stills indiscriminately. Men such as Gallatin and Brackenridge, substantial local landowners, could agree about the excise with more marginal men whom their large purchases threatened to dispossess. Resident speculators were different from absentee speculators such as George Washington. The president owned sixty-three thousand acres in western Pennsylvania. For a variety of reasons, including self-interest, he wanted a peaceful, even docile, population. Rough behavior and political extremism had to be repressed.[99] But Gallatin, Brackenridge, and rising strivers such as Findley had to live among their fellow westerners. Furthermore, if the government provoked violent reactions, they, too, or at least their property, could become targets. They had to oppose a government that provoked the west, especially when that government did so to raise revenue to strengthen a national state whose legitimacy, under the Federalists at any rate, was dubious in the first place.

As discontent over the excise grew, local elites endorsed the calling of and chaired committees that produced antiexcise petitions. But they called for peaceful and legal opposition and declared that republican government could not exist if any section of the union felt justified in violently disobeying any laws it disliked.[100] Forceful resistance, urged committees like that of Fayette County, chaired by Gallatin, was acceptable only when constitutional remedies were unavailable. The American and French Revolutions were just. But in this instance those temporarily in power disobeyed the fundamental laws and obligations of the land. The remedy, then, was to elect proper men and manage the government so that fundamental law bound both government and governors. Gallatin, Brackenridge, and Findley were nonplussed by the armed rebellion that flared up in western Pennsylvania in the summer and fall of 1794. It attracted upwards of seven thousand men and, at its most dangerous, threatened to seize the federal arsenal at Pittsburgh. The Federalists' response was to send in a massive army of thirteen thousand, almost double the number participating in the rebellion. By the time the army arrived, the most incendiary had melted into the Ohio wilderness, and those who remained were searching for more viable and less dangerous methods of protest.[101]

Though local leaders did not condone the violent acts, they did defend the right of the rebels to engage in violent speech. Furthermore, they accepted the rebels' insistence that they had legitimate grievances against the government. This willingness to act with more marginal men built solidarity. So, too, did the Federalists' conviction, soon common knowledge in western Pennsylvania, that men such as Gallatin, Brackenridge, and Findley were responsible for the entire incident. These men's reputations suffered by their involvement, but more obscure westerners acknowledged the risks they had taken.[102]

In the aftermath of the rebellion the Federalist-dominated Pennsylvania assembly annulled the state elections in the four rebellious western counties, Westmoreland, Washington, Fayette, and Allegheny. The elections had taken place during the rebellion, and Gallatin was one of the assemblymen unseated by the decision. In a lengthy speech to the state legislature he denounced the annulment and reminded his fellow congressmen that westerners were citizens of a republic and not subjects in a monarchy. Gallatin acknowledged that the rebels might have influenced the election, but republics, unlike monarchies, did not have the luxury of behaving arbitrarily without evidence. Republics had to show themselves superior to "despotic governments [that] eagerly seize every opportunity which the faults and the temporary folly of any part of the nation may afford them in order to add new energy to their powers, to justify the arbitrary exercise of jurisdiction to new objects."[103]

Gallatin's reputation was made. In the new elections all those who had been turned out were returned, and Gallatin's reelection was nearly unanimous. By 1795 most western Pennsylvanians were united in a belief that the gravest threat they faced came from the Federalists in Philadelphia. They joined behind figures such as Gallatin, Brackenridge, and Findley, who clearly had no place to go except to join the emerging Jeffersonian opposition. These leading westerners, like the successful master craftsmen of Philadelphia, did not fit the Federalists' political, social, cultural, and economic conceptions of the proper republican gentleman. Upwardly mobile entrepreneur that he was, Gallatin could talk in ways that no one in the Federalist circle ever could. Gallatin could denounce power and social arrogance. He could defend those who resisted them, and he could channel their energies into the Jeffersonian opposition.

Gallatin became a Jeffersonian party leader in the national House of Representatives. Findley would become a senator in the same building, and Brackenridge became the first Jeffersonian appointed to the Pennsylvania Supreme Court. Gallatin would be the most prominent of the three. He denounced Federalists for describing the whiskey rebels as Jacobins. Revolution and Jacobinism, Gallatin maintained, were extreme reactions to the extremity of despotic excess — the very thing the Jeffersonians resisted. Revolution and Jacobinism were reactions to hierarchy, obnoxious arrogance, and the violation of individual liberty — behavior the Jeffersonians sought to eradicate. If the United States wished to avoid Jacobinism, it needed to defeat the Federalist Party that provoked violent reactions.[104] Despite the obvious potential for internal divisions in the west, the threat posed by the Federalists transcended all else. Pennsylvanians such as Gallatin, Brackenridge, and Findley were able to lead men into the Pennsylvania Jeffersonian party who, in another context, might have considered them the enemy.

By 1794 an opposition begun by southern planters attracted urban craftsmen and radical politicians in northern cities and farmers and entrepreneurs, especially in the west. In Pennsylvania this development served to paper over divisions and conflicts just emerging that were driven by the social and economic developments of Philadelphia and the rural interior. As the Jeffersonian opposition formed in Pennsylvania, it absorbed tremendous social and economic diversity. This complexity meant that at a future date, when the Federalists were no longer viewed as the source of the Republic's ills, there was little likelihood that this diverse coalition would remain unified. The Pennsylvanians privileged enough to shape Jeffersonian political ideas in the state did not necessarily reflect the full range of the social and economic conditions experienced by all in Pennsylvania attracted to the party. But significantly, this group had to consider that full range. Certain of its members would forge close connections with Pennsylvanians who had little in common with citizens of the state whom other Pennsylvania Jeffersonian thinkers viewed as cherished constituents. Thus, Pennsylvania Jeffersonians would face conflicts that states and regions with less social and economic diversity did not experience. The conflict over the content of Pennsylvania's Jeffersonian political thought resulted from the conditions that led to the opposition's formation.

By 1794 the Pennsylvania Jeffersonian opposition was already quite multifarious, but the inclusion of easterners and westerners experiencing wildly varying social and economic conditions was not the extent of the diversity. In the early and mid-1790s an additional group of Pennsylvanians became attracted to the party. This group was more amorphous and can be difficult to characterize. It could often bleed into the ranks of the master craftsmen and entrepreneurial landowners. In Philadelphia, in rural market centers, and in rising county seats across the state, men on the make, professionals not grand enough to be invited into the great sartorial whirl of gaiety of Federalist Philadelphia, also became alienated by this hierarchical and often condescending elite.

The Jeffersonian party began in Pennsylvania to attract men from all but the most elite level. Because of this development the many potentially explosive differences within the opposition increased, a fact that concerned many prominent Jeffersonians. The inclusion of these men on the make can perhaps be rendered less abstract with the use of anecdote. For example, men such as the future Jeffersonian governor of Pennsylvania Thomas McKean were alienated from the Federalists. McKean, like Governor George Clinton of New York, made himself during the Revolution and left behind the obscure origins of his family. But that did not qualify him to meet grand Federalist gentlemen as an equal. McKean, a lawyer and chief justice of the state supreme court before he became governor (and appointed before there was a Jeffersonian opposition), had real social aspirations. He had taken full advantage of the social space opened in Pennsylvania by the American Revolution. Men such as McKean had risen far higher than had similar men elsewhere because the Revolution had produced a greater upheaval in Pennsylvania than it did in other states. The Federalist Party was a serious obstacle to rising state officeholders such as McKean, who could rise no further if conditions remained as they were. But in defeating the Federalists, men such as McKean were determined not to create a political climate so fluid and raucous that it would not respect their own talents and achievements.[105]

Perhaps a better example is the early career of Alexander James Dallas. It is more revealing because it was quite similar to Hamilton's, but the opportunities available to Dallas during the 1790s were far fewer, primarily because of Hamilton's policies. Like Hamilton, Dallas was born in obscurity in the West Indies, in Jamaica in 1759.[106] Like Hamilton, he received legal training and for a time practiced law. Like Hamilton, he became secretary of the Treasury, though he served under Presidents Madison and Monroe. But unlike Hamilton, who arrived in America in 1768, Dallas did not come until 1783. And the fifteen-year gap made quite a difference.

Hamilton was a bold man who arrived at a time when bold men could seize the moment. He soon combined his own talents with impeccable family connections and social credentials. Dallas was not able to embark on a public career until 1786, the year he was admitted to the Pennsylvania bar. Thus, he had to carve a career while Hamilton was busily shaping policies that offered little to unknowns such as Dallas. Dallas quickly proved a brilliant lawyer, made a considerable amount of money, and was recognized as a leading mind in the narrow sphere of Pennsylvania affairs. He even became Secretary of the Commonwealth during the 1790s. But he played no part in the Revolution, he had not made enough money to speculate in debt, and, most important, he had to work a bit too hard for his money and earn it within living memory. He was unknown to Hamilton's circle, and those Pennsylvanians of that circle who did know him, such as Robert Morris, refused to socialize with him. By 1794 Dallas was a staunch Jeffersonian.[107] Still, men such as Dallas had to strike a delicate balance. They had to galvanize the people to defeat the Federalists without endangering their own positions.

Men such as McKean and Dallas were not merely self-interested. The same hierarchy that limited their opportunities also produced what they viewed as intrusive, tyrannical taxes such as the excise and sought to assist Britain as it struggled to contain the spread of republican revolution. It made no sense to distinguish among any of these acts. To chafe at a society structured so that its highest levels were closed was, in this context, a political act that encouraged a further and deeper politicizing. The analysis that explained the presence of a Federalist moneyed elite also explained the hostility to the needs of craftsmen, the contempt for farmers, and the antirepublican impulses that engendered fear of ordinary people mobilizing and putting to use their political energies. By 1794 Dallas was vice president of the Democratic Society of Pennsylvania.

Dissatisfaction with one's place in the society the Federalists were building was intimately connected to a body of internationalist republican and revolutionary ideals. As various groups for different reasons grew concerned about Federalist policies, they engaged in a politicizing education that encouraged them to see their particular concerns as part of a larger whole. This process was responsible in Pennsylvania for creating the diverse and potentially conflicted opposition that by 1794–95 had largely formed.

The Pennsylvania Jeffersonian opposition of 1795, then, was angrier and more diverse than the Philadelphia gathering that had mistreated Jay's effigy. By the time Jay returned with his treaty, Pennsylvania Jeffersonians had grown even less willing to respect his and other Federalists' efforts. Benjamin Franklin Bache first published the treaty in the *Aurora*. It immediately sparked a wave of protest and became the main Jeffersonian issue in the Pennsylvania elections of 1796. Jeffersonian activist Blair McClenachan exhorted one rambunctious Philadelphia crowd to "kick the treaty to hell."[108] Alexander J. Dallas led the antitreaty forces. He published a lengthy pamphlet and newspaper articles arguing that the treaty violated American neutrality and many guarantees of the Alliance of 1778. Dallas also insisted that it constrained American commerce, dangerously empowered the president and Senate at the expense of the House of Representatives, and allowed Great Britain to dictate the Republic's future, particularly in foreign policy. Dallas carefully linked the treaty to an elite, pro-British faction in America and equated that faction with the Federalist Party. This faction, Dallas insisted, was determined to silence the popular branch of government and was almost willing to return the United States to the status of a colony to do so. Though he was confident that Americans would resist pro-British Federalist aristocrats, they had to do so quickly. Already "a great part of our trade [is] monopolized by British subjects, under the mask of American citizenship." British influence had "already formed a considerable party in our government and among our merchants," and it had become necessary to fear and combat "that paramount interest which Great Britain has already insidiously acquired in our commerce, our navigation, manufacturing, territory, and government."[109]

The denunciations were bolstered by descriptions of British atrocities against American mariners. The treaty only confirmed for laborers on land and sea that the Federalists were pro-British and that Britain hoped to curtail American prosperity. The more prominent Pennsylvania Jeffersonians such as Dallas, McKean, Bache, Leiper, Muhlenberg, Leib, and the merchant John Swanwick organized campaigns around opposition to the treaty. In the House of Representatives Albert Gallatin led the effort to deny funds to carry out the treaty after the Senate ratified it.[110] Pennsylvania's Jeffersonian leaders continued to insist that the Jay Treaty was part of a Federalist plan to create a political oligarchy and an economy in which working people would always be subordinate.

By 1795, then, the Pennsylvania Jeffersonian party was recognizable. In Philadelphia it was led by new men who had risen a great deal and hoped to rise further. But these men were stymied by the united and more powerful front of the Federalists. During the 1790s Jeffersonian candidates in Philadelphia enjoyed a mean wealth of $4,891. Though this was considerably more than the journeyman or laborer could ever hope to possess, it was considerably less than the mean wealth of Federalist candidates, which was $9,526.[111] The Jeffersonian candidates emphasized the greater wealth of their Federalist adversaries, and the grandeur and arrogance of Federalist Philadelphia only bolstered their populist arguments.

To defeat this emerging ruling class, Jeffersonian candidates had to appeal to men whose interests they often shared only imperfectly. The men to whom they appealed could potentially expect to demand from victory a set of policies vastly different from those the candidates themselves wanted. But the need to defeat the Federalists was more pressing, and so the candidates appealed, and more marginal men listened. The appeals worked. In 1796 Thomas Jefferson carried Pennsylvania in his failed bid for the presidency. That same year Republicans triumphed in the journeyman neighborhood the Northern Liberties and the laboring and mariner neighborhood Southwark with 82.5 percent and 86.9 percent, respectively, of the votes.[112] Leib was invaluable in securing such totals, which held through the remainder of the decade. Something similar occurred in western Pennsylvania, where former whiskey rebels continued to elect Gallatin and Findley. Candidates who insisted that ordinary men should have the vote and an equal chance at land and independence were a qualitative improvement over the Federalists. Of course expectations would probably rise throughout Pennsylvania if the Federalists were ever defeated.

By 1795 Pennsylvania Jeffersonians were politically conscious enough to subsume real and growing economic and social tensions within their party. They concentrated instead on the unifying desire to defeat Hamilton and his fellow Federalists. Yet the tensions, though muted, could surface. They were seen in the journeymen's strikes against their masters that occurred periodically during the 1790s and in Gallatin's and Brackenridge's discomfort over the whiskey rebels' violence. During the 1790s these nascent divisions could not be the Jeffersonians' primary concern. But in Pennsylvania the possibility of Jeffersonian division after victory was acute. The party was shaped by a broad conception of republican social and political revolution that could be defined and imagined in a variety of ways. But in Pennsylvania the Jeffersonians were also shaped by the actual social and economic conditions of the late eighteenth century. The Federalists threatened a complex, diverse, and potentially divided Pennsylvania opposition.

By 1795 this peculiar Jeffersonian Party was fully mobilized. Between 1795 and 1799 it defeated the Federalists in Pennsylvania. In 1799 Jeffersonians elected Thomas McKean governor. The following year Pennsylvania Jeffersonians played an integral role in electing Thomas Jefferson president. But the political extremity of the second half of the decade meant that some could view the final Jeffersonian victories as legitimizing a more radical brand of politics. Immediately after victory, Pennsylvania Jeffersonians would be confronted with their internal divisions and contradictions.

In 1795 Hamilton left the Treasury, and in 1796 the Hamiltonian Federalist era officially ended with the election of John Adams. Adams was no Hamiltonian, and during the second half of the 1790s the two men came to despise each other. Indeed, during the election of 1800, after Hamilton tried to replace Adams with a Federalist more to his liking, Adams exclaimed, "Hamilton is the leader of a pro-British faction, a bastard, and as much an alien as Gallatin."[113] After 1795, programs such as the Society for Establishing Useful Manufactures were no longer pursued. But the rest of Hamilton's policies remained intact, so Jeffersonian craftsmen continued to get no satisfaction from tariff policies. Still, Adams's plainer New England Federalism, though no friendlier to popular politics, was not as determined to shape a mutually reinforcing political, social, cultural, and economic elite. For one thing, the new president rarely entertained.[114] And yet the Federalist Party under Adams alienated Pennsylvanian Jeffersonians even more than it had under Hamilton and Washington. Pennsylvania Jeffersonians described the years 1798–1800 as the Federalist "reign of terror."

There were real connections between the first and second halves of the 1790s. Adams kept Washington's cabinet intact. This decision meant that his secretaries were Hamilton loyalists, particularly Secretary of State Timothy Pickering and Hamilton's handpicked successor at Treasury, Oliver Wolcott. In addition, virtually all the issues that Adams confronted as president stemmed either directly or indirectly from the Jay Treaty.

The French had been furious when the Federalists adopted the treaty, and they insisted that American neutrality was a fiction that masked favoritism for Britain. After 1795 the French intensified their molestation of American shipping. They refused to desist unless the United States honored the treaty alliance of 1778. Doing so would have violated promises made in the Jay Treaty. James Monroe, the American minister to Paris, denounced the course of American foreign policy, which, no doubt, encouraged French belligerence. Adams soon recalled him and replaced him with the South Carolina Federalist Charles Cotesworth Pinckney.[115] France was not happy with the change of ministers and refused to recognize Pinckney, thus breaking diplomatic relations. Many Federalists would have happily declared for Britain at this point. By 1796 the French Revolution had begun its violent and radical phase, the French seemed determined to conquer Europe, and the Jeffersonian opposition, including the former minister to Paris, appeared to want them to succeed. More important, and more dangerous, the Jeffersonians had almost captured the presidency in 1796 and controlled crucial state governments such as Pennsylvania's.

Adams ignored the discourtesy shown Pinckney. Instead he sent Jeffersonian Elbridge Gerry and moderate Federalist John Marshall to join the minister in Paris and attempt to reopen negotiations. Their efforts led to the infamous XYZ affair, the demand by Talleyrand's secretaries that the United States help fund the French war effort and bribe Talleyrand $225,000 for an audience. Negotiations stalled, and upon Marshall's return, the Federalists prepared for war with France. An alliance with Great Britain, with Britain as the dominant partner, seemed assured.

In May and June 1798 the Federalists mobilized the nation for war. They called for weapons to be manufactured, the assembly of a fifty-thousand-man army, the construction of a navy, and the creation of the United States Marine Corps. The Adams administration renounced the alliance of 1778, allowed the arming of merchant vessels, and authorized privation of French ships by both those vessels and the navy. To pay for the undeclared war Congress appropriated $2 million to be raised by a series of taxes, including the first direct tax ever assessed in the United States. Of greatest symbolic importance was the stamp tax on documents. Republicans quickly made the obvious comparisons to the British Stamp Act of 1765. But the Federalists were also sensitive to symbolism, and they passed their land tax on Bastille Day 1798. The tax would be levied on the assessed value of land and dwellings and would be calculated by counting the number of windows in each house. Congress calculated Pennsylvania's share as $237,177.27.[116]

The war measures infuriated the already galvanized Jeffersonian opposition. Both in Congress and out, especially through incendiary newspaper editorials and broadsides, the Jeffersonians denounced the Adams administration's drift toward Britain. One of the more obstreperous figures in this intensified war of political words was Benjamin Franklin Bache, the editor of the *Aurora*. Bache, the grandson of Benjamin Franklin, was a member of one of Philadelphia's leading families. He was profoundly influenced by the French Revolution, and his commitments made him anathema to the city's Federalists. They ostracized him, and their treatment pushed him closer to men such as Leiper, Muhlenberg, and Dallas, who were quite happy to link shared international enthusiasms to their domestic differences with the Federalists. Bache became a severe critic of Washington and, after a brief period of quiet in early 1796, of Adams as well.[117]

The Philadelphia that Bache addressed was also changing, and the nature of this change threatened Federalist control of the city and the state. Between 1790 and 1800 the city's population grew from 45,000 to 61,560. Most of this increase was due to immigration, with the majority of the immigrants English and Irish refugees fleeing the increasingly repressive measures of Pitt's ministry. Migration rose sharply after the failed Irish uprising of 1798. Overwhelmingly the newcomers supported the Jeffersonians. Those who could vote did so, and those who were not yet citizens swelled meetings, jeered the Federalists, and contributed to the raucous nature of city politics. The Federalists reserved their strongest condemnation for Jeffersonian newspaper editors and "wild Irishmen."[118]

The Federalists longed to do something about both groups, and the Jeffersonians soon miscalculated, giving them their chance. As the war measures passed the Congress, opposition congressmen insisted that Adams had never given negotiations a chance. They demanded that he justify his foreign policy. Their demands gave Adams the opening he needed, and on April 7, 1798, he published the XYZ papers. The brazen demands of Talleyrand's ministers angered most Americans. For a time Adams's popularity rose, and the Jeffersonians looked rather silly. Abigail Adams noted the change and happily reported, "We are now wonderfully popular except with Bach [*sic*]and co who in his paper calls the president old, querulous, bald, crippled, toothless Adams."[119]

The Federalists quickly moved to capitalize on their seemingly altered fortunes. Here was their chance both to humiliate the opposition of upstarts and nobodies and to cut off their supply of foreign malcontent supporters. The Federalists, as always, were moved by their hierarchical conception of a proper republic. They had long maintained that misguided freedom produced license, anarchy, and finally despotism. Since the early 1790s these Friends of Order had grown increasingly convinced that the society around them was slipping beyond the control and guidance of the virtuous and far-sighted. At long last they felt that in 1798, as the people praised Adams and denounced France, America's republican citizens had come to their senses. Republican citizens finally perceived the wisdom of their leaders and felt respect for their republican superiors. At last the people looked to their leaders to restore order and save the republican experiment. This thinking provided the context for the notorious Alien and Sedition Acts. Yet as the Federalists enacted these repressive measures, they mistook anti-French sentiment for actual support for themselves. They moved to take advantage of a popularity that was fleeting and accidental.

In June and July 1798 the Federalists attempted to deal a mortal blow to the Jeffersonian opposition. During these two months they passed the Sedition Act aimed at silencing political dissent. They also passed a new naturalization act, which increased the period of naturalization from five to fourteen years, in response to Irish votes in the midterm election of 1798. Those Irish who voted were part of the first major wave of immigration, which had coincided with the first repressive acts passed in Pitt's Britain in 1793. Completing the legislation, the Federalists passed the Alien Friends Act and the Alien Enemies Act, measures that empowered the president to punish or deport disorderly aliens and incarcerate all subjects or citizens of nations at war with the United States.[120] The Federalists sincerely hoped the legislation would produce a more orderly and stable republic. Indeed, the Sedition Act expanded protections for speech by making truth a defense, though it was not one in common law. Yet these efforts only showed how fast the society, politics, and culture of the Republic were transforming around the Federalists. Their opponents took for granted that they could say anything that was true. And truth, in a political sense at least, was subject to debate and argument that no citizen, regardless of where he felt he stood in a hierarchy, had the luxury of avoiding or silencing. Thus, despite the Federalists' republican commitments, the conclusion of the foremost scholar of the Alien and Sedition Acts is still apt forty years after its publication: "In the face of the emergence of an effective grass roots democratic opposition to their domestic and foreign policies, they retreated to repression as a means of retaining power. The authoritarian alien and sedition system was the logical culmination of Federalist political philosophy."[121]

The Alien and Sedition Acts and the taxes levied to pay for the coming war with France terrified and infuriated Pennsylvania's Jeffersonians. Once again hostility to Federalist initiatives led to further social, economic, and ethnic diversity within the opposition, for the Federalist program also managed to alienate additional parts of the state, particularly the previously Federalist Germans of southeastern Pennsylvania. As early as the beginning of 1799, support for the Federalists and for war with France was waning. The *Aurora* published insurance figures for the second half of 1798, showing that whereas France had caused $260,000 in damage to American vessels, Britain was responsible for $280,000 worth of harassment. Pennsylvanians began again to question the Federalists' amazing fondness for Britain.[122]

In addition, many Pennsylvanians were concerned about the direct taxes levied to fund the war. That war might not even be declared against the nation's most destructive enemy made the taxes harder to bear. In January 1799 the predominantly German citizens of York County, Pennsylvania, petitioned against the Federalist legislation. The Federalists should have heeded this petition, for the Jeffersonians had never carried York County. Indeed, the Federalists had triumphed there and in the rest of southeastern Pennsylvania during the 1790s. Nevertheless, in 1798 the Jeffersonians had done better in the region than ever before and had managed to carry some counties. Now the petitioners told the Federalists why they were losing ground. The petitioners stressed that "while we are warmly attached to the union, we cannot but express our concern at several acts passed in the two last sessions of congress: the law for erecting a standing army, the Sedition and Alien laws, the stamp act, the direct tax on land, and the great increase in revenue officers."[123]

The final complaint was as important to Pennsylvania Germans as was any other. The direct tax required a host of intrusive assessors, and the Federalist state government appointed those conservative, socially acceptable men on whom the Federalists always relied. In the case of southeastern Pennsylvania this inclination meant the appointment primarily of Quakers and Anglicans, who not only were the wealthiest residents of the region but also had been neutral or loyalist during the American Revolution.

These appointments angered the Germans as much as the taxes and other acts. In January and February 1799, a group of armed German militia forcibly prevented the tax collectors from doing their jobs.[124] The obstructers were quickly arrested, and news spread that they would be transported to Philadelphia for trial. The change of venue infuriated their neighbors. Most of the imprisoned were Germans, yet in the city they would be prosecuted and judged by anglophones using Anglo-American law. Furthermore, Philadelphia was the locus of the hated acts, taxes, and collectors in the first place. Already convinced that Federalist behavior violated their liberties, southeastern Pennsylvania Germans now feared that their neighbors would not be judged fairly. Thus on March 7, 1799, led by the auctioneer John Fries, 140 armed men surrounded the Bethlehem, Pennsylvania, tavern where the prisoners were held and forced their release. The Fries Rebellion had begun.[125]

The rebellion ended almost before it started. With the freedom of the prisoners secured, the crowd dispersed. Yet the implications were considerable. Fries, like most Pennsylvania Germans during the 1790s, had always voted Federalist. By 1798–99 the Germans no longer believed that the Federalists were the upholders of the Constitution or the leaders of a nation in which they could live comfortably. Influenced by Pennsylvania's democratic politics, they began to interpret the meaning of the Constitution for themselves. They concluded that the Federalist program of 1798–99 was unconstitutional. By 1799 Fries and his followers believed that they had behaved lawfully to prevent unconstitutional acts.[126]

For some time the extremity of the 1790s had bred a disposition to overreact, and the Federalists responded to Fries out of all proportion to his conduct. He and a few of his followers were quickly arrested, tried, found guilty, and sentenced to death. The death sentence came despite the efforts of defense counsel Alexander J. Dallas. If Fries was not a Jeffersonian before, he certainly was now. The Federalists wanted to execute him; the Jeffersonians hoped to return him safely to Bucks County. During Fries's trial President Adams supported the death penalty. Like his fellow Federalists, he felt besieged. The Federalists simply could not cope with or function well in the atmosphere of sustained popular politics that had existed in Pennsylvania since 1793. Fries's death, Adams hoped, would awe and quiet the state, for, the president complained, "Pennsylvania is the most villainous compound of heterogeneous matter conceivable."[127]

Luckily for Fries, his lawyers were able to show that one of the jurors had stated before the trial his intent to find the defendant guilty. The presiding judge declared a mistrial and scheduled a second trial for March 1800. Between the two trials a great deal changed. The hostility and contempt that the Hamiltonian wing of the Federalist Party felt for Adams became public knowledge. It also became clear that there would be no war with France, and the near inevitability of Jefferson's presidential victory in 1800 became increasingly acknowledged. Finally, Adams humanely concluded that the death penalty for Fries was too harsh. Arch Federalist justice Samuel Chase presided over Fries's second trial and upheld the death sentence. This time

Adams pardoned Fries. Yet Federalist mercy stopped with him. Hamilton denounced the clemency, and Secretary of State Pickering, Secretary of the Treasury Wolcott, and Secretary of War James McHenry promptly resigned. The majority of Pennsylvania's Germans were forevermore Jeffersonians. Fries died in 1818. Beginning in 1800, he never again voted Federalist.[128]

The southeasterners were latecomers to the Pennsylvania Jeffersonian coalition, and the men who impressed them most were those who shared their commitment to the Constitution and who would interpret it in ways that protected their persons and interests. Dallas was well regarded by many in the southeast after he defended Fries. For many of the rural folk of this region, joining the Jeffersonian party did not automatically mean sharing the Atlantic world radicalism that fueled the international politics of the 1790s and that had focused the reaction to Hamilton's program. This radicalism truly did animate Jeffersonian politics in Philadelphia. Thus, the Federalists played their final move in the city. Philadelphia was the foremost challenge; there the ideas were the most explosive. The Federalists wanted to make an example of John Fries, but they truly despised newspaper editors Benjamin Franklin Bache and newcomer William Duane.

Bache's *Aurora* gained a brilliant assistant editor when Duane returned to America in 1796. Duane was born in 1760 in what would eventually become Vermont.[129] His Irish parents soon returned to Ireland, and Duane grew up on that troubled island. Needing to make his own way, Duane went to India in 1786 and started the *Bengal Journal*. He remained in India until 1794 and during that time became a severe critic of the British presence on the subcontinent. He also endorsed the French Revolution. His prorevolution editorials angered British officials, and his anti-imperial stance infuriated the East India Company. In 1795 Duane was arrested and jailed for two weeks. Rather than prosecute the journalist, the British simply deported him. In 1795 he returned to the British Isles.

Duane came to London and was thrust into the midst of the younger Pitt's crackdown on republicans, French Revolution sympathizers, and critics of British society. In response Duane joined the radical London Corresponding Society and immersed himself in the United Irish Movement. Duane came of age in the middle of the age of the democratic revolution. By the mid-1790s he was a zealous critic of the imperial system that allowed Britain to dominate much of India. Duane also denounced the conditions in rising industrial cities such as Birmingham and Manchester and the poverty that he claimed typified England's rural shires. Political repression convinced Duane that only the overthrow of Europe's old regime could create and preserve republican societies. But Great Britain seemed strong enough to stem the tide in Europe. Thus, in 1796 Duane sailed for the United States. There a bold republican experiment had managed to avoid the full hostility of Britain. A committed republican, indeed, an emerging democrat, Duane arrived convinced that men such as himself had to forever warn the United States about the threat Britain posed. Radicals had to show their fellow citizens how to build a pure republican society able to defeat its enemies.

Duane quickly decided that republican America was in grave danger. Pittite legislation such as the Seditious Meetings Bill and the Treasonable Practices Act seemed closely related to the Alien and Sedition Acts.[130] The Federalists appeared willing to build their own Manchesters with their own version of the Bank of England. Duane's talents and convictions attracted Bache, through whom Duane acquired access to the *Aurora* and the opportunity to continue his life's work.

The two editors rapidly turned the *Aurora* into the most important opposition daily in the nation. Bache alone, or with Duane after his arrival, denounced the Society for Establishing Useful Manufactures; the Jay Treaty; Federalist candidates in local, state, and national elections; the Quasi War; the taxes of 1798; and especially the Alien and Sedition Acts. Indeed, the Federalists enacted the Sedition Act primarily to silence the *Aurora*. In Bache's case the Federalists could not even wait for the act to become law. In 1798 Bache was accused of seditious libel, a charge that began a decade-long campaign by the *Aurora* to expunge the common law from American jurisprudence. The Federalists also boycotted the *Aurora*, and in 1798 the Friends of Order assaulted Bache. A wealthy shipbuilder's son whose father had government contracts and the son of a prominent Federalist newspaper editor accosted Bache and beat him. Eventually Bache was also charged with violating senatorial privilege when he printed a piece of legislation still being deliberated. Unfortunately for Bache, the yellow fever epidemic that swept Philadelphia in 1798 silenced him before the Federalists had their chance.[131]

If the Federalists thought that Bache's death brought them a reprieve, they quickly learned otherwise. Bache left the paper to his widow, who soon married Duane. Duane made the paper an even more vicious opponent of Federalist policies. Duane, who had left the colonies as an infant before the Revolution, and whose citizenship was therefore dubious, campaigned against the Alien and Sedition Acts. He mounted a vigorous defense of free speech, insisting that free speech was essential for direct popular involvement in politics and that without such involvement no society was genuinely republican.

The Federalists quickly made silencing Duane their chief goal. Though there was some talk of deporting him, the question of citizenship was too tricky. The *Aurora* exuberantly denounced the Federalists, and, after 1798, the Federalists saw public disagreement as treason. Between 1798 and 1800 Duane was arrested numerous times for violating the Sedition Act. Alexander J. Dallas defended him. His willingness to do so helped strengthen the connections between members of the fractious city opposition. Prior to Dallas's and Duane's cooperation the Duane-led *Aurora* had mostly attracted Michael Leib and his constituency of Northern Liberties journeyman. Additional support had come from Irish and English immigrants, especially the radical group that arrived after 1798.

Dallas's defenses of Duane, a response to a Federalist offensive that threatened all Jeffersonians, tied all wings of the party together. The *Aurora* became the organ of the opposition. Between 1798 and 1800 it devoted itself to defeating the Federalists. Thus, in opposition Duane and the paper truly did speak for all Jeffersonians. In the midst of this campaign Duane was finally found guilty of sedition and forced into hiding. The *Aurora* continued to appear, and its content did not change. Ultimately, President Jefferson allowed the Alien and Sedition Acts to expire and cleared Duane of all charges. He also credited the *Aurora* with playing a crucial role in his victory.[132]

Jefferson's election, which included his victory in Pennsylvania, was foreshadowed by Thomas McKean's gubernatorial triumph in 1799. A fractious opposition, which was ethnically, socially, and economically diverse, had been firmly united by its determination to defeat the Federalist Party. In 1800 that same coalition was determined to deliver the nation to Jefferson. But the Federalists had one final card to play. Republicans were so disciplined in 1800 that Jefferson and the other candidate acceptable to Republicans, Aaron Burr, received an equal number of electoral votes. The Federalists quickly began to negotiate with the urbane New York lawyer. The response in Pennsylvania shows just how extreme and volatile politics in the state had become by the end of the Federalist era. McKean, a former state supreme court chief justice, a cautious, pragmatic man who truly hoped his reign would usher in stable prosperity and opportunity for all, convinced himself that the Federalists plotted civil war. McKean was a moderate who in the Revolution had been more committed to home rule than to the most radical notions about who should rule at home. Nevertheless, he allowed his allies to appeal directly to the city crowds to intervene, and he promised Jefferson that he would call out the state militia to prevent the inauguration of anyone other than the Jeffersonians' true choice.[133] Adams Federalists finally broke the electoral tie, and for the first time in many years under the Federalists, the wishes of the people were respected.

Thus, the Jeffersonians triumphed in Pennsylvania as they had in the nation, and Pennsylvania gave Jefferson crucial support outside the South. Yet victory in Pennsylvania occurred in a potentially violent context, one that seemed to justify extremity and extreme popularity in mainstream politics. This seeming justification was potent and explosive because the Jeffersonian victory in Pennsylvania was immensely complex, and this complexity would quickly lead to bitter division. Those excited by the *Aurora*'s increasingly democratic voice began to make profound and far-reaching demands of Jeffersonian victory. Once they made those demands, they placed a severe strain on Pennsylvania's Jeffersonian party, a strain that quickly led to its acrimonious division. What did they demand, and why did they think they could do so? Those grouped around the *Aurora* quickly began to insist on something that they called democracy. The quest of these Philadelphia Democrats for a truly just and equal society provoked the bitter debate over the proper content of Jeffersonian political thought that fueled Pennsylvania's Jeffersonian politics for the next thirty years.

In 1800 the Jeffersonians triumphed, and the seat of the national government moved from Philadelphia to the new city named in General Washington's honor. The move was fitting. Washington, an excellent judge of land, picked a spot that should have been bucolic and pastoral. But the impact of too much building too quickly turned the area into a second dismal swamp.[134] In the abstract, at least, this muddy place could only please the leaders of the Jeffersonian party. In the new capital country gentlemen could preside in a city that most people could not wait to leave. With the elegance and grace of Philadelphia only a memory, the move south denied the grandeur that Federalist elites believed the national state needed to establish a proper tone and hierarchy. The living conditions of early Washington made such aspirations ridiculous.

In 1800 Pennsylvanians were left to themselves. In every sense the national Federalist elite that had brought them together was gone. The Jeffersonian party that triumphed in Pennsylvania would not remain united long in the absence of a Federalist threat. As it divided, it brought to the center of Pennsylvania politics for over a generation the economic, social, and ultimately political concerns that increasingly divided the diverse, amorphous group that the Federalists had lumped together as inferior, common, untrustworthy, and dangerous. Quickly after 1800 the various elements of the Jeffersonian opposition began to realize that they disagreed with each other and wanted very different — even irreconcilable — outcomes from the victory they had all produced. The thinkers and activists who articulated Jeffersonian political thought in Pennsylvania after 1800 could not ignore this realization. As they began to articulate ideas that reflected the complexity and diversity of the opposition they had led, the content of Jeffersonian political thought in Pennsylvania became a bitter debate about what precisely the triumph of those never considered among the great actually meant. This debate and the conflict it engendered centered around protracted arguments about the proper definition of democracy and the precise relationship a democratic government had to an economy increasingly characterized by private consolidation of productive property and wage labor. Only with victory did Pennsylvania Jeffersonians come to understand how much they disagreed with one another. Once they realized this, they engaged in quarrels so fundamental that out of them they produced some of the earliest and clearest articulations of beliefs that later generations would accept as quintessentially American. These early-national Pennsylvanian Jeffersonians produced these beliefs through bitter conflict. This conflict was driven by some of them equating with the ideal of democracy ideas that other Jeffersonians in the state feared would threaten liberty in previously unimaginable ways.

Chapter Two

The Radicals Emerge:
"The European Condition of Society"
and the Promise of Democracy

The Pennsylvanians who elected Thomas McKean governor in 1799 and Thomas Jefferson president in 1800 were startlingly diverse, a fact that had been masked by the common concerns of the 1790s. As President Jefferson took office in 1801, most Pennsylvanians assumed that they agreed on most things. They believed that newspapers such as the *Aurora* and editors such as William Duane spoke for all of them, that their public responsibilities would shortly become far less onerous, and that public life would soon be placid. Very quickly they came to realize that the members of their diverse coalition did not desire or expect the same things from its victory. Nor did Pennsylvania Jeffersonians agree about the proper use of their newfound political power. Within three years, every assumption these Jeffersonians had made about what would follow Jefferson's victory proved wrong.

Between 1801 and 1803 it became clear that William Duane and those close to him, a group that would eventually be called the Duane-Leib faction, the *Aurora*-men, the Malcontents, or Jacobins, and that I have named the Philadelphia Democrats, did not speak for all. Indeed, the Philadelphia Democrats' support of Jefferson was informed by an understanding of history and conclusions drawn from this understanding that many other Pennsylvania Jeffersonians did not accept. The vision the Philadelphia Democrats articulated helped them forge a temporary but vital coalition with many rural Pennsylvanians, and it provoked an intense political conflict between the supporters of Jefferson in and around Philadelphia.

The Philadelphia Democrats were primarily those Philadelphians who viewed their local actions as part of an international effort to spread republican revolution. The ideologically incendiary, and those predisposed to associate the strength of republican revolution in America with the spread of other such revolutions, were vital participants in forming this group. Of this

74

group of indigenous and immigrant radicals, Duane and Michael Leib were the leaders. But many others circulated in and out of the *Aurora* office, including the Philadelphians Joseph Clay, Frederick Wolbert, George Bartram, James Carson, Andrew Geyer, John Steele, and William Binder. Another prominent member of the circle was Thomas Leiper. Eventually the Philadelphia Democrats drew support from younger radicals such as James Thackera and Stephen Simpson. The core of their constituency was the artisan and mariner suburbs, the Northern Liberties and Southwark. Many of the ideas they championed appealed to these laboring people. Leib in particular was a resident and spokesman of the Northern Liberties, and he could count on steady majorities there even when, after 1803, many of the city's more prominent Jeffersonians despised and denounced him.[1]

In the *Aurora* the Philadelphia Democrats articulated a view of the history of the West, and particularly of Great Britain. They did so because they believed a proper understanding of European history made clear the profound relevance of democracy to human affairs. Once these historical lessons were learned, the roles and responsibilities of citizens, the proper structure of the state, and the relationship between citizens and the state would be clear and could cease to be a source of conflict. The *Aurora* identified the 1790s as a "reign of terror" and connected the Federalists' efforts in that decade to long-standing European attempts to limit freedom.[2] The paper insisted that only a careful inquiry into the human past could demystify the sources of inequality and injustice. Once the Republic's citizens understood why people in Europe were unequal, they could better preserve liberty and overawe those Americans such as the Federalists who sought European social relations in the United States. The virtuous citizens of the United States had won a reprieve. "Placed at a vast distance, separated by an immense sea from the scenes where ambition, usurpation, and despotism have acted so many tragedies," the Republic could seek to understand the European nations, it could "calmly consider their histories."[3] Only by doing so could the new nation avoid Europe's fate and protect itself from the dangerous schemes of self-proclaimed gentlemen.

Britain's history, according to the *Aurora*, produced one cataclysm after another: "85 wars independent of 18 civil wars, and 23 invasions . . . in none of which neither the happiness, the interests, nor the true glory of the people had even the remotest share; every war is to be traced to the ambitions or avarice of their kings or nobles; the lust of power and of wealth."[4] Duane and his allies insisted that the absence of equality in Europe guaranteed that government would be perverted from its only just purpose, preserving each citizen from molestation. European aristocrats were able to abuse power for their own purposes because experience from almost time out of mind reinforced the subordination of the many to the few and concentrated wealth and power in the hands of the privileged. Thus Michael Leib explained that in "the transatlantic world despotism embrace[d] all." In Europe "a chief, sustained by a military or a proud domineering nobility, dictate[d] the law by force, or by corruption. The labour of the subject [wa]s made to minister to the ambition of the pleasures of the ruler; and his property, his liberty, and his life, in almost everyone, [we]re literally held by courtesy."[5] Human relations of this sort the *Aurora* denounced as "the European condition of society," and it was this European condition that had threatened to arise during the 1790s.[6]

Jeffersonian triumph, then, was a momentous event in human affairs. With only a few exceptions, and then only among a few people in a small area, humanity knew only abuse, tyranny, want, and fear. The Philadelphia Democrats believed that they could participate in structuring a society that transformed the human condition, and that advanced equality and liberty, thus forever ending human suffering. They drew confidence for this bold vision from what they identified as the democratic legacy of the American Revolution.

The Philadelphia Democrats believed that the American Revolution was the most profound event in history. The *Aurora* doubted "that the founders of the American Revolution knew how far they were to go [or] . . . where they ought to stop."[7] As the Revolution progressed, an entire people began to struggle to transform their earthly condition. Ordinary Americans, craftsmen, seamen, and farmers had seized "the inherent right of altering, abolishing, or forming a new government upon the most perfect principles of social and individual equality."[8] The Philadelphia Democrats insisted that the efforts of common citizens had allowed the United States to defeat the British, and they railed against the assumptions that awarded the wellborn special praise. Citing the achievements of generals and statesmen meant explaining victory in "the American Revolution without noticing a single revolutionary expedient that was used to affect it." Far more important than the efforts of gentlemen were "our town meetings, our committees of correspondence, our mobs; or Indians who destroyed thousands of property in tea, our paper currency, our tender laws, our confiscations and proscriptions."[9]

The collective and revolutionary actions of the people had defeated the British. Equally important, the process of creating a popular revolution provided the means to construct a society that smashed the social, economic, and political relations that produced the European condition of society. The Revolution taught ordinary Americans that political power belonged to them, and that no particular class had the right to make decisions that would affect the lives of all. Further, by dignifying a vast experiment in rule by the many, in democracy, the American Revolution provided ordinary people with the means to prevent a few from consolidating the materials that provided them unaccountable power. The Revolution, the Philadelphia Democrats insisted, had forever transformed American society. Though it began as a struggle against George III, with the emergence of popular and democratic activity "the contest was no longer that of resistance against foreign rule, but which of us shall be the rulers." Ordinary people "from weighing the rights of colonies . . . came to weigh the rights of men."[10]

Ordinary people able to structure the society around them could ensure that the European condition of society never arose in the United States. The antidote to that condition was democracy. Democracy allowed for widespread social and economic equality, and those conditions reinforced commitments to democracy. Of that supposition, through its discussion of European history, the *Aurora* was convinced. The Philadelphia Democrats posed an important question in the years just after Jefferson's victory. Why was Great Britain tyrannical? Thomas Paine had begun to provide an answer. The descendants of "a French bastard landing with an armed banditii" had forced feudal despotism upon England.[11] But in 1800 Britain was clearly not a feudal society. In fact, in Britain more so than in any other nation, the achievements of the modern world, which the *Aurora* identified as the expansion of knowledge and the explosion of commerce, flourished. The European condition of society required the ignorance of the ruled and a monopoly of all productive enterprise by the rulers. Yet the proliferation of cheap available print should have made it impossible for an educated minority to prevent the people from reading, learning, and criticizing. The dynamic expansion of commerce in the seventeenth and eighteenth centuries should have made it impossible for a small, crude, and backward feudal oligarchy to monopolize new wealth and opportunities.

Commerce and knowledge should have been intrinsically liberating in Britain. They were, the *Aurora* insisted, congenitally hostile to feudal barbarity, and with their rise in England "the *exclusive classes*, those few for whose service and pleasure alone the mass of society appeared to exist[,] soon found that the newly discovered powers of the *press and* the *mint* would overwhelm them."[12] But they had not been overwhelmed. The achievements of the modern world had not liberated Britain's subjects. The traditional elite had contrived to control political power even as new developments and men rose to challenge them. To defend the assertion that a grand struggle with fatal consequences had taken place at the dawn of the modern world, the *Aurora* discussed what it considered the significance of the experience of Cosimo de'Medici.[13]

Though men such as de'Medici embraced knowledge and created new commercial opportunities that should have provided them the means to escape from feudal beliefs and abuses, the political power of the beleaguered aristocracy remained. The aristocracy, therefore, had much to offer Europe's de'Medicis and a real capacity to hinder or destroy their industrious efforts. Feudal lords had forced men to cooperate with them who would have behaved differently in other contexts. The *Aurora* argued that political power surrounded all individual action and enterprise. Regardless of the intentions of modern, forward-looking thinkers such as de'Medici, men who hoped (according to the *Aurora,* at any rate) to burst antiquated limits imposed by the aristocracy, such thinkers could not do so if political power remained concentrated. If aristocrats continued to govern those who sought to move the world away from the limits of a past dominated by feudal lords, then new knowledge, new economic opportunities, and broader horizons could never be adequately explored. The significance of entrenched political power, the *Aurora* argued, was manifest in de'Medici's story. In the end his ability to act was so constrained that he had no choice but to placate those who shaped the laws and customs under which he lived. Energy, hard work, and talent came to little and could not improve society for those who labored, unless the people redistributed and democratized political power.

By co-opting men such as de'Medici, aristocrats were introduced to and began to control those pursuits that should have overthrown them. Aristocrats gradually came to control "all that was imposing or fatal to barbarous institutions." Thus "nobility at length found a pedigree in a bale of silk . . . a hogshead of sugar, or a pig of tobacco." The talented energetic commercial men were not merely the aristocrats' dupes. If a man such as de'Medici "forgot the dignity of his character and . . . consented to degrade himself into a noble at the expense of his country's liberties," by choosing this alliance he received access to political power. Political power combined with modern achievements allowed those with privileged access to them to amass fortunes far beyond the capacity of those who merely used their own resources to accumulate with their own labor. Thus in the modern world "nobility [was] in fact riches," and with nightmarish irony the potent capacities of the modern world produced societies far more despotic and unhappy than the feudal nations of the past.[14]

Commerce and intellectual forces capable of liberating an entire people by providing them with opportunity and material independence had been consolidated in the hands of a few. This modern minority had become the most awesome and terrifying ruling class the world had ever known. Its rise held desperate consequences for those it ruled. British laborers, the *Aurora* grimly explained, endured "tedious and unnecessary servitudes" where "labour commences with the dawn and ceases not for hours after the sun has disappeared." Modern achievements such as the development of manufacturing only increased inequality, making the few wealthy and the many desperate.[15] By declaring this modern European condition of society unnecessary, the Philadelphia Democrats made it clear that they did not believe it inevitable. The United States could avoid this tragic development; its people could enjoy the benefits of economic opportunity, personal betterment, and modern knowledge because they had already experienced a democratic awakening and had seized political power.

By examining British history, the *Aurora* concluded that modern achievements were not intrinsically liberating — they required democratic control and access. If states were oligarchic, then the opportunities and advances promised by commerce and knowledge would be enjoyed only by oligarchies. The legacy of the American Revolution became the vital source for maintaining equality and independence. Americans could structure their politics, their decision making about public life, so that modern achievements did not reinforce but instead undermined traditional social and economic hierarchies. Doing so required considerable effort. Building such a society demanded much from the nation's citizens, who would have to accept responsibility for virtually perpetual engagement in public affairs. But that of course was why a people struggled for republican government in the first place.

If Americans could structure their social and economic relationships so that they conformed to the values of the Revolution's democratic legacy, they would forever escape the European condition of society. With oligarchy and entrenched privilege "the effects of manufactures as conducted in Europe [were] the decrepitude, delibility [*sic*], and degeneracy of those who inhabit manufacturing cities, the evils of monopoly and the pernicious influence which large capitalists obtained over a large number."[16] But in the United States, where "the general will w[ould] take the place of the ambitious views of the interested few," Americans "would open a new science [that] would occasion so much communication of sentiment through the neighborhood, that in another generation it would change the condition of society [and] bring men nearer on a level."[17] Constant engagement and democratic decision making would allow the United States to pursue all modern advances while "preserv[ing] and promot[ing] that happy mediocrity of condition, which is our greatest security and our best preservative against the gradual approaches of arbitrary power."[18]

Building on their insights about the modern sources of inequality, the Philadelphia Democrats sought to explain how ceaseless democratic engagement in public life and decision making would work. They planned for this political structure to place key economic decisions into a purely popular and immediately responsive political realm. Their goal was to ensure that through the expression of majority will American citizens could prevent abuses of those modern advances that made citizens vulnerable and dependent on others. Democracy could ensure that laws and policies served the needs of the citizenry. Developing the nation's resources and expanding and diversifying economic activity would only compound inequality unless the capacity to oversee this dynamic economy belonged to those whose labor produced the new sources and forms of wealth. Democratic decision making would accommodate, for example, the need to promote manufactures and the desire of artisans "to be stimulated by that interest which animates those who work for themselves." Democracy would allow the people to structure their economy and society to meet their needs and not those of aristocrats or would-be aristocrats such as the Federalists.

In the pages of the *Aurora* the Philadelphia Democrats devoted considerable thought to how political power and economic dynamism needed to combine to produce a society they considered just. From the very beginning of their efforts to conceive and implement democracy, their discussion revealed serious limitations in their thinking. The reality was that the people about whom the Philadelphia Democrats rather blithely generalized were already beginning to separate themselves. Their own behavior was leading to their social and economic differentiation. What if in the future the entrenched political power in the United States (and there was certainly far less of it than in Europe) was undone? At that point, what if certain of the people used their freedom and talent to produce conditions for others of the people that did not meet the Philadelphia Democrats' idea of the necessary conditions for independence, autonomy, and citizenship? Were that to occur, it was not at all apparent that their analysis could help them to think through this unexpected problem. The Philadelphia Democrats started with the fascinating premise that democracy required a rough equality of condition. At the very least no citizen could be allowed to depend for long on the resources of another. They then went beyond this insight to argue that all would live in the "happy mediocrity of condition" if decision making were democratized and citizens were freed from the political manipulation of aristocrats or self-proclaimed republican superiors. In other words, once a people established democracy, the natural state of society was the rough equality of condition. The Philadelphia Democrats would soon face a situation where Pennsylvania's politics became more and more democratic, but their social and economic conception of a democracy would continue to elude them. As that conundrum became manifest, the Philadelphia Democrats would face a serious problem. For this unexpected situation did not cause them to rethink their initial position that quasi-aristocratic manipulation of political power was the sole source of social and economic inequality. Instead, they concluded that Pennsylvania and the nation had to be further democratized. They began to demand political structures and practices that might very well have mandated their ideal, but that were also very hard to reconcile with cherished individual rights and certain fundamental American Revolutionary values.

This problem of seeing no option but to embrace extremity lay a few years in the future. Between 1800 and 1803 the Philadelphia Democrats conceived their vision of democracy because they were committed to a popularly derived public good and a value system that prized the happiness of the community and the independence of the individual over the desire, or even the right, to amass great wealth. The Philadelphia Democrats imagined a vibrant commercial society built on widespread access to productive property. They insisted that the concentration of such property was illegitimate and dangerous. They called for democracy because they believed that direct and popular determination of crucial economic and legal disputes would allow small property holders, the beneficiaries of the "happy mediocrity of condition," to prevent the efforts of any who sought to accumulate at their expense. Democracy would prevent the concentration of property and ensure that the United States became a society of citizens enjoying widespread ownership of productive property. Dependent labor, which in the modern world was increasingly wage labor, would never become a significant part of the American economy or democratic society.

But what was democracy, and how could it be justified? Since the classical age philosophers had warned, the *Aurora* admitted, "that the people are not to be trusted with themselves, that they are too ignorant to judge of the characters proper to be brought forward as their governors, and that the interests of the people will always be sacrificed by the ignorance or violence of those they are apt to raise into office on the score of temporary popularity and democratic turbulence."[19] By explaining the American Revolution as they did, by minimizing the significance of gentlemen, by calling into question a republic's dependence on the natural aristocracy, the Philadelphia Democrats rejected the wisdom of the ancients and the classical legacy. The *Aurora* denounced "the dialectical syllogism of Aristotle" that a government of mixed and balanced rule by the one, few, and many could best prevent the danger each form posed alone, despotism, oligarchy, and anarchy.[20]

Democracy could work in the United States because the nation enjoyed unique circumstances. The new nation could escape the European condition of society because "of the greater number of freeholders in the United States than in any other country." Thus "landed property is here more safe: and so in America the more general possession of landed property renders all property more safe."[21] Unadulterated rule by the many was dangerous only when the many were degraded and abused. Of course if they then acquired political power, they would seek revenge. But if the many were largely equal, violent or vengeful politics would only upset the desirable conditions that largely existed. Given American realities, the *Aurora* insisted, "the people were the mildest governors."[22] Abuse of power would result only if those who were interested in curtailing or undoing social and economic equality gained access to a greater share of political power than that possessed by their fellow citizens. Those whom the Philadelphia Democrats included within the category "the people" would never injure themselves.

The only threats to the democratic people were the few self-proclaimed gentlemen who believed it their prerogative to rule. In the United States democracy alone could guarantee peace and widespread respect for the rights of the many. It was axiomatic that the people would never long abuse themselves, particularly when the vast majority lived as justice dictated the vast majority should. In such a society people should have no fear of the absence of Aristotle's mixed and balanced government. True popular decision making might at times be messy; it might roughly or rudely proclaim the rights of the community over individual actions that threatened first principles and ideals. Democracy might at times produce incoherence. But "this evil [wa]s subject to daily detection by the spirit of inquiry or discussion." A democratic nation best ensured justice because it fostered "the *equal* rights of every citizen to examine [another's] conduct . . . and to determine how far it com-

ports with private and public good."[23] Only those who hoped to place themselves above their fellow citizens needed to fear democracy. The Philadelphia Democrats despised such self-proclaimed natural aristocrats. Thus, a
satirical editorial in the *Aurora* mocked the lament of those who considered
themselves great:

> I am constantly occupied by the melancholy state of mediocrity to which
> the studious and learned are doomed in this semi-barbarous country,
> where the order of social authority is reversed, and the vulgar pretend
> to the knowledge of what is good for them, and to an equality with their
> superiors: I often look into myself and think how I should have flour-
> ished if I were in a great metropolis of the world, London . . . where the
> chilling breath of democracy cannot offend true greatness. . . . Here
> doomed to dwindle in the dreary darkness of dull and dizzy democracy,
> let me cheer my spirit eager to flit to regions where order is distinguished
> by gradations, where each grade gradually grows greater from the low-
> est degradation to the highest grandeur.[24]

If democracy alone ensured justice, if the majority had to rule, how did
a majority govern? By the first decade of the nineteenth century, most
Americans could explain that the people were sovereign and that all law,
including fundamental law, derived from them. But clearly majorities did
not always or automatically govern. Upper houses checked lower houses,
executives vetoed legislatures, and some even maintained that judges could
declare the acts of representatives unconstitutional.[25] In fact, the declaration
of popular sovereignty had done much to legitimately undermine arguments
for direct majority governance. In effect, the popular will of the sovereign
people had established constitutions that constrained them from acting too
popularly.[26] In calling for majority rule, then, the Philadelphia Democrats
had a great deal to prove and a great deal more to articulate for the first time.

The Philadelphia Democrats began to champion democracy and majority rule by dismissing concerns about direct popular governance. They
hoped to discredit those concerns by associating them with the Federalist
Party, with the travails of the 1790s, and with the European condition of
society. As they began to discuss how democracy should work in practice,
they insisted that accountability become the cardinal value of American life.
This demand for accountability led the *Aurora* to criticize the patently undemocratic features of American government: appointed judges who served
during good behavior, small infrequently elected upper houses, and executives who could veto more popular legislatures. But the most significant

influence on the Philadelphia Democrats, causing them to call for extreme alterations in the structure of American politics, was their reaction to the conduct of the judiciary. The behavior of judges, both in Pennsylvania and at the national level, convinced the *Aurora* that the United States was far from a democracy. Unless the judiciary was transformed, the United States would never become one, despite the glorious events of 1776 and 1800.

Between 1800 and 1805 the Philadelphia Democrats came to identify an independent judiciary and the centrality of English-inspired common law in American jurisprudence as fundamental threats to democracy and equality. During these years the Philadelphia Democrats and many other Pennsylvania Jeffersonians viewed the judiciary as a source of unaccountable decision making and a protector of privilege and inequality. The causes of these concerns were both specific and general. Two particular incidents focused Pennsylvania Jeffersonians' thinking on the judiciary: the behavior and impeachment of Pennsylvania judge Alexander Addison, and the conduct and subsequent failure to impeach federal (and Federalist) judge Samuel Chase.

Alexander Addison was an old, cantankerous Federalist from western Pennsylvania despised by Jeffersonians of every stripe. In his charges to juries and in other remarks he insisted on the supremacy of the judiciary over the legislature and questioned the competence of legislators. Addison had enthusiastically enforced the Alien and Sedition Acts. He also so overawed a fellow judge, the Jeffersonian John Lucas, that he in effect silenced him while both were hearing a case. It was this discourtesy that gave Pennsylvania Jeffersonians their chance, for they accused Addison of denying the right of Pennsylvanians to make use of and present their cases to all their judges. Addison's actions, Jeffersonians concluded, were unconstitutional.

Addison's impeachment was both popular and successful. Nevertheless, by January 1803, when his trial began, the democratic ideas of the Philadelphia Democrats were making it impossible for impeachment to be a straightforward affair. Pennsylvania Jeffersonians were unified by the idea of impeaching Addison. The prominent Jeffersonian lawyer and former Secretary of the Commonwealth Alexander J. Dallas handled the impeachment, but he did not argue for the impeachment on grounds that satisfied the Philadelphia Democrats' democratic sensibilities. Dallas argued instead that Addison was impeachable because he had actually committed a crime.

By 1803 the Philadelphia Democrats were attracted to a different philosophical conception of impeachment, one that made it a much more popular and democratic instrument. They agreed that Addison had broken the law, but they insisted that impeachment in general did not require criminal behavior. Addison's high-handed conduct and his very political opinions were dangerous in a democratic republic. Using a philosophy of impeachment for what they considered to be dangerous tendencies, radical Jeffersonians argued that the simple fact of Addison's hostility to democracy was grounds for his removal from the bench. Hostility toward democracy should not be borne from agents of a democratic state.[27]

For the time being, the Philadelphia Democrats' more radical theory, and the real threat it posed to the independent judiciary, had little impact. Addison was stripped of his position, and Pennsylvania Jeffersonians went home happy. But the failed impeachment of Samuel Chase further radicalized the Philadelphia Democrats, causing them to articulate more carefully their views on the judiciary. This articulation began to win them allies among certain Pennsylvania Jeffersonians and made it clear to others that the Philadelphia Democrats had moved beyond where they themselves were prepared to go.

Chase the federal judge was more prominent than Addison and more despised by Jeffersonians. Like Addison, he had eagerly enforced the Alien and Sedition Acts, most notably against James T. Callender. He had also presided over John Fries's second trial and had bullied a conviction. Though Chase was wildly unpopular, when his trial began in 1805, no one could point to any obvious criminal act. The Delawarean Caesar A. Rodney, largely at the insistence of the House impeachment manager, John Randolph, pursued a charge based on dangerous tendency. Rather loosely, they maintained that Chase's conduct undermined the republican efforts of legislatures. In the end the notion came too close to undermining the separation of powers for the comfort of Randolph's fellow congressmen, and Chase was acquitted. Chase's exculpation, according to John Quincy Adams, then a young congressman still two years away from his defection to the party of Jefferson, forever established that only actual crimes were impeachable offenses.[28]

But the Philadelphia Democrats did not agree with Quincy Adams's observation, though the subsequent history of impeachment has demonstrated its cogency. The *Aurora* paid close attention to the Chase affair and printed the judge's jury charge that led to it.[29] In the charge Chase violated the Philadelphia Democrats' most cherished ideals, informing the Maryland jury hearing the case over which he presided that "true liberty did not . . . consist in the possession of equal rights, but in the protection by the law of the person and property of every member of society, however various the grade in society he filled." Chase, the *Aurora* informed its readers, therefore claimed that liberty did not result from a particular form of government. Certain monarchies protected property more assiduously, and so guarded liberty more carefully, than did some republics. Finally, Chase lauded the independent judiciary, castigated legislatures for encroaching on it, and denounced universal suffrage as dangerous to property rights. Chase informed the jury that the framers of the Maryland constitution "had not imagined . . . that property would best be protected by those who had themselves no property." If universal suffrage was established, Chase had concluded, "instead of being ruled by a regular and respectable government, we shall be governed by an ignorant mobocracy."[30]

Although nothing Chase said was illegal (indeed, though the Philadelphia Democrats probably did not know it, Chase was correct about the Maryland framers), Chase's charge, the *Aurora* editorialized, was "the most extraordinary [statement] that the violence of Federalism has yet produced."[31] Here was a clear example of the need for the principle of impeachment based on dangerous tendency. Indeed, the Chase episode spurred the Philadelphia Democrats to pursue this principle further toward its logical conclusion. Judges such as Chase showed that the judiciary should not be appointed to serve during good behavior. "The office of a judge," the *Aurora* concluded, "like that of any other magistrate should be subjected to a period test, when his conduct might be investigated at the tribunal of his superior — the people." Chase, the paper insisted, should be impeached because he exhibited the dangerous tendency of believing "that our government is not a *democracy* and that an opposition or enmity of democracy is compatible with republicanism."[32] The failure to remove Chase on grounds of dangerous tendency fueled the Philadelphia Democrats' radicalism and bolstered their hostility toward the independent judiciary.

The Addison and Chase affairs helped the Philadelphia Democrats turn from abstract speculations about the desirability of democracy to concrete criticisms of the structure of American politics. But these two specific events, though important in focusing Pennsylvania Jeffersonians' thinking on the judiciary, were supplemented by Pennsylvanians' general experiences with state judges. The criticism of the judiciary was part of a growing concern about the legal structure and legal culture of Pennsylvania. Starting in 1802 and 1803 an increasing number of vocal Pennsylvania Jeffersonians exhibited these concerns.

According to the Philadelphia Democrats, the judiciary's independence was not the only source of danger. The *Aurora* also questioned an entire legal apparatus based on English common law.[33] Common law, the Philadelphia Democrats maintained, threatened democracy. Unwritten, twisted by unaccountable judges, originating in a nation poisoned by the European condition of society, independent judges wielding this common law subverted the general will. The *Aurora* insisted that Pennsylvania had "to lay the foundation of a law which should curb the *arbitrary power* assumed by the courts over the liberty of the citizen in defiance of the constitution as unauthorized by any *law* but the indefinable doctrines of English common law."[34] The Philadelphia Democrats believed that common law provided judges with a "doctrine which . . . would . . . swallow our liberties by making them depend not upon written constitutions or laws made by ourselves for ourselves, but upon the constructions of our own courts of law, of decisions of foreign courts, which however applicable to another country, and to remote periods, cannot be considered as applicable to our state of society, and which have neither been made for or by us."[35]

The Philadelphia Democrats, then, identified two separate but related threats to democracy, the independent judiciary and the prevalence of common law. To deal with the judiciary they embraced the philosophy of impeachment for dangerous tendency. The *Aurora* became one of the few places where Americans could find accessible explanations of this doctrine. The paper gave the notion of dangerous tendency coherence and applied it to everyday political events. By doing so, the Philadelphia Democrats encouraged in Pennsylvania a discussion about the nature of the judiciary and its role in a republic. If judges held their offices in good behavior, then it was necessary to force good behavior to conform to the needs and rights of a democratic people. "The point," the *Aurora* insisted, "was to ascertain what is and what is not good behavior." The Philadelphia Democrats believed that a democratic definition of a violation of good behavior had to be much broader than "a crime punishable as a felony in private." A proper democratic definition of such a violation included the display of judicial hostility toward democracy or partiality for decisions or decision making that the majority considered undemocratic. This partiality, the *Aurora* suggested, included criticism by the bench of the legislature. Impeachment could prevent judges from thwarting or criticizing democratic bodies if "partiality [was] a grounds for removal."[36]

The *Aurora* rejected the very ideal of an independent judiciary arguing that "independence [existed] to enable judges to do wrong." Wrongdoing included "the right of the courts to set aside laws as unconstitutional." Democratic impeachment, removing judges whenever they displayed dangerous tendencies toward democratic institutions or beliefs, was a fitting punishment. The Philadelphia Democrats championed impeachment based on dangerous tendency, insisting that "removal from office . . . is the most harmless of punishments, and ought to be employed for the slightest offenses." Good behavior, the Philadelphia Democrats maintained, was a matter to be determined by the majority, and the majority had to be able to punish those in positions of power that opposed it.[37]

The judiciary's independence threatened democracy, but equally dangerous was the power provided by the common law. To counter it the Philadelphia Democrats conceived a democratic and populist alternative legal structure, which they championed in the *Aurora*. Such an alternative was essential because a democratic society had to "be directed by reason, equity, and a few simple and plain laws." Those laws had to be "few in number, written in plain simple language [and] liable to frequent revision." Such laws could frequently "be repealed as being contrary to the general voice," a right a democratic people had to have.[38]

Complicated law was easily manipulated. The Philadelphia Democrats argued that if Pennsylvanians simplified the legal structure, they could make it useful and usable. At that point citizens could settle their disputes more equitably and be guided by the larger values of the democratic community. A simpler legal system would be more likely to arrive at justice and equity because it would be freed from the domination of judges and lawyers. The Philadelphia Democrats argued that litigants should be able to avoid the courts by appearing before arbitrators whose decisions would be binding. Arbitration, the *Aurora* imagined, would significantly lessen the role played by law courts in deciding disputes, particularly of property.[39] The Philadelphia Democrats presented arbitration as a democratic alternative to courts of law presided over by judges who could ignore popular opinion. Courts determined outcomes from statutes and common-law precedents. But arbitrators, the *Aurora* argued, were more concerned with equity. Arbitrators were "as attentive to law as juries where the question is a question of law, but in the ordinary course of a dispute arising in society, not one in ten requires a legal opinion, but an equitable adjustment."[40]

The Philadelphia Democrats suggested that arbitrators could be justices of the peace, especially if they were elected. They could be chosen by the legislature or elected by the people. However arbitrators achieved the position, the Philadelphia Democrats imagined that they would come from the community in which the case originated. They would be much closer to the people than any current officer of the court. Arbitrators would feel a part of the community and would share its values and sense of justice in each case. Arbitrators would have a keen sense of what the community considered just and would depend on the community's good will to retain their positions. Taken together, the attacks on judicial review and an independent judiciary, and the call for a more democratic form of adjudicating vulnerable to majority opinion, added up to a fundamental critique of the nation's legal system. The notion that democratic justice demanded that democratic politics and legal decision making move much closer together hinted at a wholesale critique of the Whig political science emerging from the 1780s.

But critique and rejection amount to challenge only if more than a few participate. The Philadelphia Democrats were a small group of radicals motivated by Philadelphia's particular problems and their era's great events. But by 1803 they began to find allies outside of the city. Between 1803 and 1805, particularly in the rural southeast, the focus on the undemocratic role of the judiciary and the common law began to resonate with preexisting rural concerns. In addition, fears grew in the Pennsylvania interior about economic inequality and the danger it posed for democracy. After 1803 the Philadelphia Democrats learned that, at least to a point, theirs were not purely city concerns.

By 1803 the city radicals found allies in the south and west of the state because the state supreme court's use of common law began to make it many enemies. Many Pennsylvanians believed that the hierarchical structure of the state courts and the judges' use of common law threatened the equality and independence they cherished. The Pennsylvania Supreme Court's commitment to the unshackled development and alienation of property did encourage it to rely on common law selectively. Much of the common law of real property, particularly in decisions made prior to 1750, placed constraints on the development and transfer of property. But other parts, particularly those decisions treating commercial disputes and mercantile property, encouraged alienation and free exchange. After 1750 English common-law judges began to interpret much of the common law in ways that protected and encouraged commercial exchange and development. The judges largely ignored the dislocating impact these decisions had on the nation's poor.

The Pennsylvania Supreme Court relied on post-1750 common-law decisions (including those made after 1776) and those more antiquated interpretations that encouraged entrepreneurial conceptions of property. The court justified its stance by asserting that Pennsylvania was a commercial society, that common-law decisions less amenable to economic development were not useful to Pennsylvania, and that Pennsylvanians wanted and needed speedy, unshackled development. Pennsylvania's Supreme Court justices, then, were part of the general transformation of American law in which judges began to interpret common law much more completely as an instrument of rapid economic development.[41]

The state supreme court benefited from a hierarchical structure of the state courts that allowed supreme court justices to preside at the appellate level. The state constitution of 1790 made it easy for property title and other commercial disputes to go from local courts to the appeals courts, where this developmental vision of the common law dominated. Bolstered by the hierarchical court structure, the supreme court imposed its vision on the state. The court's behavior helped further the consolidation of landownership in Pennsylvania between 1770 and 1800 and strengthened the claims of entrepreneurs in disputes with more traditionally minded claimants to land. The court's actions led to a general hostility toward it and the common law, hostility felt by far more people than merely the Philadelphia Democrats.[42]

In 1803 rural figures emerged who would build important political careers by demanding democracy and offering their views on how a nation of equal and independent citizens could best be built. In no region of the state was this politicization more important than in the south, extending from Chester and Montgomery Counties to the market towns of the Lehigh Valley and the counties of Northumberland and Dauphin. This region stretched from Lancaster and Easton to Harrisburg and Sunbury. It produced a future governor, Simon Snyder, and was the home of some of his most important followers, men such as John Binns, William Findlay, Thomas Rogers, Samuel D. Ingham, James Buchanan, and above all Snyder's chief ally, Nathaniel B. Boileau of Montgomery County.[43]

The southeast and the counties to the immediate west have been called by historians the best poor man's country, a place where, in virtually unprecedented fashion, settlers could start with little and gain a degree of comfort and independence, a competence, to use the contemporary term.[44] The counties that would produce the Snyderite movement were intensely commercial and produced mostly wheat. During the eighteenth century, wheat culture, unlike tobacco monoculture, encouraged economic diversity and development. In this region, therefore, vibrant market towns arose such as Easton, Sunbury, Selinsgrove, Bethlehem, Lancaster, and Harrisburg.[45] These communities, often county seats, served as local points of transfer to Philadelphia, Baltimore, and the larger Atlantic economy.

By 1800 southern Pennsylvania had come to expect real prosperity and had developed a mature economy with complex social relations. Particularly in Chester County, but also in Lancaster and other parts of the region, tenancy became a common feature of rural life. Despite, or indeed perhaps because of, the American yeoman's commitment to the competence, widespread tenancy did not produce nagging social tensions.[46] Indeed, tenancy increased as economic opportunity became more generally available. Tenants were usually able to lease enough land to participate in the regional market economy. They often combined agricultural labor with artisan production. Tenants paid taxes and regularly participated in politics. The distinction between landowner and landholder does not seem to have been critical in the region for much of the eighteenth century. The seasonal nature of the wheat economy also encouraged a flexible free labor workforce. During the eighteenth century there emerged a class of agricultural wage laborers who also cultivated small plots, engaged in truck farming, and played a vital role in the area's economy and social structure. These inmates and freemen, as they were known in local parlance, also appeared on the tax lists, though not as frequently as the tenants. Many were eventually able to accumulate capital and rent land. In fact, it was commonly believed that the social structure of southeastern Pennsylvania corresponded to the life cycle. Young inmates and freemen lived in others' houses. Gradually they saved enough to rent, and with industry and thrift they eventually became landowners.[47]

It appears that many laborers realized their happy expectations during the first half of the eighteenth century. But after 1750, as wealth grew steadily more concentrated, and as an identifiable possessing class emerged, expectations grew harder to meet. Emerging rural elites could afford to improve their lands without relying on the largely autonomous labor of tenants. For the first time during the 1760s the economy grew, but the tenant population declined because fewer inmates and freemen managed to achieve that status. In previous periods of growth the population of tenants had risen.[48] In 1800, though control of wealth in Chester County was stratified, it was still evenly distributed enough to keep expectations alive. The top decile owned 38 percent of the county's wealth, and the bottom 60 percent controlled but 17 percent. Nevertheless, though there were palpable differences between much of the county and its wealthiest residents, a middling group constituting 30 percent of the population still owned 45 percent of the wealth in Chester County.[49] This substantial and visible portion of the population was a constant throughout the region. It legitimized the social structure. But at the same time, as wealth grew more concentrated, joining the middling group became harder. Southeastern Pennsylvanians would seek various political solutions to ensure that this group expanded rather than disappeared.

The foremost authority on the region has commented that, by 1800, "a century of development brought prosperity to many southeastern Pennsylvanians. Quite possibly, for the time more of them lived better than any other population of similar size in the world."[50] Still, the goal was to keep it that way. By the 1790s southeasterners were growing less confident that their formerly typical life cycle could be lived. The region grew more concerned as the political turbulence of that decade convulsed southeastern Pennsylvania. The fears contributed to the Fries Rebellion.

The southeast joined Pennsylvania's Jeffersonian coalition late in the decade. The radical and extreme arguments of Philadelphia were never as effective there. Southeastern Pennsylvanians hoped that Jeffersonian victory would restore, or perhaps simply perpetuate, the economic prosperity and general social mobility on which their fathers, grandfathers, and neighbors had confidently relied. By 1799 they believed that the Federalist Party threatened this mobility. Southeastern Pennsylvania's Jeffersonians expected their party to reform the political structure. Once reformed, the state would encourage development and more easily and speedily resolve the inevitable disputes that development provoked. The demands of the Jeffersonians of this region would push them into the thick of what would soon become a vitriolic Jeffersonian debate.

The Jeffersonians of southeastern Pennsylvania received a real boost when John Binns fled Pitt's Britain. An Irishman and republican associated with the English Jacobins and a former member of the London Corresponding Society, he joined fellow radical exiles Thomas Cooper and Joseph Priestly in Northumberland, Pennsylvania, in 1802.[51] Once there, his friends introduced him to Simon Snyder, a resident of the county since 1784. Snyder was living proof of the possibilities available in this part of the state during the late eighteenth century. Though he had some formal education, having attended a night school kept by local Quakers, he was largely an autodidact. Working as a journeyman tanner and as a scrivener, Snyder accumulated some capital and eventually purchased land. He also built a mill and kept a store. He became a principal citizen of Selinsgrove, Northumberland, and was appointed justice of the peace and a judge for the Northumberland County Court of Common Pleas.[52] By the time he met Binns, Snyder was a rising member of the state legislature and soon to be Speaker of the House. Snyder introduced Binns to his fellow legislator, Montgomery

County's Nathaniel B. Boileau. Boileau, the descendent of Huguenot immigrants, had managed to matriculate at the College of New Jersey (later Princeton) and then joined the Pennsylvania bar. Comparing Snyder's life to the Britain of the Treasonable Practices Act, Binns must have concluded that he was three thousand miles closer to paradise.[53]

Binns was a talented journalist, and his backers soon helped him launch the *Northumberland Republican Argus,* which began publishing on January 7, 1803. From the beginning it was committed to the political fortunes of Simon Snyder and the vision of the past and future held by those residents of southeastern Pennsylvania who had prospered in the region. By the time Binns arrived, Snyder and other southeasterners, such as the entrepreneurs and politicians Daniel and William Montgomery, Samuel D. Ingham, and William Findlay, were thoroughly Jeffersonian. Binns shared their enthusiasm, and the *Argus* regularly applauded the gains made by Jefferson's party.[54]

By 1803 the demands of the Philadelphia Democrats for legal reform began to merge with the concerns felt by Jeffersonians in the rural southeast. From the west came similar demands to alter the legal structure and lessen the power of judges.[55] Southeastern Pennsylvania had its own reasons to consider such issues, and by 1803 these questions increasingly drove the state's Jeffersonian politics. Population had increased in the southeast as in the rest of Pennsylvania. Furthermore, a growing economy brought more legal business and a rising tide of legal disputes. By all accounts courts were overworked, and reaching decisions at law took an inordinate amount of time.[56] After 1803 Jeffersonians controlled counties such as Northumberland, and they began to participate in the discussion increasingly dominating their party.[57] Convinced that the Federalists had planned a hierarchical society that would have granted a small elite political, economic, social, and cultural preeminence, southeastern Pennsylvania Jeffersonians were willing to consider much criticism of the judiciary. Here was the one branch of government over which the Federalists retained considerable influence. Three of the four state supreme court justices, for example, were Federalists. As politicians such as Snyder and Boileau, and editors like Binns, entered the Jeffersonian discussion about law and the bench, they were immediately attracted to those demanding reform. Binns soon began to praise democracy, and he reprinted articles from the *Aurora* denouncing the Federalists as pro-British and secretly monarchical.[58]

By entering this discussion, southeastern Jeffersonians saw a chance to gain control of the state government and remake Pennsylvania in their image. It is important to keep in mind just how obscure the backgrounds of men such as Snyder and Boileau were. In addition, with no entrance into Philadelphia society, and thus with little experience of the world beyond rural Pennsylvania (though this point was less true of Binns and to a certain extent Boileau than it was of most future Snyderites and of Snyder himself), they concentrated on state-level transformation. While the Philadelphia Democrats cast their nets wide, seeking, it seemed at times, almost perpetual world democratic revolution, southeasterners remained firmly grounded in their fecund Pennsylvania soil.

Thus the *Argus* happily reprinted an article from the *Washington National Intelligencer* discussing the demands for arbitration beginning to gain ground in Pennsylvania. The *Intelligencer* suggested that too many Americans concentrated on the national government when "such, indeed, is the nature of our system, that the state governments are the great guardians of our internal happiness."[59] By introducing bills for arbitration into the Pennsylvania legislature, as Snyder and Boileau would soon do, by joining the movement for legal reform, southeastern Pennsylvania Jeffersonians believed that they were participating at the most critical level of government. It had to be, for the state level was all that these men could reasonably expect to influence.

In 1803, as the *Argus* was just entering the movement for legal reform, it relied heavily on reprints from the *Aurora* to defend arbitration. These reprints insisted that lawyers threatened to undermine republican government and demanded that arbitration be available and binding even when only one party to a suit desired it.[60] Indeed, Binns reprinted from the *Aurora* often enough that some accused him of being the *Aurora*'s "deputy press," and Duane's mouthpiece in the southeast.[61]

During 1803 the careers of Snyder and Boileau blossomed. Both became leading figures in the state legislature, and Snyder built the base of support that would make him Speaker of the House and a leading candidate for governor in 1805. Further, it was clear to all that something rare and vital was transpiring. Urban and rural radicals were making common cause and supporting each other's efforts. By 1803 many prominent Pennsylvania Jeffersonians were growing alarmed. A coalition of urban and rural radicals suddenly seemed impressively organized, highly vocal, and determined to take power. The coalition's determination seemed to augur sweeping changes in the legal and political system, with serious implications for the institution of private property. In 1803 the gubernatorial election of 1805 appeared uncomfortably close, and, suddenly, established Pennsylvania Jeffersonians could all too easily imagine Snyder, or worse yet Leib, in the governor's chair. Fear and the fact that demands to alter fundamental beliefs and first principles were rapidly becoming the stuff of mainstream state politics meant that the months between 1803 and the gubernatorial election would be momentous and explosive. By 1803 moderate Pennsylvania Jeffersonians believed that they had to organize against the deluge.

Chapter Three

The Quid Challenge:
Political Economy, Politics, and
the Fault Lines of Conflict

By 1802 the influence of William Duane and Michael Leib concerned many prominent Pennsylvania Jeffersonians. The emergence of the urban and rural coalition provoked alarm, and midway through Jefferson's first term the party in Pennsylvania began a bitter internal quarrel that continued for over a generation. The opponents of the Philadelphia Democrats and their rural allies were called at various times the Rising Sun Party (after a tavern where they first met in 1802), the Third Party, the Tertium Quids (Third Whats), and more often simply the Quids. The Quids hoped to tame popular politics by discrediting the radicalism that they blamed on the Philadelphia Democrats. To do so, they emphasized the nation's future greatness and the prosperity each citizen would enjoy in a vibrant economy with a peaceful representative politics committed to promoting internal economic development. Accepting, even welcoming, democracy in Pennsylvania, the Quids attempted to redefine the term. Popular politics would remain the instrument the citizens used to create the conditions that produced material independence. But democracy would only provide such independence of circumstances when Pennsylvanians realized that their power should not be used to disrupt or hinder private energies or the use of property.

The Quids hoped to teach the rest of Pennsylvania what they already believed: that the United States, in ways that no other nation did, possessed the materials to create a liberal democratic republic. The nation's unprecedented abundance of productive resources meant that material independence was within the reach of every citizen. Democracy properly conceived meant soberly and sensibly electing those trustworthy men who would mobilize and develop resources in ways that encouraged widespread independence. By stressing nearly inevitable economic prosperity and independence, the Quids hoped to turn Pennsylvanians toward private concerns and so convince them not to dwell on political disagreements. Economic opportunity, then, would ease political conflict and defuse the explosive situation within the Jeffersonian party.

In the end, the Quids hoped, Pennsylvanians would come to agree with them that the turbulent politics of the Philadelphia Democrats and their rural allies would not bring independence and equality. Those desirable conditions could never arise from a politics that encouraged wild and unpredictable change and frenzy. The future the radicals wanted would be realized by electing those sober men who understood that with the defeat of the Federalists little needed to be changed in the new nation. In their battle against the radicals, the Quids introduced many ideas that would quickly become significant for subsequent efforts to merge democracy and capitalism. They played a crucial role in shifting the nation's economic energies from the external to the internal market, perhaps the most important development to occur in nineteenth-century American political economy. They also labored to link democracy to internal economic development and the pursuit of wealth in a way that no group of Americans had done before with any sustained coherence. The Quids proved able challengers of the radicals, and the thoughtful though vitriolic debate that followed forced the participants to enunciate all the more clearly their beliefs about the meaning of democracy and its connection to a capitalist economy. The care with which these ideas were thought out and articulated owed everything to the length and ferocity of the conflict within the Pennsylvania Jeffersonian party.

The Quids had all become Jeffersonians during the 1790s and had helped elect Thomas McKean governor in 1799. But they came primarily from the upper stratum of the Jeffersonian coalition; indeed, in their battle with the urban and rural radicals they soon enjoyed the support of Governor McKean. Men such as the jurists Alexander J. Dallas and Hugh Henry Brackenridge; prominent landowners such as John Dickinson, George Logan, Joseph Heister, and Peter Muhlenberg; rising businessmen and merchants like William Jones, Manuel Eyre, Matthew Carey, Frederick Muhlenberg, and Tench Coxe; and successful politicians such as the governor's son Joseph B. McKean, William Barton, and John Kean all hoped that the Jeffersonian victory would lead to a stable and orderly political peace. They wanted to replace Federalist oligarchy with the dignified pursuit of prosperity and personal betterment. The radical coalition seemed to threaten any chance for this stable peace. The Quids feared that if ungovernable passions continued to shape American politics, then the resulting turbulence would destroy, and so forever discredit, the American political experiment that sought to eradicate rule by the privileged and mighty.

From the beginning the Quids tried to end the conflict that had characterized the 1790s. Having defeated the Federalists, they believed that individual republicans who had been Federalists should be allowed to participate in the republican experiment. The Quids insisted that they were "in principle decidedly opposed to the Federalists, as a party, and will remain so; yet conceiving that genuine republicanism and persecution are the two most complete opposite things in nature, they cannot find themselves warranted by the laws of God or man to keep up that system of everlasting hatred, persecution, and detraction which unhappily pervades the breasts of too many of our fellow citizens."[1] This spirit of persecution was "anti-republican and in a high degree injurious to the community" because it "tend[ed] to keep the public mind in a constant state of ferment." The best course for the victorious Jeffersonians, therefore, was "to allay that spirit of bitterness and animosity which has so long existed."[2]

It was no mystery whom the Quids were criticizing. By 1802 the Quids had grown concerned about the influence of the Philadelphia Democrat leader Michael Leib. Even when the Quids gained statewide prominence, their chief hostilities remained focused on the Philadelphia Democrats, and they devoted most of their energies to opposing the city radicals. Leib ran afoul of Quid ideals. One of the activists most responsible for the tone of politics in the 1790s, Leib sought to sustain angry political passions after 1801 by proscribing the Federalists.[3] As early as 1802, Leib's conduct and ideas began to anger prominent Pennsylvania Jeffersonians. Leib's fellow Jeffersonian congressmen Andrew Gregg, Robert Brown, John Smilie, John A. Hanna, Isaac Van Horne, and John Stewart publicly opposed his demand that all Federalists be stripped of office.[4] But chief among Leib's critics from the congressional delegation was William Jones, a close friend of both Alexander J. Dallas and the recently appointed secretary of the Treasury, Albert Gallatin. A rising Philadelphia merchant, Jones had turned against the Federalists during the 1790s. Though a merchant, he was not part of the established trade protected and furthered by the Jay Treaty. Indeed, after 1800 he would become one of the first Americans to penetrate the China market, where he dealt in silk and opium.[5]

Jones spearheaded opposition to Leib. He was particularly angered by Leib's effort to make proscribing all Federalists a test of one's commitment to the Jeffersonian party. Jones publicly opposed Leib's position and privately criticized him to the president. Starting in late 1802, Jones began a campaign to discredit Leib with Jeffersonian leaders by insisting that Leib's brand of republicanism was dangerous.[6] While a congressman, Leib managed his personal affairs in a manner that further convinced Jones he deserved no place among respectable Jeffersonians. In 1804 Leib's heated exchange with a fellow Jeffersonian led to a brawl in the congressional lobby that lasted for over an hour.[7] By 1804 others shared Jones's views of Leib and his allies, particularly William Duane. A correspondent of Matthew Carey's, though Carey had at one time contributed to the *Aurora*, complained of Duane's hostile treatment of material that did not agree with the positions espoused by the Philadelphia Democrats.[8]

The early campaign to expose Leib convinced Matthew Carey. Before 1804 Leib had seen that Carey received lucrative printing contracts. Yet by 1804 Carey could no longer reconcile accepting this business with his political principles. Carey denounced his patron and worked to depose him by supporting candidates backed by Jones and Dallas. Carey signed a public statement of his intentions forever disassociating himself from the Philadelphia Democrats. Other signers of the open letter published in the *Freeman's Journal* included the prominent Philadelphia merchants and manufacturers Blair McClenachan, William McFadden, Stephen Girard, Manuel Eyre, Tench Coxe, and Samuel Wetherill.[9] Coxe helped Carey over the lean period that loomed with his loss of patronage. In 1804 and 1805 he made loans to Carey at the latter's request of some $2,850. Coxe's assistance emboldened Carey, who joined him in writing a letter to Duane protesting the editor's conduct.[10] By 1805 the Quids would go so far as to compare Leib to Robespierre.[11]

By 1803 such concerns had spread from Philadelphia to Lancaster, the state capital. The Lancaster lawyer James Hopkins was terrified by the attacks on the judicial system, particularly the plan for arbitration promoted so forcefully in the *Aurora*. He feared that demands for arbitration in the state legislature would cause "a total destruction of all those blessings which result from a republican government organized according to the constitution." The behavior of the legislature was evidence that something had gone wrong in American politics. Narrow-minded men were "urged on to the work of innovation, destruction, and new creation, by a few unprincipled, groveling, ambitious demagogues."[12]

Hopkins wrote Alexander J. Dallas that only true republicanism could defeat such vicious proposals. The Jeffersonian party had opposed the despotic innovations of the Federalists. Now it must fight against anarchic innovation proposed from within the party. Hopkins insisted to Dallas that those who shared their concerns must organize. They had to run their own candidates and build their own political movement. It was imperative, Hopkins believed, that moderate Jeffersonians be heard in Philadelphia and its suburbs, where the danger was greatest. In his letter he informed Dallas that his fellow Lancastrians William Barton and Andrew Ellicott were traveling to the city. The two would "explain our ideas fully to you, and will be glad to communicate with you, and our other friends, on the best means of rescuing the state, and republicanism, from the vandalism which threatens both." Barton had written a pamphlet denouncing arbitration. Hopkins told Dallas that Lancaster and Philadelphia supporters planned to reimburse him $110 and take over the future printing and distribution costs.[13] A movement was being born.

For Barton, denouncing arbitration followed inevitably from his commitment to a developing economy that encouraged the material independence of actual producers. In addition to opposing radical political and legal reforms, Barton lobbied for a Lancaster branch of the Bank of Pennsylvania, citing the support it could give to the "considerable population, as well as the manufacturing interest of Lancaster." In a letter to Matthew Carey, Barton enumerated the manufacturers he thought the branch would encourage: "millers, brewers, tanners, hatters, gunsmiths, and tobacconists." More extensive credit would create greater opportunity, particularly for businessmen "of small capitals." Barton's efforts helped secure the branch in 1803.[14] Opportunity, prosperity, and mobility, not dangerous and anarchic innovation, would ensure the future for Pennsylvania's producers and citizens that all Jeffersonians insisted they wanted.

The Jeffersonians who would become Quids did not begin to organize in 1802 and 1803 merely because they worried about the influence of unsavory men. By 1803 the inchoate theorizing about democratic alternatives such as arbitration cohered into a political program. In 1803 urban and rural radicals led by Snyder and Boileau in the state legislature introduced arbitration bills. By 1803 the radicals had gained enough support to push these bills through both houses. Their success made the nascent divisions within the party obvious and then widened them, for Governor McKean vetoed each bill.[15]

Thus by 1803 the radicals were beginning to associate McKean with the threat to democracy and with what they considered the perfidious efforts of Jeffersonians like Coxe, Dallas, Carey, and Barton. At the same time that McKean thwarted arbitration, the state supreme court became embroiled in a lawsuit between the Philadelphia merchant Thomas Passmore and the Philadelphia insurance underwriters Andrew Petit and Andrew Bayard. In the normal course of business Passmore sued the insurers, who were defended by Dallas. The case went to the supreme court, where it was heard by three of the four judges, Edward Shippen Jr., Thomas Smith, and Jasper Yeats, all Federalists. The fourth justice, the Jeffersonian, Hugh Henry Brackenridge, was absent. The court found for Petit and Bayard. Furious, Passmore posted a diatribe in a city coffeehouse attacking Bayard. He said nothing about the judges' decision. But his attack infuriated prominent Philadelphia Jeffersonians. Petit and Bayard were leading citizens, and the former was also the brother-in-law of Governor McKean. By late spring 1803 the atmosphere in the city was already charged because of angry reaction to McKean's vetoes, and his supporters were sensitive about any criticisms of people close to the governor.

Dallas therefore went before the court and suggested that by denouncing Bayard, Passmore showed contempt for the decision. He should, under the common law of contempts, be found in contempt of court. This reasoning was flawed, for the action had not taken place in the courtroom and in fact occurred after the case had been closed and the court had adjourned. But the three judges agreed with Dallas, fined Passmore, and imprisoned him for thirty days.[16]

The *Aurora* leaped to Passmore's defense. The merchant's travails put a human face on all the complicated theorizing about democracy. Unaccountable judges used the common law to assist the powerful as they preyed on the weak. The *Aurora* printed a memorial Passmore wrote to the legislature begging redress. In a supporting editorial it denounced the judges and demanded their impeachment.[17] Thus, by spring 1803, as moderates began quietly to seek each other out, the radicalism that frightened them grew. The urban and rural coalition demanded dramatic innovations in the legal system, denounced McKean and his circle, and hoped to use its democratic theory of impeachment to strike at the despised Supreme Court.

By mid-1803 moderate Jeffersonians were convinced that they had to take action. Though some Pennsylvanians hoped to defuse the growing division by insisting that they were angry only at the obnoxious Leib, a Lancaster correspondent of Tench Coxe's knew better. Even if the cause of division was "confined to Dr. Leib," he wrote, "the effects, I apprehend, are by no means so." It was clear by 1803 that demands for democracy appealed to and energized many Pennsylvanians. The radical coalition, and for now most prominently Duane and Leib, were the Jeffersonians associated with demands for democracy. Thus the term belonged to them. Here was the chief danger. If the Philadelphia Democrats were not discredited, if the capacity to define and possibly implement democracy was not seized from them, if "this kind of intemperate conduct [was] countenanced by the Republicans as orthodox democracy," then American politics would remain legitimately and perpetually explosive and turbulent.[18] The Quids had to show that democracy was indeed the true legacy of 1800. But further, they had to convince Pennsylvania that democracy was incompatible with the ideals and policies championed by the radicals.

The leading Quids were primarily from Philadelphia. Though they were concerned about Snyder and his supporters, they considered the Philadelphia Democrats the main authors of their troubles. They were supported in this view by Quids away from the city. Coxe's Lancaster correspondent implored the Quids in Philadelphia to confront the city radicals, for, he wrote, the "effects of Duane's and Leib's principles are spreading, or at least becoming more manifest, throughout the whole state. . . . The most discreet, intelligent, and uniform friends to our representative system of government [are] denounced as Tories [and] apostates. . . . [P]rivate acts, and private character, and even life itself, I believe, were there no laws, would fall an easy sacrifice to these . . . followers of Duane."[19]

By 1803 the Quids feared that Pennsylvania politics would soon lapse into chaos. It was imperative that they discredit the Philadelphia Democrats, and to do so they had to confront them and their *Aurora*. The chief organ in this campaign was the Quids' own newspaper, the *Philadelphia Evening Post*, edited by William McCorkle, which began publication on February 20, 1804. The Quids could no longer afford to let the *Aurora* remain the only Jeffersonian newspaper in the city. The *Evening Post* changed its name to the *Freeman's Journal* on June 12, 1804, after the Quids tired of the *Aurora*'s reminding the voters that it shared a name with the Hamiltonian *New York Evening Post*.

The *Freeman's Journal* regularly denounced what it described as the *Aurora*'s "abuse and threats." It castigated the paper's columns as "Robespierrism, denunciation, and proscription."[20] The paper insisted that the *Aurora*'s tone had no place in a free society. Such language prevented the quiet, unimpeded discussion that made republican, or democratic, or representative politics possible. Whenever the *Freeman's Journal* took notice of the *Aurora*, and increasingly its only object was to respond to that paper, it described it as some variant of "the abusive and tyrannical paper up Market Street."[21] The *Freeman's Journal* also devoted much space to attacking Duane and Leib and blaming them for the regrettable style and content of politics now preponderant in Pennsylvania.[22]

The paper also insisted that Duane and Leib maintained complete control over a small faction determined to dominate the entire state. They did not speak for the people, and so were demagogues, not democrats. Regardless of what one thought of the two Philadelphia radicals' style, this case was difficult to make. Duane's paper was easily the most widely read Jeffersonian periodical in the North, and it enjoyed an interstate circulation.[23] Leib was appointed to the U.S. Senate by the state legislature and elected to the state legislature by an anonymous urban electorate in elections that were usually contested. The very existence of the Quids suggested their concern that the beliefs of the Philadelphia Democrats could resonate throughout Pennsylvania unless challenged. Thus the *Freeman's Journal* hedged its bets. Of course Duane and Leib dominated a self-interested minority. But it was also true that a principled minority, such as the Jeffersonians during the early 1790s, could legitimately oppose the majority.[24] Each person had the right to pursue his own conscience on every issue at any time. This right was the cornerstone of a democratic society. Whether the majority or a principled minority, the Quids were right, and the Philadelphia Democrats were wrong.

The Quids were quite serious about changing the tone of politics. Though they became quite good at character assassination, they did try to avoid it. They sought to make the *Freeman's Journal* a source that provided Pennsylvanians with a proper political education and grounding in Jeffersonian belief. The *Freeman's Journal* devoted as much space as did the *Aurora* to discussions of history, politics, and proper legal structure and values. It is remarkable how regularly and ably complex political and economic issues were discussed and debated in these Jeffersonian newspapers.

The *Freeman's Journal* insisted that it was simplistic to divide governments into the categories despotic, aristocratic, and democratic as the *Aurora* insisted on doing. According to the Quids, the Philadelphia Democrats with such distinctions championed antiquated and unworkable conceptions of democracy. Once they equated democracy with an impossible and undesirable ideal, any form of government that did not meet their fallacious definition could be denounced as impure and tyrannical. The Philadelphia Democrats, then, held up "Athens, Rome, etc. where the people were assembled or convened, for the purpose of enacting laws, and even administering executive and judiciary powers" as true democracy and thus the only legitimate political structure.[25] This method of argument meant that sensible "republican democrats have been, by this means, implicated in an alarming tendency to disorganize our established political rules, and our representative government." Democracy was desirable, but Jeffersonian victory had established it. Democracy was simply a political system in which the people were sovereign.[26] True popular sovereignty meant that all citizens were treated equally by the government they created, and by the representatives they elected in those areas where the government legitimately acted. But what were those areas, and which sort of public behavior characterized adequate representation?

The question of representation was crucial to the Quids, for "the conflicting interests of an extensive population naturally produce the representative form, in which energy is necessary to preserve it from anarchy."[27] Recognition of the complexity of American society forced the Quids to acknowledge the implausibility of one common good that the whole Republic could move toward or mutually share. But they did not want the competition between those interests to be the sole driving force of American politics or the only sinews of democracy. A politics driven only by such conflicts, "subjected to varying influences of passion and interest; controlled by local prejudices, and their comprehensions confined to their peculiar situation," was mean and little. Because of their provincialism, "the majority of a nation must ever remain incapable of judging of general interests. Hence governments have been instituted and the affairs of many confided to the management of a few."[28]

Their experience in raucous and divided Philadelphia and growing market towns such as Lancaster taught the Quids to expect disagreement and conflict. But the violence of that disagreement caused them to long for Madisonian umpires who would oversee and adjudicate those conflicts. The only problem, and it was momentous and perhaps perennial, was that the Quids sought to be those umpires while also either representing or constituting some of the most talented, entrepreneurial, and successful of those competing interests. While the Quids tried to defeat the Philadelphia Democrats, they also sought to resolve this nettlesome quandary within their own movement and within their own minds. How they fared tells us much about the future course of Pennsylvania and the nation they did much to shape.

The Quids insisted that they were democrats. They understood that they would lose all chance for political legitimacy if they resisted the term. Accepting democracy was more than a gesture. The Quids understood that Pennsylvania politics would continue to be animated by popular involvement. Unlike the Federalists, the Quids accepted a society in which political success depended on demonstrating the cogency of their beliefs to an electorate rapidly approaching universal white male suffrage. Thus, the Quids were forever committed to redefining what democracy meant. They had to convince their fellow Pennsylvanians that the Philadelphia Democrats' beliefs were not democracy. Indeed, they sought to show that only creating a genuinely democratic society could save Pennsylvania from the Philadelphia Democrats. The Quids insisted that true democracy in a complex nation such as the United States was representative democracy,[29] which looked much like the United States under Jefferson. Certainly, improvements and reforms were needed, but they could be achieved with little difficulty.

From the beginning, then, the Quids faced a profound dilemma that was difficult for them to articulate or address. They grasped sooner than the Philadelphia Democrats that those included in the category "the people" were a much more variegated group than the city radicals' conception of democracy allowed. Those that the Federalists did not consider fit to govern were already creating their own social and economic differentiation, which meant that the citizens who constituted "the people" had increasingly varied living conditions and experiences. Yet the Quids could not simply accept, or ask their fellow Pennsylvanians to accept, that the democratic freedom to pursue one's talents would naturally and legitimately cause this differentiation — this inequality.

The Quids could not confront the growing likelihood of social and economic inequality for two reasons. First, they drew intellectual and ideological meaning and sustenance from the Jeffersonian opposition movement of the 1790s. This opposition, to which those who eventually became Quids contributed so much, took for granted that a homogeneous and virtuous people had detected and defeated the self-interested tyrannical faction that threatened republican justice. It would go far toward undermining the achievement of 1800 if nagging conflict and division did not melt away with the waning of Federalist influence. Quite simply, after 1800 there was not supposed to be discord.

Though the Quids were beginning to sense that conflict could have sources other than Federalist aspirations, they could not bring themselves to acknowledge these sources for a second reason. The fact was that the Philadelphia Democrats were arguing something the Quids largely accepted — that inequality and suffering were unnatural and resulted from the manipulation of political power by the undeservedly mighty. If the Quids followed their insight about differing interests, and the suspicion that some interests would fare better than others, this conclusion would become difficult to justify given the assumption the Pennsylvania Jeffersonians made about the cause of inequality. Since Pennsylvania Jeffersonians believed that undemocratic political manipulation by a quasi aristocracy was the source of inequality and injustice, the Philadelphia Democrats could rather easily portray the Quids' nascent and subtler understanding of differences among the people as a defense of inequality. Given the assumptions that shaped the state's Jeffersonian political thought, if the Quids could be associated with a defense of inequality, that defense could be presented as support for consolidated political power in the hands of a quasi aristocracy.

The emerging crucible of conflict forced the Quids to develop a body of thought that was less subtle, and less likely to minister to the needs of all people, than was their initial insight that the people were an increasingly complex group whose varied needs the state would have to consider. The Quids were eager to embrace democracy. Yet their fears of the Philadelphia Democrats, their need to accommodate their own loyalty to the legacy of the Jeffersonian opposition, the city radicals' potential capacity to discredit them, and their own unwillingness to confront their own insights created a significant intellectual and ideological conundrum. Attempting to resolve it led the Quids to a definition of democracy that was quite compelling but that ultimately intensified the process already begun that was making untenable the late eighteenth-century Jeffersonian notion of a homogeneous people.

The Quids had no choice but to join in an argument about the meaning of democracy (not that they did not want to). By 1803 something unprecedented was happening in Pennsylvania. A large portion of the polity was deciding that something called democracy would be the dominant political idea. Urban and rural radicals had begun to provide one definition of democracy, and the Quids struggled to negotiate the complicated and unmapped terrain of perpetually popular mainstream politics. The journey was arduous to begin with. It became even more so because of the Quids' own misunderstandings and miscalculations.

Though they insisted that they, too, were democrats, the Quids relied on more traditional denunciations of the sorts of men who produced and were most influenced by the *Aurora*. It was unfortunate that such men had any influence. They enjoyed it not because of legitimate conclusions drawn by the voters but because of a "want of attention to the public concerns by the men of respectability and talents of the party to which they attached themselves, and which they have at length the extreme arrogance to attempt to lead. . . . These upstart demagogues . . . must sink into their original nothingness. . . . They should be told . . . you will please to fall back, and take your stands where nature intended you should."[30] Though there was a natural, organic political order, and though it required a virtuous elite to set things aright, elites could not lead until they convinced the people to elect them. The majority had to decide to follow the Quids voluntarily and to declare to the Philadelphia Democrats, "Neither your virtue, your talents, nor your standing in society entitle you to preference."[31] The Quids hoped to maintain a society of political deference. But they wanted the people to reconsider who deserved this deference and legitimate their new leaders by giving them popular endorsement. Deference would be put to a regular vote. No longer would the virtuous elite be those few who could secure preferment from an oligarchic state or live without laboring. Rather, they would be the rising men of the Jeffersonian leadership, men who were busily making themselves prosperous, and who believed that if the nation was left to their care, then all Americans would share in the prosperity.

Thus the *Freeman's Journal* wrote of natural stations in society, and of policies pursued by the farsighted that would benefit all. But the paper also insisted on the individual's right to make decisions about his own future based solely on a calculation of his own interests.[32] A crucial part of the Quids' plan to discredit the Philadelphia Democrats was to insist that the free pursuit of self-interest would lead to a general prosperity that would make their opponents' concerns irrelevant. There was nothing wrong, the Quids maintained, with the representative democracy Pennsylvania currently enjoyed. The state had almost universal white male suffrage, there were no "aristocratical distinctions" drawn between citizens, and there was a general commitment to developing natural resources and expanding market opportunities.[33] Pennsylvania simply required a political system that could guarantee the protection of private property and the qualitative economic development that would create more opportunities for each citizen. The gravest threat to this prospect was a turbulent political system that would make instability and uncertainty perpetual. Under such conditions property rights would be unstable, and sober men would refuse to accept the legitimate risks necessary for increased opportunity and greater prosperity.

The Quids promoted a view of the nation quite different from that of the Philadelphia Democrats. They stressed the nation's inevitable future greatness and the general prosperity that came when each citizen was able to exploit his property and improve his position. The Quids insisted that the "country experiences the full tide of prosperity; . . . we are obtaining new acquisitions of territory; making rapid strides in the cultivation of the arts and sciences; advancing fast towards a state of refinement, enjoying peace and plenty at home, respected abroad; commanding an elevated station amongst the greatest nations of the world; and every circumstance both physical and political conspiring to make us a great and happy people."[34] The only threat to this glorious prospect was misunderstanding and misusing democracy. If Pennsylvanians established a political system in democracy's name that obliterated "the just and wise lines of distinction which have been marked out for the different branches of our government," their act would be replete with tragic irony.[35] If the legislature became overmighty, it would destroy the political, social, and economic conditions that permitted pursuit of one's interests, and the political and economic freedom that produced general prosperity and public happiness. The maintenance of those conditions was real democracy.

The Quids conceived a vision of the nation's future that they believed made sense and could appeal to a majority of Pennsylvanians. Prosperity would embrace all, but the Philadelphia Democrats called for policies that, threatened, even doomed, this chance for widespread prosperity and independence. The Quids stressed as frequently as they could the inevitability of the Republic's future greatness if they, and not the city radicals, were permitted to shape the future. The new nation was daily "increasing in population; progressing rapidly in every branch of agriculture, manufactures encouraged as far as is politic with the extent of our territory, and our present state of population; commerce extending her banners through every quarter of the globe; education expanding the ideals of her sons."[36] Leading Quids such as Tench Coxe and Matthew Carey organized the Pennsylvania Society for the Encouragement of Manufactures and the Useful Arts. They published their views in the *Freeman's Journal* and so associated the Quids with the support for protective tariffs, laborsaving machinery, and the development of manufacturing in growing interior market towns such as Pittsburgh.[37]

The Quids were clearly committed to the development and diversification of the internal American market. But a careful discussion of the political economy of the Quids and the radicals, particularly the urban Philadelphia Democrats, reveals several things. First, it reinforces the fact that surveying political economy in isolation cannot reveal the reasons for these Jeffersonians' disagreements. The Philadelphia Democrats, the Snyderites, and the Quids were all committed to development of the internal market. Only by concentrating on the ways in which the groups thought that political power should intersect with political economy can we begin to understand what separated radicals from moderates in Jeffersonian Pennsylvania. Second, an examination of the political economy of the various groups of Pennsylvania Jeffersonians reveals that each group identified material independence and a rough equality of condition as essential for productive democratic citizenship. Though the three groups disagreed about how best to ensure those conditions, they all sought them. Examining the political economy of the Pennsylvania Jeffersonians reveals much. But only by seeing how political economy intersected with political power can we explain why the three groups disagreed.

The Quids' political economy marked them as very different sorts of Jeffersonians from party leaders such as John Randolph or even Madison and Jefferson. The Virginians were imbued with a suspicion of dependence informed by classical thought and sharpened by the ideas of the eighteenth-century British country or commonwealth opposition. They associated deviation from a primarily agrarian political economy with dependence. Jefferson believed farmers to be the chosen people of God and hoped that the workshops would remain in Europe. Madison feared that craftsmen such as the shoe buckle makers of London, dependent on the whimsy of fashion and the patronage of the great, could never be independent enough to be trusted with republican responsibilities.[38] Jefferson and Madison were far subtler than the ideologue Randolph. But even Madison, the most sophisticated of the three, chased the dream of a bucolic agricultural republic primarily engaged in foreign commerce into the second decade of the nineteenth century. When he gave up the dream and dropped most of the qualifications that had adorned his endorsement of manufactures and the development of a domestic economy, he did so with an air of melancholy that in no way matched the Quids' early and unchanging exuberance.[39]

The political economy of the Quids shows that one must look beyond the national party leaders to comprehend Jeffersonian belief more completely. The Quids imagined a diversified and developing economy and society that was as hostile to the dreams of Hamilton and other Federalists as was any policy of the party's more agrarian-minded leadership. Indeed, Quids such as Matthew Carey proposed policies such as protective tariffs that would directly assist craftsmen. By conceiving such a political economy, they were democratizing the process of economic development and providing a Jeffersonian version of economic diversification and expansion.

The Quids, by fully supporting manufactures and development of the nation's resources, were at odds with many southern Jeffersonians.[40] But their beliefs regarding political economy did not cause the conflicts among the Jeffersonians of Pennsylvania. The Philadelphia Democrats and the Snyderites were unequivocally committed to the same diversified economy based on an expanding internal market for agriculture, commerce, and manufactures. Like the Quids, the Philadelphia Democrats and the Snyderites believed that the United States should remain a place where most citizens enjoyed direct control of productive resources. Like the Quids, they both assumed that agriculture would remain the fundamental economic activity of most Americans. They agreed that a vibrant, diversified internal market best served the needs of these independent farming families.

The Philadelphia Democrats never failed to praise internal improvements or policies that would assist American manufacturers. "Roads," the *Aurora* insisted, "like rivers, enrich and enliven a society, by the facility which they give to intercourse and to trade — roads draw men and towns and states into closer neighborhood."[41] The *Aurora* lauded projects to build turnpikes connecting Pittsburgh with Philadelphia, and canals to link eastern rivers to the Ohio and Mississippi.[42]

The Philadelphia Democrats made clear that the source of debasement in Europe and Britain was the working conditions of the nascent industrial revolution. They abhorred manufacturing enterprises such as "those of Manchester and Lyon, Birmingham and Sheffield, where population and poverty abound and render labour cheap."[43] Manufacturing in Europe reinforced inequality and exploitation. The Philadelphia Democrats deplored "the effects of manufactures as conducted in Europe, the decrepitude, debility, and degeneracy of those who inhabit manufacturing cities, the evils of monopoly, and the pernicious influence which large capitalists obtained over a large number." If such conditions were unavoidable in "the establishment of manufactures, the United States ought to forbid their encouragement." If the only option was Manchester, "better to be forever dependent on foreign nations . . . than to introduce the baleful and degrading system of Europe."[44]

Yet the Philadelphia Democrats championed domestic manufacturing. They insisted that manufactures should be, in the favorite metaphor of the early Republic, the handmaid of agriculture. A nation that supported a respectable number of industrious nonagricultural producers would provide a safe and stable market for the nation's farmers. "Our country," the *Aurora* insisted, "must be eminent in agriculture, manufactures, commerce, and navigation[,] those pillars of national grandeur."[45] Like the Quids, the Philadelphia Democrats supported protective tariffs. The city radicals enthusiastically listed the variety of industrious craftsmen and crafts such policies would support: "iron works, smithies, breweries, distilleries, kilns, potteries, brickyards, coopers, joiners, cabinet makers, wharf and bridge builders, wheelwrights [and] coach and carriage makers."[46]

Regarding a political economy of diversified production and an expanding internal market, the views of the Snyderites were identical to those of the Quids and the Philadelphia Democrats. Binns's *Argus* equated paving and flagging the streets of Sunbury with the public good. Contributors to the paper, such as the famous and highly regarded British exile Thomas Cooper, called for roads linking Philadelphia to Easton, Easton to Wilkes-Barre, and Wilkes-Barre to Sunbury. The expense, Cooper suggested, would easily be offset "by the increased prosperity."[47] The *Argus* also supported projects linking all of southern Pennsylvania to Philadelphia and Lake Erie.[48] The Snyderites agreed with the Quids that democracy required widespread prosperity. A democratic society had to be market oriented and intensely commercial and needed to promote values that encouraged the full mobilizing of all resources.[49]

Thus the *Argus* reported on meetings in Northumberland County organized to petition for the incorporation of turnpike companies to improve the region. One such gathering explained how economic development provided material independence for Pennsylvania's diverse producers, the independence without which a just and democratic society could not survive. The Northumberland petitioners informed the state legislature that they resided "in the most central part of the state, and in a fertile country." But they were unable to "profit of the advantages of their situation, from not having the means of taking their produce to market, at a moderate expense. . . . The capitalists are discouraged from the employment of their capitals in undertakings useful to themselves and the public, which they would not be were the communication between this country and the sea ports more easy." The petitioners reminded the legislature that internal improvements were too expensive for townships, counties, or even the state to undertake alone. Given proper encouragement and protection by the state through corporate charters, however, internal improvements could "be accomplished by individuals whose private interest is connected with that of the public. . . . [T]hat system of turnpikes by which the capital of the individual is called forth with the prospect of profit . . . is the most effectual and desirable." When the petitioners "consider[ed] the numerous advantages that w[ould] result from the undertaking to society at large, by facilitating the means of intercourse to farmers and manufacturers by furnishing them with an easy vent for their produce, and to landholders by bringing their lands so much nearer to market, and thereby increasing their value, they ha[d] little doubt but that the capital w[ould] easily be found requisite for the undertaking."[50]

In 1803 and 1804, as the radical urban and rural coalition emerged, the Quids formed to confront it. Yet the Philadelphia Democrats, Snyderites, and Quids agreed with each other about the principal features of political economy. They all championed vibrant and diverse economic development, they all insisted that the nation's future lay with an expanding internal market. The Quids, by supporting manufactures, did not follow the more agrarian ideals of certain prominent southern Jeffersonians, but neither did the Philadelphia Democrats nor the Snyderites.

Why, then, did they disagree? The Jeffersonians in Pennsylvania splintered over precisely how their differing political ideals, which they all called democracy, should intersect with this political economy of internal development. All three groups hoped for a society of materially independent citizens. They all concurred that this society could only come from a dynamic political economy that provided widely distributed control of productive property. But they differed over how to establish and maintain this political economy, and as their arguments continued, the groups found they agreed about less and less.

The Quids, as we have seen, were quite sanguine about the nation's future. Well-established men, they had identified and defeated what they considered aristocracy in 1800. The Quids felt that Pennsylvania had already secured the conditions necessary for democracy. Confident of future prosperity, the Quids dismissed the concerns of the radicals. After all, the Quids reminded Pennsylvania, "just when we should be happiest, when we are at our most triumphant—we divide amongst ourselves, we trample our unity."[51] Prosperity, material independence, and democracy could come only if Pennsylvanians rejected a politics that conflated democracy with the innovations proposed by the urban and rural radicals. "Our country," the *Freeman's Journal* insisted, "is flourishing by arts and manufactures, yet persons have been weak enough to make attempts at innovations, which if accomplished will dangerously affect the judicial branch of government, which has protected the commerce by which they flourish." Arbitration would end any security of property rights. The Quids acknowledged that the judicial system could stand some reform, but the radicals were "not satisfied with pruning the luxuriant branches of so venerable a system, but they must pluck from the very root of that tree which was planted in liberty, and protected and cherished by independence. . . . By our present method of trial, no citizen can be ousted of his property, but by the consent of twelve of his equals . . . [but] what can we expect of men with whom there is every opportunity to tamper; men confined by no rules, but such as they may make and break at pleasure?"[52] The Quids believed that their political economy could provide the material independence that allowed each Pennsylvanian to function as a democratic citizen only if those citizens rejected radical political innovations. These innovations would frighten men of property, undermine property rights, and create such instability that citizens could never be content or secure.

This argument could resonate with many Pennsylvania Jeffersonians, particularly since so many of them were property holders. In addition, the Quids held out the happy prospect that the rewarding feelings that came from working hard and seeing this labor bear fruit would also contribute to a general prosperity and republican equality that established justice and the common good. Allowing temporary, unproved local majorities to undermine the laws and institutions that protected the conditions necessary for justice and the public good was contrary to democracy. In this argument the Quids revealed the profound virtues and limits of their thinking. The virtues were manifest; the most significant was that the Quids challenged political proposals that would have had difficulty protecting individual rights. At the same time, the Quids did not address the fact that, though the Philadelphia Democrats' methods might very well be illegitimate, the concerns about economic and social inequality that led the city radicals to conceive them were not so.

The Quids believed so firmly in the unjust ugliness of the Philadelphia Democrats' proposals that they refused to consider carefully the fears that led to them. They would not think about them, though the Quids' own initial insights — that the people were increasingly heterogeneous, and that democracy required a rough equality of condition — demanded that they confront the same fears that drove the democratic theorizing in the *Aurora*. Thus, the Quids increasingly relied on a uniform and inflexible response to a complex issue. They insisted that uncontrolled, rapid economic development would solve the problem of creeping social and economic inequality that threatened democracy. For the Quids, their solution had to be correct. If they were wrong, the implication was that the people simply did not have common interests, and at that point a choice had to be made between preserving a rough equality of condition or embracing disparities in wealth and power. If the Quids' solutions failed, the choice that followed meant either embracing the ideas of the Philadelphia Democrats, and so abandoning private property, or building a society increasingly characterized by extremes of wealth and poverty and dominion and subjection, and so forsaking democracy. The prospect was chilling in either case, and so from 1803 the Quids insisted ever more shrilly that rapid economic development alone could bring democracy to the people.

The Philadelphia Democrats could not have held that notion in greater contempt. They insisted that unless it was overseen by democratic politics, a political economy that fully mobilized the nation's resources, and that allowed for the creation of immense wealth, would inevitably become a source of injustice and inequality. The Philadelphia Democrats insisted that a developmental political economy would be liberating because it would arise in a democracy that could continually adjudicate disputes as they arose, and so protect the ideals of individual autonomy and independence. Though the Philadelphia Democrats championed a developmental political economy, they never ceased to criticize any feature of it that they believed fostered an unequal distribution of the benefits. As much as the Quids, the Philadelphia Democrats supported canal construction to link rivers such as the Susquehanna and the Delaware, for example. But the city radicals thought that how the canals were built and who controlled them was just as significant as erecting them. They could imagine a future in which the presence of internal improvements was worse than never having built them. Thus, though the Philadelphia Democrats supported internal improvements, they opposed the efforts of the Susquehanna Company, a corporation they feared was beyond the people's control. The company hoped to build a canal linking Pennsylvania, Delaware, and Maryland. The *Aurora* acknowledged that "the opening of a canal through Delaware would be of the utmost importance, and tend to the enrichment and advantage of the three states. . . . That the work would do honour to the country is equally true, and the more necessary it is that the pernicious patrons of private avarice should not be suffered to interfere, to retard, or cramp its execution. In the hands of a few men invested with the monopoly, it might become a source of great mischief."[53] For the Philadelphia Democrats the qualification was as important as the initial commitment. In a democracy each plan could be scrutinized and organized to ensure the greatest opportunity for the greatest number. Economic development bolstered social autonomy and political independence, but it did not do so automatically. It was, in fact, the difficult and unending task of a democratic people to structure a democratic political economy. If they did so, then "a fair spirit of national exertion [could] be made, jealous of foreign interference and exclusive corporations, and emulous to promote American prosperity upon American principles, free, open, and impartial, making private property secondary not superior to public good."[54]

It is easy to misunderstand this political economy and so judge the Philadelphia Democrats by standards that were not theirs. Duane, Leib, and their supporters were motivated by hostility toward inequality, and they understood that often the most pernicious example of it was the wide disparity in wealth. Their ideals, not surprisingly, attracted most of Philadelphia's laboring poor, the main reason that Southwark and the Northern Liberties amounted to safe seats for Michael Leib.⁵⁵ But the Philadelphia Democrats were not nascent socialists. They had no conception of class as Marx taught the world to understand that term. Indeed, they did not think that the market, or economic activity itself, was the chief source of inequality. The overwhelming support of the laborers can confuse the issue. The Philadelphia Democrats believed that the primary source of inequality was the unequal distribution of political power. Thus, in societies that were not democracies, people whom Marxists call the petite bourgeoisie were as oppressed as the free laborers Marxists describe as the proletariat. The solution to inequality was not a redistribution of property, an assault on private property, or a breakthrough in class consciousness that allowed wage laborers to fashion a common identity. Instead, all those denied access to politics had to alter the process of political decision making so that a particular group could not wield political power for its own ends and remain unaccountable. The distinctions the Philadelphia Democrats drew were between the few and the many or the idle and the industrious.

The Philadelphia Democrats argued that the social and economic conditions that they called the European condition of society were intimately bound up with recent usage of political power and the state, and nowhere was this truer than in Britain, the nation that the Philadelphia Democrats despised the most. The city radicals assumed that no person could ever accumulate enough to pose a danger to others if he was forced to rely only on those resources that he could naturally control, whether through accumulation from his own labor or by employing others. People accumulated dangerous amounts of wealth when they were able to use public power for private purposes — when, for example, private interests received monopoly charters of trade or finance, or the state distributed public revenue in the form of pensions or places to a privileged few.

The Philadelphia Democrats theorized that Cosimo de 'Medici would have prospered if he had been left alone. He would have been wealthier than most of his neighbors. But he only became dangerous when he was granted access to public power that few others were able to have. At that point he could cut off opportunities for other people, he could control resources that he himself had not produced, and so he could increase his wealth and power far beyond his natural capacity to do so as a private industrious man. Great and exclusive wealth was dangerous, but the source of this great wealth was unequal access to the power of the state.

The answer for the Philadelphia Democrats was not Adam Smith's. They did not believe that the state could or should be neutral. A democracy wielded power for the many; all other governments were structured by the few to aggrandize themselves. The question was not whether political power ought to be used to fashion the social, economic, and legal customs and relations that connected humanity. That had always happened. The issue was whether the majority could create a government it controlled. If it could, it would prevent the few from using political power to mobilize resources, interpret law, and dictate custom and culture for interested purposes. Government benefited either the few or the many because it was composed of either the few or the many. If the many gained access to political power, they could wield it in ways that hurt the few. They could pursue the happy mediocrity of condition that gradually lessened the distinctions between the few and the many. By definition, then, democracy improved the condition of the great majority at the inexpensive price of forcing the small number who had been great to settle for merely living comfortably and independently. Once the few accepted that they deserved no more than did others, there would only be the many — "the people." And "the people" was a broad category that included small property holders of every description, skilled laborers, workingmen on land and sea, lesser merchants, and anyone else who enjoyed only what he acquired naturally.[56]

Thus, the distinctions that the Philadelphia Democrats drew had little to do with modern conceptions of class or criticisms of capitalism. The city radicals began with the assumptions that the United States could naturally promote the widespread ownership of productive property, and that only a government hostile to democracy could prevent this rough equality of condition. They assumed that democratic control of political power would produce a society in which almost no adult white man had to depend on the resources of others. There would be little wage labor. Since the many controlled the government, they would prevent the interested use of political power that allowed the few to become unnaturally wealthy and powerful. If unanticipated threats to the happy mediocrity of condition arose, a democracy could conceive solutions that allowed the many to protect themselves.

From the beginning, then, like the Quids, the thought of the Philadelphia Democrats revealed real strengths and profound weaknesses. In many ways it made sense to think as seriously as they did about political power, as the events of the 1790s or the economic development of Britain after 1715 under the Whigs showed.[57] But at the same time, the Philadelphia Democrats assumed that all citizens (except a tiny minority of Federalist elites) —

"the people" — would think and act in the same way. The Philadelphia Democrats took for granted that mercurial local majorities and the arbitrators they elected would only impose on those few who sought to use the state to injure their neighbors. "American principles" as filtered through local majorities would, then, without difficulty protect the many. Given this assumption, the Philadelphia Democrats could announce that private property was secondary to the public good and base their idea of democracy on the belief that democracy required widespread ownership and protection of private property. The only source of inequality was a quasi aristocracy manipulating political power. Thus, certain of those among the people making use of certain American principles — the right to acquire property, improve it, profit from it, and mobilize resources to continue doing so on a larger scale — could always comfortably coexist with local majorities empowered to determine whether the conduct of their neighbors was conducive to the public good.

The Philadelphia Democrats could not (at least initially) conceive that master craftsmen and the journeymen they employed might have separate interests. They had difficulty imagining that the entrepreneurial process of production and accumulation could produce disparities in wealth and power capable of assaulting the happy mediocrity of condition. Despite the entrepreneurial dynamism of certain of Pennsylvania's people, the city radicals concluded that purely private efforts could never seriously threaten their society of independent producers. In a democracy no private interest would ever enjoy the exclusive assistance of the state, and so there was little reason to worry about the private efforts of people as long as they were confined to the private resources they acquired naturally.

Given these assumptions, the Philadelphia Democrats paid no special attention to wage laborers. Their condition was probably temporary. If they were abused it was because the state was insufficiently democratic. An undemocratic state allowed for the unnatural consolidation of property that produced permanent wage laborers who could not be protected from abuse. Once the United States was sufficiently democratized, commerce, credit, and a growing and diverse economy would perpetually encourage the desire and the opportunity to acquire property. In a democracy that desire would consolidate the happy mediocrity of condition and so allow a greater number to become independent than in any other society at any time ever before.

This faith in rapid economic development managed by locally based, immediately responsive majorities was nowhere clearer than in the Philadelphia Democrats' attitudes toward banks. The city radicals absolutely supported banks and paper money. They believed that little economic development could take place without them. But their commitment to banking was careful and qualified. Contributors to the *Aurora* wrote repeatedly that banks could be agents of injustice. They had been so in the 1790s, when "the banks were used by the late administration [of John Adams] as political engines [to] . . . the injury of real solid credit [and] the beneficial uses of banking conducted upon liberal and equitable principles."[58] The banking system had been so manipulated because it was controlled by the Bank of the United States, which had not been "kept within due bounds." The immensity and unaccountability of the national bank, and its domination of the other paltry sources of domestic credit, had "the effect of this sudden creation of nominal and fallacious wealth of one bank alone . . . [which] created a spirit of speculation . . . [and] a luxurious style of living far beyond the profits of real wealth to support it."[59] The Philadelphia Democrats feared this fallacious wealth. They reasoned that without artificial assistance, such as exclusive government charters or monopolies, no Americans could produce enough wealth with their own resources and labor to obtain a position in the economy that allowed them to pose a danger to others. Thus, the way banks should function in a democracy still had to be worked out.

Michael Leib considered determining the proper places of banks in a democracy as part of his mandate when the state legislature led by Speaker Simon Snyder elected him to the U.S. Senate. Leib demanded that federal deposits be removed from the national bank and that federal revenues be placed in state banks. Back home the *Aurora* suggested that if Leib's motion passed, "an aristocracy which has actually drawn much of its influence from the public wealth, at their disposal, will be placed more on a level with the community at large."[60] Leib was not at all opposed to banks. His plan would in fact have strengthened state and local banks and encouraged the chartering of new ones. But Leib did not believe that a developing economy would automatically serve the needs of most Americans. A developing economy was not intrinsically liberating. Rather, a democratic people, who presided over a democratic nation, had to be provided the means to determine when and if banks were harmful.

This notion of a democratized economy was clearest in Leib's stance during the 1811 debate on rechartering the Bank of the United States. Leib did more than simply oppose recharter. He brought the Philadelphia Democrats' brand of pure democracy directly into Congress, much to the disgust of many of his fellow Jeffersonians. Leib opposed the bank on principle and argued during the debate that though "the Bank of the United States was a check upon other banks [it was] a check like that of a shark upon the little fish around him. It was in the power of the Bank of the United States, by means of its great capital and the governmental patronage, to prey upon the other banks whenever it pleased." But, Leib continued, even if he had no objection to the bank, he would still oppose its recharter. Those he represented, he reported, wished to see the charter denied. Leib assented "to the right of constituents to instruct, and was ready to yield in obedience — it was in accordance with his political maxims; and he should ever consider himself bound to obey instructions as long as they did not require the performance of an act which would violate the oath which he had taken. On this occasion he yielded in obedience with pride and pleasure, as the instructions corresponded with his own impressions of solemn obligation."[61]

The rechartering issue showed how the Philadelphia Democrats hoped American democracy would function. The people empowered a popular body to decide a fundamental question. Representatives such as Leib participated, accepting that they acted as the mouthpieces of the majority. It was this democracy that could safely pursue banks and a diverse economy. Many of Leib's fellow congressmen chafed at the constraints he hoped to place on them. In response to Leib they complained about "restraining the free exercise of opinion in the deliberation of this honorable body."[62]

Yet the Philadelphia Democrats did support the chartering of banks that they believed would further the needs of democratic citizens. Between 1802 and 1804 the Pennsylvania legislature debated whether to charter the Bank of Philadelphia. The *Aurora* endorsed granting a charter, insisting that the threat certain banks posed would be alleviated by diversifying sources of credit and decreasing the influence of each particular bank. The *Aurora* also believed that unlike the other three banks in Pennsylvania — the Bank of North America, the Bank of Pennsylvania, and the Bank of the United States — the Bank of Philadelphia would be conducted on "liberal principles," and that "persons of almost every class [i.e., occupation] are stockholders." The *Aurora* argued that the newest bank lent for longer periods than did the other three. Shorter loans could assist only established merchants, who received them expecting a profit from business conducted within the period covered by the loan. Journeymen hoping to become master craftsmen, masters seeking to expand their businesses, and lesser merchants (of which there were many in Philadelphia) hoping to enlarge their concerns needed longer than the short-term loans of a few months to see their investments bear fruit. Thus, the *Aurora* concluded, at the Bank of Philadelphia "the tradesman and mechanic have an equal chance with the merchant."[63] The bank received a charter in early 1804.

The Philadelphia Democrats wanted Americans to concentrate on developing the domestic economy and creating a legitimate home market. They hoped that credit would be so generally available that those who did the actual work of building this economy would always have access to it. Democratic prosperity came when urban and rural producers controlled the resources of the vibrant domestic economy. The Quids agreed on every point. The crucial difference was that the Philadelphia Democrats believed that democratic distribution of such resources could come only with perpetual popular intrusion into the economic and legal issues that so affected the lives of all citizens. The Quids thought that such a vision of democracy would encourage disrespect for property and ruin any chance for the vibrant domestic economy both they and the city radicals considered to be essential in order to have an equal society of democratic citizens. The Snyderites agreed with the Quids and the Philadelphia Democrats that economic development was necessary for the material independence of most citizens, and thus an essential condition for democracy. Snyder, Binns, Boileau, and the rest were also committed to developing the domestic economy. They expected this domestic economy to serve the needs of the state's producers, its farmers and artisans. The *Argus* insisted that developing the domestic economy directly assisted laboring people in ways that committing to foreign trade never could.[64]

Thus, as the Quids organized in 1803 and 1804, much of the political economy they promoted overlapped with the aspirations of the urban and rural coalition. Yet the radical political program of arbitration and hostility to the less popular branches of government was intimately connected to the economic ideology of the radicals. The Philadelphia Democrats and the Snyderites sought to lessen the power of the courts so that the people who would labor in the vibrant economy could more directly administer it. The Quids feared that such an intersection of popular politics and economic activity would produce a fluctuating undependable protection of property rights that would destroy the all-important vibrant internal economy.

In 1804 the shared commitment to development of the domestic economy for the sake of the nation's producers could not prevent the Pennsylvania Jeffersonian party from shattering. The urban and rural radical coalition feared that the Quids' refusal to link economic development to a transformation of the legal system would create in America the European condition of society. Thus, in 1804 the radicals redoubled their efforts to enact arbitration. They placed tremendous pressure on Governor McKean. As criticism of the Jeffersonian McKean mounted in the Jeffersonian *Aurora,* the governor struggled to explain to himself and to his president why he was in such an undesirable position.

The denunciations stemmed from his veto of arbitration bills. McKean explained to Jefferson that "with the best intentions in the world our legislators are attempting innovations; but as their bills have been generally . . . too dangerous even for an experiment, I have been compelled to interpose my qualified negative. I wish for a few Gentlemen of science in law, history, and government in each House . . . but I despair of being so gratified and must therefore submit to my destiny."[65] McKean, like his fellow Quids, "dread[ed] the consequences that may be produced from the present apparent spirit of innovation and change in establishments." In his veto messages the governor sought to convince his constituents that they should resist "tampering with established systems or forms of government." He hoped that they would be public-spirited enough to "submit to small real injuries [rather] than set everything afloat."[66]

Demands for arbitration and condemnation of the judges who incarcerated Thomas Passmore also renewed the fears of Alexander J. Dallas. He, too, began to try to convince the Jefferson administration that it should be concerned. Writing to Secretary of the Navy Robert Smith, Dallas lamented, "It is allowed here . . . that lawyers, men of talents and education, men of fortune and manners, ought not to participate in the formation or administration of a democratic government. . . . [I]n short, every occurrence indicates a spirit and a scheme to involve our country in all the revolutionary passions and sufferings of the first convulsive throes of France."[67] By February 1804 Dallas received information that intensified his fears. From a correspondent in the state legislature, he learned that city ideas also flourished in Lancaster. In the state capital, the desire for "reformation was visionary only, innovation instead of reformation is instead tried, and of a most dangerous kind, new roads are opened and untrodden paths are searched merely for the sake of novelty, and where all will end only time will show." Dallas's correspondent lamented attacks on the law and agents of the courts, for he "believe[d] the life, liberty, and property of every individual depend[ed] upon the law and honest lawyers." "What it is coming to," he sadly informed Dallas, "I will not divine."[68]

During 1804 the Quids' inchoate fears formed into a clear purpose. In the process of carrying Pennsylvania for Jefferson in the presidential election of that year, they would also seek to discredit Michael Leib. The Quids insisted that Leib's behavior divided the Jeffersonians and weakened Jefferson's chances. They called for unity in 1804, but they also mounted a campaign to oust Leib from Congress. The Quids held their own meetings, some of them chaired by McKean himself, seeking suitable alternatives.[69] To a man, they insisted that Leib was unfit for office. His morals were questionable, his temper unseemly, his principles terrifying, and he was, "moreover, in avowed hostility to the commercial interest, upon which the prosperity of this district and of the numerous mechanical and manufacturing branches so materially depend." The Quids backed the Philadelphia merchant William Penrose, a "man of business, industry, and regularity . . . independent in pecuniary resources."[70] They denounced Leib because he sought "to make invidious distinctions between the rich and the poor. . . . Leib wants to read and write for the Northern Liberties, that he might cajole the people there."[71] Indeed, between June and the first week of October, the months of political campaigning, the *Freeman's Journal* devoted thirty-five days to attacking Leib. In more than a few cases entire issues were spent vilifying him. On September 12, the *Freeman's Journal* announced that certain of Leib's followers planned to murder Penrose if he won.[72]

The desire to discredit Leib stemmed from the Quids' broader sense that a workable democratic politics depended on a political culture drastically different from that encouraged by the Philadelphia Democrats. The inclusive and expansive political economy the Quids envisaged would function best if associated with a sober and judicious vision of politics that discouraged frenzy out of doors and a general climate of instability. This climate the Quids associated with the personalities of Leib, Duane, and the other Philadelphia Democrats.

Thus, as the Quids promoted their political economy, they also struggled to describe a more sober and responsible method of democratic politics, a method much more likely to take hold if men such as the Quids governed democratic Pennsylvania. The Quids took the opportunity provided by the Louisiana Purchase to discuss how "democratic citizens" could best participate in public life. The *Freeman's Journal* insisted that it was useful to "ask if the way in which public jubilees have been observed be worthy of a free, an enlightened and independent people? It is well known, that by the method formerly observed, the labor of a whole day is in the first place lost."[73] While this loss was beneath the dignity of democratic citizens, it was not as unfortunate as what generally followed. For usually citizens form themselves into large companies, dine at some tavern, spend from two to six dollars, and many of their families are the worse for weeks, by celebrating one grand holiday — By this, can the state be profited? Can the principles of liberty be promoted? Will the cause for which we contend be strengthened? Will morality be extended and a Christian disposition inculcated? If each of these three queries must be answered in the negative, would it not be worthy the attention of a discerning public to pause; to consider if a better way might not be devised of evidencing our patriotism than by eating costly dinners and swallowing down bottles of wine; in drinking toasts which may, nay, only flatter weak men, but never profit society.[74]

Rather than indulge in waste and demagoguery, the Quids advised dignified democrats to "form and walk in procession to some public place, where an oration may be delivered depicting the blessings of peace, and the happiness we enjoy when compared with the inhabitants of the old world; then, let everyone go quietly to his own home, and enjoy the sweets of liberty in the circle of his family."[75] Such placid, edifying conduct would help the Quids' political economy to solidify the conditions in which a free, equal, independent, and democratic people flourished. By autumn 1804 the Quids had no difficulty explaining why Michael Leib was the gravest threat to such a happy condition.

As the bitter conflict intensified in Pennsylvania, the division of the party became something of a national preoccupation. It especially troubled Jeffersonians in Washington who were busy planning the president's reelection. As more Jeffersonians learned of the division, however, they were less likely to seek reconciliation and more inclined to take sides. The issues that divided Pennsylvania's Jeffersonians were too momentous, too fundamental, for anyone involved in Jeffersonian politics to ignore them. Whether they wished it or not, Jeffersonians had to concede that party politics in Pennsylvania had become a debate about exactly how popular and accountable government should be, and precisely how much obedience a minority owed the majority, and in which areas of life. Thus, Joseph Nicholson, a congressman from Maryland and an in-law of Gallatin, wrote William Jones that congressional sessions were growing increasingly bitter. It was not because of the Federalists, Nicholson lamented, but because "our friends [are] bickering very much among ourselves." One did not have to look far to see who was responsible. Nicholson blamed an obscure Philadelphian named Michael Leib.[76]

The Quids' campaign against Leib and the radicals exposed their own weaknesses. Though they sought to discredit the ideas found in the *Aurora*, they also insisted that Duane's prominence in Pennsylvania politics was unjustified because his "standing in society d[id] not entitle him to take the lead."[77] The Quids believed that they alone could ensure the safety of the republican experiment. In order to do so, they had willingly defeated traditional elites who sought traditional privileges. The Quids did not expect, or think that they needed, the same exalted status. However, as they saw the sorts of men who were emerging to lead their party, they could not help but conclude that a measure of political deference would be salutary.

The 1804 campaign in Philadelphia and Philadelphia County showed both the Quids and the Philadelphia Democrats at their worst. Both groups were motivated by a sincere conviction that the fate of the Republic depended on the outcome of their congressional election. In Philadelphia County the Philadelphia Democrats enjoyed a majority and insisted on nominating candidates at a mass meeting. Though certain areas of the county supported Penrose, most citizens lived in the Northern Liberties and Southwark, which were overwhelmingly for Leib. The Quids demanded district meetings within the county, insisting that one mass general meeting would allow demagogues to dominate and would be too unruly for rational discussion. In the city, the Quids believed that they enjoyed majority support but knew that they might be challenged in those wards that bordered the suburbs. Thus within Philadelphia the Quids insisted on a general meeting. The Philadelphia Democrats feared that the Quids had judged the situation correctly and so demanded district meetings in each Philadelphia ward.[78]

In general, the popular nature of the campaign helped the Philadelphia Democrats and hurt the Quids. For example, at one point the Quids called a general town meeting in the city, their supposed stronghold, to nominate Penrose. When the Philadelphia Democrats turned out more people than the Quids, the Quids refused to attend the meeting they had called.[79] The Quids' campaign did have some affect, but from their perspective far too little. The Philadelphia Democrats swept the elections, but Leib won by fewer votes than the other candidates backed by the group. Still, Leib had defeated Penrose, even in Philadelphia, though only by eighteen votes. Elsewhere Leib won the suburbs of Southwark, the Northern Liberties, and Germantown. Laborers dominated the first two districts; Leib won 60 percent of the vote in Southwark and 69 percent in the Northern Liberties.[80] Thus Leib was reelected; for the time being, suburb politics had defeated the Quids.

During the months they spent failing to oust Leib, the Quids had learned valuable lessons. They realized that they could mount a sustained popular campaign and that they could weaken those they believed to be dangerous. Still, they had not defeated Leib, and the coming year promised to be crucial for their efforts to reshape the conception of democracy. In 1805 McKean's second three-year term as governor would end. Clearly the radicals had plans to challenge him. Having weakened Leib, the Quids could safely assume that he was no longer a viable candidate, but that would mean little if the radical coalition elected the next governor. Though the Quids could take some pride in their first efforts to alter the understanding of democracy, they had little time to congratulate each other. Leib secured his narrow victory in October. Autumn was fast turning into winter, and 1805 would quickly prove a most momentous year.

Chapter Four

The Crucible of Conflict: 1805

Though the Quids had not defeated Leib in 1804, Jefferson had been re-elected in a landslide, and the party had made substantial gains in still-Federalist New England. The Quids did not celebrate. Their defeat showed that although they had made strides, they had not yet mastered Pennsylvania's democratic politics. They devoted the gubernatorial election year 1805 to learning how to do so.

Despite Jefferson's victory, William Jones confessed to Joseph Nicholson that he was glad the election was over. His letter also revealed the continuing problem of the *Aurora*'s prominence. Jones assumed that Nicholson knew the outcome of the Philadelphia election, and that "the *Aurora* will have appraised you of the result." It was a difficult letter for Jones to write. He crossed out several opening lines, including a denunciation of "the popular character of the *Aurora*." The Quids were learning, even in private, that one could not belittle popularity in politics or the exuberance of the majority. Accordingly, Jones started over and described the Philadelphia Democrats as a well-organized demagogic minority. Still, Jones would not give up hope that those he considered the most rational and reasonable would win the day if they only spoke clearly and were heard. "There are," he informed Nicholson, "more men of respectability opposed to Leib than are to be found among his adherents." If they had only been more active, and perhaps had sought the support of Federalists willing to vote for Quids, Leib would have been defeated. At any rate, Jones could definitely conclude that he was "heartily sick of suburb politics." He was also frightened by it. Jones feared, he admitted to Nicholson, that the Philadelphia Democrats would seek to unseat McKean, and perhaps achieve national influence.[1]

Alexander J. Dallas also took little comfort from Jefferson's reelection. Leib had spoiled everything. One week after the election Dallas wrote to

126

Secretary of the Treasury Albert Gallatin, "Thank Heaven the election is over! The violence of Duane has produced a fatal division. . . . He menaces the Governor. You have already felt his lash. And I think there is reason for Mr. Jefferson himself to apprehend that the spirit of Callender lives."[2]

Lamentations about Leib's reelection and concerns for the future became a leitmotif in Quid letters. John Vaughan believed that the Philadelphia Democrats were "more dangerous to republican liberty than Hamiltonian aristocracy."[3] Indeed, concerns about Leib and his supporters spread far afield. Tench Coxe received letters from as far away as Georgia denouncing the *Aurora* and requesting subscriptions to the *Freeman's Journal*. One Georgian was terrified by the effects of the *Aurora*'s influence, since "ours is the last stand of democratic principles, and if liberty perishes in America, we may contemplate . . . nothing but the gloomy prospect of bondage." Denunciations of the Philadelphia Democrats and praise for the Quids also began to appear in the New York City papers.[4]

The radical coalition, especially in the city, was emboldened by the Quids' failure to unseat Leib. Leib's survival suggested that the radicals could move to complete the transformation of the legal system. But during the election the struggle for democracy had become much clearer. The Quids were more identifiable than ever before, and it was obvious to those Jeffersonians who accepted the radicals' assumptions that the Quid-dominated judiciary and executive were hostile to democracy. After Leib's reelection the radicals began to broaden their conception of what the establishment of democracy in Pennsylvania required.

In November, the month after Leib's victory, the *Aurora* took stock of the efforts to enact arbitration. In response to McKean's vetoes of more potent arbitration bills, the legislature had finally passed a more qualified bill popularly called the $100 Act. McKean had neither vetoed nor signed it, allowing it to become law without his endorsement. The new law allowed justices of the peace (who were appointed by the governor) to act as arbitrators in cases not exceeding $5.33 if one party requested arbitration. Their decisions were final. Disputes valued at less than $53 arbitrators could hear if both parties agreed, and those decisions, too, were final. Arbitrators could hear cases between $53 and $100 if both parties agreed, but such cases could be appealed by either party to a law court. Arbitrators were forbidden to hear disputes valued at over $100 and could hear no suit dealing with ejectment or replevin regardless of value.

The Philadelphia Democrats were contemptuous of the $100 Act. It did not prevent judges from shaping the legal beliefs and culture of the state. The

Aurora dismissed the new law, commenting that "the result is a kind of half way matter which the Governor was too wise to negative, but which many friends of reform wished him to have done, believing the agitation more useful than the law. He sees, or thinks he sees, you have missed the mark."[5]

The *Aurora*'s position exposed potential strains that had always existed within the urban and rural coalition. The intensity of the conflict of the coming year would allow the Quids to place pressure on these strains, with significant repercussions for the subsequent contours of Jeffersonian belief in Pennsylvania. The Snyderites did not share the Philadelphia Democrats' position about the $100 Act. In fact, Snyder and Boileau had been among those responsible for its passage. The act itself showed the differences between the two reform groups. The Snyderites realized that the act was a compromise, and they had willingly called for much stronger arbitration laws in 1803.[6] But they thought that the act was a significant step in the right direction. Shaped by the culture of mobility that had long flourished in the counties of Chester, Northumberland, and the rest of Snyderite country, they saw a virtue in such laws that the Philadelphia Democrats did not. Indeed, given that most artisans earned less than $100 per year, the Snyderites were right to conclude that the $100 Act would have a real impact on the radicals' constituents.[7]

The differences between the rural and urban radicals show that from the beginning demands for arbitration could be divided into two categories, which were shaped by the different origins and assumptions of the two groups. The first category was a commitment to commonsense reforms that would speed the judicial process and make an adversarial legal system more amenable to the rising needs of a growing economy and its litigious participants. The second category was a more utopian impulse radically to alter the legal system and link this alteration to a general transformation of American society. This latter reform spirit was often connected to internationalist hopes for a general European democratic revolution. As the Snyderites and the Philadelphia Democrats joined together, these two strains were compatible. Both categories of reform allowed for substantial changes in the legal system and stemmed from the belief that local majorities needed to play a more active role in influencing decisions that affected their communities. But the Snyderites were animated by the sense that they needed to protect, possibly restore, a past that largely met their democratic needs. Philadelphia Democrats such as Duane and Leib were convinced that they needed to lead a brash and unprecedented movement that would largely break with the past. The city radicals were shaped by the greater disparities in wealth and power found in Philadelphia and were much more intimately connected to the rhythms of Atlantic-world radicalism. They were generally animated by the second category of reform, whereas the Snyderites were motivated by the first. The Snyderites saw real progress in the $100 Act. Furthermore, they were less prone to ideological flights, of either fancy or inspiration. Rooted in their fertile southern Pennsylvania soil, they were always somewhat skeptical of the most grandiose of the Philadelphia Democrats' claims.

The *Argus*, for example, satirized a purported reformer who "would have every man to be his own lawyer, hatter, blacksmith, tailor, shoemaker etc." Since said reformer's deepest antagonism was for lawyers, he thought it best "to abolish the subject matter of their profession — that is to say the laws — and also one principal means whereby the profession is attainable — I mean the schools."[8] The Snyderites were sincerely critical of a legal structure that they believed threatened the material independence of Pennsylvania's producer citizens. However, they came from a region where inequality was less pervasive than it was in Philadelphia and where one's experience was generally not that different from one's neighbors. Thus, they were willing to see the threat of the courts as a combination of factors. Certainly the state was insufficiently democratic, but it was also true that the courts were overburdened. Even careful and conscientious judges and lawyers had trouble settling disputes with dispatch. Thus, the *Argus* defended arbitration in ways often unlike those found in the *Aurora*. One *Argus* editorial announced that "none will pretend that arbitrators will understand the subject they are called to investigate better, or that they will be furnished with any more honesty by being chosen [instead of] a court [to hear a dispute]." "But arbitration," the editorial continued, "makes an immense difference to the parties. If the cause is decided before it is entered in the court the expense is perfectly insignificant — if after it is ruinous."[9] The Snyderites saw demands for arbitration as compatible with calls to increase the number of courts and judges in Pennsylvania. An increase would complement arbitration, and such demands came while the Snyderites fought for the $100 Act. "Would it not be prudent," one correspondent to the *Argus* queried, "to let the two measures go hand in hand, and thereby prove that the friends of an adjustment law are not for tearing up old approved systems by the roots, but only for accommodating them to the present state of society?"[10]

The differences between the urban and rural radicals, then, were in part due to temperament and instinct. Bu these vaguer notions shaped by emotion and sensibility were influenced by something entirely concrete — the growing difference in access to and distribution of property between Philadelphia and the rural southeast. By 1805 Philadelphia was very much in the vanguard of a nineteenth-century process that included the transformation of craft production, the growth of permanent wage labor, and an unprecedented creation and consolidation of capital. These developments occurred far more gradually in the rural southeast. The city radicals and the Snyderites agreed that widespread access to productive property was the foundation of a democratic citizenry. But the Snyderites could more comfortably conclude that measured legislation such at the $100 Act would address threats to this widespread access. The threats required concern, but that concern need not be acute. The Philadelphia Democrats believed along with all other Pennsylvania Jeffersonians that the power of a privileged quasi aristocracy lay behind all inequality. They could only look around at the many examples of this inequality in Philadelphia and conclude that a quasi aristocracy was near to extinguishing the possibility of democracy. The democratization of public life needed to be sweeping and needed to happen quickly. This differing position concerning the availability of property would, over the course of 1805, prove a key weak link between the urban and rural radicals, one that could not survive the pressure placed on it by the dizzying development of Jeffersonian political ideas produced by the crucible of conflict.

Nevertheless, differences between the urban and rural radicals should not be overemphasized or given too much explanatory power too quickly. They would matter much more by the end of 1805 than they did at the beginning. As the urban and rural radicals reached out to each other in 1803 and 1804, something vital began to happen in Pennsylvania. A vibrant coalition of rather ordinary people began to insist that they were the most fit to make the important decisions that would shape the Republic. They argued that their very lack of distinction, that they labored, that at times they struggled to live comfortably, made them superior statesmen for a democracy than were more well educated professionals and gentlemen. If one read both the *Aurora* and the *Argus* carefully in 1803 and the first months of 1804, one saw obvious differences; however, they were outweighed by the vitality of this shared purpose. For a brief time a vocal coalition of Pennsylvania Jeffersonians considered turning a radical democratic consciousness into the primary ingredients of mainstream politics.[11]

In 1804 the Quids saw no reason to distinguish between the urban and rural radicals. They saw arbitration as an attack on private property, while all the radicals associated Governor McKean with animosity toward the democratizing of state institutions. Thus, 1805 became the crucial year of the Jeffersonian era in Pennsylvania, for in 1805 McKean was up for reelection. Ever since his first vetoes, the radicals had planned to unseat him. As Snyder helped shepherd the $100 Act through the legislature, and as rural and urban radicals combined to elect him Speaker of the House, he emerged as the logical challenger. The Philadelphia Democrats quickly linked Snyder's gubernatorial campaign to a widespread program that would make 1805 year one of the state's democratic revolution. McKean would be unseated, making way for a much more complete arbitration law, and the legislature would impeach the three supreme court judges who had so abused Thomas Passmore.

The effort to impeach Edward Shippen, Jasper Yeats, and Thomas Smith showed the solidarity felt by the radical coalition. The radicals assumed it would be the first great victory of 1805 and would pave the way for Snyder's election and the arbitration laws that would improve but also alter the legal system. The trial to impeach the judges began in 1804 and culminated in January 1805. Snyder and Boileau were the leading House managers, and the *Aurora* championed their efforts on the grounds of dangerous tendency.[12] Initially, the Philadelphia Democrats believed they could use the trial of the judges to link the Quids with the Federalists and so discredit them. The *Freeman's Journal* had published the defense of their conduct written by the three Federalist judges.[13] Alexander J. Dallas, who had been in the thick of the Passmore business, was one of the lawyers now defending the judges. Since 1803 the Quids had defended an independent judiciary and the common law. With the trial these positions were attached to the three Federalist supreme court judges. But linking positions the Quids took solely to Federalist justices became impossible when Pennsylvania's fourth supreme court judge, the Jeffersonian Hugh Henry Brackenridge, publicly defended the conduct of his colleagues. Brackenridge's intervention underscored that the impeachment battle, arbitration, and the coming gubernatorial election were all major campaigns in the struggle to define democracy and shape Jeffersonian belief.

The *Aurora* quickly denounced Brackenridge and called for his removal. The *Freeman's Journal* rejoiced when McKean praised Brackenridge and refused to strip him of his position.[14] Brackenridge next published a vigorous defense of judicial review in the *Freeman's Journal*. The judge insisted "that without this power in the judiciary . . . the Constitution will vary with the flux and reflux of representation in the legislative body." Brackenridge hoped to supplement the Quids' effort to equate democracy with a more sober and cautious method of decision making that nevertheless somehow accommodated popular politics. Thus Brackenridge insisted that "the judiciary is not a mere subordinate functionary in the administration of the laws, but a branch of the government itself, coordinate with the law making power and bound to regard the constitution and compare the law of the legislature with the superior law of the people."[15]

The move to impeach the judges began to focus the Quids' position. Over the course of the trial, and increasingly as the radical program cohered in 1805, the Quids sharpened their definition of what democracy was and how it should function. This careful statement of belief became the first part of an increasingly desperate response to the radical challenge. The second part was to emphasize the grave danger posed by the most extreme beliefs of the radicals. Though it took some time for the Quids fully to conceive what would become a brilliant political strategy, gradually, as they sought to discredit the most extreme beliefs of the radicals, they began to place unbearable pressure on the connections between the two categories of reform. The effect would be to sever the two reform impulses from each other. After 1805 utopian aspiration and the hardheaded workaday world that would come to be defined as democratic politics would find it ever more difficult to coexist.

As the debate within the Pennsylvania Jeffersonian party developed in 1805, it did much to shape the future boundaries of permissible thought in mainstream politics. In response to the impeachment effort, the Quids initially concentrated on promulgating a coherent explanation of what democracy ought to be. They insisted that constitutions were pure embodiments of popular will shaped by constitutional conventions that were "the people" distilled to their essentials. It was government's chief responsibility to ensure that it did not violate these popular documents. This task was immensely difficult and complex. The simpler the government's structure, the easier it was to act immediately on day-to-day convictions, the more likely it would be that the people's original desires would be trampled and forgotten. This view left room for a great deal of day-to-day governance based on popularly perceived needs. For the Quids insisted that constitutions covered only those few essential issues and questions, such as guarantees of free speech, trial by jury, and rights to property and full enjoyment of it, that all rational men agreed were necessary for a free and just society. Daily concerns, such as how to choose candidates, where to build roads, and when to charter banks, normal majorities in legislatures could decide. Popular politics was eminently desirable, but it should not concern itself with fundamental questions. Popular legislatures were ill equipped to debate such issues. The Quids maintained that

the courts of justice are to be considered as the bulwarks of a limited constitution, against legislative encroachments. The exercise of power
implies no superiority in the judiciary to the legislature. It implies nothing
more than that the people are superior to the legislature, and that the judiciary, as a coordinate branch of government, charged with the execution
of certain powers, is bound to regard the will of the people, as expressed
in the constitution, in preference to the will of the legislative body. . . .
The judges are the interpreters of law. The constitution is itself a fundamental law.

Any contrary view endangered "the life, liberty, and property of the individual citizen . . . the public weal, and even the national existence."[16] The
legislature should carry out the day-to-day concerns of a democratic people. But the judiciary ensured that the legislature continued to confine itself
to those areas of life that it was constitutionally qualified to manage.

The impeachment trial culminated in January 1805. Sixteen of the
twenty-four senators had to agree to impeach. The radical campaign fell
short by three, garnering only a simple majority of thirteen.[17] Quids such as
William Barton experienced a deep release of pressure and were almost
giddy at the radicals' defeat. "Lo triumph — Lo triumph — Lo triumph,"
he wrote to Jared Ingersoll. "All is well — Law (even the common law) with
common sense (tho' not Tom Paine's) and common honesty have triumphed — The arch fiend Duane is done and the Jacobins are in conster-
nation." Pennsylvania, Barton wrote, had narrowly avoided "the abyss of
anarchy."[18] The Quid James Hopkins, in a letter to Alexander Dallas, hoped
that acquittal would "teach the unprincipled, the fractious and anarchical,
that Republicans will never sacrifice conscience, truth or justice to obtain
favor with Jacobins, Demagogues, and Levellers."[19]

Failure to remove the judges infuriated and galvanized the Philadelphia
Democrats. With only a toothless arbitration bill and the survival of the
supreme court, the city radicals concluded that they had to make a much
more complete assault on the state's political structure before they could
hope to democratize the legal system. Looking back on the efforts since 1802
to build democracy, the *Aurora* concluded that "the abuses of the executive
power — of the judiciary — and the lawyers, ha[s] become after three or
four years of struggle, intolerable to be borne." Judicial reform was not
enough, for between 1803 and 1805 "the executive became outrageous,
tyrannical, insolent, scurrilous, and abusive."[20] The time had come to confront the enemies of democracy completely. Only after three years of

conflict, the survival of an unaccountable judiciary, and the seeming betrayal by the executive and senate, did the *Aurora* demand a constitutional convention. It did so on February 28, 1805, less than one month after the judges were acquitted.[21]

In its appeal, the paper insisted that democracy could be preserved only if Pennsylvanians "express[ed] themselves in their sovereign capacity." The *Aurora* insisted that the only true test of a good government was the experience of living under it. Frequent reconsideration and alteration were thus desirable, and the last few years only reinforced this observation. The *Aurora* criticized several features of the state constitution. Among them were the four-year terms for senators, which it considered far too long. Annual elections for senators would force them to adhere more scrupulously to majority will. More complete obedience by senators was desirable, for the *Aurora* maintained "that the agents of the people should feel at all times their responsibility to those who have constituted them — the will of the people is the paramount law."[22]

The paper also took aim at McKean, complaining that he had far too much patronage and citing as proof that every seat on the bench was in his gift (as was every position of justice of the peace). The governor's patronage coupled with his veto "put it in his power efficiently to controul the acts of the legislature, to the utter subversion of the principle that the majority shall govern." Both patronage power and the veto had to be denied the governor.[23]

The *Aurora* called for a convention hoping to lessen the power of a governor and senate that it believed had set themselves against majority will. But the executive and the upper house, though dangerous, were not the most frightening agents of government. When placing its hopes on a constitutional convention, the paper primarily concentrated on "the *judiciary department* of our government," arguing that "this anxiety is rendered more poignant by recent occurrences." A constitutional convention, the *Aurora* argued, had to eliminate judicial tenure during good behavior, "a provision which gives existence to a set of officers still further removed from responsibility [than the governor and senate,] if not entirely above it." The very idea of an independent judiciary was "incompatible with, and hostile to our republican system." The *Aurora* also insisted that the convention declare once and for all that the judiciary could not "decide on the constitutionality of all acts of the legislature." Efforts by the legislature to alter the judiciary had failed, and the paper believed it a "consequence of the root of the evil lying so deep as not to be reached by any legislative act — that your hands have been tied by the constitution."[24] Thus the constitution had to be altered, as did the offices of governor, senate, and judge.[25] The *Aurora*, then, laid out the reasons for an immediate constitutional convention. Thereafter, each time it called for the convention, it reiterated its support for the annual election of senators, seizure of the governor's patronage, abolition of the executive veto, the election of judges, a constitutional rejection of judicial review, and the enactment of arbitration legislation that would provide a real alternative to courts of law.[26]

The Philadelphia Democrats' demand for a constitutional convention was bold and promised sweeping changes in the way Pennsylvanians experienced politics and public life. Nevertheless, the Snyderites agreed with the demand, which suggests the profound sense of purpose shared by urban and rural radicals in 1804 and 1805. McKean's vetoes had also caused the Snyderites to consider structural inadequacies in Pennsylvania's democracy. After one veto of an arbitration bill the *Argus* announced that "the power given by the constitution of this state to the governor by which he is enabled to nullify the act of the legislature is a very high, and permit me to say, a very dangerous power . . . for the minority to rule the majority is the very essence of aristocracy."[27] Starting in March 1805, the Snyderites and the *Argus* joined the Philadelphia Democrats and the *Aurora* in demanding a constitutional convention.[28] During that spring this demand and Snyder's campaign for governor appeared to be connected. A truly democratic governor would usher in a convention to purge the state of inequality and aristocracy.

This unity terrified the Quids. It appeared to them as if 1805 would be the last chance to provide a sane idea of democracy. If Snyder defeated McKean, as alarming as that was, the convention would follow, and the Quids could only assume that fundamental law would begin to molest private rights. From the beginning of the desperate year 1805, the Quids focused on the Philadelphia Democrats. Like that group, most Quids lived in Philadelphia, and they reasoned that already dangerous notions were made all the more extreme by the grievances and sensibility unique to the city. John Kean, one of the Jeffersonian state senators who had voted for the acquittal of the supreme court judges, encouraged this thinking. He wrote Dallas that since the previous winter "the legislature exhibited symptoms of anarchy and disorder, but at the commencement of the present session [a] plan appeared to be deliberately formed." Kean had "early perceived a marked hostility to the governor [and] . . . immediately on the acquittal of the judges the plot against the constitution appeared and no effort has since been left untried to effect their purpose." Memorials demanding a constitutional convention had begun to arrive regularly, and Kean stressed the importance of drafting countermemorials. The situation was bleak, for "the extensive circulation of the *Aurora,* and the implicit confidence put in it may do infinite mischief. . . . The evil effects of his [Duane's] poisonous columns can only be counteracted by hand bills, no paper having an extent of circulation or standing with the community capable of rebutting his pernicious doctrines." In the Congress, Kean figured that those Jeffersonians he called Constitutionalists were sorely outnumbered: "We stand as 30 to 111 . . . so is that republicanism to anarchy."[29]

Dallas agreed with Kean. One month before receiving the senator's letter, he had predicted to Albert Gallatin that unless Jefferson took "decisive measures Republicanism will moulder into anarchy and the labour and hope of our lives will terminate in disappointment and wretchedness." He complained bitterly of "your Duanes, Cheethams, Leibs etc."[30] After receiving Kean's letter, Dallas expressed fear of "some wild irregular step after the adjournment [of the legislature] aimed against the Governor as well as the constitution." Leib and Duane maintained that they represented Jefferson's views. Dallas urged Gallatin to have the administration intervene to discredit the Philadelphia Democrats' leaders, for while they possessed "influence, the state, the United States, will never enjoy quiet."[31]

Between April and October 1805, the true meaning of democracy and the extent of the majority's political power was the stuff of Pennsylvania's politics. Who ought to decide the justice and injustice of alleged property rights, contracts, and virtually all other matters concerning economic development? Democracy, the Quids insisted, meant defending the constitutional system already established. It meant a separation of powers that included an independent judiciary, and it meant a public commitment to economic development that would organize the American economy so that each individual would have a likely chance of prosperity.

The Quids stressed the lessons of history. England's chance for a republic had died when the parliamentary forces had failed to produce a written constitution between 1649 and 1660. A document that established fundamental law and inviolable rights was priceless. Pennsylvania's democratic citizens should rejoice at how lucky they were. England had never possessed such a document; France had quickly rendered it a dead letter. The horrors were palpable. Why would any sane man wish to repeat them?[32]

The *Freeman's Journal* applauded "the principle of universal suffrage." But the paper insisted that "this delightful principle of equality cannot be tolerated without endangering liberty unless the stays or restraints upon public volition are proportionally powerful." The Philadelphia Democrats,

the Quids argued, wished "to give the House of Representatives an unqualified control over the judiciary departments, and other extensive attributes to be taken from the executive; also lessening the powers of the senate."
These changes would "render property perpetually unstable." If property
were threatened, the otherwise reasonable expectation that each American
would flourish and prosper would be lost. Freedom, security, and happiness
depended on representative instead of immediate democracy, and "divisions
of power in the representation; the law making, the law expounding, and
the law executing power." Equally essential was a division in the lawmak-
ing power between an upper and a lower house and an executive empowered with a qualified veto. Thus Americans already enjoyed something far
closer to democracy than the vision demanded by the Philadelphia Democrats. Daily life would materially worsen should things change.[33]

The proposed changes, the Quids insisted, were unprecedented. Once
such a transformation began, it could not be limited or bounded. They pitied
those Pennsylvanians who supported the call for a constitutional convention
on the assumption "that only some partial changes are contemplated." The
articles in the *Aurora*, the Quids suggested, contradicted that sanguine view.
The *Aurora*, they asserted, favored absolute legislative power and the belief
that at any time "the opinion of the majority shall be the law of the whole."
From the chaos that would ensue under such a system, "out of the cabals,
the intrigues, the jealousies, and consequent weaknesses of a legislative
body, possessed of such undefined and unlimited powers, monarchy would
inevitably rear its horrid crest." But before the inevitable despotism arrived,
the citizens would experience the grossest treatment in the name of democracy and justice. Pennsylvanians needed to dread such a future for "when
the happy era arrives, in which all power shall be absorbed by the legislature . . . [then] these exclusive patriots shall proceed on, with undeviating
steps, unrestrained and unchecked by any constitutional provisions, until
they arrive at the acme of perfectibility, on such destructive and wild ideas is
the attempt for calling a convention founded."[34]

For the Quids, 1804 and especially 1805 were years of acute anxiety. The
thinking of Hugh Henry Brackenridge during this period illustrates the
extent of the Quids' fears and their real commitment to theorizing and articulating a usable democracy. Brackenridge's ordeal, particularly the impeachment episode and the assault on the independent judiciary, deeply influenced
him. The personal attacks shocked Brackenridge, who had long associated
himself with the Revolution's themes and with the promise of Jeffersonian
politics. Before becoming a lawyer and then a judge, Brackenridge had

attended the College of New Jersey (later Princeton) and aspired to be one of the American Revolution's men of letters. With his poet friend, fellow Princetonian, and subsequent Jeffersonian editor Philip Freneau, Brackenridge composed the epic poem *The Rising Glory of America*, which anticipated independence. In the early 1790s he wrote one of the first American novels, *Modern Chivalry*. Royalties did not roll in, and for the next decade he devoted himself to Jeffersonian politics and the law. He sincerely hoped to help build a nation whose free and independent citizens could be an example to the world. Why, he had to wonder by 1805, was he vilified?

Brackenridge's experiences in 1804 so affected him that they reawakened his artistic impulses. In that year he was moved to return to literature and resumed *Modern Chivalry*. Brackenridge's novel told the story of an American Don Quixote, except in the new nation the protagonist was the sage and the world foolish. An educated gentleman, Captain Farrago, and his ignorant Irish manservant, Teague O'Regan, travel throughout the Republic, meeting all different sorts of people. In the 1804 volume they return to their native state to discover a chaotic mess. In the captain's own village a scurrilous printer has irrevocably divided the community, and the more unseemly his prose, the more his readership grows. The captain, having realized during his travels that the people will consider legitimate only a popular or democratic solution, proposes an orderly town meeting to decide whether the editor has committed libel. He also calls on the lawyers of the community to give advice, reasoning that "if it were a case of digging a trench or building a road the mechanic's opinion is given the most respect. So on this occasion, the gentlemen of the long robe will not be wanting to develop a case that involves in it a nice question of law and municipal regulation."[35]

At the start of the town meeting the townspeople agree that a free press is essential, that all should have access to it, and that it should not merely be aimed at the wellborn and well educated. These opinions are commendable, and so the captain and his friends conclude that the people can conduct popular discussions and engage in popular decision making that do not lead to vitriol and leveling.

Brackenridge sought to contrast this desirable behavior with the irresponsibility and crude anti-intellectual immaturity he ascribed to the Philadelphia Democrats. Those attitudes and their dangerous effects he sought to discredit by having the town meeting suddenly take a turn for the worse. After some at the meeting conclude that newspapers are useful, many townspeople begin to defend the irresponsible editor. One defender wondered, "Are there not amongst us those who have not relish for disquisitions on the balance of power, or forms of government, agricultural essays, or questions of finance; but can comprehend and relish a laugh raised at the expense of the master of a family; or a public character in his station; if for no other reason, but because it gratifies the self-love of those who cannot attain the same level of eminence?"[36]

Brackenridge sought to demonstrate the silliness of the boisterous democrats. Thus he lampooned the actions of his characters at the meeting. The captain and his friends, a lawyer and a schoolmaster, hope that, by congregating, the people would reach a useful conclusion. Instead they decide to start another newspaper that will use the same tactics against the editor and his supporters. Furthermore, they choose Teague to be the new paper's editor. The captain protests that Teague is ignorant, knows no restraint, and while in Paris became a Jacobin. But the villagers ignore him. In an aside, Brackenridge states that the first editor is modeled on William Cobbett, the arch-Federalist propagandist. It was easy to deduce that the Irish, pro-French, and Jacobin Teague was intended to invite comparison with William Duane. The dilemma, then, was clearly stated. The people had the best intentions. They met sincerely, seeking to correct an obvious problem, but by doing so they had made the situation worse. Democracy was inevitable and essential. Yet the people when they practiced it only seemed to create new problems.

Democracy was also liable to burst out of control. In the novel, once the town meeting assembles, it refuses to confine itself to the issue that caused it to meet. That problem, of course, would not have surprised a Pennsylvanian concerned about the implications of convening a constitutional convention. The discussion of the newspaper's behavior at the meeting leads to a general demand to extinguish nuisances and "an incendiary proposed to abate, or burn down the college. Because, said he, all learning is a nuisance." A town meeting is thus called to vote on the issue of torching the college. The proposition is carried, and several villagers set off with torches. In the democratic world of *Modern Chivalry,* once a majority votes, its will is law. The captain realizes that he can save the college only by convincing the mob that its destruction is unnecessary. The captain convinces the villagers to spare the college by arguing that learning is already held in such contempt in the area that all schools are, for all intents and purposes, already burned.

The crowd acknowledges the wisdom of this view, but on the way back to continue the meeting the majority decides that "if they had not burned the college, they would burn or pull down a church."[37] By destroying the church the village can silence the preacher, who quotes the English religious commentators when only American commentators are acceptable to them. The captain argues that religion, like the common law, transcends its origins. He points out that their discussion took place in the English language. He tries to convince the mob that the denunciation of learned men such as lawyers and clergymen, who have access to traditional knowledge, is harmful. The captain provides an analogy. He reminds the mob that the art of medicine, too, was cultivated in Britain, yet nobody thinks of denouncing doctors. But this strikes the majority as a good idea. The crowd sacks the apothecary's shop and drives the surgeon out of town.

The same villagers who denounce the common law and call for the destruction of the legal system commit these excesses. During the course of the novel the villagers make Teague an editor, an apothecary, a lawyer, a judge, and a public orator. Throughout *Modern Chivalry* the captain and his reasonable minority of educated friends fear for the safety and property of all citizens. At one point the captain encounters a former leader of the Whiskey Rebellion. He tells the captain that he has found a safer method of achieving his goals: "Abolish the courts and demolish the judges, and the laws will go of themselves."[38]

Throughout the novel the captain remains committed to a political system called democracy. He seeks to convince an ever-decreasing number of listeners that meaning well is not enough, and that support from the majority on any given question does not prove that one was right and could suggest that one was wrong. Still, Brackenridge acknowledged that "talk out of doors" had to be respected, and that "representatives must yield to the prejudices of their constituents even contrary to their own judgement. It is therefore into this pool that I cast my salt. It is to correct these waters that I write this book."[39] In his closing statement Brackenridge begs not to be dismissed as an interested pleader. It is true that he has experienced difficulties, but "the talk of abolishing the courts and judges . . . is more general than imagined. I am afraid it may affect ultimately the democratic interest: to which I feel myself attached; for I aver myself to be a democrat." Yet the democrat was, by 1805, "positively more afraid . . . of the honest man than I was of the resentment of the knave at a former period."[40]

Brackenridge's fears were typical of the Quids' concerns. The stakes, they believed in 1805, could not be higher. Gradually during the spring and summer the Quids conceived the strategy of equating the call for a constitutional convention with support for Snyder, and of insisting that both positions were synonymous with commitment to the ideals espoused by the Philadelphia Democrats. By doing so they gained the tactical advantage of having to rebut only those ideas they considered the most readily discreditable. But there was more to the strategy than its tactical advantage. In 1805 the radicals genuinely shocked the Quids, who were profoundly concerned because it was so difficult to discredit ideas that they believed should have collapsed of their own weight. They focused their energies on the Philadelphia Democrats because they considered them the graver threat.

Thus when the Quids sought to expose their enemies, they ignored everybody except the radicals in Philadelphia. Who provoked division and threatened anarchy? It was "William Duane. A man . . . who should have swung beneath a gallows tree [and] . . . his artful coadjutor Dr. Leib."[41] Simon Snyder might be Speaker of the House, but "who is it we ask, directs the state puppets in the grand design to enslave our country? Do they or do they not, obey the nod of the *Aurora*? Is not that paper become the arbiter of the legislature?" This view was not the result of Philadelphians focusing on Philadelphia. The preceding remarks were written by the Constitutional Republican Society of Carlisle in Cumberland County. Cumberland was but one county removed and slightly southwest of Northumberland, where Snyder resided. Even Quids in the countryside claimed that he was the creature of Duane and Leib. They wanted to defeat the Philadelphia Democrats, and they wanted to ensure that victory in 1805 demonstrated forever the rejection of suburb politics.

The enemy was the Philadelphia Democrats, and they were beyond the pale. The *Aurora* "with Robespierrian power rule[d] the commonwealth, and even influence[d] the union." If the Philadelphia Democrats triumphed, they would probably "propose a division of all property, or agrarian law." Afterward they might even set their sights on the federal Constitution, and then "the reign of vandalism and anarchy [would] open on us in all its horrors."[42] The Quids insisted that they were paying the voters of Pennsylvania a great complement. They believed that the people were sensible and dutiful enough to defeat this palpably unworthy group. They also offered the blandishment that, if Pennsylvanians did so, the entire union would be in their debt, "for the views of the Friends of the People [the Philadelphia pro-convention society started by the Philadelphia Democrats] are not limited to the state of Pennsylvania; they extend to the union in general, and to each state in particular. Nothing but universal revolution will satisfy their ambition."[43]

The Quids constantly repeated the charge that the Philadelphia Democrats were not democrats but Jacobins, and that there was a substantial difference between democracy and the Mountain. The Quids insisted that Pennsylvanians were in an analogous position in 1805 to that of the French in 1792. The *Freeman's Journal* pointed out that "Marat and Robespierre form[ed] associations under the delusive title of the Friends of the People." Unlike those bloody men, the Quids insisted that Pennsylvania's democratic citizenry realized that "ameliorations should gradually be effected, as defects in our system may become evident by experience."[44] "Pure democracy" produced the Terror and Napoleon. The people of Pennsylvania could become the first group of citizens in the history of the world to save themselves and their progeny by skillfully and responsibly wielding democratic political power.[45] To assist the people in their momentous task, the *Freeman's Journal* began printing excerpts of *Modern Chivalry*.[46]

The conflict of 1805 ensured that popular participation and competition would characterize Pennsylvania's political culture. Further, participants would have to demonstrate their commitment to popular politics and democracy. The Quids, unlike the Federalists, did not simply resist and then fulminate against the inevitable democratizing of politics.[47] The Quids had helped guide popular enthusiasms into mainstream politics. They had helped to create a political culture in which common men no longer acted on the margins of public life.[48] At times the Quids had participated in this profound shift somewhat reluctantly, but they had never opposed it. As genuinely moderate Jeffersonians, they were able to function far more effectively in American politics than could the illegitimately conservative Federalists. The Quids encouraged broad participation in elections precisely because they understood that these contests would become increasingly popular affairs. Those who hoped to retain political legitimacy could do no less "in a democracy such as ours, where the people are the source of all authority."[49]

The Quids hoped to show that democracy did not have to be chaotic or perpetually argumentative. The best democracy preserved the people's power by constraining their elected officials and by forcing them to operate within known boundaries that did not threaten first principles. The greatest threat to stability in a democracy was political actors who sought to blur or even obliterate those boundaries. Those who did so were overly zealous and dangerous. They were not content to participate in the regular and common commitment to seeing the nation improve by allowing each citizen the opportunity to prosper. The Quids portrayed the Philadelphia Democrats as having no interest in quiet, orderly, productive citizenship, the behavior that, in the context of rapid, dynamic economic development, allowed democracy to flourish. Instead the city radicals survived by provoking the tumult that increased the circulation of the *Aurora* at the ultimate expense of liberty, property, and democracy. Speaking in particular of the threat to the constitution, the *Freeman's Journal* insisted that

> a few men are undermining it with incessant zeal and activity. And do you think fellow citizens that these individuals, in the city and Liberties, whom you see so continually employed in politics, are impelled solely by such pure disinterested patriotism, that you can safely trust them with your dearest interests. . . . Look at their employment in life. They are not, like most of you, pursuing the regular and orderly means of gaining a livelihood, but they are occupied solely in carrying on the intrigues of faction by conversations and cabals in the streets and public places, by false and scurrilous publications in their prostituted press, and even by traveling into distant counties, fomenting division and sowing the seeds of discontent and agitation. Having no other employment, these men make a trade of intrigue, and depend for their substance on public discord.[50]

The Quids also started the Society for Constitutional Republicans to challenge the Philadelphia Democrats' Society of the Friends of the People. They elected George Logan president and Israel Israel, the Philadelphia businessman and father of the Quid newspaper editor John Israel, vice president. Samuel Wetherill Jr., the Philadelphia manufacturer, served as secretary. The corresponding committee included Alexander J. Dallas, Wetherill, and the merchant Blair McClenahan. Manuel Eyre also joined, as did the governor's son, Joseph B. McKean, and the Philadelphia judge Moses Levy.[51] The Quids' society showed that it was willing to participate in the rough-and-tumble of city politics. When "one of the *Aurora*'s devils" tried to infiltrate a meeting, he was forcibly removed.[52] The society also printed manifestos and statements meant to be read by large numbers. A long address on the gubernatorial campaign and other issues written by Dallas in 1805 was widely distributed. It was also published frequently in the *Freeman's Journal,* and five thousand copies were printed in German.[53]

The pamphlet, titled *An Address to the Republicans of Pennsylvania,* was adopted by the Philadelphia Society for Constitutional Republicans on June 10.[54] It reiterated the Quids' main themes. The Revolution had declared, and victory in 1800 had forever confirmed, the sovereignty of the people and their right to form whatever government they desired. This achievement had been a tremendous success, and at present "the character of the American people and their government is rising, with unrivaled luster, in the estimation of the wise and the good throughout the world." Thus, "domestic prosperity present[ed] its blessing as the reward of virtue and industry, without distinction of persons, places, [or] pursuits." Therefore, Dallas demanded, "Who can hear without surprise the cry of social discontent, or view without apprehension a spirit of political innovation? But the painful crisis has arrived."[55]

The *Address* insisted that the wrongs trumpeted were "imaginary," and the reasoning of the Philadelphia Democrats "specious." Yet Dallas insisted that all would be put right because Pennsylvanians were responsible democrats. Thus he was "convinced that there is yet safety by an appeal to the virtue, intelligence, and power of the people." The very condition, interests, and beliefs of the democratic citizens of Pennsylvania ensured the Quids victory. Thankfully, Pennsylvanians did not live in a nation

> whose overgrown population is tainted with crimes and enervated by want, where the inequities of property and rank produce envy on the one hand and contumely on the other, where labor has no excitement for its movements nor any security for its accumulations. Far different is the condition of Pennsylvania, where no material change can be projected without involving the hazard of a material injury. . . . [T]he people, neither insensible to the bounties of providence nor regardless of the dictates of prudence, will hear, examine, and decide for themselves.[56]

The bulk of the *Address* sketched the emergence of the Philadelphia Democrats (whom Dallas called the Malcontents), reiterated Quid arguments against their irresponsible and dangerous politics, equated them with the Jacobins, and vigorously defended the state constitution. It also praised both those portions of the common law that Pennsylvania's revolutionaries had accepted and the full separation of powers. Each of these essential institutions was under attack, and "such fellow citizens is the crisis at which your decision is required upon the great questions." The people had to reject the Philadelphia Democrats, who sought "the agency of a convention to organize a political millennium upon the ideal scale of human perfectibility."[57]

The *Address* reminded Pennsylvanians that under the state constitution they enjoyed universal (free, white, and male) suffrage; each citizen was eligible for every office, and the executive and the upper house were directly elected. Under this system the legislature was free to concern itself with the material prosperity of the citizenry but was constrained from endangering inalienable rights to life, liberty, and property. Summing up the necessity of government for building internal improvements, protecting property, and enforcing criminal and civil law codes, Dallas reminded fellow Pennsylvanians that "the use of power is essential to the order and peace of society, and the hazard of its being abused must therefore be encountered." It was essential, then, both to "confer power [and] extract responsibility." The Quids insisted that the state's constitution did so, but that the crazed schemes of "men deranged by utopian theories" never could. What legitimate apparatus would replace the constitution? No sane man could answer along with the Philadelphia Democrats "the direct and constant agency of the people. . . . Let it not be answered the exclusive authority of the legislative agents of the people."[58] Anarchy could not preserve liberty and property.

Under McKean and the constitution, Dallas explained, people were protected and had prospered. In Pennsylvania the common law had been "stripped of its feudal trappings." It thus embraced "the law of nations, the law of merchants, [and] the customs and usages of trade." Thankfully it did, for the growing economy and thriving commerce, which made securing an independent democratic republic worthwhile, would not survive without Pennsylvania's common law. Dallas argued that "for the varying exigencies of social life, [and] the complicated interests of an enterprising nation, the positive acts of a legislature can provide little fundamental protection alone." The common law and the current political structure protected the liberty and property of each individual "from the encroachments of a popular assembly, whose numbers serve at once to abate caution and dismiss responsibility."[59]

The *Address* closed with a stirring defense of McKean. The governor had overseen the first responsible and sustained commitment in Pennsylvania to the dynamic economy by and for producers that a democracy needed. McKean was a true democrat, for "agriculture ha[d] received his aid in his exertions to extend our roads and improve our navigable communication. Commerce ha[d] been advanced by his assiduity in employing the best means to preserve the health of our capital. Of mechanics and manufacturers he had been the unaffected friend and patron."[60] McKean's reelection would make a fundamental, crucial, and as yet unacknowledged point. The Quids earnestly pleaded with the citizens of Pennsylvania that "it [was] time to evince to the world that a democratic republic can enjoy energy without tyranny, and liberty without anarchy."[61]

The popular efforts of the Quids worked fairly well. Throughout the state, imitation Constitutional Republican Societies arose, often after a member of the first organization was dispatched to assist locals in their formation. In addition, counties such as Chester began to have separate party meetings based on the stance toward McKean and the constitution. The Quid meeting from Chester County was representative of these efforts when it urged that Jeffersonians not allow their "zeal for republicanism [to] carry us beyond the bounds of moderation, let us be content with true liberty, secured by the constitution without grasping at licentiousness, thereby running the hazard of anarchy and confusion: a state worse than monarchy itself." The meeting then endorsed McKean.[62] Constitutional Republican Society or pro-McKean Jeffersonian party meetings met in Philadelphia, Chester, Northampton, Butler, Lancaster, and Cumberland Counties.[63] In addition, the Society for Constitutional Republicans sponsored an alternative Tammany Society to the one dominated by Duane and Leib.[64] The Quids also held an alternative Fourth of July celebration.[65] These popular organizing efforts were bolstered by the emergence of other Quid newspapers. Chief among them was the *Harrisburg Dauphin Guardian*. The *Guardian* and the *Freeman's Journal* were supplemented by the *Lancaster Constitutional Democrat* and the *Greensburg Farmer's Register*.[66]

From June through October the Quids continued to try to redefine democracy and discredit the Philadelphia Democrats. The legislature was the most dignified branch of government if it pursued its legitimate purpose. The separation of powers preserved freedom, and "the present political crisis in Pennsylvania [was] the most important which has occurred since the revolution." Almost daily the Quids reiterated that "if the constitution of Pennsylvania falls, that of the United States will follow, and the union is dissolved. . . . The constitution of Pennsylvania [is] the citadel in which rational republicanism will now make its decisive stand." Pennsylvanians had the most momentous decision to make, for "life, liberty, and property [were] in danger of being cast afloat on the boisterous sea of anarchy."[67]

Still, despite the Quids' successful entrance into the raucous world of Pennsylvania's popular democratic politics, they were not as comfortable there as were their radical opponents. At their most frustrated the Quids registered amazement that the radicals could command attention. Were the people not aware that "the best and wisest men in the community [were] opposed to their mad schemes?" As the election drew nearer, and as Simon Snyder continued to appear capable of winning, the Quids denounced "new fangled doctrines introduced by party spirit, and advocated by anarchists, none are perhaps more dangerous, in a republican country, than those which flatter the prejudices and lull into listless security, the unthinking multitude."[68] As the potentially leveling arguments of their enemies grew shriller, the Quids could not keep from denouncing members of the legislature who were nothing more than "backwoods bumpkins." Such men returned to their rustic constituents, harangued them about the need for a convention, and "with a little whiskey circulated, at the time [seemed] equal to Demosthenes or Cicero."[69] Their constituents were the gullible fools who would choose the members of a constitutional convention.

Governor McKean embodied the Quids' ambivalence toward the new democratic nature of public life. During the campaign a group of legislators led by Snyder met with him about reforming the courts. McKean lost his temper and shouted at the delegation. The Quids insisted that McKean had denounced only one legislator, who had boasted that he would do his "utmost at elections to prevent all men of talents, all lawyers and rich men, from being elected." All agreed that McKean, a member of the Pennsylvania bar, had responded, "Why are not lawyers and rich men to be as trusted in the administration of legal affairs as any others?" But the *Aurora* insisted that the governor had belittled all of his opponents as "a set of clodhoppers who had no more understanding than geese." The Quids maintained that he intended the remarks for the unruly legislator alone.[70] The truth is unclear. But certainly McKean had described the legislature unflatteringly in the past, and the unguarded remarks suggested the Quids' discomfort with democratic politics.

The Quids' lapses and contradictory impulses showed how new the notion of a truly egalitarian mainstream politics was. The Jeffersonian Quids functioned far better than had the Federalists in this politics. They were able to imagine ordinary citizens with the power to make decisions that would affect the Quids themselves. That was the essential philosophical difference between the Quids and the Federalists. The Quids assumed that the people wanted justice for all and were capable of administering it. The Federalists, at their best, could only believe that the people wanted it. But clearly, the Quids insisted, the people needed and deserved careful guidance from both their leaders and the structure of their politics. The combination of all of the Quids' beliefs and impulses added up to an ideology that remained legitimate, in the way the Federalists' had not, while still calling for strong constraints on popular impulses. The Quids were forced in 1805 to defend these constraints, to explain why popular decision making was essential in certain areas of American life and catastrophic in others.

They stressed their developmental political economy and insisted that the democratic legislature was responsible for overseeing it. The true duties of the legislature were to maximize the opportunities that resulted from allowing private citizens to use the resources they controlled in entrepreneurial

ways. If management of such an economy was the job of the democratic legislature—its quintessential task—then democracy demanded that the rest
of government be empowered to stymie this legislature when it violated that
task. The legislature could be stopped if it strayed beyond the duties that the
Quids assigned to it, and it would be so arrested in the name of democracy.

The Quids in 1805 articulated essential ingredients of what would emerge
in the nineteenth century as the dominant strand of modern American belief,
the nineteenth century's classical liberalism.[71] The Quids struggled to articulate these ideas in the midst of violent struggle and a profound absence of
consensus. The notions that would eventually be so central to mainstream
thought surfaced early in Pennsylvania. The Quids were the first in the state
to try to organize these ideas into a coherent worldview. As they did, they
understood all too well that their beliefs would take hold not because they
resonated with and thus captured the spirit of their fellow Pennsylvania Jeffersonians, but only if the Quids themselves could somehow prevail in a terrifying conflict.

The Quids insisted that a properly structured democracy would produce
an economy that continually grew and diversified, providing unprecedented
opportunity. In a properly conceived democracy, entrepreneurial producers
would be assured that temporary popular whims could never threaten their
labors. By properly distinguishing between the rolls of different branches
of democratic government, the people would protect the economy, which,
when left to itself, produced the social relations of independence and equality that alone maintained the democracy the people had built.

At times the Quids were ambivalent democrats, but though it is important to recognize the first term, so it is equally important to remember the
second. Their ambivalence, and their profound concern about what Pennsylvanians might produce in 1805, was mixed with their deep faith in the idea
of democracy they propounded. The Quids held out to their fellow citizens
a world where "our state command[s] that respect due to a virtuous and independent people—our citizens happy, agriculture and the arts flourishing,
and indeed, to see you possess every advantage which good government is
intended or can be expected to bestow. Our present government . . . is calculated to secure those advantages:—It is founded on justice and equity;—
possessing those qualities which will protect the boundaries of private
property." They contrasted this world with a future that they considered
savage and violent, one where demagogues "instigated by the Devil and
William Duane" dissolved government and the protection it provided with
a "politically omnipotent convention."[72]

In 1805 the Quids showed that they could mount a popular campaign and largely meet the demands of democracy. The campaign was successful, for over the course of 1805 the Snyderites concluded that they had to distinguish themselves clearly from the Philadelphia Democrats. In two ways the campaign had a lasting impact on mainstream Pennsylvania Jeffersonian conceptions of democracy. First, the Quids placed unabsorbable pressure on the connections between the two reform categories, utopian aspiration and incremental reform. Much of the vitality of the reform movement came from the belief of ordinary legislators that they could conduct the state's daily business and have their efforts approach or even open on the grandest dreams of the age of the democratic revolution. In 1805 that connection was broken. The Quids skillfully suggested that the grand innovations would so upset daily business that no life would be worth living. The second achievement of the Quids was to forcefully champion their political economy and the political structure that sustained it. The Quids in 1805, then, sought to explain what democracy was and what it must not be.

Their efforts had a dramatic effect on the Snyderites, whose commitment to reform, while just as real as the Philadelphia Democrats', had emerged from different assumptions and a much more sanguine view about the future. The Snyderites could support legislation such as the $100 Act, though the Philadelphia Democrats dismissed it, because they believed that small and meaningful reforms would help to produce a society and economy able to sustain democracy. As the Quids sought to equate all reform with the most extreme statements in the *Aurora*, the Snyderites began to seek their own distinct reform voice. They stressed the sensible limits of that reform which had actually become law, such as the $100 Act. They pointed out that law's monetary ceiling and the right to appeal almost all cases to law courts. As the conflict sharpened, the Snyderite *Argus* sought to distinguish essential reform demands from those it considered fanciful and even dangerous. One editorial took stock of the reform campaign and discussed the "number of proposals for a reform of our judiciary, considerably variant from each other." The *Argus* reminded its readers that the chief goal of reform was to make the legal system more accessible and quicker to reach decisions. Much could be accomplished with the existing legal structure. Archaic names and perplexing language could be updated or expunged. Other reforms could prohibit lawyers from reading English decisions verbatim in court. Unlike the Philadelphia Democrats, the Snyderites did not insist that English precedents be declared irrelevant to American jurisprudence. Rather, lawyers should merely cite the cases they considered precedents, and perhaps read short, salient passages. Then the issue "without any pleading" could be left "to the determination of the judges, who are supposed to be competent judges of the law, and can see how far the cases referred to, go to establish the point before the court, without having the public time wasted in decisions of little or no value."[73]

Assuming correctly that some form of limited arbitration, such as the $100 Act, would remain part of Pennsylvania's legal system, the editorial turned to the subject of lawyers. Again the *Argus* tried to distinguish itself from the *Aurora*. Given the system established by the act, most civil cases could end up in law courts. Thus it was irresponsible to seek to discredit lawyers. "It would appear," the *Argus* insisted,

> to be absolutely necessary that some person used to speak in public, and who is in the habit of clothing his ideas in words, pertinent to the case, be employed in every cause, to open it up before the court and jury, so as to make as clear and intelligible as possible, what the real demand of the plaintiffs is, and what points he will rely upon and endeavor to prove in the course of the investigation; in order to establish this demand it is necessary also that a person of skill attends to the examination of witnesses, to take care that everything be inquired after that can throw light on the controversy. . . . When the plaintiff's case is thus before the court and jury, the defendant will require the same talents and attention to be employed on his behalf, so that his defense may be clearly understood.[74]

Nevertheless, the acquittal of the supreme court justices reminded the Snyderites of how many concerns they shared with the city radicals. The *Argus* was incensed by the judges' escape and printed the vote of each senator so that citizens could remember.[75] Snyder and Boileau had been leading managers of the impeachment.[76] After the acquittal they joined with the Philadelphia Democrats in demanding the constitutional convention. Their commitment to the convention reinforces much of what can be learned from this momentous year about Jeffersonian politics and early American democracy. It shows how committed ordinary rural Pennsylvania politicians were to the notion that prosaic reform legislation and sweeping initiatives could supplement each other. It should remind us of their profound faith in mainstream politics and the possibilities this politics held — at once radical and concerned at the same time with individual rights.

Starting with past experiences and assumptions about the availability of property so unlike the Philadelphia Democrats', leading Snyderites approached the demand for a constitutional convention differently. In early

1805 they still sought to merge the two reform impulses into a movement of careful, even incremental, change informed by a radical commitment to a democratic recasting of everyday life. Thus in March 1805, in the thick of the campaign to unseat McKean and convene the convention, Boileau wrote to Alexander J. Dallas. The two men had recently opposed each other during the judges' impeachment trial. Boileau wrote candidly that he disagreed with Dallas and thought a convention necessary. Still, he did not believe that a convention should consider every issue causing political conflict. Boileau assured Dallas that he, Snyder, and their supporters had "no idea of throwing up everything into the wind, but that if delegates should be chosen they should be instructed by their constituents and limited to certain points." Nevertheless, Boileau insisted that a genuinely democratic society could not be afraid to allow its first principles to be debated and determined by the people. Concentration of power in an executive, or in any public officials beyond the people's reach, encouraged oligarchy, a dangerous political form with which the Republic was sadly too familiar. But Boileau urged Dallas to involve himself in the reform campaign and so provide it with his wisdom. Were Dallas to do so, reform could be accomplished "without tumult and difficulty or danger."[77]

Boileau's and Dallas's differences should not be minimized. Boileau did his best to impeach the judges because he believed that an independent judiciary was incompatible with democratic politics. Furthermore, Boileau willingly participated in a political coalition with the Philadelphia Democrats. He was committed to the $100 Act and to strengthening the legislature at the expense of the judiciary. He believed that essential reforms depended on a constitutional convention, and he was willing to allow the people to ask fundamental political questions in a forum where first principles could potentially be reconfigured. These convictions placed him closer to the Philadelphia Democrats than to the Quids. Yet Boileau sought a political space that the Philadelphia Democrats had no wish to occupy. Had Duane learned of Boileau's letter, he would have considered it political treason. Through public debate and personal correspondence, the Snyderites made it possible for the Quids to realize that there were distinctions worth drawing between different elements of the reform coalition. But in 1805, banking on McKean's victory and terrified of any administration in which Duane and Leib would have influence, the Quids had no interest in abandoning their campaign.

At the beginning of 1805 the two goals of the reform coalition were to defeat McKean and convene the constitutional convention. Initially these two goals were compatible. However, from the beginning the Philadelphia Democrats wanted the convention first and Snyder's election second. If forced to choose, the Snyderites' preference was the reverse. This subtle distinction could have remained insignificant. But it became crucial once the Quids devoted all of 1805 to denouncing the ideas of the Philadelphia Democrats and to equating the call for a convention with the introduction of anarchy. Early in 1805 the *Argus* called for Snyder's election and a constitutional convention. By late summer, the high point of the campaign, Snyderites were convinced that Snyder could be elected only if they distanced themselves from demands for a convention.

During April and May the *Argus* was unambiguously pro-convention.[78] By the end of May, Snyderites from Lancaster and Montgomery Counties were suggesting a meeting merely to consider the propriety of calling a convention.[79] There were still demands from Northumberland for a convention in late June, but by July these were qualified with the caveat "to amend, not destroy the constitution."[80] During the summer, sentiment grew among the Snyderites that linking their candidate so completely to demands for a convention hurt rather than helped him. Thomas Cooper, writing in the *Argus,* reminded Snyderites that they did not have to endorse "every crude innovation" emerging from Philadelphia. If the Quids opposed all reform, then of course they had to be defeated. But that did not mean that dissatisfied Jeffersonians should begin "ridiculing all moderate and gradual reform, denouncing all those to whom experience has taught caution, and who are desirous of setting some bounds to political innovation." "Is there no middle term," Cooper asked, "in republican government between hereditary rank and privilege, and the state of confusion and anarchy? I think there is."[81]

By late June the *Argus* was seeking to implement reform without calling a convention. The paper began to insist that the legislature was the most important branch of state government, that it had the power to increase the number of courts, maintain arbitration, and pursue developmental policies that allowed all Pennsylvanians to prosper.[82] The threat to this legislature was a hostile governor wielding his veto. More and more, the goal of the Snyderites became electing Simon Snyder. After May the *Argus* tended to air its more radical statements in the form of a dialogue between a Connecticut man and a Pennsylvanian. Statements more likely to harm Snyder's candidacy came from the Connecticut man, while the Pennsylvanian went so far as to defend the good intentions of the members of the constitutional convention of 1790.[83]

During July and afterward, talk of a convention grew infrequent in the

Argus, while denunciations of McKean mounted, particularly for his many vetoes.[84] The Snyderites made much of the clodhopper episode. Snyder and his fellow Northumberlanders Abraham McKinney and Daniel Montgomery were among the delegation that provoked McKean's outburst. During the summer the Snyderites cheerfully began to call themselves clodhoppers — genuine men of the people — and not aloof, would-be aristocrats.

On May 31 the *Argus* had reported Montgomery County's suggestion for a meeting to consider the necessity of calling a convention rather than automatically convening one should Snyder win. By mid-August Boileau's county had reached a decision. Its party meeting voted to endorse Snyder but said nothing about a convention.[85] Washington, Cumberland, Huntington, Dauphin, Delaware, Berks, and Bucks Counties joined Montgomery in endorsing Snyder and remaining silent about a convention. The Snyderites of Allegheny County explained their thinking. The county meeting unanimously resolved "that the real substance of the address shall be to support Simon Snyder as Governor." The meeting further resolved "that the call of a convention be introduced in the address as a secondary consideration to our fellow citizens, it having no *immediate* connection with the election of governor."[86]

The question of a proper governor was paramount, the meeting insisted, and all men who cared about the future prosperity of Pennsylvania had to vote for Snyder. The *Argus* asked Pennsylvanians to compare the two gubernatorial candidates. The Quids, the paper reminded them, mocked Snyder's obscure origins. But "the trouble of publishing that Mr. Snyder served his apprenticeship to a trade [is] his friends everywhere know it, and boast of it. We know well that he is, and has been, a mechanic, a farmer, and a merchant, and he has discovered skill and dexterity in each of these situations and integrity in all of them."[87] Snyder, the ordinary man of business, the dignified clodhopper, could be relied on to encourage all occupations. He would treat none with contempt but instead would grant all equal gravity and respect. Could the clodhoppers of Pennsylvania receive the same from McKean? A reprint from the *Lancaster Intelligencer* asked Pennsylvanians to compare the governor's clodhopper remark to Jefferson's paean to laborers in his *Notes on the State of Virginia.*[88] McKean felt contempt for those who toiled; he was not a true Jeffersonian. In a democracy, the Snyderites insisted, only a clodhopper should govern the people.

The Snyderites insisted that McKean had forfeited any right to support from the party. Unfortunately, the *Argus* lamented, "there are many honest and worthy men who are led to believe that McKean and the constitution are inseparable, and that if one falls the other must necessarily go and do like-wise," but this belief was not the case. "The truth is," the *Argus* insisted, "there is no sense or reason in the supposed connection between McKean and the constitution, and Snyder and the convention. If after the election of Mr. Snyder there shall not appear to be a necessity of calling a convention, or a majority of the people after a full and fair discussion shall be averse to that measure, in either case it will be given up."[89]

Seeking to reassure those Pennsylvanians influenced by the Quids, the *Argus* suggested that there was little wrong with Pennsylvania's political structure. The problem was, rather, the closed elitist circle that controlled it. The paper proposed that the executive's veto and power to grant pardons were necessary prerogatives. But when placed in the constitution, they, like all executive impositions on the legislature, were "intended to be exercised very rarely and always with a judicious and sparring hand. But the Gover-nor has exercised these salutary prerogatives so promiscuously, and so fre-quently, as to render them highly pernicious rather than beneficial." Snyder, on the other hand, was "possessed of a spotless character, extensive infor-mation, a clear and luminous intellect, he is mild without timidity, prompt and firm without rashness, and affable without mean condescension."[90] The implication was clear. If Pennsylvanians replaced an aristocrat with a clod-hopper, there would be no need for a convention.

But the Philadelphia Democrats would stand for none of it. Ignoring the wishes of those closest to Snyder, they continued to demand a convention until the last few days of September, one week before the election. On Sep-tember 13 the *Argus* reprinted an article from the *Aurora* demanding a con-vention and Snyder's election. It was not enough to elect Snyder, for if the political structure remained intact, "a future governor entertaining the same principles with the present executive, might present the same obstructions to the salutary views of his constituents."[91]

In the same issue the *Argus* responded to the *Aurora*. The Snyderite paper wished to apprise its "friends and fellow citizens of the gravity of this elec-tion," but "we will not wander into the fields of fancy, nor will we magnify real evils to call forth your resentments against those who have adopted other ideas in politics, than we think consistent with the real interests and safety of the liberties and happiness of the good people of this country." The real problem was McKean, not the state's political structure. Jefferso-nians had elected him in good faith, "but no sooner did our legislature begin the work of reformation, than he began to discover his real temper." As long as McKean was governor, reform would be blocked. Once Pennsylvanians

elected Snyder, he and his supporters would usher in the Jeffersonian prosperity stymied by McKean's fear of a fully independent and powerful people. Once exposed, oligarchy could never again secure election.[92]

The *Argus* hammered away at the importance of a Snyder victory and
continued to insist that Snyder's election would make a convention unnecessary. But McKean's reelection would leave the legislature "humbled in the dust
before the judiciary . . . your legislature will be rendered nugatory and your
judges completely sovereign." The lawyers, the paper insisted, "know well,
unless controlled by the results of this election, what the decisions of the
judges of the supreme court will be; and that no attempt of theirs, however
audacious, will be met in any degree with their disapprobation; but on the contrary these efforts will be viewed as brave attacks on legislative sovereignty."
But Snyder's election would make all the difference. Pennsylvanians had a
clear choice: "Either our legislature must be supported as the highest dele-
gated power under our constitution; and that they as a distinct, and all important branch of our government, should be kept entirely separate from and
independent of any of the other branches, or powers of government, *or* our
liberties are at an end."[93] Snyder would accord the legislature this support and
respect; McKean had shown that he would not. Still the *Aurora* refused to
cooperate. Less than two weeks before the election, the *Argus* reprinted one
of its articles demanding a convention. Wearily, the Snyderite paper reiterated that Snyder's election itself would be enough to end the delay and expense of justice.[94]

In response to the Quids' efforts to discredit them by equating them with
the more extreme city radicals, the Snyderites began to connect democracy
more to a culture of the common man and a desired personality than to
sweeping changes in the structure of political society. Their efforts infuriated the Philadelphia Democrats, who had come to equate democracy with
the successful convening of a convention. As the Snyderites began to distance themselves from the convention, the Philadelphia Democrats began
to demand it more forcefully than ever before. In the process, they made
their clearest, most complete, and most radical statements about what
democracy was and how it was best achieved. The increasing extremism that
typified *Aurora* editorials in the summer and autumn of 1805 made the Quid
campaign more potent and the Snyderites more anxious to articulate their
own version of democracy before they were dismissed as rash mouthpieces
of the Philadelphia Democrats.

In response to the Quid definition of democracy and the Snyderite response, the *Aurora* insisted that democracy was quite simply a government

designed to ascertain majority will and then immediately enact it into law.
"It is a correct maxim," the *Aurora* announced, "that the will of the people
ought to rule, and that the will of the majority is the will of the people.
Therefore, every part of the Constitution, which prevents the will of the
people from becoming the supreme law, whenever that will can be conve-
niently ascertained, is unjust, and dangerous, and ought to be abolished."[95]

By midsummer 1805 the possibility that there might never be a convention had become very real. If there were no convention, if the Society of
the Friends of the People failed, it would prove that an aristocracy ruled
Pennsylvania. Aristocracy was not simply rule through privilege or birth,
but rather any effort to prevent majority will from being put into immediate affect. Clearly, the *Aurora* insisted, the clauses of the constitution that
established the process of reform did just that.[96] If aristocracy could not be
defeated through the established methods of convention or amendment,
then those methods were insufficient protections for democracy. The *Aurora*
demanded a constitutional convention, but if that remedy failed, the
Philadelphia Democrats were prepared to go even further for the sake of
direct and immediate rule by the majority.

Thus, while the *Aurora* called for a constitutional convention, it also
began to argue that constitutions themselves were aristocratic documents.
They were illegitimate whether or not the aristocrats they empowered managed to prevent their alteration. The Pennsylvania constitution was unac-
ceptable because it contained measures "contrary to the will of the majority,"
and any person, body, or document that thwarted the majority was "repug-
nant to the principles of the revolution."[97] Majority rule was the only acceptable form of government. In a democracy "the will of the majority shall give
law." If the people were sovereign, if it was their duty to govern, to decide
what was best for themselves, then any check upon their attempt to decide
and implement their decisions undermined their popular sovereignty. If the
majority voted one way, nothing should hinder its desires.[98] Concerned that
the constitutional convention would be prevented by the entrenched power
of the aristocracy, the *Aurora* began to insist that citizens should ignore the
procedures established by that aristocracy to challenge its measures or alter
the political structure that served it.

By trying to show why Pennsylvania's constitution was illegitimate, and
thus why the procedure for changing it was as well, the *Aurora* ended up insisting that constitutions themselves were the result of aristocratic efforts to
check democratic majority rule. All sovereign power belonged to the people. Logic and the experience of Pennsylvania showed that the purest and

best representative of majority will was the state legislature. Anything that prevented the lower house from implementing what the people told it to implement, be it a senate, a governor, a judge, or a constitution, simply allowed the few, the aristocracy, to prevent majority will from governing.[99]

The Philadelphia Democrats, then, came to reject the emerging American orthodoxy of constitution making first elaborated in Massachusetts in 1780 and enshrined at Philadelphia in 1787.[100] Proponents of this orthodoxy argued, the *Aurora* observed, that constitutions stood above legislatures, and that the fundamental law established by constitutions could not be altered by a normal legislative session. This position, the paper contended, resulted from a "disposition to controul future time. . . . [T]he fact is, if the people of this year discover a bad law, or wish a good one, they have as much right to it as the people of last year or those who made the constitution, for the constitution is but the self same act of sovereignty resolved into an irrepealable act, which a convention can have no more power to make than a legislature who comes after them." Calling a second constitutional convention to alter the work of the first one was "tedious and expensive," as the Philadelphia Democrats were discovering. Equally so was following the amendment procedure, a process established to strengthen the enemies of democracy in the first place. The entire elaborate and ludicrous enterprise resulted from "the same spirit of *dictating to future times.*" The only democratic solution was to allow the legislature to make and amend fundamental law.[101]

By rejecting constitutional orthodoxy, the *Aurora* demanded for the American legislatures the same power that the British Parliament had claimed for itself during the 1760s — complete powers of legislation. But the similarities were superficial. Parliament had insisted that it was sovereign, it could decide the best course for the nation and empire through internal debate among its members, and its decisions were irresistible. The *Aurora* did not claim that the legislature was sovereign. It was instead the most reliable, though still imperfect, mouthpiece of the sovereign people. It could be relied upon to accurately represent the majority will more frequently than any other political body. But at times the legislature, too, would err, and if the people once established that it had done so, the representatives would have no protection from the people. Sovereignty had not been extended to the legislators, even temporarily. Rather, they were simply allowed at a given time to say efficiently what the majority would say if it were possible to assemble it. The legislature, then, existed solely to discover what a majority of the people wanted, and then to enact it as swiftly as possible.[102]

Once the proper political structure for a democratic society was finally fully imagined, it became easy to see just how wrong much of American government was. The separation of powers was clearly an obnoxious, antidemocratic idea. Popular sovereignty led inexorably to majority rule, and if they were "true principles in theory why shall they be destroyed in practice?" Bicameral legislatures, executive vetoes, and independent judiciaries guaranteed that "the most numerous branch in the most cases [is] entirely excluded from any power, and in all cases may be controlled by a minority, or even by a single individual."[103]

Anyone who feared the results of democracy, then, was simply afraid of "the people," that venerable category on which the Philadelphia Democrats had long relied. Those who resisted this conception of democracy merely wished to hold a privileged position above "the people." Only democracy could preserve the equality that would allow the United States to leave the European condition of society behind. If all men were equal, and if equal and independent citizens could come together to discuss what was best for themselves and each other, then "the only danger must proceed from interests at variance with the principles of the government," for "from equality itself nothing is to be apprehended."[104] Once "the people" denied the aristocracy any political foundation from which to secure a dangerous concentration of political power, it would be stripped of its undue influence in American life. If the majority decided what fundamental law was, based on its perception of justice as events occurred, then it could prevent the developments that permitted the European condition of society in the first place.

The Quids seized on these statements, insisting that finally the secret beliefs of the entire reform movement had been revealed. Clearly, the choice was now between sanity and insanity. The *Freeman's Journal* ran articles arguing that though Duane was Irish and Leib and Snyder German, all sensible Irish and German Pennsylvanians supported McKean. In this campaign, the Quids sought the support of Joseph Heister, the wealthiest and most prominent German in the state. In private letters they described the tyrannies that would follow a McKean defeat.[105] These efforts worked, and the Quids were able to announce that Heister and an almost-as-prominent German, Peter Muhlenberg, both opposed Snyder.[106] Muhlenberg and Heister provided invaluable service when they allowed a private letter to be published announcing their opposition to both Snyder and a convention. In the letter Muhlenberg insisted that the "call for a convention and the election of the Governor are so intimately connected, that they cannot be separated." Muhlenberg also expressed concern if McKean lost for "him who has a large farm, particularly when others possess none." The letter appeared in Quid newspapers throughout Pennsylvania.[107] By September the Quids were confident. They pointed primarily to the Muhlenberg-Heister letter and their success at linking Snyder's election to the call for a convention as reasons for their probable victory.[108]

By August the reform coalition was terrified. The Snyderites had finally arrived at a position that called for Snyder's election and incremental reforms such as the $100 Act. Yet the Quids were skillfully equating Snyder's candidacy with at best an unpredictable convention and at worst the rejection of all fundamental law. The reform coalition was so alarmed that on September 28, scarcely a week before the election, the *Aurora* wrote that it would not automatically demand a convention should Pennsylvanians elect Snyder.[109]

By then it was much too late. Since early August the Quids had been preparing for McKean's landslide victory and the imposition of sobriety and sense on the idea of democracy. Only a complete victory could provide an irrefutable endorsement of Quid belief, and so the Quids reached out to all good citizens regardless of party. They reminded Pennsylvania that

> it is of importance not only that the old Governor be carried at the present time, but that the force in his favor be a great majority; because in proportion as the malcontents approach their purpose, they will be encouraged to persevere. . . . Should the present Governor be elected with but a small majority, and should no great change be made in the representative bodies, things will go on in the same way; the administration of justice will be kept at a stand, and the public be poisoned by blasts out of doors, and defamation within. . . . Thus at length the object will be accomplished and a revolution brought about. Then we shall see a renovation of all things. Those that stop short will be denounced; it will be necessary to be violent in order to be something.[110]

The turbulent and draining battle ended on November 10, and the results shocked the Quids. McKean won, but by the slimmest of margins. His majority of almost 40,000 votes in 1802 was reduced to 4,766 in 1805. The final tally was 43,644 to 38,483, with 395 votes for Samuel Snyder discounted because of the voters' error. Snyder and McKean each carried seventeen counties. The Quids delivered Philadelphia to McKean, but despite the fifteen-month effort to discredit Duane and Leib, despite their alarming beliefs, the Philadelphia Democrats carried the suburbs and the rest of the county for Snyder. For the most part, McKean's strength came from counties that had previously voted for the Federalists. Indeed, Albert Gallatin estimated that as many as two-thirds to three-fourths of the Jeffersonians voted for Snyder.[111] Though this estimate is perhaps too high, all contemporaries realized that McKean had not been supported by a majority of Pennsylvania's Jeffersonians and had needed Federalist votes to win. This dependence almost immediately jeopardized the Quids' legitimacy. Despite victory, the Quids had a lame-duck leader and faced a bleak future. Many of their fellow Jeffersonians distrusted them, and the reformers would make much of the Federalist support for McKean.

The Quids were profoundly relieved to have survived "such a lamentable crisis."[112] Yet William Barton understood that "our victory . . . was not so complete as to have disheartened the enemy: They will assuredly rally their broken squadrons, and perhaps give us a signal defeat in their turn." Barton insisted that it was imperative to consolidate victory by demonstrating the jurisdiction of the judiciary over all fundamental economic and political questions.[113]

Thus despite their victory, the Quids had grave concerns. In addition to the stigma of Federalist support, McKean was constitutionally prohibited from seeking reelection in 1808, having served three successive terms. In 1808 Snyder would be the most prominent candidate. Though the differences between the Philadelphia Democrats and the Snyderites had become apparent in 1805, having been exposed by the pressure of the Quids' campaign, the Quids had to believe that in a Snyder administration the influence of the Philadelphia Democrats would only grow. The Quids had an impotent governor. They had articulated a safe and sane vision of democracy, but a majority of Pennsylvania's Jeffersonians had rejected it. The Quids could only conclude that the men whom the majority of Jeffersonians endorsed threatened a rational understanding of democracy.

By late 1805 the Quids were desperate to protect what they considered true democracy by demonstrating how a democratic government both encouraged and constrained the citizenry. If in the future they could not expect to control those branches of government elected by the people, it was all the more crucial to demonstrate the centrality of the nonelected branch to democratic life. Suddenly, in the weeks after the election, the Quids got their chance. In late November one of the "blasts out of doors" predicted by the *Freeman's Journal* occurred. Philadelphia's journeyman cordwainers struck their masters, and their actions led to *Commonwealth v. Pullis* in January 1806, the first labor conspiracy trial in the nation's history. The Quids could not count on the voters to respect true democracy, but in *Commonwealth v. Pullis* they were determined to demonstrate that the soberer branches of government still retained the capacity to enforce respect for fundamental law.

The master cordwainers hoped to discipline their employees, not articulate a theory of moderate democratic belief. Labor strife in the trades, and especially among cordwainers, had disrupted the crafts in Philadelphia since the 1790s. Indeed, the concerns of free wage laborers that flared into a national movement in the late 1820s and 1830s were already present in Philadelphia a generation earlier. They were part of the more strident and acrimonious atmosphere that gave the Philadelphia Democrats such a different tone from the Snyderites.[114]

Philadelphians rightly saw the trial as the continuation of the Jeffersonian political battle that had raged with increasing intensity since 1802 and that had clearly not ended with McKean's narrow victory. The trial carried into the courtroom presided over by Recorder Moses Levy vast disagreements about the proper intersection of economic activity and democratic politics, and precisely what obligation property holders owed to their fellow citizens. The Philadelphia Democrats probably influenced the accused journeymen. The organization they created put many of the Philadelphia Democrats' theories into practice. Majority will was law, and once it was declared, the minority of cordwainers were expected to follow the majority's declaration. Much of the testimony at the trial concentrated on the cordwainers' efforts to force individual journeymen to strike against their wishes. In addition, the *Aurora* published the defense of their actions written by the accused cordwainers and printed supportive editorials. No other newspaper in the state did so.[115]

The trial began in early January 1806. The Federalist attorneys Joseph Hopkinson and Jared Ingersoll represented the master cordwainers. Hopkinson was just middle age and had come of age after the Revolution. He had to spend the bulk of his public career in an America dominated by Jeffersonians. By 1806 he had begun to act accordingly. Both Ingersoll and Hopkinson had supported McKean in the recent election, and both were moving away from the Federalist conception of organic hierarchy and a hierarchical political economy. Indeed, Ingersoll would be Dewitt Clinton's running mate in 1812. His son, Charles Jared, would later be influential in turning the Pennsylvania Jacksonian party in a pro-tariff, pro-bank direction. Ingersoll had always been independent-minded and committed to internal development for its own sake. In 1795, though a Federalist, he had opposed the Jay Treaty.[116]

Hopkinson and Ingersoll opened their case by denouncing the *Aurora*, which had "teemed with false representations and statements of this transaction" and so endeavored "to poison the public mind, and obstruct the pure streams of justice flowing from the established courts of law."[117] The master cordwainers' lawyers were reminding the court that if the Philadelphia Democrats had their way, "established courts of law" would have little power to decide cases such as this one. The presiding judge, Moses Levy, needed no reminder. A Jeffersonian and an officer of the Philadelphia Society for Constitutional Republicans, Levy was a McKean supporter and one of the original Quids.[118] Prosecution, defense, and bench all agreed that the trial resulted from disagreements about the nation's political and economic future. The Quids were determined to show that their tenuous hold on popular political power would not prevent them from shaping that future.

Trial testimony demonstrated the significant changes that had occurred in the Philadelphia economy during the final decades of the eighteenth century. Both bench and prosecution defended the transformation of the crafts, though these developments had provoked the journeymen's organizing efforts. The trial, in part, would either justify or discredit the emerging capitalist social relations that contributed to growing disparity of wealth and social status between masters and journeymen, and that created divisions among the journeymen themselves.[119] Victory was crucial for the Quids because the journeymen challenged the Quids' insistence that opportunity and development would bring general prosperity and economic independence. The journeymen's defeat in the trial could discredit their criticisms.

Not all journeymen cordwainers were angry about the transformation of their craft, but they all agreed that it had occurred. During the trial, journeyman Job Harrison testified as a witness for the prosecution. Harrison stated that his master, John Bedford, employed as many as twenty-four men. His business was too substantial to be housed in one shop, and Harrison lived over a mile from Bedford.[120]

Bedford was one of the many rising Pennsylvania craftsmen seeking to expand his business and hoping to take advantage of the new economic opportunities of the Jeffersonian era. Masters such as Bedford were converting production from bespoke work to order and shop work. Indeed, Bedford was seeking to tap the growing demand of large slaveholders for cheap shoes. The strike had cost him $4,000 worth of contracts with buyers in Charleston, Petersburg, Richmond, Norfolk, and Alexandria.[121] Other masters testifying for the prosecution also sought to become producer-merchants, expand their markets, and profit by producing larger quantities of cheaper shoes with lower labor costs. Master cordwainer William Montgomery had secured orders worth $2,000 from St. Thomas, New Orleans, and Charleston. He testified, "I could not afford to give the rise in wages without a loss in executing those orders." Master Lewis Ryan made the concerns of his fellow employers explicit during his testimony. A successful combination by the journeymen would make it impossible to bargain far afield with a reasonable expectation of what labor costs would be. Such conditions meant "that we [are] not able to do any work for exportation, but rather would have to confine ourselves to bespoke work only."[122]

Both masters and journeymen understood what was at stake. Journeyman Philip Dwyer testified that wages for order work had been cut and that this type of production increasingly dominated the trade. Profits were being made on the labor of journeymen, and Dwyer understood that "either the customer or the employer put it in their pockets." Journeyman John Hays echoed this sentiment. The statement by the accused journeymen published in the *Aurora* explained why the masters now had the power to materially alter the living conditions of the journeymen. The masters were "the retailers of our labor, and in truth live upon the work of our hands [and] are generally men of large property." This unequal relationship was undemocratic and unjustifiable because it prevented the workingman's inalienable right to "obtain a fair and just support for our families."[123] The stakes were clear. Could a majority decide to prevent the actions of individuals it found reprehensible? In the process, how coercive could that majority be? And, of course, given the explosive political context in which the trial took place, in what venue would these questions be decided, and how popular and accountable would the decision makers be?

The prosecution understood that it had to accomplish two things. First, it had to show that a democratic republic benefited from the activity of entrepreneurs such as the master cordwainers. Second, it had to demonstrate that the gubernatorial election had settled the conflicts within the Pennsylvania Jeffersonian party. The issues at stake in the trial would be decided in a law court presided over by an independent judge. If that judge did not commit a crime, he was not impeachable, and so was beyond the reach of the legislature and the voters.

First, the prosecution defended the entrepreneurial behavior of the masters. Joseph Hopkinson built on themes used by the Quids in the recent election. He invoked Philadelphia's magnificent industrial future. If nothing prevented the master craftsmen from accumulating, expanding, and transforming production, opportunity would abound, and all would prosper.[124] Indeed, the masters embodied the public good when they pursued their own interests. Hopkinson implied a subtle if potentially contradictory message. He suggested that there was a discernible public good that society could

collectively move toward, and that the masters contributed to this movement through their entrepreneurial activities. But he also suggested that a
society secured the public good when it allowed entrepreneurs to fully exploit the resources they were able to acquire.[125] The latter viewpoint had increasingly become a Quid rallying cry during the gubernatorial campaign.
In conjunction with the insistence that opportunity would generally arise
with development, the Quids argued that this definition of the public good
was legitimate in a democracy. Even if it did not yet command majority support, after 1805 this notion of the public good had been defended skillfully
enough for many Pennsylvanians to believe it deserved a hearing. Clearly,
then, the prosecution concluded, the coercive tactics of the journeymen hindered the development that made democratic independence possible. The
solution to inequality was not intrusive majority rule but encouraging the
entrepreneurial behavior of each individual. Finally, the prosecution also
insisted that the journeymen were guilty under the common law of criminal conspiracy. Common law was applicable to civil and criminal cases in
Pennsylvania. An independent judge was responsible for interpreting the
common law and instructing the jury in its meaning.

The defense, represented by Caesar A. Rodney and Walter Franklin,
was as concerned with distancing itself from the debates over legal reform as
it was with defending the cordwainers. Rodney felt compelled to explain to
Judge Levy that it was "not my interest, nor would it comport with my character, holding a seat within this bar, to stir up opposition against the due
course of proceedings, or the legal settled practice of the court. I am sure,
sir, you know me better."[126] The defense sought to defend the cordwainers
without giving any support to the ideas of the Philadelphia Democrats.
Rodney and Franklin tried to conduct the trial without reference to the
debates and disagreements that were shaping politics in the state.

The defense also expected a rising industrial future.[127] But it insisted that
this future could be achieved only if the economy was truly shaped by individuals acting as individuals. It was clear, the defense maintained, that the
master cordwainers had colluded in their efforts to drive down wages and
discipline recalcitrant workers. If the court prevented all individuals from
combining, and thus forced each person to depend only on his own labor
and the labor of those he could afford to pay and convince to enter his
employ, then "the market will sufficiently and correctly regulate these matters."[128] The market free from all combination naturally provided for the
needs of all. Franklin believed that the only real problem with Philadelphia's
economy was the presence of combinations by both parties and "a want of

regular demand" for manufactures. The solution was a completely free market for capital and labor that eschewed collective action by both masters and journeymen. This market, and the construction of a great warehouse in the city where all artisans could market their goods, would provide abundant opportunity and end Philadelphia's labor struggles.[129]

The defense had an even more difficult time carving out an independent space to discuss the common law. On the one hand, Franklin and Rodney did not want to cede the arguments about the common law to the prosecution, for those arguments purported to establish the journeymen's guilt. On the other hand, they did not want to anger Levy by associating themselves with the Philadelphia Democrats. In addition, the defense did not agree with the extreme positions taken in the *Aurora*.[130]

Rodney and Franklin made it painstakingly clear that they did not approve of a wholesale rejection of the common law. That they felt it necessary to qualify their arguments with this disclaimer suggests the explosive context in which the trial was taking place. Rodney insisted that at the time of the American Revolution much of the common law had been "declared to be binding and obligatory."[131] But the defense insisted that the journeymen could not be tried for conspiracy merely for assembling, for the Pennsylvania constitution guaranteed their right to do so. Given that the defense wanted to distance itself from the issues everybody else wanted to discuss, it had the narrowest of channels to navigate. It had most likely conceded too much by its willingness to condemn all combinations. But it did maintain that one could endorse the independent judiciary, and much of the common law, while acquitting the journeymen.

The trial could not be divorced from the political events that made it so important to the Quids and those Federalists who in 1805 saw the Quids as their only option. The extent to which individuals could be made accountable to the majority had to be determined. Echoing the Quids, the prosecution linked the individual's untrammeled right to pursue his self-interest to the defense of the common law and the current political structure. Those things were under attack. The journeymen's efforts to organize, and the radical democracy of the Philadelphia Democrats that most observers believed inspired them, would stand or fall together. Thus, demonstrating that supervision of conflicts such as the cordwainers' belonged to judges like Levy was as imperative in January 1806 as electing McKean and preventing the constitutional convention had been in 1805.

Therefore, the prosecution ignored whatever subtleties there were in the defense's arguments. In response to the defense's position on the common law, Ingersoll insisted that the common law itself had been rejected during the trial. He then asked, "Whence comes this enmity to the common law? It is of mushroom growth. Look through the journals of congress during the revolutionary war, you will find it claimed as the greatest charter of liberty."[132] Clearly the prosecution was using the trial as an opportunity to respond to the greater debate that convulsed the state. Ingersoll's defense of the common law did not actually differ from Rodney's. The stance they both took was identical to that taken by Dallas in the *Address to the Republicans of Pennsylvania*. Ingersoll insisted that "the common law, as adopted and practiced in Pennsylvania, is the least exceptionable criminal code in the world."[133] Ingersoll then denounced the wholesale rejection of the common law as adopted by Pennsylvania and predicted a lawless anarchy if the adherents of this position ever came to power.[134] The prosecution was determined to make the trial a contest between the entrepreneurial and legal vision espoused by the Quids and the beliefs of the Philadelphia Democrats regardless of what the defense actually said.

Moses Levy supported the prosecution's effort. Indeed, he was even more responsible for turning the trial into a denunciation of the Philadelphia Democrats. Levy accepted the prosecution's arguments that the public good was both served and met by the master cordwainers' entrepreneurial efforts. He also denounced the wholesale rejection of the common law, ignoring the fact that no participant in the trial had called for such a rejection. But he also castigated efforts to undermine the independent judiciary, though the defense was at pains to show that it wished for no alterations in the legal system. Levy hoped to consolidate a legal and political vision that was under siege. Thus, he insisted that the independent judiciary had to be preserved for "the moment courts of justice lose their respectability[,] from that moment the security of persons and property is gone." It was his duty, Levy insisted, to remind Pennsylvanians of that. Lamentably, "much abuse has of late teemed upon its [the law's] valuable institutions."[135] Levy then rejected the Philadelphia Democrat's ideals. "The acts of the legislature," the judge declared,

> form but a small part of that code from which the citizen is to learn his duties, or the magistrate his power and rule of action. These temporary emanations of a body, the component members of which are subject to perpetual change, apply principally to the political exigencies of the day. It is in the volumes of the common law we are to seek for information in the far greater number, as well as the most important causes that come

before our tribunals. That individual code has ascertained and defined, with a critical precision, and with a consistency that no fluctuating body could or can attain, not only the civil rights of property, but the nature of all crimes from treason to trespass.[136]

The common law and the courts that administered it were more responsible for preserving fundamental rights than was the ephemeral and popular legislature. Thus Levy instructed the jury to decide guilt or innocence based on that law "regardless of what the world may think . . . or of popular abuse." If fundamental questions were decided other than by strict application of the law, then "numbers would decide all questions of duty and property, and causes would be hereafter adjudged, not by the weight of their reason, but according to the physical force of the parties charged." Once this state of affairs came to pass, "the rights, the liberties and privileges of man in society could no longer be protected within these hallowed walls [of the court room.]"[137]

Levy described the common law as complex and insisted that only highly educated and trained lawyers and judges could understand it. He then instructed the jury that the prosecution had interpreted the common law correctly. The jury, then, should find the journeymen guilty.[138] The jury summarily did so, though the journeymen were merely lightly fined. But the insistence on retaining the jurisdiction of the independent judiciary over questions of property rights and labor relations was upheld. Levy thus summarized the views the Quids had propounded for the last three years. Popular bodies should represent a democratic republic, but they had to recognize their limitations. The most fundamental questions had to be resolved in less popular (possibly entirely unpopular) venues. There, learned justices could guide common citizens to proper decisions based on common law. Levy made sure that the trial would answer the Philadelphia Democrats. The response came from an independent judge, a source beyond the reach of their popular, immediate democracy, and one that survived only because of the constitution. The cordwainers were discredited, in part, by the implication that they demanded the same changes as the radical Jeffersonians who supported them.

The trial of the journeymen brought into sharp relief the problems that had plagued Pennsylvania's Jeffersonian party since its inception. Rodney noted during his argument that the trial pitted two Jeffersonian constituencies, master craftsmen and journeymen, against each other. Distinguishing between productive master craftsmen and those Americans "who have inherited large fortunes . . . [and who] have been born with silver spoons in their mouths," Rodney wondered how the former, self-made working men, could seek to reduce "to a state of vassalage and want" their fellow mechanics.[139] This was a question Pennsylvania's Jeffersonians could not answer, at least if they continued to cling to their category "the people." Interestingly, Rodney would get a cogent answer four years later when Joseph Hopkinson tried once again to defend the common law. In his pamphlet *Considerations on the Abolition of the Common Law in the United States*, Hopkinson identified the crucial dilemma that the Pennsylvania Jeffersonians could not bring themselves to face. The discord they so abhorred was not the result of the common law, for "these difficulties and embarrassments [we]re not created by the law or by lawyers; they ar[ose] out of the very nature and intricacy of human affairs; from the variety of transactions between man and man."[140]

Yet this shrewd assessment of the way they lived now in Jeffersonian Pennsylvania obliterated the assumption at the core of Jeffersonian political belief and political mission. Since Jeffersonians in Philadelphia would not accept an observation such as Hopkinson's, *Commonwealth v. Pullis* exposed the strengths but also the even greater weaknesses of the thought of both the Philadelphia Democrats and the Quids. For the Philadelphia Democrats, had they chosen to face it, the trial posed a grave problem. It simply was not credible, as Rodney understood, to equate master artisans with a quasi aristocracy that could exploit fellow citizens because of its privileged access to political power. The real problem for those who viewed democratic citizenship as intimately dependent on a rough equality of condition was that the creative endeavors of certain citizens were causing inequality to grow among citizens. The master cordwainers needed no special privileges from government to begin to take advantage of more reliable commercial routes, expanding markets, and broader access to credit. Indeed, the loosening of elite Federalist control over manufacturing processes and policy and bank credit that resulted from Jeffersonian victory was a major cause of the conditions causing tensions in the Philadelphia crafts.

The master craftsmen, then, had they wanted to, could have plausibly argued that their behavior was entirely justified within the Philadelphia Democrats' own belief system. The masters simply exercised their "American rights, based on American principles," to improve their conditions through the free use of their private property. They did not seek political power, they did not attempt to deny others access to politics, and they did not rely on special relations with any who did pursue power or attempt to limit access. A dispassionate view of the trial strongly suggested that the

Philadelphia Democrats' explanation of the source of inequality could not reveal why the journeymen lived in increasingly vulnerable conditions. Yet, undeniably, those conditions did not reflect the social and economic relations that the Philadelphia Democrats insisted were necessary for all citizens to remain secure in the possession of their democratic rights.

The Philadelphia Democrats' theories could not explain why a conflict supposedly between "the people" and a minority of antidemocratic quasi aristocrats was being conducted between two groups that both fell within the city radicals' conception of "the people." But the trial, at least in a limited way, confirmed the Philadelphia Democrats' assumptions to the point that it discouraged them from thinking about the implications of certain citizen-producers being in conflict with fellow citizen-producers. For the master-journeyman conflict did overlap with the use of common law and with the least accountable branch of government wielding and interpreting that law. By focusing on the presence of common law and the survival of independent judges such as Levy, the city radicals could claim vindication. They could ignore that the source of the conflict predated the court's hearing the trial. At a deeper and more troubling level, they could ignore that in this case their version of democracy would potentially trample the rights of a group of men that the city radicals' own ideals demanded had to be protected, cherished, and encouraged for democracy and justice to be present. *Commonwealth v. Pullis* exposed a profound weakness in the thought of the Philadelphia Democrats, a weakness they refused to confront. Instead, they concluded that the trial confirmed their most extreme positions, those they had drawn when the crucible of conflict was at its most heated.

Commonwealth v. Pullis posed profound intellectual and philosophical problems for the Quids as well, problems that they were as unwilling as their opponents to confront. The concerns and actions of the journeymen that led to the trial were understandable and logical reactions to the dynamic and precocious economic changes occurring within the Philadelphia manufacturing community. Had the final months of 1805 been less charged, less polarized, less contentious — had they not, in other words, been the product of the crucible of conflict — thoughtful Quids (and there were many) might very well have been forced to ponder the conundrum the trial exposed. Philadelphia, more than any other region of the state, resembled the Quids' ideal of a dynamic economy populated by industrious citizens seeking to fully mobilize their resources. Yet within the manufacturing community, the outcome of this activity was not what the Quids had predicted (or sincerely expected and hoped for).

The trial could not be separated from the atmosphere that produced and surrounded it — the vitriolic conflict among Pennsylvania Jeffersonians over the meaning of Jeffersonian political ideas. The crucible of conflict had by 1806 created a political climate that simply could not accommodate nuance, flexibility, or compromise. The choices seemed so stark that the Quids could believe that there were only two options. Either their political economy was the prescription for a placid democracy based on widespread access to and protection of property and commitment to the rights and interests of all, or Pennsylvania faced the anarchy of the Philadelphia Democrats. Thus, the Quids felt an irresistible desire to see the problem of the journeymen cordwainers as an aberration. They continued to insist that the solution for the cordwainers and their fellow citizens was a more complete commitment to the politics and political economy the Quids championed.

The Quids' unwillingness to address the concerns of the journeymen revealed that the people about whom all Pennsylvania Jeffersonians generalized were more complex than their theories allowed. The Quids' stance did not end in their political oblivion, though it did guarantee that they would be unlikely to gain the trust of certain of those included in "the people." But the Quids' ideas did resonate with many others among those who were understood by all Jeffersonians to be a part of "the people." Quid ideas were particularly exciting to those who looked forward to an entrepreneurial future, those who thought the best days of the nation lay rather smoothly ahead, and most of those who, with their own labor and talent, had secured productive property and expected to acquire more. These portions of "the people" found in the Quids' ideas a deeply powerful defense of democracy, justice, and their own creative aspirations. If the trial proved anything at all, it was the cogency of Caesar Rodney's concerned query (and Hopkinson's observation). The natural constituency of the Pennsylvania Jeffersonian party was fracturing along with the party itself. If the various Jeffersonian factions remained entrenched, it would be impossible for Pennsylvania Jeffersonian political thought to speak meaningfully at the same time to all those whom Pennsylvania Jeffersonians had originally assumed possessed the same ideas, needs, and concerns. *Commonwealth v. Pullis* should have caused both the Philadelphia Democrats and the Quids to think more sensitively about their own ideas. It should have encouraged both groups to consider the limits of their thought, to dwell on what their competing definitions of democracy could not explain. The impact of the crucible of conflict was that after the trial both groups did precisely the opposite.

In the short term *Commonwealth v. Pullis* reinforced McKean's election.

Yet ultimately, the Quids' experience between Leib's reelection in 1804 and *Commonwealth v. Pullis* showed that they could not contain the charged politics that daily forced fundamental differences to become the subject matter of mainstream political discussion. The Philadelphia Democrats were eminently discreditable. They challenged orthodox constitution making and the separation of powers though both were legitimated by the Constitution of 1787. They suggested murky and nebulous alternatives to existing legal and constitutional structures. Most important, they never successfully dealt with the nagging question of how to ensure the rights of the individual if the community or the majority was able to declare on a question of fundamental law. And yet, the Quids — generally wealthier, better educated, holding most of the prominent public positions, and enjoying the support of possibly three-fourths of the state's newspapers — had barely beaten Snyder, the relatively obscure son of a tanner. They had been only narrowly victorious though they ran a member of the Stamp Act Congress, a signer of the Declaration of Independence, and easily the most prominent Jeffersonian in the state.[141]

In the end the Quids could not convincingly lead a political movement over the new democratic terrain. The concerns raised by the radicals were real, and the popular efforts of the Quids, mixed as they were with ambivalence and condescension, were unconvincing to a majority of Pennsylvania's Jeffersonians. When the election of 1805 revealed how tenuous their control of political power was, the Quids rushed to declare their core beliefs in a venue that could ignore the majority of their party. What the popular surge in Pennsylvania would come to mean was not yet clear, but everybody realized that the position the Quids finally had to fall back to was untenable.

Though the Quids' future looked bleak, the Snyderites emerged from Snyder's narrow defeat bitter and angry. They had run a true man of the people who represented everything they felt McKean did not. They promised a desirable future where ordinary men used the state legislature to responsibly pursue the business of opportunity and independence for all citizens. Yet the Quids had been able to cast doubt, to misrepresent them just enough to thwart their emerging conception of democracy.

For the Snyderites the events of 1805 exposed two grave threats to the democratic future they wanted. First, the Quids had shown that they could skillfully taint all efforts at reform by connecting them to the most extreme ideas being propounded. Though Snyder was clearly in a strong position looking ahead to 1808, what the Snyderites understood as his manifest virtues had not been enough to withstand the Quids' strategy in 1805, and might still not be enough in the future. The second threat was even more frightening. Over the course of 1805 the Philadelphia Democrats had ended up equating democracy with ideas that the Snyderites had to acknowledge could threaten property. The Philadelphia Democrats proclaimed their commitment to the rights of all people. But the Snyderites as easily as the Quids could see that the Philadelphia Democrats' final understanding of democracy could render some of the people's rights uncertain. The Snyderites had always possessed a more sanguine view than the city radicals of the general ability of citizens to acquire the propertied independence necessary for democratic citizenship. By 1806 they feared that the Philadelphia Democrats' conception of democracy was potentially a graver threat to that citizenship than even the Quids' unwillingness to consider necessary reforms.

After 1805 the Snyderites no longer considered the Philadelphia Democrats useful allies. Together the two reform groups had guaranteed that Pennsylvania Jeffersonian politics would be democratic. Over the course of 1805, weighty though disparate understandings of the term had emerged. By the end of the cordwainers' trial there were three main sources of dispute: (1) How much power to affect fundamental law should popular bodies have? (2) what precisely was the connection between these popular bodies and the expansive political economy all Jeffersonians desired? and (3) which people could most credibly claim to be democrats? Battling over these questions had split the Jeffersonians between the urban and rural radical coalition and the moderate Quids. But the crucible of conflict — the need scrupulously to articulate and triumph in polemic and argument — had been as crucial in shaping belief as had initial assumptions and ideals. Within the crucible of conflict, particularly in 1805, the Snyderites began to realize their significant disagreements with the Philadelphia Democrats as well as the Quids. With Snyder poised to become governor in 1808, the Snyderites were determined to make coherent what was confused. By doing so they would show Pennsylvania why neither the Quids nor the city radicals spoke true democracy. They would do so by finding their own democratic voice and by providing a definition of that term that challenged the equation of democracy with either wild anarchy or elitist arrogance. During 1805 the arguments about democracy became apparent to all. But if there were so many competing meanings of the term, then democracy, as yet, had no definition. After 1805 the Snyderites were determined to provide one. And that meant moving to Philadelphia.

Chapter Five

"Perpetual Motion—Perpetual Change— A Boundless Ocean without a Shore": The Final Meaning of Democracy in Pennsylvania

In 1807, four years after setting up shop in Northumberland with the *Republican Argus,* John Binns started a new newspaper in Philadelphia. It is unclear whether Binns began the *Democratic Press* intending to provoke a schism with the Philadelphia Democrats. But starting in 1808 the rural and urban radicals began to denounce each other as enemies of democracy. The divisions between the Snyderites and the Philadelphia Democrats had profound implications for the meaning of democracy in Pennsylvania and the relationship between democracy and a capitalist economy. In Pennsylvania between 1807 and 1814, the Snyderites fashioned the rudiments of a political culture and a political economy that later generations would identify as inherently American and essentially modern and liberal.

Little hint of the coming political split could be detected as the Philadelphia Democrats welcomed John Binns to Philadelphia in February 1807. The *Aurora* announced that the *Democratic Press,* "a new shield for principles," would soon begin publication, and that John Binns, "a faithful, undaunted supporter of the rights of man," would edit it.[1] The Philadelphia Democrats also provided Binns with financial support. At a party meeting, leading Philadelphia Democrat Thomas Leiper recommended that fifteen democrats from the city and fifteen more from the Northern Liberties subscribe to Binns's paper to popularize it with democrats in the city and county. The *Aurora* also gave Binns much press and published his Statement of Farewell to the democrats of Northumberland County.[2]

During the first few months of 1807, the *Aurora* and the *Democratic Press* worked together, with the *Press* publishing in the morning and the *Aurora* in the evening.[3] They supported each other, and Binns advertised William Duane's recently published pamphlet, *Politics for American Farmers.*[4] By May 1807 Binns seemed fully accepted by the Philadelphia Democrats. He was

173

elected to membership in the Society of the Friends of the People, and Duane, Leib, and Leiper made him an officer in the Tammany Society. Binns was even invited to give the long talk to that organization, a rare honor for a newcomer. In his speech Binns sounded the proper themes, insisting that "in truth there are but two names in our language which designate the principles and views of the two parties [in America]. I mean the words democrats and aristocrats — the friends of the rights of the many — and the advocates of a privileged few."[5]

But there were intimations of future trouble as the Philadelphia Democrats sought to sustain the political debates of the recent gubernatorial election. After McKean's victory they concluded that the next logical step was to impeach an executive so hostile to democracy. In addition, from 1807 through 1809 Michael Leib sat in the state legislature. For the first time Snyderites were pushed into close and regular contact with the Philadelphia Democrat leader. They were forced to deal with the divisions and intense reactions he provoked. Leib lost little time calling for an inquiry into impeachment.[6] He insisted that McKean could be impeached on six counts, ranging in importance from accusations that he had ignored the results of the Philadelphia County sheriff's election to the charge that he had violated the constitution by using a facsimile stamp of his name rather than sign every public document.[7]

Leib managed to organize a committee of inquiry and secured the chair. But impeaching McKean did not serve the Snyderites' interests. After 1805 Snyder was the most prominent gubernatorial candidate. Having already been narrowly defeated, the Snyderites wanted to get as many votes as possible from those Pennsylvanians who did not consider themselves Federalists. Thus the Snyderites sought to postpone the impeachment inquiry. In early 1807 McKean suffered an attack of gout, and Nathaniel B. Boileau insisted that he should not be forced to undergo impeachment while ill. He refused to promise to support the inquiry. A former Quid who had recently joined the Snyderites, Samuel D. Ingham, openly campaigned to vote down the inquiry.[8] Ingham's willingness to confront Leib was the first step in his rise to subsequent party prominence. The *Aurora* continued to demand McKean's impeachment, and initially the *Democratic Press* supported it.[9] But Binns quickly began to follow the lead of Snyderites like Ingham and Boileau, who continued to oppose the impeachment.[10]

Through late spring 1807 the *Democratic Press* printed statements opposing the impeachment.[11] The *Press* also began to print Leib's speeches alongside careful responses that came increasingly from Boileau.[12] Typically Leib would harangue the legislature with the fiery oratory for which he was famous. Leib insisted that the impeachment was essential for democracy. Executives had to be brought under the control of legislatures. "Do you," Leib thundered at his fellow legislators, "consider the will of the people expressed by a majority, as the vital principle of a republic?"[13] Boileau would then provide a measured response, seeking to demonstrate to the Quids that they could safely elect Simon Snyder. It was necessary, Boileau insisted, to proceed cautiously. Impeachment was "a question of extreme delicacy. The spirit of party is still but too prevalent: should we finally put the governor on trial, we may expect that our conduct will be attributed to impure motives, we probably may be charged with a vindictive and unrelenting spirit, that we are pursuing him, not only to a bed of sickness but even to the grave."[14]

There was another reason for caution. The Snyderites realized in 1807 that they occupied a position in Pennsylvania politics that the Philadelphia Democrats did not. They were actually close to taking power in the state. They did not want to antagonize any potential voters, nor did they wish to do possibly irreparable damage to institutions they might soon control. Boileau pointed out that impeachment of an executive in the new nation under the Constitution was unprecedented. It should not be undertaken lightly.[15]

In the legislature Leib proved a constant irritant and obstacle to the Snyderites, and particularly to Boileau, their floor leader. A fine example was the debate over Boileau's legislation aimed at reforming the legal process in state courts. The legislation sought to prevent lawyers from reading English legal precedents in court. Boileau noted that lawyers, rarely content to summarize precedents, often read them verbatim. This practice, "instead of having the tendency to elucidate the subject before them, only serve[d] to bewilder and confound the jury." Boileau made pointed remarks about the use of English precedents, particularly of common law. He also admitted that he wanted his legislation to force lawyers to rely less on British jurisprudence. He hoped that in the future Americans would "gradually acquire a common law of our own." But Boileau acknowledged that "it would not be practicable to reduce the common law at once into a text." He carefully explained that his legislation would not forbid reference to English common-law precedents and that judges and lawyers could still make use of them. They simply could not read them in their entirety. Boileau pushed the legislation to "prevent the present delays of justice, produce a greater uniformity of decision in our courts, and have a tendency to render our law less complex, and of course easier understood."[16]

Boileau's was a classic piece of Snyderite legislation. It suggested certain utopian impulses, but it was much more likely to bring about incremental, albeit concrete and substantive, reforms. It was by no means a craven piece of legislation. Horace Binney, the prominent Philadelphia lawyer, quickly rose to oppose it. He sought to discredit Boileau's motion by damning it as part of a "fever for innovation." After 1805 innovation was a loaded term guaranteed to revive memories of the acrimonious gubernatorial election. Binney spoke of threats to property if legislators attacked the common law.[17]

Boileau had an obvious rejoinder, for he had not called for the abolition of common law. But before he could give it, Leib seized the floor. Leib began by denouncing Binney. Boileau had called for no alteration in the common law, but Leib announced that he was "of the opinion that the abuses of the common law require reformation." He supported Boileau's legislation because it would lead to more general reforms. Binney had spoken of a fever, and Leib "acknowledge[d] that I have a fever to take into consideration this thing called common law; and if it is such a fever to which the gentleman alludes that brought about the reformation of Luther, or produced the independence of the United States, I am proud to acknowledge I feel the effects of such a fever, a fever of innovation which has so eminently contributed to promote the happiness of mankind." Leib demanded that the state expunge all British cases from the law code and insisted that all laws in the United States be codified.[18]

Boileau and Samuel D. Ingham quickly moved to repair the damage. Ingham carefully reminded the legislators that Boileau's legislation did not require codification of the common law, nor did it outlaw reference to British precedents. Boileau reiterated that his legislation did "not contemplate prohibiting judges and lawyers or any other persons from reading British reports or any books they think proper, in their own chambers." Precedents could be cited and summarized, and court officers could take them into account.[19] Boileau and Ingham were so busy responding to Leib, who believed that he had helped their cause, that they did not have time to answer Binney's charges. Pennsylvanians like Binney continued to insist, regardless of Boileau's actual stance, that Leib's demands were the Snyderites' true intentions. As long as Federalists such as Binney could equate Boileau with Leib, the Snyderites feared that they might lose the Quids to the Federalists. They might never be in a position to implement reform of any kind.

Thus, as the Snyderites worked to pass more moderate arbitration legislation, they began to oppose Leib. In 1807 they passed an arbitration law that covered all civil suits except ejection and replevin, and that allowed either party to force arbitration and appeal to a law court.[20] By that summer they concluded that they had to rid themselves of Michael Leib. In early June the *Aurora* denounced an anti-Leib pamphlet published by the Philadelphia printer Joseph Lloyd. The paper dismissed it as the latest Quid libel.[21]

But Lloyd, the printer who had published the cordwainers' pamphlet defending their actions (which had also been printed in the *Aurora*), was not a Quid, and he insisted that he sought to save the Jeffersonian party from a demagogue and an intriguer. The *Aurora* refused to publish his explanation. Prior to 1807 that would have been the end of it. Lloyd would have either let the matter rest or defended his actions in the *Freeman's Journal*, thereby fueling accusations of his Quid sympathies. But now Lloyd had the option of the *Democratic Press,* and the Snyderites were looking to challenge Leib in Philadelphia. The *Press* published Lloyd's letter. In it Lloyd denounced McKean and the Quids but insisted that Leib cared only for self-aggrandizement and would sacrifice democracy for personal power.[22] In the pamphlet Lloyd accused Leib of intriguing with certain Quids against the Snyderites in exchange for office. The actual backroom politics are murky, and indeed Lloyd subsequently retracted his accusation.[23] It was far more significant that the differences among the reformers were now public. Henceforth the Snyderites would battle the Philadelphia Democrats for supremacy in Philadelphia and Philadelphia County. The political struggle would force both sides to clearly articulate exactly what they meant by democracy, and the winners would most likely gain the power to impose their vision of democracy on the Pennsylvania Jeffersonian party.

With Leib now the enemy, the Snyderites struck at the base of his power, the general democratic meetings to elect candidates held annually in Philadelphia and Philadelphia County. The Philadelphia Democrats enjoyed majority support in the county and a near majority in the city. The Quids had nearly always demanded that both city and county be divided into districts, for there were parts of both that were hostile to Leib. He was especially unpopular in the wealthier city wards near the waterfront. The Snyderites adopted the demand for district meetings. They argued that unruly general meetings were the last refuge of demagogues and served to silence the majority rather than discern its will.[24]

The Philadelphia Democrats denounced this argument as a Quid attack and held their general meetings over the protests of the *Democratic Press*. At the meetings they nominated Leib for the state assembly and Duane for the state senate.[25] The *Democratic Press* dismissed the meetings as poorly attended and the work of a minority. It argued that the nominations of the two leading Philadelphia Democrats were illegitimate.[26] The *Aurora* spat back the worst insult Duane could conceive. Unfathomably, the supporters of Snyder demanded "the Quid project of district meetings."[27]

The Snyderites proved quite capable of participating in the rough-and-tumble of Philadelphia's democratic politics. The *Democratic Press* mounted an impressive and sustained campaign to destroy Duane's and Leib's political reputations. The Snyderites blamed Leib for Snyder's loss in 1805 and for divisions among the democrats in the legislature that prevented the passage of salutary reforms. Indeed, they insisted, Leib's hostility for Snyder continued unabated. This alleged man of the people and instrument of majority will connived to prevent the victory of the democrats' strongest gubernatorial candidate.[28]

The Philadelphia Democrats responded in kind. The *Aurora* warned democrats to beware of a new political coalition of Federalists, Quids, and those who supported Snyder for interested reasons. The paper dubbed this new coalition the Quadroons. The Quadroons were supported by "efforts made in a paper, which in the very moment that it is violating every principle of *democracy,* calls itself the *Democratic Press.*"[29] It is not necessary to recount every twist and turn of the schism. In began in April 1807, and it never ended. Binns and Duane could be depended on to denounce each other into the 1820s.[30] Quickly the *Aurora* moved from attacks on anonymous Quadroons to denunciations of Boileau.[31]

The battle between the Philadelphia Democrats and the Snyderites broke new ground in Pennsylvania politics. For the first time both groups involved openly and proudly identified themselves as democrats from the beginning. The Snyderites managed to push the Philadelphia Democrats onto uncertain terrain. For the first time that group's enemies could not be dismissed as hostile to arbitration, in support of McKean, opposed to the impeachment of the supreme court judges, or scions of the Philadelphia entrepreneurial, manufacturing, commercial, and financial Jeffersonian community. The Snyderites boldly denounced the Philadelphia Democrats and shouted just as loudly that they were democrats and plain common men.

The Snyderites were ingenious politicians. They managed to invest lasting legitimacy in the category of Philadelphia politics that the Quids, in fits and starts, had begun to construct — the democrat who believed that the Philadelphia Democrats were the greatest threat to democracy. In folksy and even semicomic editorials, the *Democratic Press* introduced this new political character to the Philadelphia region. One editorial was written by "a steady and uniform Whig from the commencement of the revolutionary war to the present day." This writer had habitually taken no paper but the *Aurora*. He admitted that he had initially assumed that the recent charges against Leib were simply part of the latest Quid plot. But coming across an issue of the *Democratic Press*, he suddenly remembered a deeply held belief, "that although accustomed to storms and tempests, I am not without fears and apprehensions that, with bad management, and the poison of political hypocrites, our political barge may be upset; indeed it would betray the greatest weakness to suppose that anything can injure us so much as division among ourselves." With that concern in mind, the Whig read the *Democratic Press* and was shocked to learn that Leib was provoking such divisions.[32] Such editorials created a new position, one from which very ordinary men could oppose Leib in the name of democracy. The Snyderites were protected from the charge that they were secret Federalists, for they could counter that they were actually capable of placing a clodhopper in the governor's chair. Indeed, it was Leib who threatened their chances.

The *Democratic Press* continued to print editorials and letters to the editor from self-described former Leib supporters who were now grateful to the Snyderites for providing them with a way to support democracy and defeat a demagogue.[33] The Snyderites also made this campaign more credible by attracting Philadelphians who were well-known opponents of the Quids. Chief among them was Walter Franklin, who along with Caesar A. Rodney had defended the journeymen cordwainers. The debate in Philadelphia at the time of the trial had ignored Franklin's position. He joined the Snyderites believing that they more closely represented his commitment to an economy shaped entirely by the market and a government determined to allow unfettered competition between producers in that market. By attracting Franklin the Snyderites were able to publish the views of a prominent Philadelphian who was anti-Quid and opposed to Leib. Franklin wrote in the *Democratic Press* that "happily for the cause of Democracy . . . the proscriptions of the *Aurora* have lost their terrors — and a difference of opinion with William Duane is now no longer considered as a crime against Republicanism." Franklin became a Snyderite leader and later served as attorney general in Snyder's cabinet.[34]

Anticipating Snyder's victory in the next gubernatorial election, the Snyderites were determined that the Philadelphia Democrats would receive no credit or gain from his success. The *Democratic Press* even denounced the *Aurora*'s efforts to assist Snyder and insisted that Duane and Leib could not pretend to be his supporters.[35] By fall 1807 the Snyderites had managed to make the breach all but irreparable. The Philadelphia Democrats expelled Binns from the Society of the Friends of the People, and the Snyderites began to create their own democratic societies and held separate democratic meetings.[36] By the time of the off-year election, the *Democratic Press* was printing articles by Boileau praising Binns for courageously denouncing candidates Duane and Leib.[37]

Not surprisingly, given the sustained attack on him and the divisions among city democrats, Duane lost his bid to become a state senator. He ran in Philadelphia, where the Philadelphia Democrats were weakest. Leib, running in the much safer Northern Liberties, managed reelection, but he received the fewest votes of the six representatives elected from the county. None of the six were Quids. The Snyderites argued that the results proved that Duane and Leib did not enjoy the trust of the majority and should be prevented from holding important positions in the party. The Philadelphia Democrats countered that the two had done quite well, given the unprecedented attack by those whom they had once considered allies and fellow democrats.[38]

But Leib had been reelected. He stayed in the state legislature in 1808. In 1808 Snyder would again run for governor. The Snyderites were determined that by the election Leib would be out of the party. They would build such a following for Snyder that they would not need whatever votes the Philadelphia Democrats could deliver. The Snyderites founded the Society of Independent Democrats and at its meetings planned the proscription of Duane and Leib. The group gave Walter Franklin a prominent role in the new organization, easing the concerns of those Philadelphia Jeffersonians who did not trust the Quids.[39]

But the Snyderites wanted Snyder to win convincingly. They hoped to show that he was the overwhelming choice of virtually all Pennsylvanians while simultaneously demonstrating that the Philadelphia Democrats were vicious opponents of the state's first genuinely democratic governor. Thus, starting in late 1807 the Snyderites began to allow the Quids back into democratic politics. They bargained from a position of strength, offering the Quids the chance to join the ascendant political party. They also made a convincing case that by joining them, the Quids would prevent the Philadelphia Democrats from enacting their frightening legislation. As a show of good faith, the Snyderites stopped McKean's impeachment inquiry.[40] But the Snyderites also demanded that the Quids accept arbitration, popular politics, the likelihood of obscure men in positions of power, and an economy intended to encourage social mobility and a basic equality of condition. The Quids could participate in democratic politics, but by doing so they would help to build a world that did not readily identify the notable men whom the Quids considered the obvious leaders and thinkers, those sorts whom they fancied themselves to be.

Alexander J. Dallas resisted this amalgamation more than most. He wrote to Caesar A. Rodney that Pennsylvania had become a "tyranny of printers." Democratic newspapers were "no longer the agents but are become the masters of party." The only issue left, Dallas feared, was "the question whether Binns or Duane shall be the dictator."[41] But Dallas was in the minority among the Quids. The Snyderites sincerely sought the Quids' support, and the Quids were grateful to them for so forcefully and successfully challenging Duane and Leib, something the Quids had tried and failed to do. Furthermore, by 1807 the Quids had to make a decision about their political future. After 1806 the tensions with Great Britain that would eventually lead to the War of 1812 returned. From 1807 to 1809 the Jefferson and Madison administrations pursued their most vigorous foreign policies to date, the Embargo and Non-Intercourse Acts.[42] The years 1807 and 1808 were difficult ones in which to emphasize differences between Jeffersonians. The Quids could never accept the Philadelphia Democrats, but, at least during those years, most Quids found it difficult to justify attacks on the Snyderites. The Madison administration expected all Jeffersonians to unite in troubling times during precisely those two years when Snyder emerged in Pennsylvania as the nearly inevitable future governor. These were not years that would suffer subtle distinctions or qualifications. After the British frigate *Leopard* fired on the USS *Chesapeake* off Cape Henry outside Norfolk, most Quids found it impossible to denounce all but the most heinous Jeffersonians.

The Quids and their fellow Jeffersonians were furious about the renewal of British hostilities. They supported the Embargo and Non-Intercourse Acts and tentatively accepted Snyderite overtures.[43] Thus, as the Snyderites denounced Leib and Duane, the Quids began to make suggestions that appealed to the Snyderites. Leading Quid and revolutionary hero John Dickinson privately urged McKean to consider reform. With McKean's reelection "a check ha[d] been given to dangerous projects; but no decisive victory ha[d] been obtained over the body of the revolutionists." Dickinson insisted that the majority of Pennsylvanians had been successfully agitated because there were real problems with the legal system and the judiciary. The state needed more courts and judges to curb delay, and the statutes needed to be reduced and simplified. Most grievances could be redressed within existing constitutional boundaries.[44] In a speech given to the legislature shortly after receiving Dickinson's letter, McKean announced that every fair criticism of the judiciary could be remedied by the legislature without violating the constitution. McKean acknowledged that

> the law which they [the legislature] dispense, whether statute law or common law, may be annulled or modified. The delay of justice may be obviated by increasing the number of judges in proportion to the obvious increase of judicial business; or by instituting local tribunals where local causes demand a more constant exercise of jurisdiction. With this view of the subject, and anxious to destroy every pretense for an attack upon our constitution, I pray you gentlemen to engage head and heart, in every necessary, in every salutary reform.[45]

The governor's son and cabinet member Joseph B. McKean also discussed judicial reform with McKean's comptroller general, Samuel Bryan. Joseph McKean acknowledged that the Quids had to alleviate the pressure on the courts, for "the delay is now so great it amounts, in effect, to a denial of justice."[46]

During McKean's final term, additional judicial districts were added, and the legislature lessened the domination enjoyed by the state supreme court over the lower courts. The Quids also accepted the limited $100 Act that had been passed by the legislature. The act denied jurisdiction to arbitrators over all questions of property title regardless of value and required that both parties to a suit valued at over $5.33 accept the arbitrator's decision for it to be binding. Joseph B. McKean credited Quid flexibility with easing political tensions.[47] As the Quids became reconciled to the likelihood of Snyder's ascendancy, and began to accept the Snyderites' overtures, the Philadelphia Democrats found it difficult to set the terms of debate. Though the Philadelphia Democrats considered McKean and the judiciary as obnoxious as ever, the governor skillfully worked to give other concerned Jeffersonians reason to trust him. McKean began to instruct his judicial appointees to work to accommodate the concerns of the people. During his final term, for example, he appointed Federalist William Tilghman to the state supreme court. In his letter of acceptance Tilghman made clear that he understood the political climate in which he was expected to function. He accepted his appointment with "real diffidence and humility" and was "well aware of the difficulties and dangers of my situation."[48]

As the gubernatorial election of 1808 and the end of McKean's career neared, the Quids' original concerns and the disgust they felt for the politics of the Philadelphia Democrats remained. For most Quids the indecision they felt about throwing themselves on the mercy of whichever palatable Snyderites would have them disappeared in 1808. As McKean's term ended, the Federalists demanded a return of the favor they had done the Quids in 1805. No radical of any stripe was acceptable to them. Thus the Federalists were "resolved not to be under the direction of the Quids" during the upcoming election. Instead, they would run their own candidate, perhaps James Ross, whom McKean had defeated in 1799 and again in 1802. Joseph Hopkinson reasoned that "the Quids, if they value their offices or professions will be obliged to join us." Hopkinson also thought that what he considered the anticommercial measures of Jefferson's administration made the Quids' presence in the Jeffersonian party untenable.[49]

The Federalists' potential revival due to the frustration with embargo and nonintercourse, and the demands they made of the Quids, served to remind most Quids of why they had become Jeffersonians in the first place. Though the Federalists tried gamely to function in the new world of democracy, their attitudes toward this world, which ranged from profound ambivalence to contempt and disgust, could not be disguised. Federalist unwillingness to fully embrace the ideal of democratized opportunity and social mobility was clearest in New England. But even in Pennsylvania the differences remained pronounced between the Quids' faith in rising, prosperous citizens selecting the proper candidates to ensure mobility and prosperity for all, and James Ross's continued commitment to a naturally ordered society of social distinctions. The Federalists' possible resurgence in 1808 ultimately served to force most Quids, particularly Quid leaders, to reiterate their commitment to the party of Jefferson, and in Pennsylvania to Snyder.[50]

The Federalists soon realized "that the Quids [were] at present determined to yield to no man who is not of their party." The Federalists suggested both Ross and William Tilghman, who were respected by Dallas and other leading Quids. But most Quids understood that they had no choice but Snyder, and those who could not, as yet, vote for him were equally opposed to supporting a Federalist as that party denounced the policies of Jefferson and Madison. Those Quids ran one of their own for governor, John Spayd.[51] Eventually the Federalists concluded that "a cordial union with the Quids under [the Federalist] banner is not to be hoped for." The Pennsylvania Federalists, following the suggestion of the party's New York Corresponding Committee, futilely but "decidedly [were] of the opinion, that the Federalists, as a party, ought to nominate and support . . . candidates *of their own*."[52]

The Quids soon realized that Spayd's effort was equally futile. Further, given the gravity of the international situation, it was essential to keep Pennsylvania Jeffersonian. Splitting the party, with the Federalists again running their own candidate, courted disaster. If Snyder was to be the next governor, then the Quids had to show that they were worthy of his attention and deserved his ear. Quietly the Quids abandoned Spayd for Snyder. Federalist state supreme court justice Jasper Yeats reported to Chief Justice Tilghman that leading Quids, such as their colleague Hugh Henry Brackenridge, had decided to vote for Snyder.[53]

The Quids' decision was momentous. They soberly concluded by 1808 that they could not be leaders in Pennsylvania's democratic political culture. Their wealth, talents, inclinations, and expectations meant that they would lose the battle for the majority. But though they could not lead, they still might influence. The Quids had conceived and articulated certain crucial ideas, ideas that if wielded by less suspect figures might prove convincing to the voters. Most significant among them, the Quids had connected democracy to the protection of individual prosperity and accumulation and had provided a well-structured defense of entrepreneurs such as the master cordwainers of Philadelphia. They had made a consistent argument for a redefinition of democracy. They had insisted that a democratic people lived in a society built on the right and capacity of individuals to pursue their own interests and control whatever resources they could accumulate through their own labor. Quid democracy emerged in response to the democracy of the Philadelphia Democrats. Because of the Quids, popular politics of a sort and a brand of economic development based on the internal economy and expected social mobility were linked. Without the challenge of the Philadelphia Democrats, the Quids would probably not have been so willing to take democracy seriously. But because they did, they were among the very first Americans to fuse democracy and capitalism so openly, completely, and coherently.

The Quids' political economy was one of the earliest and most articulate statements of a body of thought that was emerging in a variety of places. Indeed, what made the Quids exceptional was how little they had to change their thinking over time to arrive at the conclusions they did. But after 1805 even some of the most prominent Jeffersonians, particularly Madison and younger men influenced by him, were beginning to support a more diverse and dynamic domestic economy than late eighteenth-century republican theorists had generally sought.[54] Increasingly after 1805, Quid ideas did not stand out as sharply as they once had in the party of Jefferson.

Though the Quids were among the most vocal Jeffersonians when conceiving these ideas, by 1808 they had realized that they could not set policy in Pennsylvania. Nevertheless, they hoped that their participation in Jeffersonian politics would continue to shape the state's political discussion. The Quids had articulated what they hoped would be a politics and a political economy that would moderate Jeffersonian democracy and defuse the tensions within Pennsylvania's Jeffersonian party. They ended up contributing crucial beliefs that shaped a democratized and capitalist economy and society, beliefs that would emerge in the nineteenth century as the core of what was uniquely American.

By 1808 the Quids were willing to support Snyder, hoping that the rural radicals would shape democracy in Pennsylvania in ways compatible with the Quids' ideals. The Snyderites were thus able to rid themselves of many troublesome issues left over from 1805 while seeming to engage in meaningful compromise with the Quids. As part of their campaign, the Snyderites declared that they would not support a constitutional convention after Snyder became governor. They argued that the majority had rejected a convention by reelecting McKean in 1805.[55] The Snyderites' efforts were tremendously effective. They convinced the Quids that it was safe to vote for Snyder.

By 1808 Snyder's election seemed increasingly likely. Thus, those Quids whose greatest priority in the end was thwarting the prospect of seemingly radical democracy in Pennsylvania felt that they could not waste their votes on the Quid protest candidate, John Spayd. They moved closer to the Federalists and their perennial gubernatorial candidate James Ross, though in the end a minority of Quids actually abandoned the Jeffersonian party. Among those Quids who backed Ross was William McCorkle, editor of the *Freeman's Journal*. With the *Freeman's Journal* now a Federalist newspaper, the *Democratic Press* gave space to those Quids opposed to Ross. In return, Quids such as Matthew Carey agreed to denounce the *Freeman's Journal* in the *Democratic Press*.[56]

The Snyderites accomplished all their goals by the end of 1808. Pennsylvanians voted overwhelmingly for Snyder, who defeated Ross and Spayd 67,975 to 39,575 to 4,006, respectively. Snyder was clearly the choice of the democrats, the democrats were obviously a large majority in Pennsylvania, and Duane and Leib had played no role in the democratic victory.[57] Snyder's landslide victory occurred because the Snyderites managed to unite most Jeffersonians in Pennsylvania behind him while excluding the Philadelphia Democrats. They succeeded because they provoked the split with the Philadelphia Democrats and managed to emerge with their democratic reputations intact. The Snyderite campaign truly did ensure that democracy would be the only political ideology and cultural style in Pennsylvania.

The experience of Philadelphia lawyer Charles Jared Ingersoll provides a good example of the lasting implications of the Snyderites' achievement. The son of the Federalist prosecutor of the cordwainers, Charles Jared Ingersoll came of age considering himself a Federalist. Enamored of Thomas McKean, he soon became a Quid, but he continued a friendly correspondence with the New York Federalist Rufus King.[58] In 1807 Ingersoll got into trouble when he was overheard saying that in 1776 the Tories had possessed more talent and intelligence than the Whigs. At the time he was a member of McKean's cabinet, and the *Democratic Press* demanded his resignation.[59] Ingersoll was a young man in 1807, just twenty-seven, and his political future was in jeopardy. Thus, he had every reason to convince himself that a state governed by Snyder would not descend into a Philadelphia Democrat–dominated, Jacobinic anarchy. To elect their man in the fashion they wished, the Snyderites needed the support of Pennsylvania's Charles Jared Ingersoll. Ingersoll realized by 1809 that there was no Pennsylvania politics other than clodhopper democracy. He joined the Snyderites and by 1813 had a mutually beneficial working relationship with John Binns. Ingersoll remained a democrat, eventually supported Andrew Jackson, and even flirted with Locofocoism.[60]

Perhaps the single most dramatic example of the Snyderites' success was their alliance with Tench Coxe. Coxe, initially a member of Alexander Hamilton's staff at the Treasury, had been a leading Quid. The Snyderites took special care to recruit him. A Philadelphia supporter of Snyder, William Petrekin, wrote to Coxe during the gubernatorial campaign that "I was informed, some time towards the last of the year 1805, that you had seceded from the democratic party and joined the Federalists in the character of what is called a Quid — this I could not account for on any known principles. I always thought since our first acquaintance, that if democracy was in any man inherent, constitutional, and an intrinsic quality, you were that man." Petrekin knew that Coxe could not believe "the absurd wicked story respecting the division of property" propagated by the Quids in 1805. Petrekin could only conclude that Coxe had been driven from the Jeffersonian party by character assassination and demagoguery. Petrekin wrote that Coxe and many others "who I still believe are democrats in their hearts" had been forced to leave the party. But Petrekin assured Coxe that most Philadelphians "deplored the wanton and unqualified abuse poured out in the *Aurora* against every man of our party who dared express a sentiment different from the editor, and those attached to him. I had often my fears that this system of fulmination and intolerance would one day or other produce a fatal schism in the party, and I have no doubt but it was this that engendered Quidism in Pennsylvania."

But times had changed, and Petrekin argued that the *Democratic Press* now protected true democrats from the *Aurora*'s libels. Petrekin offered Coxe a chance to return to where he belonged: "If I have not entirely mistaken your character, you must long for an opportunity to escape from every appearance of communication with [the Federalists] . . . which opportunity now presents itself. The *Aurora* party in the state is now comparatively nothing. . . . If you and the rest of the sound principled of the third party will unite with those democrats whom Duane . . . calls dangerous, you will annihilate that faction." Petrekin insisted that Coxe should forget past concerns. He could comfortably support Snyder, "a man of business, intelligence, and independence." Petrekin felt that men such as Coxe and Matthew Carey, whom he named in the letter, would find much to support and celebrate in Snyderite Pennsylvania.[61] Coxe accepted the Snyderites' offer, and by November 1808 he was working for Snyder's election. Coxe died in 1824 after helping to deliver Pennsylvania to Andrew Jackson.[62] In addition to Ingersoll and Coxe, the Snyderites won the support of prominent Quid activists such as Blair McClenachan.[63]

The Snyderites did not just secure support from the Quids. After 1809 the Philadelphia Democrats faced political oblivion. Between 1809 and 1814 Philadelphia Democrats such as Thomas Leiper, Joseph Clay, Frederick Wolbert, George Bartram, Michael Bright, James Carson, and Andrew Geyer also joined the Snyderites.[64] As early as 1807 Duane was beginning to feel the pressures of political proscription and defeat. He also faced financial ruin from libel suits and physical danger from challenges to duels. Duane complained that "the state I am kept in is almost intolerable, between law suits and assassins." He promised to "kick as long as my boots land" and spoke of "my resolution . . . not to be driven from my post."[65] This last promise Duane could not keep. The *Aurora*'s circulation plummeted after 1807. In 1809 Binns announced that a "very great increase of printing and newspaper business" forced him to relocate to a larger press "at present known by the name of the *Aurora* office."[66] The Snyderites had finally succeeded where all others had failed. The Philadelphia Democrats were defeated.

Upon arriving in Philadelphia, and particularly as they moved closer to taking power, the Snyderites articulated the democratic political economy they planned to pursue. They hoped that Pennsylvania's economy would provide the general prosperity and social mobility that would make the entire state flourish as their rural counties once had. The key element in their vision was a sustained economic growth and development in which all Pennsylvanians would participate, and from which they would all benefit.

The *Democratic Press* called for a bankruptcy law, "some fixed regulation which while it protect[s] the unfortunate, should not do injustice to the prosperous, or deprive the commonwealth of the industry of any of its citizens."[67] The Snyderites sought a system in which credit was readily available and entrepreneurs could borrow without worrying that bankruptcy would mean utter ruin. The Snyderites also criticized imprisonment for debt because it deterred many energetic men from borrowing.

But the Snyderites opposed the way the nation's credit networks were organized in the early nineteenth century. Geared mostly toward the needs of large-scale merchants engaged in foreign trade, banks generally made only short-term, ninety-day loans. The Snyderites argued that such loans primarily met the needs of "the speculating foreign merchant, the stock-jobber, the adventurer," who were "the principal borrowers; while the farmer, the manufacturer, the mechanic, and those who would really improve the interior of the country, by roads, by canals, and consequently by an increased population, find no encouragement to do either, in any facility hitherto afforded by the legislature, nor in the inclination of the money lenders to loan the necessary sums, for periods which all similar improvements require for their completion." But the Snyderites were confident that they could achieve "a diversion of the public mind from exterior commerce to internal trade, improvement, and intercourse."[68]

The Snyderites hoped to alter the way banks issued credit so that as many producers as possible would acquire access to productive resources. Thus the Snyderites praised banks and considered them a vital part of their effort to build a democratic political economy. But the Snyderites believed that "the establishers of banks have hitherto neglected to attend to the accommodation of the industrious lower classes in society."[69] In the legislature the Snyderites approved additional branches of the Bank of Philadelphia and also voted to incorporate the Farmers and Mechanics Bank. The charter of this new bank required that "a majority of the directors . . . be farmers, mechanics, or manufacturers actually employed in their respective professions." The Snyderite state legislature also provided a charter for the Bank of the Northern Liberties.[70]

The Snyderites planned to increase the number of banks and to incorporate banks administered by actual producers. By doing so they intended to extend access to credit farther down the social ladder, to most farmers and mechanics. The solution to monopolies of credit and perceived disparities in economic power was to dramatically increase the amount of capital and distribute it to new and energetic men seeking to develop the internal economy.[71]

To develop the domestic market, Snyderites in the legislature and through their newspapers continually promoted internal improvements calling for turnpikes, bridges, and canals. The Snyderites wanted roads to link the west and east and canals to connect the state's rivers to each other and to the Ohio River system.[72] Snyderites such as state legislator Abraham McKinney kept alive the original Snyderite insistence that such development be a joint venture between the state and private capital.[73]

Leading Snyderites such as Nathaniel B. Boileau captured this Snyderite spirit for improvement and led the campaign to develop the state. As a legislator, then Speaker of the House, and eventually as Secretary of the Commonwealth under Governor Snyder, Boileau constantly argued that economic development was a positive good. He insisted in the state legislature that

> the making of roads, improving the navigation of rivers, and cutting canals, is highly conducive to the promotion of manufacturing, commercial and agricultural interests of every country, particularly those situated like the United States, the extent of which embraces such a diversity of climate; affords such a variety of productions, intersected by so many streams of navigable waters, that if properly improved, it would furnish its inhabitants all the necessaries and most of the luxuries of life, independently of any other nation.[74]

The Snyderites called for a diversified economy, and legislators like Boileau wanted internal improvements to help stimulate the development of domestic manufacturing. The Snyderites also called for bounties and premiums. But unlike the Federalists, the Snyderites simultaneously championed a protective tariff so that American artisans would be able to compete with British manufacturers and be in a position to earn the premiums and bounties. The *Democratic Press* suggested raising the impost to 20 percent.[75] The Snyderites scoffed at any who imagined that the United States could not develop manufactures to supply its own needs. Bursting with confidence as they came to power in one of the nation's most prosperous states, the Snyderites lauded Pennsylvania's already extensive manufacturers:

our leather branch such as the tanners, shoemakers, saddlers, coach and harness makers, and parchment makers. . . . To these, add the complete manufacture of all the iron, copper, tin, brass, wool, flax, and hemp we can produce, procure, or import: To these add a very considerable domestic and shop manufacture of cotton: To these add our considerable breweries, and our innumerable great and small distilleries: To these add wares of lead and tin, and pewter, and various other mixed metals and composition: To these add our . . . coopers wares, and other manufactures of wood; manufactures of stone, clay, and sand; our tallow chandlers' goods, chocolate, mustard, refined sugar, the manufactures of the dairy, and of the fishery articles.[76]

The Snyderites argued that manufacturing, agriculture, and commerce were mutually beneficial. A sizable manufacturing population provided farmers a domestic market for their produce.[77] With more banks, democratized access to credit, and protective tariffs, actual producers could take advantage of growing opportunities. Indeed, as the international situation grew more turbulent after 1807, the Snyderites were able to defend domestic manufactures as a patriotic alternative to dangerous foreign trade. As fear of Britain grew, the Snyderites were able to combine their genuine patriotism with their domestic agenda. The development of the domestic economy was not simply an interested and sordid grasp for profit. Instead, the Snyderites pursued developmental measures "for such weighty reasons as the necessary support of our agriculture, the protection of our seamen, and the employment of the injured merchants and mariners, and seaport artisans and laborers."[78] The Snyderites believed that pursuit of economic development and general prosperity were patriotic acts that could end American dependence on foreign markets and provide the United States true independence for the first time.[79]

Simon Snyder dedicated his administrations to the development of a democratic political economy in Pennsylvania. In message after message he called for internal improvements and commitment to manufacturing. He regularly insisted to Pennsylvania Jeffersonians that "the union, harmony, and happiness of our constituents are best promoted by a mutual interest and dependence; a facility of exchanging produce and manufactures; and a frequency of intercourse." The governor called on the state legislature to pursue "such public measures as will best promote the real substantial happiness and prosperity of our country."[80]

The Snyderites sought to distance themselves from radical legal and political reforms intended to give poorer and more obscure Pennsylvanians greater control over economic decision making. Their peaceful control of the state depended on not reviving the issues of 1805. Thus, the Snyderites relentlessly insisted that economic development structured by the state legislature in the way that they proposed would produce basic economic and social equality. Since the market by itself would undo unequal economic and social conditions, the state government — the instrument of a democratic people — did not have to concern itself with those issues. The Snyderites sincerely intended that their political economy produce a society of independent producers largely able to avoid structural dependence on resources and capital controlled by others. They believed that Snyder's election as well as clodhopper control of the legislature meant the triumph of democracy. Snyderite political economy would protect and strengthen that democracy. Once they came to power, the Snyderites were convinced that they had secured democratic political, social, and economic equality. Snyderites could now create their ideal society, one where

> an extensive and fertile territory, an active, industrious and intelligent population, and a wise and beneficent system of government, present the materials of opulence and social comfort, which it is the duty of the legislature, by a steady exertion of the common energy of the state, to cultivate and increase. The public purse, entrusted to their care for the common benefit amply supplies the means — and the public voice, and the public necessity loudly demand their application to the purpose of internal improvement. To bring into a productive state the large masses of land which lie wholly uncultivated; to increase the value of those which are partially improved; to stimulate industry by furnishing it with a motive for activity; increase the public wealth, and distribute it in due proportions through all the parts of the state, and thereby as far as possible to equalize the condition of her citizens: and above all to draw together and bind with the ties of common interest, the citizens of the same community; are the results which the legislature, by a liberal policy, may contribute to produce.[81]

The Snyderites' reliance on the market to produce social and economic equality, essential conditions for a democratic society, terrified the Philadelphia Democrats. They were also wholly committed to diversified economic development. The city radicals continued to support policies that they considered necessary to produce it, most notably in William Duane's pamphlet *Politics for American Farmers* (1807).[82] In addition to Duane's pamphlet, from

1807 to 1814 the *Aurora* continued to support internal improvements, manufacturing, and the democratization of credit and banking. British bellicosity after 1807 only confirmed the Philadelphia Democrats' worst fears about that most dangerous nation. Developing the internal economy became a crucial way to avoid confrontation with Britain and a disastrous war. The Philadelphia Democrats hoped that by turning inward the nation would radically alter its political, social, and economic structure. Internal development would empower producers. The nation would then avoid Great Britain, lessen its reliance on foreign markets, and develop an alternative economy to the one dominated by large-scale merchants engaged in foreign trade.[83]

The Philadelphia Democrats did not believe that switching from an economy geared toward foreign trade and the interests of great merchants to an internal economy, which was intended to meet the needs of actual producers, would naturally or automatically ensure social and economic equality. They worried about the dramatic increase in banking and credit that fueled internal development. After 1806 the Philadelphia Democrats agreed that committing to the internal market was more crucial than ever and the only way to keep the nation from a dreadful war with Britain. Since internal economic diversity and development needed to occur immediately and rapidly, it was imperative that the people secure true democratic means to oversee this development. If left unsupervised by democracy, the market would simply produce new, but no less dangerous, concentrations of wealth and power. The *Aurora* nominated the internal improvement and bank corporations as the most likely threats. The paper insisted that "the alarming increase of banks and bank paper in the U.S. threatens the most serious evils, to the community, inasmuch as the corporate bodies, by whom they are issued, are too frequently mere artificial creatures." Without some form of understood and irresistible public control, the corporations' wealthy backers would disappear at the first sign of difficulty. They would be especially able to renege on their obligations to the people if bankruptcy laws limited their liability. Those who controlled the corporations would then "leave only the sad variety of note holders . . . and the miserable skeleton of what the laws call a corporation."[84]

The Philadelphia Democrats demanded public or popular control of the exciting, but potentially dangerous, new orientation toward internal development. A powerful historical consciousness and a strong commitment to the rights of the public informed their concerns. They insisted that those rights had to be favored over the interests of a powerful and privileged few when and if those rights and interests proved incompatible.

In a stunning essay titled "On the Evils Which have Proved Fatal to Republics," the *Aurora* sought to elucidate these themes. The essay defended the agrarian law — that concept so frightening to men of wealth and standing (and those possessing the most modest competences). The *Aurora* noted that people had come to shudder at the very mention of the term. But the paper insisted that this fear resulted from a selective reporting of history that served the interests of the wealthy and powerful. The agrarian law was in fact a reaction to great injustices done to the people in the past. Lest anyone think that the people's rights could never be systematically violated, the *Aurora* provided an example from recent memory. It urged its readers to recall "the plunder of the American soldiers of the Revolution, and the cruel and disgraceful sacrifice of their rights to the rapacious scheme which was an associate link of the chain of measures that accompanied the funding system."

The *Aurora* next proceeded to tell the story of the Roman world as understood by William Duane. Initially the Romans had distributed property equally and so "rendered poverty unknown in that happy commonwealth." But, as leading Romans began to awaken to the possibilities for greater wealth and power, a "spirit of greedy speculation and covetousness arose in the very body of the government." Patricians began to systematically violate public rights, "and this was first exhibited by the encroachment of the patricians on lands which were set apart as commonage for the public use." As leading citizens used the state for their own purposes, "large portions were from time to time fenced in and appropriated to the use of private individuals . . . so that the people were defrauded." This consolidation of property continued until "at length the commonage lands disappeared. . . . Stately structures and walls enclosing vast tracts occupied the space. Troops of slaves manicured and cultivated for the use of the patricians."[85] According to the *Aurora*, when the people complained, they were denounced as clodpolls and silenced by the judiciary. The paper explained that

we have been more particular in narrating this great event in Roman history because the historians, both ancient and modern, have seriously censured the Roman people for their discontent as being so seditious as to assert their rights; and applauded the most barbarous and corrupt acts of the patricians perpetrated in support of their robbery. From Livy down to Vertot every historian has loaded the Roman people with reproach and treated the agrarian law as a prodigy of sedition, as proof of the turbulent and impatient character of republics. The agrarian law, which was intended originally to wrest from usurpers and restore to the virtuous citizens the lands that were their property, has been held forth constantly as a terrible turbulence and of a disposition in republics to plunder the rich. . . . [O]ur purpose in quoting this portion of history, is to apply the principle of experience to circumstances in our own country, that we may learn to guard in early time against the dangerous consequences of the rapacious spirit of monopoly.[86]

Like the Snyderites, the Philadelphia Democrats drew a firm distinction "between the cultivator of a field, or garden, the ingenious artist or mechanic, and the dealer in stocks, the calculator of differences and chances, a biped called a broker or a banker, or an usurer, or even a merchant." Both groups of democrats longed for a time "when real wealth [is] acquired by real industry and economy." Both championed the cause and interests of "the really and substantially useful and valuable citizens, the farmers, mechanics, tradesmen and laborers of the community." But the Philadelphia Democrats believed that without direct public involvement in the maintenance of the public interest — sustained social and economic equality — economic development of any variety could "introduce also great inequality in the fortunes of the citizens, a principle which has ever been considered as subversive of republicanism, which flourishes in the greatest purity and vigor when as great an equality of property and uniformity of habits exists as is consistent with security."[87]

Thus the Philadelphia Democrats could support internal development only if the Jeffersonian party in Pennsylvania continued to champion the Philadelphia Democrats' political ideals of 1805. The *Aurora* continued to denounce the common law, and when it did so, it invoked the fate of the journeymen cordwainers.[88] The Philadelphia Democrats continued to demand a constitutional convention and insisted that the power of the state house of representatives be increased at the expense of the governor, senate, and judiciary.[89]

Because the Snyderites rejected all but moderate arbitration legislation, which included appeal to the law courts, the Philadelphia Democrats sought to expand the power of juries. Since Snyder's election would not rid the state of independent judges and of its basic legal structure, the Philadelphia Democrats began to insist that the power relations within the courtroom be altered. After all, it was still the case, the *Aurora* insisted, that

artful counsel know how to bring the cause before the court; and the court, by deciding what are called points of law, (but more properly

deciding what shall be law) on the trial, and in the particular cases, have
the power of producing what verdict they choose, and accomplishing
the most flagrant injustice. . . . [T]he decisions of judges is the key to the
lock, it is the screw to the press; and it is the most artful and terrible
engine, in a country which believes itself free, that profligate ingenuity
could deliver or credulity tolerate.

The Philadelphia Democrats continued to argue that "the judges very often
discover that the law, as written, may be made to mean something which the
legislature never thought of. The greatest part of their decisions are in fact,
and in effect, making new laws."[90]

The solution was to make the jury a real check on the judge. Since the
Snyderites were trusting in development and the market alone to cure social
ills, and because they did nothing to diminish the power of the antidemocratic elements of the government, juries of the people had to be given true
decision-making power. The Philadelphia Democrats could no longer trust
a Snyderite legislature. Thus they proposed a system where the legislature
made law with "the law to stand as a general rule, but the jury to have the
right to except out of it cases which the principle of justice would direct,
could any harm accrue? . . . If the legislators do their best to make just general laws, juries will do their best to make just special decisions, and consequently the law as a general rule will be just, and the exceptions receive just
decisions." The proposal would merely "give the jury the power of arbitration, so much approved of."[91]

The Philadelphia Democrats acknowledged that detractors would argue
that "all property will be held by the uncertain tenure of the judgments of
a set of ignorant jurors, instead of the known law of the land, guarded by
wise judges who know the law." But, they responded, judges did not know
the law; rather, they made up the law. And, incredibly, an administration that
called itself democratic did nothing about it. It insisted that economic development would serve the needs and interests of all. And it left the decisions
about disputes and injuries that resulted from that development to law courts
dominated by judges who were beyond the people's control. "What," the
Philadelphia Democrats asked,

are the prospects before us? The rapid swelling codes are increasing the
labyrinth of law, while the increase of mental refinement in nice techni-
cal disquisitions banish already every student not above a mediocrity of
talents, and exclude all hope of the people ever coming to a knowledge
of the law. There has been a constant complaint of the ambiguity of the

law. . . . [T]he remedy for this enormous evil is extremely simple and likewise very safe — A single law giving the jury the power over the law, when justice requires it. . . . If the law of the land gives you relief well and good, and if not, you have an appeal to the law of justice and equity.[92]

By keeping alive the issues of 1805, the Philadelphia Democrats placed tremendous pressure on the Snyderites. The Snyderites could maintain their coalition only by giving up demands for radical legal and political reform. To answer concerns about concentrations of wealth and power, they placed their faith in the democratization of economic opportunity. They also argued that it made a qualitative difference when this development was initiated at the state level, largely by a state legislature dominated by Jeffersonian democrats like themselves. Yet after Snyder's election the Philadelphia Democrats continued to insist that "we have been so long anxiously waiting for a reform in the state, . . . unless we commence at our first entrance into power, we shall always remain under the dominion of arbitrary and oppressive laws."[93]

In response the Snyderites only grew more forceful in their insistence that genuine and general economic opportunity would create the social and economic equality necessary for democracy. As the Philadelphia Democrats' proposed reforms did not materialize, they began to identify themselves as the true democrats, or the "democrats of the old school." Old school democrats were "not the brawlers for constitutional reform and a correction of abuses when OUT, and the idolaters of power and position when IN."[94]

Repeated demands for a constitutional convention and radical reform forced the Snyderites to insist more vociferously than ever that state-based and untrammeled development, overseen by clodhopper legislators, would make the Philadelphia Democrats' extreme plans unnecessary.[95] Needing to respond to the Philadelphia Democrats, the Snyderites more forcefully praised banks, entrepreneurs, and the worthy contributions made to a democratic society by men with capital. They had to believe that they were correct, for the Snyderites shared the Philadelphia Democrats' commitment to a basic or rough social and economic equality of condition. They had to champion their faith that state-based and unqualified economic development produced such social and economic conditions. If they did not, they would be forced back to the failed strategy of 1805 and the radical proposals to deal with inequities in wealth and power. One could rather easily imagine those solutions creating more injustice than they resolved. Further, the Snyderites were already satisfied that pushing the program of 1805 would keep them from power. In the end it came down to that. Good and decent men like Simon Snyder and Nathaniel B. Boileau truly believed that their presence in government would ensure the justice and equality without which democracy could not survive.

The need ever more stridently to promote their economic program forced the Snyderites to become uncompromising on issues of economic development and states' rights. That Snyderites — plain common men — would be in positions of power became a crucial response to the concerns and criticisms of the Philadelphia Democrats. Thus the state, and particularly the state legislature, had to remain the fundamental location of policy making. The pressures placed on the Snyderites left them little room to maneuver. Without that room they could not escape the Olmsted affair, one of the most troubling conflicts to occur during Madison's administration involving issues of states' rights and federalism. Because the Snyderites were forced into that unfortunate confrontation, their Quid allies became determined to create some place where they could again confront the Snyderites, whose control of Pennsylvania they had to acknowledge.

The Olmsted affair was the most important source of states' rights theory, and the sharpest confrontation between a state and the national government, between the publication of the Kentucky Resolution in 1798 and the Hartford Convention of 1814.[96] In brief, the Pennsylvanian Gideon Olmsted managed to seize the British ship on which he was imprisoned during the American Revolution. Two Pennsylvania ship captains insisted on helping Olmsted bring the ship into port. They then claimed a share of the spoils. The Pennsylvania admiralty court heard the case in 1778, and its jury decided against Olmsted. Olmsted quickly appealed to the wartime Continental Congress, which decided in his favor. So began a thirty-year, *Bleak House*–like dispute over whether the State of Pennsylvania or various federal institutions had jurisdiction over the case.

By the time the Snyderites took power, the relevant institution of the federal government was the Supreme Court led by Chief Justice John Marshall. Marshall already had a reputation for defending the national government at the expense of the states. The Snyderites did not support his argument for federal judicial review made in *Marbury v. Madison*. Nor would they be happy to see that power extended over state governments in *Fletcher v. Peck* one year after the Olmsted affair. The Snyderites relied on their reputations as committed democrats, and their ability to shape policies at the state level, to answer the criticisms of the Philadelphia Democrats. Now, with Olmsted, they worried that precedent would be set for the federal courts to overturn decisions dealing with property made at the state level.

The Snyderites were not that friendly to President Madison in the first place. They had initially preferred George Clinton for president, the old anti-Federalist who supported states' rights and advocated development overseen at the state level.[97] Thus, the Snyderites were willing to resist the federal government's demand that they turn over the property of the original seizure to Olmsted. At the height of the confrontation Snyder ordered the state militia to prevent federal agents from doing their duty as ordered by the national government.[98] Eventually the Snyderites backed down, and Marshall's decision was implemented.

The Olmsted affair lasted only a few months, but it had two important ramifications. First, it provided an opportunity for the Philadelphia Democrats to continue to criticize the Snyderites. The Snyderites challenged the federal government at an anxious time when Jefferson and Madison's embargo was collapsing, largely because of Federalist resistance at the state level, and when war with Great Britain seemed likely. William Duane must have quite enjoyed equating Snyder with Timothy Pickering and the Snyderites with the Essex Junto.[99] This criticism only forced the Snyderites to be more uncompromising in their positions.

A second and more important result of the Olmsted affair was the reaction of many former Quids. Alexander J. Dallas, at best a profoundly reluctant supporter of Snyder, was the federal district attorney charged with representing the government in the confrontation. He concluded that the Snyderites, though certainly better than the Philadelphia Democrats, were reckless, and that states' rights enabled the wrong sort of people to make important decisions. For the time being, Pennsylvania had the best government it could hope for. But after Olmsted, Dallas and other Quids grew determined to find a place where they could confront the Snyderites. During and after the War of 1812, they would seek to make the national government the crucial locus of policy making.[100]

The Snyderites could defend their conduct in the Olmsted affair because by 1809 they had fully articulated their democratic ideology. Democracy came with complete commitment to economic development implemented at the state level, primarily by the state legislature. When Americans made policy at the more accountable state level, the citizens were more involved in decision making. The Snyderites worked hard to convince Pennsylvania that their political economy and political philosophy would promote a demo-

cratic society. Fine examples of their efforts were the editorials by the Snyderite everyman "Simon Easy" that the *Democratic Press* ran soon after
Binns came to Philadelphia. Easy was "a plain man much better acquainted
with hogs and chickens, calves and horses, ploughing, making butter, and
driving a wagon than writing politics." But in a series of encounters he
proved able to defend Simon Snyder and democracy against all criticism.
Easy could mock the pretensions at sophistication exhibited by urban elites,
but in a folksy and inviting manner he also articulated the blessings of roads,
canals, manufactures, market day, credit, personal improvement and comfort, and the legislature that made those things available to Pennsylvanians.
Easy was the consummate man of business who could penetrate the interested disquisitions of those whom democracy had defeated. But he laughed
at long-winded soliloquies and would rather tend his farm and pass the time
in good company with his neighbors.

The *Democratic Press*'s editorial voice created a democratic vernacular;
it imagined what sort of person a democratic citizen was, how he acted, and
what he expected. Simon Easy mistrusted all airs, lampooned social preten-
sion, and understood that common sense and common men could resolve
the commonwealth's difficulties without windy pomposity. The Snyderites,
in effect, were taking the farce out of *Modern Chivalry*. The captain was the
fool, and Teague O'Regan proved capable of fulfilling the duties thrust
upon him.

Simon Easy, the *Democratic Press* suggested, was Simon Snyder. And the
most obscure man ever elected to executive office up to that point would
always protect the needs and interests of his fellow democratic citizens.[101]
Snyder was the ideal man to lead this party. Truly of obscure origins and
genuinely humble, he even refused an honor guard as he rode triumphantly
into Lancaster for his inauguration. Though his state treasurer William
Findlay suggested it, Snyder responded, "I hate and despise all ostenta-
tion — pomp and parade as anti-democratic. . . . I should feel exceedingly
awkward." Snyder's sentiments were authentic. They were not made less so
by the fact that the *Democratic Press* prominently published his views.[102]

But the Snyderite legacy proved complicated and ultimately produced
unanticipated conditions that not all Snyderites regarded as compatible with
their original ideals. On Snyder's watch, and despite his strongest efforts,
Snyderite belief quickly produced a political economy and a political ideology that rendered increasingly unstable the initial expectation of perpetual
social and economic equality based on a broad direct ownership of productive resources. The Snyderites had to govern while facing the tremendous

pressures that resulted from the Philadelphia Democrats' denunciations and the Quids' revived concerns. In response, after 1808 the Snyderites relied more and more heavily on their assumption that a state's right to control all economic issues arising within its borders and untrammeled economic development would produce the Pennsylvania Jeffersonian ideal of the "happy mediocrity of condition" and a just democratic society. It was the role of the legislature to ensure that no impediments to development arose. This vision of "profitable patriotism" attracted a great many followers.[103]

After 1809, as it grew increasingly difficult to pause and ponder the various possible implications of economic development; it became harder and harder to pose from within mainstream politics what the Philadelphia Democrats had rightly understood to be a valuable critique. The Snyderite William Montgomery insisted that the best way to ensure democracy was to accumulate "honorable wealth" by taking advantage of whatever opportunities arose to develop the domestic economy.[104] But the relentless pressure that resulted from the Philadelphia Democrats' denunciations forced the Snyderites to dispense with nuance and complexity. The more the city radicals demanded the restoration of the platform of 1805, the more the Snyderites had to rely on their answer of "profitable patriotism" — state-based, untrammeled economic development. With the Quids eager after Olmsted to discredit the Snyderites by associating them with irresponsible radical notions, the Snyderites could not safely entertain any ideas that could be portrayed as making property anything less than inviolable and its protection sacrosanct.

The Snyderites had no choice but to make their thought narrower and less supple than their original vision of an egalitarian, democratic Pennsylvania probably required. The polarized climate of Pennsylvania Jeffersonian politics discouraged the Snyderites from rethinking or qualifying as their conception of democracy proved unable to encompass the ever more diverse needs and conditions of the people. Rapidly after 1808 even the Snyderites' clodhopper-conceived, state-based economic development, intended to administer to the needs of the most obscure producer-citizens, could not keep many of those citizens from experiencing conditions that all Pennsylvania Jeffersonians identified as incompatible with democracy. The Snyderites reacted to radical ideas that were potentially quite dangerous and to a new Quid resolve to challenge their localist, clodhopper ethos.[105] In response to this political climate, the Snyderites fashioned an ideology that made it difficult to critique economic processes that quickly began to create mobility and opportunity, but that also produced consolidations of wealth and genuine distress. Had the political conditions been different, had the

Snyderites not had to fear what they viewed as anarchy from one direction and contempt for state legislators and state-based decision making from the other, they might very well have responded to such worrying developments more creatively than they did. The crucible of conflict ensured that they never had that chance.

Snyderites such as William Findlay and Samuel D. Ingham rose in Pennsylvania's Jeffersonian party by championing economic development for its own sake far more uncritically than had Snyder or Boileau. Ingham, among other things, the president of the New Hope and Delaware Bridge Company, attracted entrepreneurial-minded followers along the state's rivers. As the Snyderites demanded more banks, roads, canals, and manufactures, and as the internal economy boomed, stimulated by embargo, nonintercourse, and war, these men could not be faulted for equating "profitable patriotism" with democracy, and democracy with accumulating and developing as much productive property as possible. Increasingly this was an ever more legitimate interpretation of Snyderite belief.

The alternatives seemed to be either the city radicals' disrespect for property or the Quids' increasingly public efforts to make the national government the most important locus of decision making. The Snyderites who emerged after 1808 pursued an expansive entrepreneurial vision that appeared to many Pennsylvanians to be the most attractive option available. Indeed, it seemed to preclude the need for alternatives. Yet in little more than a decade this sanguine faith in an egalitarian outcome would be challenged by the panic of 1819. The combination of a truly inspiring body of thought and the fear to deviate from that thought — a fear that stemmed from the pressure created by the crucible of conflict — meant that when outcomes proved different from expectations, the Snyderites had not been allowed to develop the capacity to adjust. Increasingly after 1805 the answer was clodhopper, state-based decision making and wholesale commitment to economic development. This combination of ideas was the answer in 1808, when it made perfect sense and spoke to a great many Pennsylvanians more movingly than any previous amalgamation of political economy and political philosophy ever had before. It did appear that egalitarianism and capitalism would be fused once and for all. Given the real success of these ideas, and the predisposition to avoid qualification imposed by the crucible of conflict, this combination of ideas remained the solution even after shocking events showed that Snyderite thought could not ensure for all Pennsylvanians conditions that the Snyderites themselves considered necessary for democracy.

The clodhopper solution, reinforced by the crucible of conflict, was a dynamic, localist political economy overseen by clodhoppers. The letters of Findlay, Ingham, and their followers, Snyderites such as Thomas Rogers, Christian Hutter, James Hopkins, Lewis Coryell, Samuel Preston, Jacob Wagener, John Stevens, and above all James Buchanan, burst with plans to build, buy, sell, manufacture, and accumulate. The Findlayite faction of the Snyderite party also attracted energetic and creative second-generation politicians like Samuel McKean and George Mifflin Dallas. These men called for "a general system of improvement in the state" and pursued every profitable scheme imaginable.[106]

The Philadelphia Democrats denounced the full and uncritical embrace of economic development. The *Aurora* decried the frenzied charter of banks and improvement corporations and insisted that this practice allowed the wealthiest investors to control the development of the internal economy. The paper identified Reading and Easton, the Susquehanna River towns and region where many Findlayites lived, as the source of these dangerous values. "We may expect," the *Aurora* somberly predicted, "to see the whole property of this flourishing state, and all its useful industry and frugal habits, about to be sunk into the den of sordid speculation, to the ruin of innocent private families, to the enrichment of the cunning and profligate; and to the total discredit of this prosperous state."[107]

But as Snyder swept to reelection in 1811, the Philadelphia Democrats lost whatever influence in the state they had retained. A staunch Philadelphia Democrat, John Steele, wrote Leib in 1811 that most of his fellows had given up. Though he "hoped there were yet a few that had not put their principles to sleep, I fear a strange stupor seems to prevail. . . . I have not met with a single person . . . that appeared willing to engage in any opposition. They say all attempts to remove Snyder are hopeless." Steele sadly reported that even Duane no longer believed that he could influence state politics.[108]

Yet almost precisely at the time that the Philadelphia Democrats gave up, Snyder lost control of his party. The Findlayites had for some time sought rapid expansion of speculative opportunities in the state. In 1813 Snyder had successfully vetoed a bank bill that raised serious issues of corruption by including many members of the state legislature among the bank directors. But in 1814 the Findlayites passed a bill incorporating forty-two new state banks. This sudden increase was unprecedented, and it shocked more sober Snyderites, who feared that rapid riches meant dangerous accumulations and potentially rapid disasters. Snyder vetoed this bank bill also.[109] He was shocked to learn that the Findlayites had enough power in the legislature to override him. The new banks lent irresponsibly over the next several years and played a crucial role in the panic of 1819, which hit Pennsylvania hard and ruined the prospects and hopes of many. One of the unfortunates was Simon Snyder, who spent 1819, the last year of his life, lamenting the worthlessness of country paper and desperately seeking loans from friends such as John Binns to satisfy his creditors.[110]

Boileau and Binns backed Snyder's veto. The result was that Boileau, Snyder's chosen successor, lost control of the party. In 1817 William Findlay defeated him in the gubernatorial election. Binns also could not find a place in the Jeffersonian party of Findlay, Ingham, and Buchanan. But he did participate in the general consensus of mainstream Pennsylvania politics that celebrated capitalism and that required citizens to live as best they could in a society dominated by the unfettered market. Years later, in his autobiography, Binns confirmed that most of the forty-two banks had been established. The result was "an unprecedented amount of bank notes." Binns recounted that a frenzy of borrowing had occurred as farmers and artisans sought to expand their businesses and lead the good life that the Snyderites promised. Though Pennsylvania developed rapidly, many of the small producers suffered horribly in the panic. Yet, Binns concluded, "Is it not then reasonably clear that, although individuals were thus made bankrupt, the state became benefited and improved? The next inquiry is, did the passage of the law chartering the 40 [sic] banks injure or benefit the state? I have always entertained the opinion that the passage of the act was a benefit to the state. The titles of land became clear, settled, and certain."[111]

The experience of Thomas Leiper, a former Philadelphia Democrat turned Snyderite, also helps to show the final meaning of democracy in Pennsylvania and the function of a state legislature in a democratic society. He also participated in Pennsylvania's emerging democratic capitalist consensus. It is unclear exactly when Leiper switched allegiances, though it seems to have occurred between 1811 and 1815. He opposed the dissolution of the first Bank of the United States, though Duane and Leib demanded it. Leiper, a successful Philadelphia manufacturer, is something of a puzzle. He even confused contemporaries, who could not fathom his initial support of the Philadelphia Democrats.[112] By 1820 Leiper was defending the Quid Matthew Carey and large-scale manufacturing to John Taylor of Caroline.[113] An undated petition from Leiper to the state legislature, which appears to have been written just after the War of 1812, completely captures the democratic legacy, a legacy rapidly producing outcomes that few Snyderites in 1805 could have imagined.

Leiper identified himself as "possessed of a considerable property, consisting of mills and a quarry." He was "desirous to improve the same, by digging a canal." Leiper acknowledged "the personal advantage" he would gain from the canal but had no doubt that it would "be productive of great benefit to the public." Leiper described what he considered the common goal of entrepreneurial citizens and the state legislature to do what was necessary to develop the state, since the public good was synonymous with that development. Leiper informed the legislature that "the prosperity of the commonwealth, therefore, demands that these channels of intercourse should not be wantonly obstructed, nor too strict a regard paid to the territorial rights of those who possess them, at the expense of the public good." The most fundamental rights of the citizenry, and the public good, were enforced, Leiper suggested, when Pennsylvanians "enjoy[ed] the easiest and shortest access to the common market." Therefore, the only restriction on entrepreneurial seizure of and reimbursement for property, the only "political restrictions on the use of private property," should be after a demonstration of serious lasting injury. The fact was that regardless of the temporary injuries done to certain property owners because Leiper built his canal, "every other owner of property upon the creek will eventually be a gainer from the improvement."[114] Increasingly after 1814, arguments like Leiper's could be made in democratic Pennsylvania with fewer and fewer reservations.[115]

The conflict and difficulty of accommodating widely varying needs and interests implicit in Leiper's petition underscored the dilemma that the makers of Pennsylvania Jeffersonian political thought had faced since at least *Commonwealth v. Pullis*. After 1815 it became ever more manifest that the Jeffersonian category "the people" was not sufficient to explain Pennsylvania's (or the nation's) reality of social and economic complexity. Yet the Findlayite-inspired Snyderites were doing nothing more than continuing to obey the wishes of the majority of the voters when they rejected the ideas of the Philadelphia Democrats and the antilocalist values of the Quids. They respected those same voters' wishes still further when they pursued the political economy that made positions such as Leiper's legitimate. The problem was that some of the people increasingly saw the conditions this political economy created as illegitimate. Nevertheless, by 1815 mainstream politics in Pennsylvania had cohered around the assumption that falling short of a full and pristine fealty to the Snyderite legacy (as defined by Snyderites such as Findlay) meant falling short of democracy.

The eventual (and as of 1805 unanticipated) legacy of the Snyderite victory was to completely equate the securing of egalitarianism with capitalism. The continued contentiousness of state politics made it increasingly difficult to rethink that equation, even when conditions suggested the need to do so. Such a rethinking might have again legitimated the ideas of the Philadelphia Democrats and allowed them to push their radical ideas back into mainstream politics. It also would have strengthened the Quids' efforts to encourage contempt for the Snyderite enterprise. With William Findlay's ascension in 1817, the vision of democracy that unquestionably insisted that capitalism produced egalitarianism became harder and harder to challenge within mainstream Pennsylvania Jeffersonian political thought. Yet the Philadelphia Democrats had predicted something like the panic of 1819. When it struck, they sought to revive their political movement and use mainstream politics to again critique, and impose a measure of public control over, an economy producing social and economic inequality. At the same time, old Quids sought to use positions that they had taken at the national level during the War of 1812 to undermine the Snyderites in Pennsylvania by making the national government the main instrument of economic policy making. The Philadelphia Democrats failed, and the Quids partially succeeded. Their efforts and the Snyderite response meant that the battles over the meaning of democracy in Pennsylvania would play a crucial role in the formation of modern America.

In Pennsylvania after 1815 the connection became increasingly unbreakable between democracy and the right to take advantage of an expanding market economy free from radical demands. Old Philadelphia Democrats tried to challenge the mainstream political consensus of democratic capitalism that emerged from the political, social, and economic arguments of the state's Jeffersonian Party between 1800 and 1814. But the consensus about democracy held, and mainstream Pennsylvania politicians managed to make allegiance to it a requirement for participation in the second party system. By 1830 Pennsylvania's radical Jeffersonian political legacy was banished from mainstream politics.

The Snyderite eclipse of the Philadelphia Democrats by 1814 renewed the Quids' confidence. They could once again, they believed, support their own candidates without fear that the city radicals would attract enough votes in three-way races to win elections. Once again they began to push their political agenda. Their experiences in Pennsylvania taught them that politics would become increasingly popular and democratic. Their best hope was a society that confirmed through actual experience a belief in the possibility of sustained prosperity for all. If the nation continued to prosper, Americans would not embrace radical political ideas that the Quids feared threatened property and encouraged recurring political convulsion.

Yet after Olmsted the Quids worried about what they considered the Snyderites' irresponsible behavior. Even at a time of national emergency the Snyderites had pursued states' rights arguments. The Quids believed that the Snyderites were acceptable only if the alternative was the Philadelphia Democrats. Further, after 1815 the wholesale removal of all constraints on development by the Findlayites troubled the Quids. They reasoned that such an expansive political economy overseen by clodhoppers of limited vision could easily encourage overspeculation and borrowing during boom periods, and panic and widespread calamity when those periods ended. A dynamic political economy, the Quids insisted, needed to be administered by the sober, self-controlled men of standing they considered themselves to be, and not by the less accomplished clodhoppers the Snyderites proudly proclaimed they were. It was the anxiety produced by irresponsible Snyderite policies at the state level, the Quids decided, that led voters to consider truly extreme solutions such as the program of 1805. Believing that they no longer had to worry about the Philadelphia Democrats, the Quids sought to challenge the Snyderites.

When Albert Gallatin resigned as secretary of the Treasury in 1813, Alexander J. Dallas soon replaced him. From his new position Dallas sought to make the national government the primary instrument of economic policy. He conceded control of Pennsylvania to the Snyderites, but he hoped to make the triumph of their version of democracy irrelevant.

Dallas became secretary of the Treasury during the War of 1812, when bold initiatives were required. President Madison and the Congress encouraged him to borrow, seek new taxes, and make the national state more energetic and interventionist. Dallas and fellow Pennsylvanians, such as the Quid Richard Rush, understood that he had an opportunity to strengthen the national government so that it could, among other things, respond to states' rights attacks such as the Olmsted affair and the Hartford Convention. In addition, at the national level, further removed from the people than they could be in Pennsylvania, the Quids might rule in the measured and responsible way they had always wanted. Thus after Dallas's appointment Rush advised him "that something ought to be done, and at once; something distinctive, something bold; something that the people would both see and

feel."[116] Charles Jared Ingersoll, only gradually easing his way into the Snyderite Democratic Party, also rejoiced at the appointment of his father's colleague. Dallas had a rare opportunity, for "seldom, if ever, [are] the destinies
of a nation placed so entirely in the hands of one man as the destinies of this
are in yours at this moment." Ingersoll urged Dallas to secure the rechartering of the national bank. He also hoped that the national government
could responsibly restore public credit and oversee the extension of private
credit. Ingersoll was confident that "the opulent individuals with whom you
stand so well, the Girards, Astors etc," would assist in this great endeavor.
It was time, Ingersoll insisted, for "a national system."[117]

Dallas lost little time seeking to make the federal government the primary location of decision making about the nation's future. He wrote his
close friend William Jones that he planned to pursue the rechartering of the
Bank of the United States, and that he considered the constitutional issue
settled by the long tenure of the first national bank.[118] Dallas also explained
to Jones his comprehensive plan to allow the national government to oversee American economic development in a responsible manner. Dallas sought
to broaden the government's revenue base with new taxes, particularly a
stamp tax. He planned to push for a protective tariff, recharter the National
Bank, and issue treasury notes at 7 percent backed by restored public credit.
The sound notes would function as a national circulating medium.[119]

With Matthew Carey and young "War Hawks" like Henry Clay, Dallas
began to conceive what would soon be termed the American System.[120]
Carey in particular lobbied for high protective duties and described a future
of regional agricultural and industrial specialization, a well-developed internal market, and the frequent addition of productive resources through westward expansion. Carey's optimistic view of the nation's unlimited potential
appealed to Quids like Rush and Dallas and Snyderites such as Jonathan
Roberts and Walter Franklin. He popularized the demands for protection-
ism and the extension of credit as a democratic instrument. The political
economy of writers like Matthew Carey helped provide a basic area of consensus for Jeffersonians who disagreed about whether policy should be
implemented at the state or national level.[121] Writers like Carey and the German immigrant to Pennsylvania Friedrich List, who wrote at the behest of
Carey's Pennsylvania Society for the Promotion of Manufactures, constantly argued that freedom, prosperity, and democracy could only come
with protection and complete development of the internal market.[122]

Dallas received support from others besides private citizens such as
Carey and List. John C. Calhoun, in his first incarnation as secretary of war,

backed Dallas's nationalist policies. In correspondence with Charles Jared Ingersoll, he endorsed the bank and the protective tariff. Henry Clay, as Speaker of the House, shepherded the bank bill through the legislature. In return Dallas's ally William Jones, the president of the second Bank of the United States, worked closely with him to open western branches, especially in Kentucky.[123]

The Snyderites saw much to support in Dallas's policies. General commitment to the internal market furthered their agenda in Pennsylvania. They had no quarrel with a protective tariff or a national currency. They even endorsed the rechartering of the national bank, but they supported it only if it was "an independent . . . not a discordant institution." Under Jeffersonians, the Snyderites assumed that the national bank would not be allowed to dominate the nation's economy. The growth of state banks provided alternative sources of credit and healthy competition, which did "not imply hostility" between the various banks. Instead, competition would drive interest rates down and so help producers and entrepreneurs. With credit sufficiently democratized, the Snyderites appreciated the protection a national bank would provide by forcing irresponsible banks to lend more carefully.[124]

The political economy of the National Republicans is often described as neo-Federalist.[125] It was not. Rather, it was firmly rooted in the Pennsylvania Jeffersonian tradition. Commitment to protective tariffs, democratized credit, state banks, and westward expansion were anti-Hamiltonian, and in addition they intended to place the nation's productive resources in the hands of actual urban and rural producers. The Jeffersonians of Pennsylvania, as is clear by now, agreed on very little. But they never betrayed their universal hostility and contempt for the hierarchical and mutually reinforcing social, political, economic, and cultural assumptions of the Federalists.

Nevertheless, the Quids' efforts did not add up to the measured, responsible oversight of a universally beneficent and dynamic political economy. In the frenetic postwar years before 1819, the economy experienced an intense boom. In 1811, the year before the war began, Pennsylvania had 25 banks. In 1814 the Findlayites chartered 42 more. But by 1815 the number of banks in the state had risen to 111.[126] Though Pennsylvania was spectacular, it was not entirely atypical. The banks lent quite promiscuously, while postwar demand seemed insatiable and opportunities abounded. Credit was readily available, and the traditional conception of creditworthiness did for a time cease to exist.[127]

The boom period between 1815 and 1818 was the first real test for the new national bank, and it failed the test dramatically. After 1816 William

Jones, the bank's president, found himself in a difficult position. A committed Quid, Jones did want the bank to serve as a check on the thoughtless borrowing orgies that he believed resulted when men like Snyder, Boileau, and especially Findlay and Ingham governed. On the other hand, the Quids had been forced to retreat from Pennsylvania as obvious losers. They could no longer persuade the voters at the state level. If the Quids were going to convince them to trust their policy at the national level, they had to accommodate those men who mattered in the states. Jones could not simply clamp down on Pennsylvania's banks without facing accusations that the Quids sought to defeat democracy with an overweening national government.

Unfortunately, Jones's personal affairs also clouded his judgment. A pioneer in the China trade, and primarily involved in commerce, his business had been largely destroyed by embargo, nonintercourse, and war. Jones never faltered in his commitment to the Jeffersonian party and defended those policies that pushed him toward bankruptcy. But with the war's end he sought to revive his fortunes by taking advantage of seemingly endless domestic opportunities. He looked to invest in internal improvement corporations and manufacturing enterprises and borrowed $30,000.[128] Thus, Jones had a real disinclination to curtail the postwar boom and indeed had a strong incentive to contribute to it. As president of the Bank of the United States he did so. In theory the national bank was to act as a check on the state banks. In general, Americans paid their taxes and purchased public lands with state and local bank notes. Those notes flowed into the national bank. Through a judicious demand for specie redemption, the national bank could force the state and local banks to keep their paper emissions close to their specie holdings.

During 1817 and 1818 Jones did not prove equal to the image that the Quids had of themselves. His recent financial misfortunes and the exuberance brought on by the postwar boom combined to encourage him to view the rapid expansion of paper money as in his and the nation's best interests. Under his direction the Bank of the United States made no effort to check the emissions of its branches, and equally important, it and its branches did not demand regular specie redemption of the state bank notes they held. The national bank and its branches sat on the notes, which began to accumulate. The combination was a calamity. It was made more so because the national bank had far less specie than its charter originally required. It issued notes far beyond the expected specie-to-paper ratio, and it allowed the state banks to think that they did not have to worry about specie redemption from above.[129] As the state and local banks acquired national bank notes, the national bank lost the power to check the boom. If it demanded specie repayment, the state and local banks could do the same, and the national bank was increasingly unable to meet that obligation if pressed.

Thus the rate of lending increased, and by 1818 banks issued paper out of all proportion to their actual specie holdings. The borrowers assumed that they could ride the postwar boom and pay their debts with future profits. The banks simply carried the loans over as they came due, having no interest in making a demand for payment that would reverberate throughout the economy. As consumption demand peaked and then subsided in 1818, the expectation of future profits was not met. At the same time, in 1819, Jones panicked at his own business failures and at criticism of his conduct as president of the Bank of the United States. He began to demand specie repayments and started a savage contraction of credit. The state banks in turn demanded repayment from their debtors, including the national bank. Suddenly debts were not rolled over; instead, they came due. The panic of 1819 had begun.[130]

The panic hit Pennsylvanians hard. They engaged in fifteen thousand suits for debt in 1819 alone. Philadelphia wheat peaked in price at $2.41 a bushel in 1817. The panic brought a savage deflation that did not bottom out until 1821. That year a bushel of Pennsylvania wheat sold for 88 cents. At the height of the panic as many as three-fourths of Philadelphia's laborers were believed to be out of work, and the *Democratic Press* estimated the number at twenty thousand.[131]

For a time the abysmal conditions revived the fortunes of the Philadelphia Democrats. They had been staunch opponents of rechartering the Bank of the United States, the only group of Jeffersonians in Pennsylvania to take such a stand. They had also predicted the irresponsible behavior of the state banks.[132] The panic briefly allowed the Philadelphia Democrats to force their radical views back into mainstream Pennsylvania politics. They realized that their original political solutions to provide public control over private economic misbehavior would never be enacted. With their worst fears confirmed, they began to challenge directly the prevailing commitment to capitalism. In reaction to the panic, the Philadelphia Democrats began to demand a hard money economy, and they denounced banking.[133] Duane's political fortunes improved briefly, and his supporters elected him to the state legislature, the only time he achieved elected office. There he opposed all efforts to provide debtor relief, expand financial institutions, and increase the supply of paper currency. He also demanded compulsory specie repayments from all the banks, a plan that, if enacted, would probably have bankrupted every bank outside of New England. Duane hoped to retard the pace of development and make the risks of entrepreneurship and accumulation too great to be pursued.[134] Younger radicals attracted to the grand old ideals of 1805 joined him in this effort. Urban activists such as James Thackera demanded a purely specie economy, and Stephen Simpson published a series of essays in the *Aurora* denouncing banks.

Faced with the revival of radical democratic politics, the Snyderites and the Quids set aside their differences. The *Democratic Press* denounced Stephen Simpson's attacks on the Bank of the United States, even as it criticized William Jones's conduct.[135] Snyderites and Quids feared the return of the old battles in a climate where economic development pursued at either the national or the state level was in disrepute. All of the Pennsylvania Jeffersonians who were enemies of the Philadelphia Democrats began forcefully, even shrilly, to defend economic development as the solution to social and economic dislocation and inequality.

By 1817 the breach between Nathaniel B. Boileau, as Snyder's chosen successor, and William Findlay, as the leader of the faction actually taking control of the party, was complete. In 1817 Findlay's supporters elected him governor, and the so-called Family Party emerged as the beneficiary of the Snyderite triumph.[136] Binns and Boileau were now on the outs. Nevertheless, faced with the resurgence of the Philadelphia Democrats after 1819, Family men, old Snyderites, and former Quids all began to suggest similar solutions for hard times.

The only sane response, Binns argued in the *Democratic Press,* was to commit completely to a capitalist economy that could truly provide perpetual growth and opportunity. First, it was essential to ensure that the most entrepreneurial weathered the storm. The *Democratic Press* continued to support bankruptcy legislation to assist the "commercial part of the community." The Philadelphia Chamber of Commerce seconded this suggestion and also argued that debtor relief and bankruptcy legislation were the first rational steps toward dealing with economic crisis.[137]

The *Democratic Press* further maintained that the banks had been weakened and finally forced to suspend specie payments, thus precipitating the crisis of confidence, because the nation had not developed the internal economy satisfactorily. If Americans developed the nation's full industrial potential, there would be much less specie flight, since fewer foreign manufactures would be purchased. With greater specie reserves, banks could increase their paper emissions and extend necessary credit, yet not weaken paper, cause inflation, provoke a crisis in confidence, and engender collapse. Strong banks and the safe democratic extension of credit would come with more economic development.[138] The keys to recovery and prosperity were a truly reliable domestic market, a favorable balance of trade to prevent specie drain, available and reliable public and private credit, a climate in which "those possessed of property, and in want of money, can borrow it at a reasonable interest," and general bankruptcy legislation. With these necessary features of capitalism established, "the mass of the laboring part of the community are able to procure steady employment, and such reasonable wages as to support themselves and their families comfortably."[139]

Anyone who opposed developmental plans was despicable, for development was the best way to provide relief for the impoverished. Snyderites of every variety used tragic stories of poverty and dislocation to defend policies intended to extend the market and develop the nation.[140] In response to the panic of 1819 the *Democratic Press* began a sustained campaign to raise the already protective tariff and convince the nation to commit itself even more fully to manufacturing.[141] The paper also began to print the essays produced by Matthew Carey's Pennsylvania Society for the Promotion of Manufactures. The forces that had joined to oppose the Philadelphia Democrats between 1807 and 1816 once again united to provide an alternative explanation for the causes of and solutions to crisis in a capitalist economy.[142]

An article from the *Democratic Press* that appeared on May 31, 1819, provides a fine example of these efforts. The piece included one of the clearest statements yet of the emerging response of mainstream Pennsylvania Jeffersonians to the altogether unexpected crisis. It was at once an honest effort to deal with that crisis and an example of the developing mainstream consensus about the broad features of political economy and democracy that united Quids with Snyderites of all varieties. The searing experience of the panic of 1819 allowed the previous two decades of thought and struggle to cohere into a body of mainstream Pennsylvania Jeffersonian political thought that once and for all pushed the Philadelphia Democrats to the margins. Written by "A Workman," the *Democratic Press* article spoke for the "seven-tenths of the population [who] come into the world without the means of subsisting for themselves." This group was the vast majority of that political category so essential to Pennsylvania Jeffersonian political thought, "the people." It was the lifeblood of democracy. The ability of laborers to fulfill the obligations of citizenship was crucial; therefore, so was their capacity to become independent and place themselves beyond want and coercion.

There could be no dispute that government played an important role in making it possible for those people to gain independence whose "labor is the only commodity they possess to offer in exchange for those things necessary to supply their wants." How, then, did a responsible democratic government respond to the panic of 1819? By acknowledging that the most reliable market was domestic. The nation had to commit to protective tariffs; a mixed economy of manufacturing, agriculture, and commerce; and internal consumption of internal production. The dynamic internal market would provide the opportunity that allowed the seven-tenths to secure their independence through their own dignified efforts. The panic occurred not because Americans had been overindulgent or irresponsible. Rather, it happened because the nation had incompletely embraced the future. Resources, capital, and labor were not fully used; the internal economy was not fully developed. Thus the laborers, the best potential citizens, relied on the vagaries of foreign commerce.[143] Those who called for extreme solutions, procapitalist Jeffersonians insisted, frightened men of standing and capital from supporting the internal market.

The Philadelphia Democrats never understood that their radical solutions frightened more than just men of standing. Although they were still claiming to speak for all of "the people," their rising hostility to economic development could also terrify master craftsmen, smaller landowners, and indeed any who believed they could build a future brighter than the past. As early as 1805 the Philadelphia Democrats had found it difficult to appeal to more than a portion of the people. By 1820, with social relations in the United States even more fractured and complex, they had no hope of inspiring the entirety of this diverse category whose needs, the Philadelphia Democrats still insisted, could be simultaneously met with policies increasingly able to attract only the most frightened and vulnerable. Perhaps the nature of their appeal was a final clue to the Philadelphia Democrats' marginal position. The city radicals generalized based on conditions that few citizens wanted to face or acknowledge they might have to endure. Given the very tangible and attractive policies committed to upward mobility and renewal offered by the Quids and Snyderites, virtually no property-owning Pennsylvanians wanted to believe that they needed the Philadelphia Democrats. Pennsylvania Jeffersonians could conclude that the demands of the city radicals would simply keep workers idle and undermine independence and genuine citizenship. Those who attacked the sinews of the domestic economy — banks, paper currency, credit, internal improvements, and protective tariffs — were in fact demagogues who would reduce the people to dependence. Such men sought to keep the people angry and desperate so they could ride to power on a dangerous and destructive wave of popular fury.

The answer to the panic of 1819, most Pennsylvania Jeffersonians concluded, was a great deal more democracy — a more complete commitment to economic development and a stronger faith in the power of the market created and expanded by and for producers. This market guided by true democrats would produce the conditions for independence that all Pennsylvanians understood were essential for democracy. Snyderites and Quids responded to the Philadelphia Democrats by focusing the ideas they had been articulating with increasing coherence for close to two decades before the panic. When the economic crisis struck, they were able to answer demands for direct popular interference in the economy. They could do so because they, and particularly the clodhopper Snyderites, credibly denounced such popular intervention in the name of democracy and "the people."

The efforts of the Snyderites and the Quids succeeded. By 1821 the Philadelphia Democrats had not managed to keep their ideas alive in mainstream politics. The panic of 1819 had not boosted their fortunes as they had expected it to. Thus in 1822 the Philadelphia Democrats sought to break the Snyderite control of democracy by linking democracy in Pennsylvania to a figure of their choosing, General Andrew Jackson. They did not select Jackson at random. In Tennessee Jackson opposed the same measures that Duane did in Pennsylvania and first articulated the hard money, antibank policies he would later pursue as president.[144] Stephen Simpson, among the Philadelphia Democrats, the leading critic of the national bank, had served under Jackson at the Battle of New Orleans.[145] Simpson and fellow Philadelphia Democrat and hard money advocate James Thackera convinced the other city radicals to support Jackson for president.[146] As early as 1822 the Philadelphia Democrats were determined to reclaim democracy and make it synonymous with Andrew Jackson.

Though the city radicals' strategy worked initially, it did expose their increasingly marginal position in Pennsylvania Jeffersonian politics. By 1822 they could not challenge those shared features of Quid and Snyderite political economy and hope to win a battle of ideas in the state. They had to attach themselves to an outsider and hope that his sudden popularity would not prove fleeting. Furthermore, they had to hope that a national movement would somehow not reflect the increasing complexity and diversity of needs and aspirations articulated by all of those whom they included in the category "the people." By attaching themselves to Jackson, the Philadelphia Democrats were reduced to the nonsensical hope that the nation would somehow prove less complicated and more manageable than Pennsylvania had been.

Nevertheless, in the short term the Philadelphia Democrats were aided by concern about the panic, widespread anger over Congress's decision to raise members' salaries, and popular frustration with the undemocratic ways in which the Republican Party continued to choose its presidential candidates in the 1820s.[147] By 1823 the Philadelphia Democrats had reason to believe they could carry Pennsylvania for Jackson. The Jackson surge in the state was very much a popular movement in which the Philadelphia Democrats were in the vanguard. Indeed, as late as 1823 and early 1824, procapitalist Pennsylvania democrats, who would later become important Jacksonians, were unaware of his strength in Pennsylvania. In 1823 Charles Jared Ingersoll believed that John Quincy Adams would be the next president and planned to vote for him. He reported years later that news of the corrupt bargain had angered him, but he had then switched loyalties to William H. Crawford.[148] In 1824 Samuel D. Ingham was confident that John C. Calhoun would be elected, and Ingham, a leader of the Family Party, assumed he could deliver Pennsylvania to Calhoun. Thomas Rogers supported Adams. Samuel Preston wrote Lewis Coryell that he was undecided but would make his choice among the worthy candidates soon. He listed them as Adams, Crawford, Calhoun, and Henry Clay.[149]

The Snyderites were quite contemptuous of the Jackson supporters when they finally recognized them. They grasped, in part, what the Philadelphia Democrats were attempting.[150] The Philadelphia Democrats could no longer influence the state from within mainstream Pennsylvania politics as established by 1820, but they argued that the crisis of 1819 had forever discredited Snyderite democracy. They insisted that Jackson was a completely new man who could make government respond to the new issues that were now clearly the chief concerns of democratic society. By supporting Jackson the Philadelphia Democrats planned to force their way back into mainstream politics. Proscribed from the political mainstream as never before, the Philadelphia Democrats sought to alter its course. Initially, supporting Jackson in Pennsylvania meant agreeing with their effort and opposing the spread of a capitalist economy by directly attacking economic development.

One thing the Philadelphia Democrats could do well was run a popular campaign. By summer 1824 Jackson had emerged as the likely winner in Pennsylvania. The Philadelphia Democrats drew on most of the strategies they had long since mastered. Greatly assisted by Tennessee supporters close to Jackson, such as John Eaton, the early Jackson men in Pennsylvania made sure he had a glowing campaign biography, which was first published in the

Columbia Observer, the newspaper Stephen Simpson started in 1822.[151] In the pro-Jackson press the general was portrayed as an outsider who had nothing to do with the major sources of danger democracy faced. Pennsylvanians were informed that Jackson abhorred privilege and was the only presidential candidate wholly unconnected to the decision-making process that ignored voters when party leaders chose candidates. Further, the campaign in Pennsylvania reinforced the notion, scattered among Jackson supporters elsewhere, that Jackson alone among the candidates endorsed a sensible tariff and the growth of the domestic economy while remaining the sworn enemy of the moneyed aristocracy. Only Jackson, then, could right the wrongs done by those responsible for the panic of 1819. The implication in Pennsylvania, at least initially, was that he would right those wrongs by endorsing policies similar to those of William Duane.[152]

In the 1824 election Pennsylvania was the only significant northern state to vote for Jackson. His local success terrified procapitalist Pennsylvania democrats. In 1824 and 1825 Jackson's victory in Pennsylvania meant the triumph of the Philadelphia Democrats. After news of the alleged corrupt bargain, Jackson had immediately declared that he would run again. It now seemed quite possible that the radicals would play a prominent role in the election of a president. Thus between 1825 and 1828 procapitalist democrats engaged in a systematic effort to take over the Jacksonian movement in Pennsylvania.

One thing the Snyderites could do well was thrive on popular democratic political terrain. Rather than resist Jackson, they quickly recognized that "the cause of General Jackson, if it was not six months ago, has now, by unprecedented circumstances, most obviously become the cause of popular government, the cause of democracy, the cause of that essential principle without which a republic is merely nominal, or rather a base deception."[153] By 1826 Samuel D. Ingham well understood that Jackson would again carry Pennsylvania as well as New Jersey and possibly New York. Middle Atlantic votes combined with southern support would give him the presidency. To preserve the victory procapitalist Pennsylvania democrats had won by 1820, they had to make sure that the right sorts of Jacksonians delivered Pennsylvania to Jackson in 1828. Ingham advised his democratic followers to "sustain the current . . . [and not] suffer some very unworthy men to thrust themselves at the head of it. . . . This is the crisis to take sides."[154]

Still, those unworthy men were the original Jacksonians. At first the procapitalist democrats had trouble seizing the movement.[155] George Mifflin Dallas reported to Ingham that "our meeting was all powerful in moral and political weight—but it was not as numerous as I had expected. We had not more than 400. The subordinate Jackson men are not yet skilled in getting numbers out, at a moment's warning."[156] Initial failures were all the more galling because original and anticapitalist Jacksonians like Stephen Simpson presided over meetings that their procapitalist democratic enemies could only admit were "enormous." George Mifflin Dallas contemptuously described one such gathering: "No preparations were made—everything was confided to a few heedless young men—and the consequences were at once injurious to the cause, and absolutely ludicrous." Simpson, Dallas reported, refused to take the chair, not wishing to impose his views on the people. Thus, no one chaired, and "as they dispersed a child took the chair—then an old crazy fellow who loiters about the streets—and on the whole, the matter ended like a farce." Dallas was furious because Simpson had called a spontaneous meeting after ignoring the wishes of the Family Party's pro-Jackson committee of correspondence. Dallas hoped that the spontaneous meeting would be "the last and worst blow to the cause of Jackson which it will ever be in Simpson's power to give. If the high and leading friends of the General still address this fool and madman as a popular instrument and organ, they must not be surprised to find everything retrograde, and every intelligent man avoid the party."[157] Still, four months later Dallas complained that "a tirade of Simpson's manufacturing was introduced" at an official and, but for Simpson, less chaotic pro-Jackson meeting.[158]

But in 1822 Leib had died, and that same year declining circulation had forced Duane to sell the *Aurora*. The Philadelphia Democrats, given the anxious circumstances of the early 1820s, were able to influence events for the next few years. But by 1828 six years had passed since they had controlled a major newspaper. Their democratic enemies also carefully forgot Leib, the Philadelphia Democrats' guiding political spirit. The times also improved, and the procapitalist democrats continued to insist on their developmental themes during a period of rising expectations.

Ultimately the Philadelphia Democrats failed to make Jackson's presidential bids a means to revive the grand old cause of 1805. Their inability to do so exposed for a final time the profound deficiency in their thought that resulted from their inability to accept the truly diverse ideals and aspirations of the people about whom they generalized. For the movement Jackson led proved, inevitably, to be at least as multifarious as Pennsylvania's Jeffersonian party. Strains of thought within it shared certain of the city radicals' concerns; indeed, they were present largely because of their concerns. But equally Jacksonian were those who chafed at national control of key economic policy. Equally Jacksonian were small and middling property holders; strivers on the make who believed that their talents could guarantee them distinguished independence, particularly when they were treated with respect and fully encouraged by democratic policy makers who shared their outlook.[159]

The Snyderites were as capable as were the Philadelphia Democrats of fitting into what has been called the Jacksonian persuasion. The best the city radicals could hope for was something like a reprise at the national level of the struggle to define democracy in Pennsylvania — a struggle within the state they had already lost. The original Pennsylvania Jacksonians believed that vicious pseudodemocrats had hijacked the state's Jacksonian movement. This view was immeasurably preferable to the alternative, given that the voters of Pennsylvania always had a choice about precisely which sorts of democrats they would elect.

By 1825 the old Philadelphia Democrats — the original Jacksonians — could only lament that they had been "pushed to the wall."[160] By the late 1820s George Mifflin Dallas, Samuel D. Ingham, Samuel McKean, James Buchanan, and the rest were the Pennsylvania Jacksonians. In Pennsylvania they could successfully deny political places to Simpson, William J. Duane (Duane's son), and those supporters of "unalloyed democracy."[161] By the late 1820s the Philadelphia Democrat survivors truly had no place in mainstream politics. Thus Stephen Simpson helped found the Pennsylvania Workingman's Party. Simpson kept the traditional concerns of the Philadelphia Democrats alive. In 1831 he sadly reported "If the mechanics combine to raise their wages, the laws punish them as conspirators against the good of society, and the dungeon awaits them as it does the robber. But the laws have made it a just and meritorious act that capitalists shall combine to strip the man of labor of his earnings, reduce him to a dry crust and a gourd of water. Thus does power invert justice, and derange the order of nature."[162] The presence of tested and creative politicians in Pennsylvania like Simpson, who could draw on the most radical version of the Jeffersonian legacy, helps explain the early and prominent labor politics of the state.[163] But the culmination of the Philadelphia Democrats' efforts was their support for the workingmen's political parties. In the end, to maintain their original vision of 1805 the Philadelphia Democrats were finally forced to acknowledge that they could speak for only a portion of "the people." Indeed, they could find a hearing only with those in that venerable category who were as marginal as they were.

The political mainstream in Pennsylvania between 1828 and 1840 belonged to the procapitalist Jacksonians. The age of Jackson in Pennsylvania meant pro-tariff, pro–internal improvement, and pro-bank politics. These Jacksonians relied on tested and refined strategies for using popular politics and developmental policies to defeat radical democratic measures. The 1830s were the high tide of their democratic triumph. These Jacksonian democrats succeeded in forging a fundamental procapitalist consensus. Even some former Federalists participated. William Tilghman could not hate the democracy built by procapitalist Pennsylvania Jacksonians. Their internal improvements developed the Delaware River, allowing his "property on the water that flow[ed] into the river [to] become much more valuable."[164]

The procapitalist Pennsylvania Jacksonian consensus was challenged, at least periodically, by an unexpected source — President Jackson himself. In the bank war, through his commitments to a hard money economy, and by veto of the Maysville Road bill, Jackson proved that the Philadelphia Democrats had not entirely misjudged their man back in the early 1820s.[165] Jackson and his successor, Martin Van Buren, at least at times, sought to slow the development of a capitalist society.[166]

The Pennsylvania Jacksonians opposed virtually all these policies. Samuel D. Ingham, whom Jackson appointed secretary of the Treasury in 1829, in particular defended his fellow Pennsylvanian Nicholas Biddle, president of the second Bank of the United States. From 1830, though they absolutely controlled Pennsylvania, the procapitalist Jacksonians did not enjoy the same degree of influence in national Jacksonian politics. Ingham, the leading Pennsylvania Jacksonian at the national level, was the big loser in the cabinet shakeup of 1831. Martin Van Burren went from being Jackson's failed nominee to the Court of St. James's to the White House. But Ingham's 1860 obituary reported that after 1831 he retired from political life.[167] The final example of the Pennsylvania Jacksonian's alienation from mainstream national party policy occurred after the dissolution of the second Bank of the United States. The Pennsylvania Jacksonians promptly offered Biddle a state charter.[168]

By the mid-1830s the procapitalist Pennsylvania Jacksonians faced a climate in which the consensus that gave them absolute control of Pennsylvania forced them into a new struggle within the Jacksonian party as a whole about the meaning of democracy. In the 1830s, and particularly during and after the panic of 1837 — the worst capitalist crisis to that point in the nation's history — the rest of the country fought the battles Pennsylvania's procapitalist democrats already knew how to win. They had been having those political, social, and economic arguments since the revolution of 1800.

Former Quids turned National Republicans quickly took advantage of the Pennsylvania Jacksonians' dilemma. They had been unable to influence state politics for the previous twenty years. Now, from the Pennsylvania perspective, national Jacksonian politics threatened to revive old Philadelphia Democrat notions, but on a far grander scale than Duane and Leib had ever dared hope for. Those Pennsylvanians happy with what the Pennsylvania Jacksonians had been delivering grew unwilling to help them elect Jacksonian presidents.

Old Quids like Richard Rush had become anti-Masons in response to Jacksonian triumph in Pennsylvania. They could not defeat the Jacksonians in the state by a direct challenge. Indeed, since the Quids were pro-tariff, pro-bank, and pro–internal improvements, very little of substance separated them from Pennsylvania's Democratic Party. But they were more nationalist and did not distinguish between Pennsylvania's brand of states' rights and Nullification. Former Quids abhorred both, even though the Pennsylvania Jacksonians claimed jurisdiction only over all economic policies arising in response to purely Pennsylvania issues. They did not demand the right to nullify national legislation resulting from Congress wielding its enumerated powers. At any rate, Pennsylvania Jacksonians supported the Tariff of Abominations and so had little sympathy for South Carolina.[169]

Anti-Masonry in Pennsylvania had always had a strong anti-Jacksonian flavor. But the political mainstream before 1835 had room only for democrats, and in Pennsylvania democrats who hoped to resonate with a majority of voters were procapitalist and Jacksonian. In order to avoid the charge of hostility to democracy, those who hoped to battle the Jacksonians for state supremacy had to organize around issues that Jacksonians ignored, such as the dangers of Freemasonry. By the mid-1830s old Quids, and those Snyderites like John Binns who had been ousted after the Findlayite ascension, were confident that they could challenge the Pennsylvania Jacksonians. They also had unquestionable Jeffersonian pedigrees and had learned, or in the case of Binns taught others, how to be democrats. Now with the radical implications of Jackson's thought seemingly exposed, the Pennsylvania Jacksonians, though they feared his ideas as much as did the anti-Masons, were vulnerable by association. From 1834 those Pennsylvania Jeffersonians who had shared in the capitalist consensus, but not in state political power, began a direct mainstream political assault on the state's Jacksonians. In Pennsylvania they conceived and founded the state's Whig Party.[170]

John Binns noted Jackson's radical politics and the stigma placed on the Jacksonian party by the Nullifiers, even though Pennsylvania's Jacksonians, and for that matter Jackson himself, practiced a very different brand of states' rights. Binns began to agitate for a party that could continue to champion the procapitalist, democratic consensus but that would necessarily do so from outside the Jacksonian party. This new party would also allow him to be a major figure once again in mainstream state politics. The Whig Party could seize the mantle of democracy from the Jacksonians, who could now be portrayed in Pennsylvania as hostile to commerce and banking and even, by association, as radical secessionists. When considering the name of the new party, Binns explained how it ought to conduct itself: "I would use a name, as well as principles, which are dear to the people to induce them to associate and preserve the institutions and with them the happiness and prosperity of our country." True democrats could now form "an association whose objects should be purely national."[171]

The Whig Party drew on the legacy of democratic opposition to radical democrats that had been pioneered by the Quids and perfected by the Snyderites. It legitimately claimed a Jeffersonian democratic legacy. Whigs like Binns led popular campaigns that directly appealed to and involved the people. Strategies like Binns's anti-Jackson coffin handbill and the popular presidential campaign of 1840 testify to the profound Jeffersonian and popular influences that shaped the Whigs.[172]

In 1840 the Whigs captured the presidency and Pennsylvania. In 1842 Henry Clay wrote a letter to the Pennsylvanian Jacob Strattan, who passed it on to the family of the late William Jones. Clay outlined the values of the Whig Party: a sound national currency, an adequate revenue, commitment to manufacturing via a protective tariff, organized sale of the public lands, and westward expansion.[173] Political fighting continued. But whether Whigs or Democrats triumphed in Pennsylvania, they preserved the democratic capitalist consensus.

By 1840 this consensus dominated Pennsylvania because the twists and turns of the crucible of conflict had made the solutions of the Philadelphia Democrats untenable to the majority of Pennsylvania's voters. The Philadelphia Democrats could not persuade enough people that they would respect property and eschew anarchy. But procapitalist Pennsylvania Jeffersonians and their beneficiaries could not impose their consensus on the nation. As the benefits of capitalism increasingly came to be distributed unequally, new challenges arose to the idea that economic development would meet the needs of all. Those challenges came partly from within the Jacksonian party and also from new and much more potentially radical voices outside of it.[174] Within the political mainstream, the battle between

Whigs and Jacksonians, and among Jacksonians, was far more complex than a simple reprise of the struggle Pennsylvania Jeffersonians had experienced. For one thing, after 1820 Americans reacted to new developments and considered significant issues that had not been given as much prominence during the Jeffersonian era. Religious disputes assumed a much more central role in the public life of the Age of Jackson. In addition, as immigration led to ever-increasing ethnic complexity, the desire of white native Protestants to assert homogeneous cultural values led to sharper conflict over the nature of American identity and citizenship and one's place in the nation.[175]

The religious, ethnic, and cultural conflicts of the Jacksonian period were far more than a repeat of the struggle to define democracy that had occurred in Jeffersonian Pennsylvania. But significantly, the results of the argument within Pennsylvania Jeffersonian political thought intersected with the new disagreements that drove public life after 1830. This intersection was particularly noteworthy for the Quids, who after 1815 embraced the American System and ultimately Whiggery. There had always been coursing through the Quids' ideas about a democratic political economy a conception of sobriety, personal betterment, and uplift that fit quite well with evangelical values and moral reform. As the Whigs became intimately associated with these values, they could draw on a democratic political economy based on expansion and opportunity that reinforced their larger cultural vision. This conception of political economy was a venerable body of thought, toughened by searing conflict — a body of thought that none had conceived earlier or defended more persuasively than the Pennsylvania Quids. Their legacy became a significant part of the ideas the Jeffersonian tradition bequeathed to the Whigs — a political economy of economic development and dynamism that nevertheless allowed those who defended it to legitimately claim the Jeffersonian legacy of promoting the democratic needs of "the people."

The Pennsylvania Quid tradition provided the Whigs a legitimacy that the Federalists had never possessed. The Whigs enjoyed this legitimacy because, between 1820 and the Gilded Age in the North, their Quid-inspired political economy was a key part of the combination of ideas and policies that provided laboring people more opportunity and mobility over a larger territory than any society had ever known. The political economy of the Whig and later the Republican Party was the mature statement of the anti-Hamiltonian economic development the Snyderites and the Quids had sought.[176] This political economy also reflected the faith in market forces and the rejection of popular intervention in the economy that was the procapitalist consensus forged by Quids and various types of Snyderites. It emerged from the visions of men such as Coxe, Snyder, Findlay, Binns, and Carey, and the latter two became Whigs. The Whigs succeeded where the Federalists of old never could because their origins were purely Jeffersonian. The American System recalled not Hamilton's Society for Establishing Useful Manufactures but the ideology embedded in Alexander J. Dallas's *Address to the People of Pennsylvania,* his actions as secretary of the Treasury, Moses Levy's remarks in *Commonwealth v. Pullis,* and especially the *Democratic Press*'s response to the panic of 1819.

The Pennsylvania Jeffersonian struggle over how to fuse democracy and egalitarianism with capitalism allowed this Quid political economy to reach mature coherence in the American Whig and Republican Parties. At the same time, it also helped ensure that when Jacksonians argued about the meaning of democracy, the results would be as contentious as they had been in Jeffersonian Pennsylvania. During the 1830s and afterward, when Locofoco and antibank Jacksonians claimed to speak democracy, fellow Jacksonians could insist that such radical notions would merely weaken the nation and undermine the capacity for the proud, dignified independence that made democracy possible.[177] They could make this clear and compelling response so effectively in large part because of the long-standing efforts of Snyderites turned Jacksonians to provide a defense of state-based, untrammeled economic development that was unquestionably democratic and Jeffersonian in its origins.

After 1825 the expansion of a dynamic capitalist economy inevitably contributed to the further fracturing of "the people" — the process that had so stymied the efforts of Pennsylvania Jeffersonians to put their various theories into practice. Participation in this dynamic economy of liberal capitalism invariably led to varying experiences and multifarious reactions. In the end this increasing complexity helped to reveal the final importance of the struggle to fuse democracy and egalitarianism with capitalism in Jeffersonian Pennsylvania. By the mid–nineteenth century American economic and social relations had become so diverse that all of the very different aspects of Jeffersonian political thought present in Pennsylvania were relevant to someone somewhere. By midcentury the Jeffersonian legacy encompassed everything, which only meant that the nation was as rife with conflict as Pennsylvania had been in 1805 — when Jeffersonian commitments were similarly ubiquitous.

Though the procapitalist consensus forged by the Quids and the Snyderites could not entirely banish potentially radical ideas from the pre–Civil

War American mainstream outside of Pennsylvania, it did have that impact on the mainstream inside the state. Nevertheless, it is too simple to argue that the Snyderites and the Quids won while the Philadelphia Democrats lost. John Quincy Adams cogently described antebellum American society in the North to Charles Jared Ingersoll as "perpetual motion — perpetual change — a boundless ocean without a shore."[178] In Pennsylvania the pro-capitalist consensus could not provide security and stability for all. Providing such shelter had always been a primary goal of Pennsylvania's Jeffersonians. The Quids and the Snyderites sacrificed steady and measured development, and the Snyderites relinquished the capacity to use public power to directly ensure widespread access to property.

The lasting legacy of the crucible of conflict was that Pennsylvania's Jeffersonian party developed a mainstream consensus at once capitalist and democratic. But from the beginning all Pennsylvania Jeffersonians had looked at the best within themselves and each other and sought a world with many ports and few storms. "Perpetual motion — perpetual change — a boundless ocean without a shore" — Quincy Adams's was a powerful and an anxious image. Despite all of their best and noblest efforts, the crucible of political conflict — the process of argument and polemic, the need to become more rigid for the sake of argumentative power, and the fundamental absence of consensus — finally produced an altogether unanticipated outcome of the Pennsylvania Jeffersonian struggle to fuse egalitarianism and capitalism. Absolute triumph over the Federalists, despite what everyone from Michael Leib to Alexander James Dallas had hoped for, led in the end to a frightening voyage for many future sailors.

Conclusion

History and Historiography

Thomas Jefferson and William Duane

In 1824 William Duane wrote to Thomas Jefferson that the nation had experienced a "revolution in speech."[1] This description of the changes in American life was profoundly dismissive. Duane suggested that all citizens now considered themselves democrats, and thus the term "democracy" could be attached to widely varying behavior, much of it harmful to Duane's idea of a democratic republic.

Such an interpretation certainly accorded with Duane's beliefs and concerns in the year of the Corrupt Bargain. Like all Jeffersonians, Duane had organized against the Federalists' decisive attempt to restore order and hierarchy during the 1790s. The Federalists sought to fortify a beleaguered natural aristocracy with policies that combined political and economic power with social and cultural grandeur. The movement that rose against them spoke bravely of unleashing human potential. Jeffersonians talked movingly about expanding equality, autonomy, and human dignity. They believed that they offered a profound alternative not just to the Federalists but to the human tradition of inequality, brutality, exploitation, and condescension that they believed had long shaped relations between rulers and ruled. This tradition they believed the Federalists sought to preserve.

As usual, Thomas Jefferson spoke more movingly than most about the differences between the two parties and about the meaning of the all-important Jeffersonian triumph. One year before Duane suggested that changes in American life centered more on the words that men spoke than on the deeds that they did, Jefferson gave his views on the same subject. In a letter of 1823 to Supreme Court Justice William Johnson, Jefferson explained precisely what he thought the revolution of 1800 had achieved. It had allowed Americans to break forever with the sorry human past. For the

doctrines of Europe were that men in numerous associations cannot be restrained within the limits of order and justice but by forces physical and moral wielded over them by authorities independent of their will — hence their organization of kings, hereditary nobles, and priests. Still further, to constrain the brute force of the people, they deem it necessary to keep them down by hard labor, poverty, and ignorance; and to take from them, as from bees, so much of their earnings as that unremitting labor shall be necessary to obtain a sufficient surplus barely to sustain a scanty and miserable life. And these earnings they apply to maintain their privileged orders in splendor and idleness, to fascinate the eyes of the people, and to excite in them a humble adoration and submission, as to an order of superior beings. Although few among us had gone all those lengths of opinion, yet many had advanced, some more, some less, on the way. And in the convention which formed our government, they endeavored to draw the cords of power as tight as they could obtain them, to lessen the dependence of the general functionaries on their constituents. . . . To recover, therefore, in practice, the powers which the nation had refused, and to warp to their own wishes those actually given, was the steady object of the federal party. Ours, on the contrary, was to maintain the will of the majority of the convention and of the people themselves. We believed . . . that man was a rational animal, endowed by nature with rights, and with an innate sense of justice; and that he could be restrained from wrong and protected in right by moderate powers confided to persons of his own choice and held to their duties by dependence on his own will. We believed that the complicated organization of kings, nobles, and priests was not the wisest nor best to effect the happiness of associated man, that wisdom and virtue were not hereditary, that the trappings of such a machinery consumed by their own expense those earning of industry they were meant to protect and by the inequalities they produced exposed liberty to sufferance. We believed that men, enjoying in ease and security the full fruits of their own industry, enlisted by all their interests on the side of law and order, habituated to think for themselves and to follow their reason as their guide, would be more easily and safely governed than with minds nourished in error and vitiated and debased, as in Europe, by ignorance, indigence, and oppression. The cherishment of the people then was our principle, the fear and distrust of them that of the other party.[2]

Duane's brief statement and Jefferson's extended eloquence provide quite a contrast. In 1823 Jefferson saw a fundamental and decisive change, an irreversible triumph. One year later, Duane did not. The Philadelphia Democrats had hoped to make popular intervention in public affairs perpetual and virtually complete. They sought to construct a politics where majorities could identify and check people or behavior that threatened the community's idea of democracy. This democratic ideal required majority deliberation of economic, political, and legal decisions, which by 1824, it was clear, would not be made by popular arbitrators, journeymen's organizations, or local majorities. Philadelphia Democrats such as Duane could detect a revolution in speech in 1824. But this revolution in speech had not produced their revolution of deeds.

At the risk of simplifying what is complex, allow me to pit Duane and Jefferson against each other. Whose sentiment was more justified in 1823–24? How significant was Jeffersonian triumph? Since the momentous events surrounding Jefferson's election to the presidency, had anything really changed? A good way to judge whether Duane's dismissal of the achievements of the Jeffersonian era was appropriate is to consider for a moment the group that he hated most: the Pennsylvania Quids. The Quids by 1824 had become, or in the case of the deceased Alexander J. Dallas had recently been, leading National Republicans. By 1824 the national bank had returned, and indeed it was four times larger than the first Bank of the United States. The national government was again in debt. As secretary of the Treasury, Dallas had asked for and been granted taxes unlike any levied since the Federalist era. The National Republicans were aggressively pursuing a diversified economy. Political economists such as Matthew Carey and politicians such as Henry Clay spoke of an American System. When they did, they drew intellectual inspiration from Hamilton's *Report on Manufactures*. Duane believed that only speech, and not deeds, had changed. His contention should be easiest to accept if one concentrates on the National Republicans and their Quid origins and influences.

Yet a careful consideration of the National Republicans' politics and political economy inescapably suggests that Jefferson's belief in a vital change, and not Duane's frustrated dismissal, more reliably characterized the United States on the eve of the Age of Jackson. The Federalists had pursued a political economy of economic development from the top down. The National Republicans pursued such a political economy from the bottom up. The National Republicans democratized American political economy. Their policies of development had as their foundation a commitment to social mobility and the betterment of citizen producers — the common man.[3]

The cornerstone of the American System was the series of protective tariffs passed by Congress between 1816 and 1828. The Federalists, we need to remind ourselves, eschewed such tariffs. They understood that such protection rewarded and strengthened artisans, a prospect that the Federalists found politically, socially, and culturally terrifying. The National Republicans rechartered the Bank of the United States, but they did so in the context of the transformation and democratization of American finance. Three banks existed in 1791. By 1820 state legislatures had chartered over three hundred.[4] Pennsylvania's chartering of forty-two banks in one legislative session was but one example of this spectacular expansion of credit. By 1820 Jeffersonians had overseen "the parade of institutions" that had so concerned Fisher Ames. Because they had done so, it was impossible for a central bank to dominate the nation's finances, just as it was beyond the means of that central bank's directors to confine the status of creditworthiness to those whom Ames had considered "safer people." Local men interested in improving their localities sought credit from others in the same position, men who shared their concerns and interests.

In this context, the National Republicans viewed the second national bank in a completely different way than the Federalists had the first one. The second national bank would receive sizable portions of local bank notes as Americans paid their taxes and purchased public lands. The national bank could then judiciously call for specie repayment and ensure that local banks did not emit paper notes irresponsibly. But if it supervised effectively, it would only further the local banks' capacities to extend reliable credit to the free, autonomous producer citizens busily and industriously improving the nation.

With protective tariffs the national government could not rely as completely on imposts to generate revenue. Hamilton's revenue tariffs would be replaced by the sale of western lands. This policy again underscored the qualitative transformation of American political economy and the significance of Jeffersonian triumph. The Federalists had feared the West and distant westerners beyond the control of centralized authority. The whiskey rebels confirmed these fears. In one of Hamilton's last acts before the incident at Weehawken, he criticized the Louisiana Purchase.[5] The National Republicans created a developmental political economy that democratized access to credit and support for manufacturing. Their political economy encouraged social mobility and fluidity. Ideally, westward expansion would replicate independence and autonomy across space. The empire of liberty would be wealthier and more economically diverse than Jefferson had imagined or probably considered salutary. But under the National Republicans, it would still be the empire of liberty. The political economy of the National Republicans was entirely shaped by the Jeffersonian tradition.

In 1824 the National Republicans were the most extreme supporters of the energetic national state and a capitalist economy. That they occupied one end of the legitimate political spectrum shows that by the 1820s the entire American world was Jeffersonian. This world was divided; it produced bitter conflict. It did so precisely because the National Republicans were not in any way neo-Federalists. The 1820s witnessed bitter division and conflict because bitter division and conflict had been intrinsic to Jeffersonian thought from the beginning. By the 1820s everyone was Jeffersonian, which meant, of course, that conflict over the future of American politics, society, and economy had only just begun. Put another way, when Jefferson called his victory the revolution of 1800, if anything he underestimated its significance and lasting influence.

Much of this significance resulted from Jeffersonian triumph in Pennsylvania. From the bitter conflict that raged in Pennsylvania between 1800 and 1820 there emerged new amalgamations of ideas that provided a foundation for what ultimately became the mainstream values of middle and late nineteenth-century America. In response to radical ideas, the Quids and especially the Snyderites began to stress two things: a cult of democratic personality connected to a democratic cultural ethos, and the spectacularly unprecedented availability of productive resources in the new United States. These two things they saw as connected. Proper self-made democratic men could mobilize and make available vast productive resources. Thus the happy mediocrity of condition would merge with social mobility, social fluidity, and entrepreneurial values. In such a culture and political economy radical political solutions would be unnecessary. Indeed, they would harm the happy mediocrity of condition by making ownership of property unstable, thus discouraging the commercial and entrepreneurial values that provided opportunity for all.

This belief system, at once capitalist and democratic, accomplished several things. First, it underscored that the Jeffersonian triumph of 1800 was definitive. The ordered hierarchical world the Federalists sought was smashed irrevocably by movement, scramble, change, and pursuit of the main chance.

Second, it grounded the faith in opportunity and social mobility in reality; there was an abundance of productive property in the nation — abundance virtually unprecedented in the Western world. This abundance allowed for the development of a nineteenth-century social and economic order — the fusion of democracy and capitalism — that just might deserve the name American exceptionalism. There was greater mobility and opportunity in the United States between 1800 and 1860 than ordinary people had ever reasonably expected to experience.[6] But, third, this belief system drove from the mainstream a set of political ideas and concerns articulated as part of an effort to critique and curb what future generations would call capitalist excess. From within the political mainstream over the course of the nineteenth century, it became ever more difficult to pose popular and political alternatives to market solutions, even when the happy mediocrity of condition grew to be in danger.

Threats to the happy mediocrity of condition profoundly troubled all of those Pennsylvania Jeffersonians who considered Duane the enemy. Men such as Carey, Binns, and the rest embraced a vision of the future where want, dependence, and indignity were vanquished. Given the extent of this hope, many of them could not help but grow concerned as the economy of boom and bust, wealth and want, developed.

By the mid-1830s Matthew Carey, for one, had become quite alarmed. The sad fact was that numerous citizens did not enjoy the conditions he deemed necessary for productive citizenship. Furthermore, the commitment, extending now for a generation, to protective tariffs, the expansion of banking, internal improvement, and an increasingly integrated national economy had not entirely delivered on the promises of procapitalist Jeffersonians. By 1833 Carey sought a solution. Nevertheless, he remained committed to the fusion of democracy and capitalism that he had done so much to construct. Thus, he sought to balance what were increasingly incompatible commitments: the desire for universal egalitarianism, autonomy, and independence, and the embrace of a largely free, unregulated market. In his 1833 pamphlet *Appeal to the Wealthy of the Land, Ladies as Well as Gentlemen, on the Character, Conduct, Situation, and Prospects of Those Whose Sole Dependence for Subsistence is on the Labour of Their Hands,* the only solution Carey could conceive was to beg the wealthy to give "a portion of their superfluous wealth" to those laborers in need.[7]

Carey did believe that the fusion of democracy and capitalism had achieved a great deal. The nation's wealthy did not have to fear for those numerous industrious citizens who were able "to save enough in the course of a few years, to commence business on a small scale on their own account." American democracy depended on the citizens being "stimulated by that interest which animates those who work for themselves," and this fusion of democracy and capitalism allowed many to be so stimulated. But this political economy also produced unforeseen and profoundly troubling conditions. The "friends of humanity, . . . all those whose views extend[ed] beyond their own narrow selfish concerns," had to acknowledge, Carey insisted, that a growing number of Americans worked permanently for wages and "when sick or unemployed, must perish unless relieved by charitable individuals, benevolent societies, or the guardians of the poor."[8] When Carey called on the wealthy to be charitable, he approached acknowledging that the fusion of democracy and capitalism did not provide independence and dignified autonomy for all. Tragically, the defeat of hierarchy and privilege, and the democratization of opportunity, produced a society where "even among the occupations of males, there are some which are so indifferently remunerated that no industry, no economy, no providence, in the times which the parties are fully employed, will enable them to save wherewith to support themselves and families in times of stagnation and during severe seasons."[9]

Though this fusion of democracy and capitalism would not succeed in eradicating conditions that Carey once believed were caused solely by artificial privilege, he could not leave behind the ideals and assumptions that he had long considered synonymous with justice and democracy. Carey could not endorse the radical proposals for redress growing ever more available after 1819. Despite systemic inequality, something the fusion of democracy and capitalism was supposed to end, this system of ideas remained for Carey the only legitimate blueprint for a just society. Hence the need for charity. When the poor inevitably felt privation, the only solution was the munificence of the rich. The self-made way by which countless ordinary people rose in American society after 1820 was quite new.[10] This social mobility owed much to the political economy of Carey and other procapitalist Jeffersonians. But as early as the 1830s Carey was forced to acknowledge that even the fusion of democracy and capitalism could not leave inequality and injustice behind.

Increasingly after 1820, and particularly as workingmen's parties and nascent socialist ideals offered alternative ideas, the defenders of this fusion of democracy and capitalism became ever more shrill.[11] Thus the ideal of a democratic, dynamic internal economy proved impossible to oppose within the American mainstream. The assumptions surrounding it held sway well after 1850, as it became increasingly less likely that this body of ideas would

build the world that procapitalist Jeffersonian defenders of the happy mediocrity of condition had always wanted.[12]

All Pennsylvania Jeffersonians sought to preserve the happy mediocrity
of condition. They thought long and hard about how to protect the material independence that democratic citizenship required. Yet Quids, and later
Snyderites, sincerely feared that the Philadelphia Democrats' ideas would
destroy the Philadelphia Democrats' ideals. Thus, they could brook no
qualification or dissent from their political economy of liberal capitalism and
their political ideology of democracy, which nurtured their political economy. To acknowledge that this liberal capitalist and democratic belief system would not deliver what it promised would open up space for dangerous
ideas that would surely destroy the happy mediocrity of condition.

Faced with the triumph of this democratic, liberal, and capitalist belief
system, did William Duane have anything relevant to say in 1824? He did
misunderstand the profound change that had occurred as a result of the
Jeffersonian triumph. Nevertheless, in misunderstanding it he was moving
closer to a deeper truth that Jefferson did not comprehend. Duane had finally come to fear that even very ordinary men would succumb to the temp-
tation of being dangerously wealthy unless a democratic majority could
remind them of their better selves. In 1824 Duane could have dwelled quite
sadly on the lessons of Cosimo de'Medici or, closer to home, Thomas
Leiper. By that year Duane was finally confronting that threats to the happy
mediocrity of condition could come from those he included within the category "the people." The Philadelphia Democrats struggled for twenty years
to articulate ways in which democratic majorities could protect themselves
from potentially dangerous men. Managing to figure out a politics that allowed majorities to do that would also protect potentially dangerous men
from the worst versions of themselves. But by 1824 those who wished to
pause, to slow down, to consider the origins of agrarian laws, the sources of
wealth and poverty and patrician and plebeian, to reflect on the ways the
actions surrounding them might contribute to human misery — those people had difficulty finding a place in the American mainstream. They confronted an aggressive and coherent political economy and belief system that
had no time or use for them. Yet despite losing the capacity to influence the
mainstream, Duane was groping toward an understanding of the true complexity of the Jeffersonian victory that Jefferson's statement suggests he
only partially possessed. By 1824 Duane had begun to realize that the variety of people who could claim to be democrats meant that the category "the
people" was useless. The United States in 1824 was undeniably a democracy.

Yet Duane could see that there was something hollow about a democracy where some of the people benefited only when others could not.

Over the course of the nineteenth century this democracy produced greater privation and inequality than any figure of the early Republic could ever have imagined. In the process, American society became something altogether unlike anything any Pennsylvania Jeffersonian had sought or hoped for. This world of aggressive individual acquisitiveness, vulnerability, anxiety, and poverty amid plenty was far removed from the time when there existed within the political mainstream ideas designed to prevent such developments. Many of these ideas were doubtless unworkable. But when they were forced out of the political mainstream in the nineteenth century, so, too, was much of the will and spirit to confront want and suffering. With that spirit banished from the ideological and political mainstream, as wealthy as the United States became, Americans were poorer for it.

Republicanism, Liberalism, Democracy, Capitalism, and the Historians

In her 2001 Presidential Address to the members of the Society for Historians of the Early American Republic, Joyce Appleby urged her audience to maintain the "intellectual effort" to explain how Americans made their nation a capitalist culture and society.[13] *Crucible of American Democracy* is very much a part of that effort. By seeking to contribute to the telling of this story through an examination of Jeffersonian political thought, this book intersects with two (at times overlapping) historiographies. The first is the scholarly work that established what historians in their shorthand called the republicanism-liberalism debate and efforts to transcend it. The second is the scholarly work treating the connections in the early national period between democracy and capitalism, most notably the work of Michael Merrill and Sean Wilentz and Gordon S. Wood's *Radicalism of the American Revolution*. I will discuss the connections between *Crucible of American Democracy* and these two historiographies in turn.

In *Crucible of American Democracy* I have discussed a set of preoccupations and developments in Jeffersonian political thought that are only somewhat compatible with the republicanism-liberalism debate and the efforts to reconcile the two positions. The original debate began when historians of Jeffersonian political thought identified what they termed a republican ideological tradition that most influenced the Jeffersonians. Historians such as

J.G.A. Pocock, John Murrin, and Lance Banning pointed to the seventeenth-
and eighteenth-century commonwealth or country tradition that had initially developed in response to the later Stuart monarchs and that cohered
in reaction to the Hanoverian state administered by Robert Walpole.[14] Since
Jeffersonian policy (and the Jeffersonian polity) laid the foundation for
nineteenth-century America's dynamic internal economy, the result had to
be seen as at least somewhat ironic and indicative of a profound transition
from the Jeffersonians' initial values. Heavily influenced by the commonwealth tradition, these initial values were, if not anticapitalist, deeply ambivalent about capitalism. The transition away from republicanism was so
searing that in certain scholarly works it was seen, in part, as both a product
and a cause of psychological trauma.[15]

The argument that the Jeffersonians were most influenced by the commonwealth tradition was challenged in the most sustained and vital way by
the work of Joyce Appleby. In a series of essays and a book, Appleby doubted
that there had ever been a significant commonwealth influence on Jeffersonian thought or a transition away from what was not there in the first
place.[16] She argued that a classical liberal tradition was far more significant
to the Jeffersonians than was commonwealth thought. Appleby was by no
means reviving an older view that posited a narrow, stultifying liberal consensus, a consensus that sharply limited possibilities for political creativity
and concerns for justice in nineteenth-century American life.[17] The liberal
tradition that she traced from mid-seventeenth-century England emphasized
the liberating potential of liberalism — the celebration of the individual —
in an age of organic hierarchy. She argued that Jeffersonians, when embracing a political ideology and political economy that placed the individual at
the center, broke with an antidemocratic past. Appleby's liberal tradition
came much closer than had the older, consensus-era view to catching the
truly subversive spirit of Locke's assault on absolutism and divine right and
Adam Smith's denunciation of state-directed economic systems shaped by
ancien régime privilege.[18]

A great debate ensued, and neither side convinced the other.[19] The defenders of the republican synthesis linked together several very important
concepts. They argued that Americans prized virtuous politics above individual self-interest. They were suspicious of activity that hindered independent landowners from making independent, well-informed decisions.
Such concerns required an ambivalent attitude toward behavior and institutions connected to commerce and profit seeking, particularly when associated with Great Britain. Thus the Jeffersonians often distrusted banks, paper

money and stock markets, and economic developments such as large-scale manufacturing that decreased the population of independent landowners. These advanced forms of commerce and production encouraged economic inequality, uncertain economic conditions, and the desire for ease and luxury. Such a culture discouraged sober devotion to the needs of the larger Republic. Ultimately the republican synthesis suggested (at times only implicitly) that the Jeffersonians were hostile to many of the features necessary for the development of capitalism.

Appleby argued that the Jeffersonians associated commerce, the market, the desire to better one's condition, and the pursuit of self-interest with freedom and the conditions that made the United States superior to tyrannical Europe. The Jeffersonians cared deeply about liberty, freedom, autonomy, and protection from injustice. Because they did, they demanded a politics that prevented the great from controlling the behavior of the citizenry. They celebrated commerce, economic development, the diversification of the market, and each citizen's right to take advantage of all opportunities. For the vast majority of Jeffersonians, those who would shape the nineteenth-century American mainstream, the commonwealth tradition was irrelevant. All Americans of significance after 1800 were liberal, and the triumph of liberalism, the celebration of democracy, and the embrace of capitalism were the logical culmination of Jeffersonian victory.

Such an impasse led to new efforts at synthesis. In seeking to synthesize, scholars sought to minimize the degree to which these two traditions, or languages, or idioms were mutually exclusive. Scholars such as James Kloppenberg and others reminded us that historians granted much more coherence and stability to categories of thought than they actually enjoyed in the past. Political languages could overlap within the same period, the same party, and even the same person. Gradually one strand of thought—in the American and Jeffersonian case clearly liberalism—ultimately overawed the others. With regard to the historians' debate, all participants were equally right (and all were equally wrong).[20] This effort to shift the terms of the debate had considerable virtues. It was deeply learned, and it provided a more realistic picture of people's muddy, semicoherent efforts to impose intellectual order on the world around them.

The scholarly effort to bridge the gulf between those arguing for either Jeffersonian republicanism or Jeffersonian liberalism was of great assistance as I sought to figure out the messy world of Pennsylvania Jeffersonian politics and political thought. Though republican concerns and preoccupations were clearly evident in Jeffersonian Pennsylvania, Pennsylvania Jeffersonians had assumptions and eventually constructed a belief system that could only be reconciled uncomfortably with the findings of the historians of the republican synthesis. Pennsylvania Jeffersonians clearly drew on the commonwealth tradition to critique the Federalists during the 1790s. They could identify with opposition leaders so completely because emphasizing luxury, corruption, and the horror of eighteenth-century Britain made sense to them. At the core of the Pennsylvania Jeffersonian understanding of the source of injustice was the fear of the corrupting influence of consolidated power, a fear around which the commonwealth tradition cohered.

Yet Pennsylvania Jeffersonians, as they moved into opposition, lived in very different social and economic conditions from those found in Virginia or idealized by the commonwealth thinkers of eighteenth-century Britain. Pennsylvania Jeffersonians desired what was already their reality: cities, advanced manufacturing, a market society, and the capacity for citizens to improve their standing within that society. As early as the 1790s these social and economic realities added up to a strong commitment to developing the domestic economy. Pennsylvania Jeffersonians felt no ambivalence or trauma as they placed rapid and diverse economic development and ever-expanding economic opportunity at the center of their democratic vision.[21]

Yet the preoccupations, concerns, and ideas of the Pennsylvania Jeffersonians who produced the crucible of conflict show that they were not merely slipping comfortably into the liberal tradition traced by Appleby. Appleby provided a brilliant discussion of this liberal tradition in the Jeffersonian era, a tradition that connected individual freedom with the ability to control productive property. But for the most part, she described a Jeffersonian commitment, primarily in the Middle Atlantic region, to a commercial economy built on widespread access to productive property. She then called this economy liberal and capitalist, and she defined capitalism as "free enterprise and greater productivity."[22] This definition invites confusion because the world of widely distributed productive property that was the foundation for democracy in Pennsylvania Jeffersonian political thought was altogether unlike the distribution of property after the Civil War, a period no one would describe as anything but capitalist. Even had the values and behavior that Appleby described inevitably produced the post–Civil War world, it would be imprecise to use the same term to describe eras with such profoundly different social relations concerning access to productive property.

The debates among Pennsylvania Jeffersonians showed that there was nothing inherent in their political and economic thought that made later developments inevitable. In Pennsylvania Jeffersonian political thought, liberal capitalism emerged from the unanticipated twists of polemic and conflict and not from original assumptions, ideas, or ideals. Even though Appleby provided the quite subtle argument that early capitalists did not realize that in time their commitment to free enterprise and greater productivity would undermine the ability of most to participate equally, this argument does not entirely work for Jeffersonians in Pennsylvania, despite its nuance.

Appleby's is a shrewd observation, and it helps to explain a part of the origins of the fusion of democracy and capitalism in Jeffersonian Pennsylvania. The category "the people" allowed different varieties of Pennsylvania Jeffersonians to avoid confronting the most critical source of the social and economic inequality they feared: the actions and competing interests of the multifarious citizens they placed within that category. They did not think threats to their original conception of democracy — a conception predicated on the happy mediocrity of condition — could come from "the people." Therefore, they were eager to remove constraints from this group, a removal that encouraged a social and economic order that threatened the happy mediocrity of condition.

As useful as Professor Appleby's insight is, it can only provide a partial explanation for the rise of democracy, liberalism, and capitalism in Jeffersonian Pennsylvania. Though Pennsylvania Jeffersonians constructed a belief system that prevented them from seeing "the people" as a threat to the happy mediocrity of condition, they were constantly preoccupied by the possibility of threats to it. The Philadelphia Democrats, and for a time the Snyderites, provided concrete (though ultimately insupportable) proposals for preventing actions conducive to inequality. But significantly, when the Quids (and eventually the Snyderites) opposed these proposals, they did not do so because they could not imagine threats to the happy mediocrity of condition. They could imagine such threats quite easily. But they also believed that the radical solutions were at least as dangerous as the inequality those solutions were intended to eradicate. Within the crucible of conflict that resulted, moderate Pennsylvania Jeffersonians did not have the option of proposing less extreme solutions. Though less extreme, such solutions were still difficult entirely to reconcile with the Quids' and Snyderites' ultimate solution — rapid, unshackled economic development. Within the crucible of conflict, ideas that could be presented as hindering this economic development could far too easily be tainted with the original extremity of calls to expunge the common law, destroy the separation of powers, and jettison written constitutions. The presence of this original body of frightening radical thought led to a reaction that narrowed options for moderates and provided an incentive for them to confine an expansive democratic vision within a political economy that ultimately could not sustain their original political philosophy.

By the 1830s Pennsylvania had as nearly pristine a version of classical liberal capitalism as was likely, given that societies are never as coherent as the belief systems created by political economists and political philosophers. Yet this version was not in place because Pennsylvania Jeffersonians easily and consensually embraced a long-standing ideological tradition and could not imagine it creating social and economic relations other than the ones they wanted. It was in place because the process of Pennsylvania Jeffersonian politics narrowed options and made certain ideas and concerns dangerous to think and voice. Liberal capitalism emerged in Pennsylvania precisely because Pennsylvania Jeffersonians could quite easily imagine threats to the happy mediocrity of condition. In acting on their fears, they lost control of the crucible of conflict. From that process of ideological formation there emerged Pennsylvania's fusion of democracy, liberalism, and capitalism. This process of engaging in polemic and argument transformed, and at times twisted, belief. Conflict, then, guaranteed that no group could pursue its original notions. Thus, no single group could either enjoy total victory or suffer the ironic fate of successfully silencing its opponents, imposing its first principles, and then seeing original ideas produce something unintended.

After the Philadelphia Democrats were pushed to the margins, the Pennsylvania Jeffersonian mainstream rapidly began to reflect the liberalism Appleby has so sensitively discussed. But this development was far more tortured and contingent than explaining it as an embrace of a long-standing intellectual tradition can allow. It was so because Pennsylvania's Jeffersonians were capable from the beginning of imagining what Appleby often suggests early nineteenth-century Jeffersonians could not foresee — that certain methods for unleashing individual potential could produce new forms of inequality and injustice.[23] In fact, the concern that rapid economic development might produce inequality if it was not structured and overseen properly was as central to Pennsylvania Jeffersonian political thought as was the commitment to rapid economic development. The difficulty of balancing these two positions produced the widely varying ideas for how to balance them, which in turn produced the crucible of conflict. And the crucible of conflict — a messy, contemporary, rational bordering on irrational, logical shading into illogical jumble of heated human action and noise — ended up producing a mainstream liberalism that resulted because Pennsylvania Jeffersonians could not consensually and calmly embrace a discrete ideological tradition.

Thus, the development of Pennsylvania Jeffersonian political thought helps to confirm the efforts of those scholars of political ideology who sought to move beyond the "either-or" quality of the republicanism-liberalism debate.[24] Yet, as I researched the process by which Pennsylvania Jeffersonians articulated their political thought, the scholarly effort to transcend the debate often left me frustrated. The scholars seeking to explain how republicanism and liberalism could overlap and blend tended to emphasize ideas and intellectual traditions at the expense of the people who spoke them. In the essays cited here, what drove ideological and intellectual development was the overlapping and intermingling of nebulous ideological traditions, a notion that often rendered the ideas themselves literally disembodied. Intellectually rigorous though this scholarship was, it encouraged historians to lose sight of the people of the era who sought to articulate their views about the republic and what it should be and do. Increasingly, what seemed to drive ideas and ideological development was the tectonic movements of ideological traditions, and not the aspirations, fears, dreams, hatreds, ideas, ideals, and jealousies of actual people. In an effort to resolve the controversies of the republicanism-liberalism debate, historians moved to a deeper level of abstraction where language and not people drove politics, and where language was, quite often, disembodied.

This degree of abstraction, quite unintentionally, revived the view that the late eighteenth and early nineteenth centuries were shaped by consensus. Americans (and particularly Jeffersonians) were all republicans; they were all liberals. Gradually, one was forced to conclude that the slow, tectonic shifts of political languages pushed liberalism up as our ideological Everest, and all Americans became merely liberal. The discussion of overlapping ideological traditions returned us to a Jeffersonian era where everybody, for the most part, agreed with the ideas of everybody else.

Quite simply, I did not find in Jeffersonian Pennsylvania this abstract process whereby Jeffersonians picked and chose from different discrete ideological traditions on their way to collectively fashioning nineteenth-century liberalism. Instead, I discovered a politics limited only by whatever very different individuals could imagine month by month, at times week by week, to deal with the very immediate conditions and events that concerned them. A bird's-eye view of the crucible of conflict might very well take on this quality of the overlapping and shifting of ideological languages. But on the ground it became a bloody, messy, chaotic struggle among actual people who discovered over time that they agreed about less and less. I have learned so much, and benefited so immeasurably, from the scholars who rigorously examined the multifarious ideologies blended together by early national Jeffersonians that it would be inexcusably ungrateful to deny that in the end the muddling through of Pennsylvania Jeffersonians can be explained with this scholarly conception. But the stress on the overlapping of disembodied political languages renders bloodless, cold, and ultimately consensual what the crucible of conflict in Jeffersonian Pennsylvania made bloody and hot.

The second historiographical issue with which *Crucible of American Democracy* intersects is the argument that the early national period irrevocably fused capitalism and democracy. The scholars who believe this fusion occurred in this period disagree about who drove the process. In seeking to explain how capitalism and democracy were yoked together during the early national period, Michael Merrill and Sean Wilentz drew on a rich body of scholarship, which showed that many ordinary Americans of the late eighteenth and early nineteenth centuries possessed values that were incompatible with the acquisitive mentality of commodity producers devoted to the market.[25] Yet Merrill and Wilentz sought to account for a decisive scholarly response that showed that virtually all American producers did in fact enter into market relations when they had the opportunity.[26] Merrill and Wilentz argued that historians were right to detect values held by early American producers that were incompatible with the political economy and belief system of nineteenth-century liberal capitalism. But they sought to redefine the debate about attitudes toward the market by suggesting that involvement in the market, and the commodity production implicit in that involvement, did not make the world of the late nineteenth century inevitable. By seeking to define more rigorously the term "capitalism" than they believed historians had yet defined it, Merrill and Wilentz argued that commerce and commodity production were not synonymous with capitalism, that in fact capitalism required a more precise definition than scholars such as Appleby had provided.[27]

Merrill and Wilentz cautioned that we must be careful about seeing what is often considered the inevitable development of capitalism in the United States, or of identifying the purportedly deep and unquestioned values that ensured its development. They acknowledged that those very few Americans who were openly hostile to commerce and economic development were quickly rendered marginal and could safely be dismissed as unrepresentative. Between the American Revolution and the Age of Jackson, virtually everybody praised commerce, and a great many championed economic diversification and the expansion of credit and banking.[28]

Though commerce and the market were nearly universally endorsed, Merrill and Wilentz argued that historians could not be satisfied with defining capitalism as simply an economy and culture based on private ownership of productive property and production for the market. It was difficult, after all, to find a period of history where people did not, or at least did not wish to, own property and produce for the market. It was useful to distinguish capitalism, which most scholars agreed was a modern economic form, from the commerce and commodity production that had occurred for time out of mind. To do so, one had to isolate what was broadly unique about the political economy of the last few centuries. One could more carefully identify an economy, culture, and society as capitalist, Merrill and Wilentz suggested, once a private group consolidated control of productive property, and when the vast majority, who could not afford to acquire productive property, were free to bargain with those who had it for access to it. These free laborers were not bound by custom or law to work for any person or region. Only the expense of moving, and the fact that they almost always bargained for access to productive property from a position of weakness, limited their mobility and their recompense for their labor. These combined conditions, Merrill and Wilentz pointed out, were relatively recent and, until the early modern period, quite rare.

Merrill and Wilentz argued that capitalism needed capitalists. Capitalism, to be meaningfully distinguished from mere devotion to private property and commodity production, included wage labor as the fundamental condition in the economy. Capitalism was in fact a system of social relations in which most of the productive property on which all depended was owned by a group — the capitalists — a group that was much smaller than those who depended on that productive property. Thus, describing the economy of the early United States — an economy predicated on widespread distribution of productive resources (a distribution that was unprecedented) — as capitalist confused far more than it clarified. Merrill and Wilentz proposed that this economy could perhaps be more usefully termed one of "democratic commerce."

Underneath the surface of alleged commitment to capitalism that historians had mistakenly associated with the ubiquitous devotion to commerce, Merrill and Wilentz argued, there existed a far more interesting nation during the period of the early Republic. Citizens of the early Republic planned to develop the land and mobilize its people, were concerned that this mobilization lead to social and economic equality and justice, and proposed a variety of suggestions for how to accomplish those things. It was past time, therefore, to discover a better term than "capitalism" to describe these economic attitudes and behaviors even though they included commitment to commerce and the market. Continuing to rely on the term "capitalism" led to careless equation of the early Republic with American society at a later date. Most Americans in the early Republic, Merrill and Wilentz concluded, wished to live comfortably, to avoid constant reliance on the resources of others, and to travel on good roads. These hopes became for too many historians the inability, or the seeds of the inability, of an entire people to imagine alternatives to what emerged later.

The insights of Merrill and Wilentz have been usefully supplemented by the work of certain economists and political theorists, in particular Robert Heilbronner. Heilbronner also provided insights that help to differentiate a capitalist economy from the commercial economy of private property Merrill and Wilentz argued characterized the early United States. Heilbronner pointed out that a capitalist society does not protect private property to the point where it allows owners to do whatever they wish with it. There are in modern capitalist societies all sorts of constraints placed on property holders. But capitalist societies do protect the right of these holders to deny access to their property. In capitalist societies, Heilbronner suggests, the great many have no productive property of their own. Thus, though they are free laborers, free to bargain for employment and to leave when they wish, the right to deny access to productive property, access which the great many must have to survive, creates a fundamental and undeniable disparity in power between capital and labor. In the world of democratic commerce described by Merrill and Wilentz, the right to deny access to property would of course exist, and would also of course remain entirely irrelevant.[29]

The theoretical conception "democratic commerce" was of immense value to me as I sought to sort out what Pennsylvania Jeffersonians hoped to accomplish, particularly the Philadelphia Democrats. Yet in the end, Merrill and Wilentz needed to explain how a desire to preserve widespread access to property, limit wage labor, and maintain an economic culture where producers owned what they produced gave way to something different—to capitalism. Here Merrill and Wilentz pointed to what could only be seen as a snake in the garden—those early Americans they identified as the moneyed men. They did not define the category moneyed men as rigorously as they did the political economy of democratic commerce, but it included great land speculators, substantial merchants, and financiers. This element in American life sought profits and power that could not be realized in an economy dominated by small property holders and modest profits. Through their manipulation of political power, through expensive development projects that raised land values and taxes, and through large-scale land speculation, moneyed men — the capitalists — destroyed the world of democratic commerce.

Quite simply, in the most capitalist state of the early national period, I did not find this process to be the case. The Federalists best fit the moneyed men posited by Merrill and Wilentz. But the Hamiltonian model for economic development was decidedly not the source of the ideas that spurred Pennsylvania's commitment to economic growth. Indeed, the Pennsylvania Jeffersonian political economy of economic development very much offered a "bottom-up" alternative to the Federalists' "top-down" plans.

The Jeffersonians of Pennsylvania who conceived a political economy of rapid economic development — editors such as Duane, the master cordwainers, smallholders such as Snyder and his followers, and even self-made professionals such as Dallas and Brackenridge — did not fit the description of moneyed men. Caesar A. Rodney was correct to point out that the conflicts developing during the early rise of capitalist social relations pitted against each other people who had not been born with silver spoons in their mouths. All Pennsylvania Jeffersonians conceived their visions of democracy by beginning with assumptions about political economy and economic and social relations that looked very much like the conception of democratic commerce provided by Professors Merrill and Wilentz. But in Jeffersonian Pennsylvania, despite what every Jeffersonian originally hoped for, the conflicts these small and middling property holders had with each other resulted in a mainstream belief system that could not tolerate criticism of economic processes that eventually destroyed the world of widespread ownership of productive resources. Capitalism was imposed from below after the defeat of America's moneyed men in the late eighteenth century. What Pennsylvania Jeffersonians could not have known was that they would lose control of what became the crucible of conflict. The mainstream belief system that emerged from this crucible sheltered new and far more powerful capitalists than any of the moneyed men Hamilton's programs could have sustained. Yet these new moneyed men were the product of the "bottom-up" nature of the fusion of democracy and capitalism.

Gordon S. Wood has been Merrill and Wilentz's most forceful and persuasive critic, and Joyce Appleby has broadly supported his alternative explanation.[30] Wood argued that the strivings and desires of middling and modest property holders at the local and state levels largely drove the fusion of democracy and capitalism. Obviously this historiographical controversy overlaps the republicanism-liberalism debate in several ways and confirms that somehow and in some way by the end of the early national period, liberal capitalism characterized American society, economy, and culture.

It is rarely a good idea for a monograph to challenge a synthesis, particularly one as fine as Wood's *Radicalism of the American Revolution*. In general *Crucible of American Democracy* fits into Wood's argument. Wood argued that between approximately 1790 and 1820 the commonwealth tradition ceased to dominate American intellectual and political life and was painfully and forcefully supplanted by a commitment to democracy, liberalism, and capitalism. Furthermore, only the nation's elite was sad to see it go. Postrevolutionary elites sought a republican future of virtuous hierarchy and self-denial that was entirely unsatisfactory to the vast majority of ordinary Americans. They were deeply suspicious of powerful and wealthy men who claimed that disinterested devotion to the commonweal required a political, social, cultural, and economic order that would, among other things, preserve their status as powerful and wealthy men. Though Wood did not doubt the sincerity of these elite convictions, he argued that ordinary Americans did. They rushed into the space in public affairs that they had forced open during the American Revolution and built a world by and for men on the make, modest striving property holders. The politicization and engagement of ordinary people destroyed the only belief system that could have contained an egalitarian, individualist liberal capitalism.

A synthesis has no choice but to smooth what is rugged; it must squeeze an ungainly collection of materials into a space smaller and more pleasingly shaped than that material demands. To work, a synthesis must de-emphasize that which falls over the sides. In the end Pennsylvania Jeffersonians did build the world Wood said they and Americans like them built. But how they came to do it is as important as where they ended up, and in the intimate details *Crucible of American Democracy* does not confirm Wood's synthesis.

This is certainly not a damning criticism. I do not believe that there can be such a criticism of *Radicalism of the American Revolution*. The first two parts of that book, more than any other single work, have influenced my understanding of the early national period as a time of profound transition and fluctuation. In the third part, where Wood makes his case for the fusion of capitalism and democracy, I follow him in seeing the main issues of the early national period as being shaped by the increasing predominance and connection of democracy and capitalism. Thus I am more in sympathy with Wood than I am with his most open critics.[31]

Yet, though I do not think I am making a damning criticism, *Crucible of American Democracy* does study the state with the most advanced economy and complex social relations of the Jeffersonian era. In Pennsylvania disagreements about the desirability of capitalism and capitalism's relation to democracy resulted from a far more thoughtful discussion of ideas than Wood allows for these years. Oddly, though ideas and grand utopian visions drove the action in the first two parts of Wood's synthesis, in the final part the ordinary folk who carried the day were shaped by a jumble of impulses, and a seething spirit of distrust, that never quite amounted to the degree of edification Wood found in the thought of elites. The grand and awe-inspiring, he suggested, gave way to the practical, hardheaded, and workaday. The result was the assault on privilege, hierarchy, deference, and elitism but also the loss of the capacity of American culture to embrace the high-minded, the idealized, and that which was larger than the immediate gratification of the individual.

Crucible of American Democracy suggests that we need not see the Jeffersonian era (at least in the arena of Jeffersonian political thought) as characterized by this rapid declension as the nation passed from a republican moment to a democratic epoch. Pennsylvania Jeffersonians, as early as William Findley in 1786 (before there even were Pennsylvania Jeffersonians), were capable of imagining a democracy as grand, as awe-inspiring, as public-spirited, and as capable of transcending individual self-interest as were any of the political philosophies of elite founders. The final mainstream incarnation of Pennsylvania Jeffersonian thought was narrower than the original preoccupations that produced the crucible of conflict. But the process of getting from original preoccupations to that final incarnation was far more thoughtful, far more painful, and far more profoundly shaped by enduring conflict among the ordinary middling property holders who made Jeffersonian political thought in Pennsylvania than Wood's synthesis can allow.

In the end what I found in Jeffersonian Pennsylvania can gesture toward the leading current statements that treat the questions that interest me most. At the start of my research I knew far less about Pennsylvania than I believed I did about the general features of Jeffersonian political thought and the relationship of democracy and capitalism in the early national period. On completing my book, I find things somewhat reversed. The current efforts to explain this period as a whole are quite good. But writing this book has convinced me that, about what used to be called "the big picture," in this case the evolving nature of Jeffersonian political thought and the advent of the fusion of democracy and capitalism, we have not yet learned enough to synthesize.

Notes

Introduction. The Crucible of Conflict

1. Thomas Jefferson to Albert Gallatin, in Henry Adams, ed., *The Writings of Albert Gallatin,* 3 vols. (New York: Lippincott, 1879), 1:119–120.

2. For the inability of either Jeffersonians or Federalists to imagine a loyal or purposeful opposition, see James Roger Sharp, *American Politics in the Early Republic: The New Nation in Crisis* (New Haven, Conn.: Yale University Press, 1993).

3. Caroline Robbins, *The Eighteenth-Century Commonwealthmen: Studies in the Transition, Development, and Circumstance of English Liberal Thought from the Restoration of Charles II until the War with the Thirteen Colonies* (Cambridge, Mass.: Harvard University Press, 1959); Bernard Bailyn, *The Origins of American Politics* (New York: Vintage, 1968); Bailyn, *The Ideological Origins of the American Revolution* (Cambridge, Mass.: Harvard University Press, 1967); Gordon S. Wood, *Creation of the American Republic, 1776–1787* (Chapel Hill: University of North Carolina Press, 1969); John M. Murrin, "The Great Inversion or Court vs. Country: A Comparison of the Revolutionary Settlements in England (1688–1721) and America (1776–1816)," in *Three British Revolutions: 1641, 1688, 1776,* ed. J.G.A. Pocock (Princeton, N.J.: Princeton University Press, 1981), 368–453.

4. This phrase appeared in the *Philadelphia Aurora,* May 27, 1805.

5. The debate is well known because Gordon S. Wood gave it a crucial place in his discussion about the advent of democracy. Readers will note the real differences between my reading of Findley and Wood's. I will discuss the historiographical implications of my study in the second part of my conclusion. For Wood's discussion of the Findley and Morris exchange, see Gordon S. Wood, "Interest and Disinterestedness in the Making of the Constitution," in *Beyond Confederation: Origins of the Constitution and American National Identity,* ed. Richard Beeman, Stephen Botein, and Edward Carter II (Chapel Hill: University of North Carolina Press, 1987), 69–109; and Wood, *Radicalism of the American Revolution* (New York: Vintage, 1991), 256–259.

6. Findley's remarks were recorded by the eventual Pennsylvania Jeffersonian (and a key figure in this book) Matthew Carey in Matthew Carey, ed., *Debates and*

Proceedings of the General Assembly of Pennsylvania on the Memorials Praying a Repeal or Suspension of the Law Annulling Charter of the Bank (Philadelphia, 1786). The significant portions of Findley's remarks are reprinted in Jack P. Greene, ed., *Colonies to Nation: A Documentary History of the American Revolution* (New York: Norton, 1975), 495–505. All subsequent references are to the Greene edition. The above quotation is from page 497.

7. Greene, *Colonies to Nation,* 496.

8. Ibid.

9. Ibid., 497.

10. Ibid.

11. Ibid.

12. Ibid.

13. Ibid.

14. Ibid., 496.

15. Ibid., 497.

16. Ibid., 498.

17. These conditions and their impact on Pennsylvania Jeffersonian politics will be discussed in chapter 1.

18. The impact of Federalist policy will be discussed in chapter 1.

19. Christopher Clark, *The Roots of Rural Capitalism: Western Massachusetts, 1786–1860* (Ithaca, N.Y.: Cornell University Press, 1990); Stephen Hahn and Jonathan Prude, eds., *The Countryside in the Age of Capitalist Transformation: Essays in the Social History of Rural America* (Chapel Hill: University of North Carolina Press, 1985); Bettye Hobbs Pruitt, "Self-Sufficiency and the Agricultural Economy," *William and Mary Quarterly* 41 (1984): 333–364; Winifred Rothenberg, *From Market Places to Market Economy: The Transformation of Rural Massachusetts, 1750–1850* (Chicago: University of Chicago Press, 1992); Lucy Simler, "The Landless Worker: An Index of Economic and Social Change in Chester County, Pennsylvania, 1750–1820," *Pennsylvania Magazine of History and Biography* 94 (1990): 163–199; Howard Rock, *Artisans of the New Republic: The Tradesmen of New York City in the Age of Jefferson* (New York: New York University Press, 1979); and Wood, *Radicalism of the American Revolution.*

20. Fine studies of Jeffersonian political ideas include Merrill D. Peterson, *Thomas Jefferson and the New Nation* (Oxford: Oxford University Press, 1970); Ralph Ketcham, *James Madison: A Biography* (Charlottesville: University Press of Virginia, 1990); Ketcham, *Presidents above Party: The First American Presidency, 1789–1829* (Chapel Hill: University of North Carolina Press, 1984); Lance Banning, *The Jeffersonian Persuasion: Evolution of a Party Ideology* (Ithaca, N.Y.: Cornell University Press, 1978); Banning, *The Sacred Fire of Liberty: James Madison and the Founding of the Federal Republic* (Ithaca, N.Y.: Cornell University Press, 1995); Drew R. McCoy, *The Elusive Republic: Political Economy in Jeffersonian America* (Chapel Hill: University of North Carolina Press, 1980); McCoy, *Last of*

the Fathers: James Madison and the Republican Legacy (Cambridge: Cambridge University Press, 1989); Norman K. Risjord, *The Old Republicans: Southern Conservatives in the Age of Jefferson* (New York: Columbia University Press, 1965); Robert Shalhope, *John Taylor of Caroline: Pastoral Republican* (Columbia: University of South Carolina Press, 1980); Herbert E. Sloan, *Principle and Interest: Thomas Jefferson and the Problem of Debt* (Oxford: Oxford University Press, 1995); and Richard K. Mathews, *The Radical Politics of Thomas Jefferson: A Revisionist View* (Lawrence: University Press of Kansas, 1986).

21. Two recent examples that splendidly epitomize the new political history of political culture are David Waldstreicher, *In the Midst of Perpetual Fetes: The Making of American Nationalism, 1776–1820* (Chapel Hill: University of North Carolina Press, 1997); and Simon P. Newman, *Parades and the Politics of the Street: Festive Culture in the Early American Republic* (Philadelphia: University of Pennsylvania Press, 1997).

22. For more on this theme, see Andrew Shankman, " 'A New Thing on Earth': Alexander Hamilton, Pro-manufacturing Republicans, and the Democratization of American Political Economy," *Journal of the Early Republic* 22 (2003): forthcoming.

Chapter 1. Background to the Struggle: The Federalist Challenge and the Origins of Pennsylvania's Jeffersonian Conflict

1. Quoted in Gary J. Kornblith and John M. Murrin, "The Making and Unmaking of an American Ruling Class," in *Beyond the American Revolution: Explorations in the History of American Radicalism*, ed. Alfred F. Young (De Kalb: Northern Illinois University Press, 1993), 27–79, quotation on 29.

2. Paul Rahe, *Republics Ancient and Modern: Inventions of Prudence: Constituting the American Regime* (Chapel Hill: University of North Carolina Press, 1994); and Rahe, "Fame, Founders, and the Idea of Founding in the Eighteenth Century," in *The Noblest Minds: Fame, Honor, and the American Founding*, ed. Peter McNamara (New York: Rowman and Littlefield, 1999), 3–36; Ketcham, *Presidents above Party*.

3. J.G.A. Pocock, *The Machiavellian Moment: Florentine Political Thought and the Atlantic Republican Tradition* (Princeton, N.J.: Princeton University Press, 1975); McCoy, *Elusive Republic*.

4. For example, one can note the terms James Otis used to describe the British constitution even after concerns about British taxation had arisen. See his "The Rights of the British Colonies Asserted and Proved" (1764). For Voltaire, see his *Letters concerning the English Nation* (1726–1727). A thoroughly enjoyable discussion of Voltaire the Anglophile is provided by Ian Buruma, *Anglomania: A European Love Affair* (New York: Random House, 1998), chap. 2.

5. For examples of the English country, commonwealth, or real Whig opposition, see the selections of Cato's letters in David L. Jacobson, ed., *The English Lib-*

ertarian Heritage (San Francisco: Fox and Wilkes, 1994); Isaac Kramnick, *Bolingbroke and His Circle: The Politics of Nostalgia in the Age of Walpole* (Cambridge: Cambridge University Press, 1968); Bailyn, *Origins of American Politics;* and H. T. Dickinson, *Bolingbroke* (London: Constable, 1970).

6. The best statement of this new view was, of course, Thomas Paine's in *Common Sense* (New York: Penguin, 1986). Paine of course was far more sanguine than men such as Jay about the future prospects of liberty in a republic.

7. David Ammerman, *In the Common Cause: American Response to the Coercive Acts of 1774* (Charlottesville: University Press of Virginia, 1974).

8. Wood, *Creation of the American Republic.*

9. On these developments, see T. H. Breen, *Tobacco Culture: The Mentality of the Great Tidewater Planters on the Eve of Revolution* (Princeton, N.J.: Princeton University Press, 1985); Richard Bushman, *The Refinement of America: Persons, Houses, Cities* (New York: Vintage 1992); and Bushman, *King and People in Provincial Massachusetts* (Chapel Hill: University of North Carolina Press, 1985).

10. For the broad cultural and social developments of anglicization, see Wood, *Radicalism of the American Revolution,* especially parts 1 and 2. On this topic the work of John M. Murrin is invaluable. See his "Review Essay," *History and Theory* 11 (1972): 226–275; "Anglicizing an American Colony: The Transformation of Provincial Massachusetts" (Ph.D. diss., Yale University, 1966); "The Transformation of the Bench and Bar of Eighteenth-Century Massachusetts," in *Colonial America: Essays in Politics and Social Development,* 3d ed., ed. Stanley N. Katz and John M. Murrin (New York: Knopf, 1983), 540–572; and "Political Development," in *Colonial British America: Essays in the New History of the Early Modern Era,* ed. Jack P. Greene and J. R. Pole (Baltimore: Johns Hopkins University Press, 1984), 345–383. See also Richard Bushman, "American High Style and Vernacular Cultures," in *Colonial British America,* 345–383; and Jere R. Daniell, "Politics in New Hampshire under Governor Benning Wentworth, 1741–1767," *William and Mary Quarterly* 23 (1966): 76–105. For the development of the politics of country harmony in Virginia and Governor Alexander Spotswood's failure to use the old corruption to forge stability, see *Proceedings of the Journals of the House of Burgesses of Virginia,* 1715, 1720, 1723–1726, 1727–1734, 1736–1740 (Richmond, 1912), 159–160, 163–170, 239–244.

11. On internal conflicts and radical revolutionary developments, see Marvin L. Michael Kay, "The North Carolina Regulation, 1766–1776: A Class Conflict," in *The American Revolution: Explorations in the History of American Radicalism,* ed. Alfred F. Young (De Kalb: Northern Illinois University Press, 1976), 71–123; Alfred F. Young, "George Roberts Twelves Hughes (1742–1840): A Boston Shoemaker and the Memory of the American Revolution," *William and Mary Quarterly* 38 (1981): 561–623; Ronald Hoffman, "The 'Disaffected' in the Revolutionary South," in *American Revolution,* 273–313; Edward Countryman, "Consolidating Power in Revolutionary America: The Case of New York, 1775–1783," *Journal of*

Interdisciplinary History 4 (1976): 645–677; and Countryman, *A People in Revolution: The American Revolution and Political Society in New York* (New York: Norton, 1981). For the Morris quotation, see page 138. See also Alfred F. Young, *The Democratic Republicans of New York: The Origins, 1763–1797* (Chapel Hill: University of North Carolina Press, 1967); Gary B. Nash, *The Urban Crucible: Social Change, Political Consciousness, and the Origins of the American Revolution* (Cambridge, Mass.: Harvard University Press, 1979); and Steven Rosswurm, *Arms, Country, and Class: The Philadelphia Militia and "Lower Sort" during the American Revolution, 1775–1783* (New Brunswick, N.J.: Rutgers University Press, 1987).

12. See Countryman, "Consolidating Power"; Hoffman "The 'Disaffected' in the Revolutionary South."

13. For these developments, see Robert E. Shalhope, "Republicanism, Liberalism, and Democracy: Political Culture in the Early Republic," in *The Republican Synthesis Revisited: Essays in Honor of George Athan Billings*, ed. Milton M. Klein, Richard D. Brown, and John B. Hench (Worcester, Mass.: American Antiquarian Society, 1992), 37–90; Jackson Turner Main, "Government by the People: The American Revolution and the Democratization of the Legislatures," *William and Mary Quarterly* 23 (1966): 391–407; Young, *Democratic Republicans of New York*; Hoffman, "The 'Disaffected' in the Revolutionary South."

14. Alan Tully, *Forming American Politics: Ideals, Interests, and Institutions in Colonial New York and Pennsylvania* (Baltimore: Johns Hopkins University Press, 1994).

15. Brooke Hindle, "The March of the Paxton Boys," *William and Mary Quarterly* 3 (1946): 461–487; George W. Franz, *Paxton: A Study of Community Structure and Mobility in the Colonial Pennsylvania Backcountry* (New York: Garland, 1989). See also Fred Anderson, *Crucible of War: The Seven Years' War and the Fate of Empire in British North America, 1754–1766* (New York: Vintage, 2000), in particular 160–165, 611–612.

16. It was not the only exception, as the Regulator movement in North Carolina and the conflict in the Hudson River Valley suggests.

17. James T. Lemon, *The Best Poor Man's Country: A Geographical Study of Early Southeastern Pennsylvania* (Baltimore: Johns Hopkins University Press, 1972).

18. Rowland Berthoff and John M. Murrin, "Feudalism, Communalism, and the Yeoman Freeholder: The American Revolution Considered as a Social Accident," in *Essays on the American Revolution*, ed. Stephen G. Kurtz and James H. Hutson (New York: Norton, 1973), 256–288; R. Eugene Harper, *The Transformation of Western Pennsylvania, 1770–1800* (Pittsburgh: University of Pittsburgh Press, 1991).

19. Thomas C. Cochran, "Philadelphia: The American Industrial Center, 1750–1850," *Pennsylvania Magazine of History and Biography* 106 (1982):323–340.

20. Sharon V. Salinger, "Artisans, Journeymen, and the Transformation of Labor in Eighteenth-Century Philadelphia," *William and Mary Quarterly* 40 (1983): 62–84; Billy G. Smith, *The "Lower Sort": Philadelphia's Laboring People, 1750–1800* (Ithaca, N.Y.: Cornell University Press, 1990); Ronald Schultz, *The Republic of*

Labor: Philadelphia Artisans and the Politics of Class, 1720–1830 (Oxford: Oxford University Press, 1993).

21. James H. Hutson, *Pennsylvania Politics, 1746–1770: The Movement for Royal Government and Its Consequences* (Princeton, N.J.: Princeton University Press, 1972).

22. For these sentiments, see Young, *Democratic Republicans of New York;* Hoffman, "The 'Disaffected' in the Revolutionary South."

23. Richard Allen Ryerson, "Republican Theory and Partisan Reality in Revolutionary Pennsylvania: Towards a New View of the Constitutionalist Party," in *Sovereign States in an Age of Uncertainty,* ed. Ronald Hoffman and Peter J. Albert (Charlottesville: University Press of Virginia, 1981), 95–133.

24. Rosswurm, *Arms, County, and Class;* Steven Rosswurm, "'As a Lyen out of His Den': Philadelphia's Popular Movement, 1776–1783," in *The Origins of Anglo-American Radicalism,* ed. Margaret C. Jacob and James R. Jacob (Atlantic Highlands, N.J.: Humanities Press International, 1984), 279–302.

25. Quoted in Rosswurm, "'As a Lyen out of His Den,'" 285.

26. Rosswurm, *Arms, Country, and Class;* John K. Alexander, "The Fort Wilson Incident of 1779: A Study of the Revolutionary Crowd," *William and Mary Quarterly* 31 (1974): 589–612.

27. Ryerson, "Republican Theory and Partisan Reality"; Wood, *Creation of the American Republic;* Edmund S. Morgan, *Inventing the People: The Rise of Popular Sovereignty in England and America* (New York: Norton, 1988).

28. Wood, *Creation of the American Republic;* John Adams "Thoughts on Government," in *The Political Writings of John Adams: Representative Selections* (New York: Liberal Arts Press, 1954), 83–92. See also C. Bradley Thompson, "John Adams and the Quest for Fame," in *Noblest Minds,* 73–96, especially 88–92.

29. Saul Cornell, "Aristocracy Assailed: The Ideology of Backcountry Anti-Federalism," *Journal of American History* 77 (1990): 1148–1172; Thomas Slaughter, *The Whiskey Rebellion: Frontier Epilogue to the American Revolution* (Oxford: Oxford University Press, 1986), chap. 3.

30. Mary M. Schweitzer, "The Spatial Organization of Federalist Philadelphia," *Journal of Interdisciplinary History* 24 (1993): 31–57.

31. Quoted in Robert J. Gouge, "The Philadelphia Economic Elite at the End of the Eighteenth Century," in *Shaping a National Culture: The Philadelphia Experience, 1750–1800,* ed. Catherine E. Hutchins (Winterthur, Del.: Winterthur, 1994), 15–43, quotation on 16.

32. Ethel Rasmusson, "Democratic Environment — Aristocratic Aspiration," *Pennsylvania Magazine of History and Biography* 90 (1966): 155–182.

33. Wood, *Radicalism of the American Revolution.*

34. Thomas M. Doerflinger, *A Vigorous Spirit of Enterprise: Merchants and Economic Development in Revolutionary Philadelphia* (Chapel Hill: University of North Carolina Press, 1986).

35. On George Washington's land speculation, see Slaughter, *Whiskey Rebellion;* Charles Royster, *The Fabulous History of the Dismal Swamp: A Story of George Washington's Times* (New York: Vintage, 1999); Lorraine Smith Pangle and Thomas L. Pangle, "George Washington and the Life of Honor," in *Noblest Minds,* 59–71.

36. Forrest McDonald, *Alexander Hamilton: A Biography* (New York: Norton, 1982).

37. Stanley Elkins and Eric McKitrick, *The Age of Federalism: The Early American Republic, 1788–1800* (Oxford: Oxford University Press, 1993); Whitney K. Bates, "Northern Speculators and Southern State Debts: 1790," *William and Mary Quarterly* 19 (1962): 30–48.

38. Bates, "Northern Speculators."

39. Jacob Cooke, ed., *The Reports of Alexander Hamilton* (New York: Harper and Row, 1964), 1–45.

40. John Brewer, *The Sinews of Power: War, Money, and the English State, 1688–1783* (New York: Knopf, 1989). See also P.G.M. Dickson, *The Financial Revolution in England: A Study in the Development of Public Credit, 1688–1756* (London: St. Martin's, 1967). See also J. H. Plumb, *The Growth of Political Stability in England, 1675–1725* (New York: Macmillan, 1967).

41. For the importance of country ideology in England and its influence in British North America see Pocock, *Machiavellian Moment;* Kramnick, *Bolingbroke and His Circle;* Dickinson, *Bolingbroke;* Bailyn, *Origin of American Politics;* Murrin, "Great Inversion," 368–453. See also note 9.

42. For Jefferson, see Merrill D. Peterson, *The Portable Thomas Jefferson* (New York: Penguin, 1975), 534–535; Banning, *Sacred Fire of Liberty;* Joseph Charles, *The Origins of the American Party System* (New York: Harper and Row, 1956).

43. Elkins and McKitrick, *Age of Federalism;* Charles, *Origins of the American Party System.*

44. Winton U. Solberg, *The Constitutional Convention* (Urbana: University Press of Illinois, 1990), 108–110; Alexander Hamilton, James Madison, and John Jay, *The Federalist Papers* (New York: Mentor Books, 1964), 77–84.

45. Cooke, *Reports of Alexander Hamilton,* 46–82.

46. Harold C. Syrett, ed., *The Papers of Alexander Hamilton,* 26 vols. (New York: Columbia University Press, 1962), 8:872.

47. W. B. Allen, ed., *Works of Fisher Ames as Published by Seth Ames,* 2 vols. (Indianapolis: Liberty Classics, 1983), 2:872.

48. Karl Friedrich Walling, *Republican Empire: Alexander Hamilton on War and Free Government* (Lawrence: University Press of Kansas, 1999); Joanne B. Freeman, "Dueling as Politics: Reinterpreting the Burr-Hamilton Duel," *William and Mary Quarterly* 53 (1996): 289–318; Gordon S. Wood, "An Affair of Honor," *New York Review of Books* 47 (2000): 67–72; Peter McNamara, "Alexander Hamilton, the Love of Fame, and Modern Democratic Statesmanship," in *Noblest Minds,*

141–162. For British policy during the 1780s, see J.C.A. Stagg, *Mr. Madison's War: Politics, Diplomacy, and Warfare in the Early American Republic, 1783–1830* (Princeton, N.J.: Princeton University Press, 1983); David J. Weber, *The Spanish Frontier in North America* (New Haven, Conn.: Yale University Press, 1992), 273–275.

49. The efforts and impact of Federalists such Duer and Nicholson are discussed later.

50. Hamilton, Madison, and Jay, *Federalist Papers*, 212; Cooke, *Reports of Alexander Hamilton*, 167.

51. Hamilton, Madison, and Jay, *Federalist Papers*, 212.

52. Ibid., 214–215.

53. The society's prospectus is reprinted in Arthur Harrison Cole, ed., *Industrial and Commercial Correspondence of Alexander Hamilton Anticipating His Report on Manufactures* (Chicago: A. W. Shaw, 1928).

54. Joseph Stancliffe Davis, *Essays in the Earlier History of American Corporations* (Cambridge, Mass.: Harvard University Press, 1917), 354.

55. Allen, *Works of Fisher Ames*, 2:873–874.

56. Robert F. Jones, *"The King of the Alley" William Duer: Politician, Entrepreneur, and Speculator, 1768–1799* (Philadelphia: University Press of Pennsylvania, 1992), 102. See also Davis, *Essays in the Earlier History of American Corporations*, 111–345; Cathy Matson, "Public Vices, Private Benefits: William Duer and His Circle, 1776–1792," in *New York and the Rise of American Capitalism: Economic Development and the Social and Political History of an American State, 1780–1870*, ed. William Pencak and Conrad Edick Wright (New York: New-York Historical Society, 1989), 72–123.

57. For these figures and the prospectus of the company, see Cole, *Industrial and Commercial Correspondence of Alexander Hamilton*, esp., 194–196.

58. Davis, *Essays in the Earlier History of American Corporations*, chaps. 2–3.

59. Syrett, *Papers of Alexander Hamilton*, 9:251.

60. Davis, *Essays in the Earlier History of American Corporations*, 416. Hamilton's ally, the Pennsylvania Federalist merchant John Nicholson, proved similarly ineffective. He courageously began a manufacturing enterprise in Pennsylvania but refused to devote capital to it at the expense of more reliable and established opportunities. In the end most of his workers left when he could not pay their wages because the bulk of his capital was tied up in land speculations and commercial ventures. See Cynthia Shelton, *The Mills of Manayunk: Industrialization and Social Conflict in the Philadelphia Region, 1787–1837* (Baltimore: Johns Hopkins University Press, 1986), chap. 1.

61. As a result of the deep influence of commonwealth thought in the colony and then state discussed earlier in this chapter.

62. Cochran, "Philadelphia." New York City did not become a major manufacturing city until after 1815, though it did have a thriving craft culture in the Jeffersonian era. See Rock, *Artisans of the New Republic;* Sean Wilentz, *Chants Democratic:*

New York City and the Rise of the American Working Class (Oxford: Oxford University Press, 1984).

63. Salinger, "Artisans, Journeymen," 62–84.

64. Ibid.

65. For the rise of free labor commitments, see Robert J. Steinfeld, *The Invention of Free Labor: The Employment Relation in English and American Law and Culture, 1350–1870* (Chapel Hill: University of North Carolina Press, 1991). For the Revolution's impact on slavery in Pennsylvania and generally, see Gary B. Nash and Jean R. Soderlund, *Freedom by Degrees: Emancipation in Pennsylvania and Its Aftermath* (Oxford: Oxford University Press, 1991); Nash, *Race and Revolution* (Madison, Wis.: Madison House, 1993). For the Revolution's impact on the white unfree, see W. J. Rorabaugh, "'I Thought I Should Liberate Myself from the Thraldom of Others': Apprentices, Masters, and the Revolution," in *Beyond the American Revolution,* 185–220.

66. Salinger, "Artisans, Journeymen." For the journeymen cordwainers' trial, see chapter 4. For wages during the 1790s, see Billy G. Smith, "The Material Lives of Laboring Philadelphians, 1750–1800," *William and Mary Quarterly* 38 (1981): 163–202; *The "Lower Sort,"* 116, 121; Salinger, "Artisans, Journeymen," 69.

67. Salinger, "Artisans, Journeymen."

68. For the rising political consciousness and radicalism of artisans and plebeian city dwellers, see Nash, *Urban Crucible;* Nash, "Social Change and the Growth of Prerevolutionary Urban Radicalism," in *American Revolution,* 3–36; Young, "George Robert Twelves Hughes"; Alfred F. Young, "The Framers of the Constitution and the 'Genius' of the People," *Radical History Review* 42 (1988): 8–18; Rosswurm, *Arms, Country, and Class;* Charles S. Olten, *Artisans for Independence: Philadelphia Mechanics and the American Revolution* (Syracuse, N.Y.: Syracuse University Press, 1975). In particular for Leveller influences on the Philadelphia craftsmen, see Schultz, *Republic of Labor.*

69. Quoted in Davis, *Essays on the Earlier History of American Corporations,* 436.

70. Ibid., 428.

71. Ibid., 449, 431.

72. *Aurora,* November 30, 1804.

73. For the impact of the French Revolution on American politics, see Elkins and McKitrick, *Age of Federalism,* 308–329; Noble E. Cunningham Jr., *The Jeffersonian Republicans: The Formation of Party Organization, 1789–1801* (Chapel Hill: University of North Carolina Press, 1957), 54–55; Sharp, *American Politics in the Early Republic,* 70–74.

74. Gary B. Nash, "The American Clergy and the French Revolution," *William and Mary Quarterly* 22 (1965): 392–412. For the concerns of more secular Federalists, see McDonald, *Alexander Hamilton,* 270–282.

75. John Brewer, *Party Ideology and Popular Politics at the Accession of George III* (Cambridge: Cambridge University Press, 1976).

76. E. P. Thompson, *The Making of the English Working Class* (New York: Vintage, 1963); Albert Goodwin, *The Friends of Liberty: The English Democratic Movement in the Age of the French Revolution* (London: Hutchinson Press, 1979); Michael Durey, *Transatlantic Radicals and the Early American Republic* (Lawrence: University Press of Kansas, 1997); David A. Wilson, *United Irishmen, United States: Immigrant Radicals in the Early Republic* (Ithaca, N.Y.: Cornell University Press, 1998). See also Richard J. Twomey, *Jacobins and Jeffersonians: Anglo-American Radicalism in the United States, 1790–1820* (New York: Garland, 1989).

77. Quoted in Eugene Perry Link, *Democratic Republican Societies, 1790–1800* (New York: Columbia University Press, 1942), 11.

78. Quoted in James Tagg, *Benjamin Franklin Bache and the Philadelphia Aurora* (Philadelphia: University of Pennsylvania Press, 1991), 34.

79. Quoted in Link, *Democratic Republican Societies*, 11.

80. William D. Barber, "'Among the Most Techy Articles of Civil Police': Federal Taxation and the Adoption of the Whiskey Excise," *William and Mary Quarterly* 25 (1968): 58–84.

81. Roland M. Baumann, "Philadelphia Manufacturers and the Excise Tax of 1794: The Forging of the Jeffersonian Coalition," *Pennsylvania Magazine of History and Biography* 106 (1982): 3–39

82. Ibid., 20.

83. *Aurora*, October 18, 1804, reprinted from the *National Intelligencer*.

84. For insights into the political economy of the Democratic Republican societies, see Philip S. Foner, *The Democratic-Republican Societies, 1790–1800: A Documentary Source Book of Constitutions, Declarations, Resolutions, and Toasts* (New York: Greenwood Press, 1976), 68, 77.

85. Michael Leib left few letters or other papers. The best discussion of his significance is Kenneth W. Keller, "Diversity and Democracy: Ethnic Politics in Southeastern Pennsylvania, 1788–1799," (Ph.D. diss., Yale University, 1971), chap. 5. The letters that reveal most about Leib's personality and beliefs are Michael Leib to Matthew Carey, October 12, 1802, Lee and Febiger Collection; Leib to John Barker, October 18, 1803, Gratz Collection—American Physicians, case 7, box 31; Leib to Frederick Wolbert, November 24, 1803, Dreer Collection—American Statesmen, all in Historical Society of Pennsylvania (HSP).

86. See Sharp, *American Politics in the Early Republic*, for elite Jeffersonian concerns about overly democratic popular behavior. A clear statement of Jefferson's fears on this matter and the need for a national aristocracy is found in Peterson, *Portable Thomas Jefferson*, 534–535. For Madison's views, see Colleen A. Sheehan, "The Politics of Public Opinion: James Madison's 'Notes on Government,'" *William and Mary Quarterly* 49 (1992): 609–627.

87. See Slaughter, *Whiskey Rebellion*, chap. 8, on these themes; also Sharp, *American Politics in the Early Republic*, on the emerging demands for democratic representation developing among the Jeffersonians during the 1790s.

88. See John R. Commons, ed., *A Documentary History of American Industrial Society,* 10 vols. (New York: Russell and Russell, 1958), 3:121, 123–124; *Aurora,* November 28, 1805.

89. For these concerns, in addition to the works cited earlier, see also Richard H. Kohn, *Eagle and Sword: The Beginnings of the Military Establishment in America* (New York: Free Press, 1975), esp. 139–273.

90. Richard Miller, *Philadelphia — The Federalist City: A Study of Urban Politics, 1789–1801* (Port Washington, N.Y.: Kennikat Press, 1976), 61.

91. For Federalists and the excise, see Barber, "'Among the Most Techy Articles of Civil Police'"; Slaughter, *Whiskey Rebellion.*

92. For Jay's earlier negotiations with Spain, see John E. Crowly, *The Privileges of Independence: Neomercantilism and the American Revolution* (Baltimore: Johns Hopkins University Press, 1993), 114–115.

93. Statistics are taken from Harper, *Transformation of Western Pennsylvania,* chap. 2.

94. For Brackenridge's acreage, see Harper, *Transformation of Western Pennsylvania,* chaps. 3–4. For Gallatin, see Raymond Walters, *Albert Gallatin: Jeffersonian Financier and Diplomat* (New York: Macmillan, 1957), 220–221. For Findley, see Wood, "Interest and Disinterestedness," 69–109.

95. Thomas Slaughter skillfully describes the violence of western Pennsylvania in the introductory vignettes to the chapters of *The Whiskey Rebellion.*

96. Albert Gallatin, antiexcise petition in Adams, *Writings of Albert Gallatin,* 1:2–4.

97. For the continuity of western Pennsylvania thinking about taxes, see Slaughter, *Whiskey Rebellion,* chap. 1.

98. For concerns about the economic implications of the excise, see "Declaration of the Committee of Fayette County," in Adams, *Writings of Albert Gallatin,* 1:4–9.

99. For Washington's acreage and attitudes, see Slaughter, *Whiskey Rebellion,* chap. 5.

100. "Declaration of the Committee of Fayette County."

101. Slaughter, *Whiskey Rebellion,* chaps. 11–13; Elkins and McKitrick, *Age of Federalism,* 461–488.

102. Walters, *Albert Gallatin,* chaps. 6–7.

103. "Speech of Albert Gallatin, Representative of Fayette County to the Pennsylvania Assembly," in Adams, *Writings of Albert Gallatin,* 3:1–68.

104. The Papers of Albert Gallatin, Princeton University microfilm, Firestone Library, reel 3, March 1, 1798.

105. These remarks were influenced by G. S. Rowe, *Thomas McKean: The Shaping of American Republicanism* (Boulder: University Press of Colorado, 1978). For George Clinton, see Young, *Democratic Republicans of New York.*

106. Two years after Hamilton's birth.

107. Raymond Walters, *Alexander James Dallas: Lawyer, Politician, Financier, 1759–1817* (Philadelphia: University Press of Pennsylvania, 1943).

108. Keller, "Diversity and Democracy," 158.

109. Alexander James Dallas, "Features of Mr. Jay's Treaty," in George Mifflin Dallas, ed., *The Life and Writings of Alexander James Dallas* (Philadelphia, 1871), 160–210, quotation on 183.

110. On the Jay Treaty and the reaction, see Elkins and McKitrick, *Age of Federalism*, 406–430; Charles, *Origins of the American Party System*, chap. 3; Miller, *Philadelphia — The Federalist City*, chap. 5; Walters, *Albert Gallatin*, chap. 8; Gerald A. Combs, *The Jay Treaty: Political Battleground of the Founding Fathers* (Berkeley: University of California Press, 1970); Roland M. Baumann, "John Swanwick: Spokesman for 'Merchant-Republicanism' in Philadelphia, 1790–1798," *Pennsylvania Magazine of History and Biography* 97 (1973): 131–182.

111. Miller, *Philadelphia — The Federalist City*, tables on pages 15 and 18 and chap. 6. Miller shows that Federalist candidates were generally wealthier than their Republican opponents at each office level. Furthermore, Federalist politicians tended to be merchants and professionals, whereas Jeffersonians were often successful master craftsmen.

112. Miller, *Philadelphia — The Federalist City*, chap. 6.

113. Quoted in John C. Miller, *The Federalist Era, 1789–1801* (New York: Harper and Row, 1960), 262.

114. For the Adams years, see Stephen G. Kurtz, *The Presidency of John Adams: The Collapse of Federalism, 1796–1800* (New York: A. S. Barnes, 1957); Manning J. Dauer, *The Adams Federalists* (Baltimore: Johns Hopkins University Press, 1968).

115. For the origins of the Quasi War with France, see James Morton Smith, *Freedom's Fetters: The Alien and Sedition Laws and American Civil Liberties* (Ithaca, N.Y.: Cornell University Press, 1956), chap. 1; Alexander De Conde, *The Quasi-War: The Politics and Diplomacy of the Undeclared War with France, 1797–1801* (New York: Scribner, 1966), chaps. 1–2; Elkins and McKitrick, *Age of Federalism*, 498–512, 537–580, 643–661.

116. Kenneth W. Keller, *Rural Politics and the Collapse of Pennsylvania Federalism* (Philadelphia: American Philosophical Society, 1982), 24–25.

117. Tagg, *Benjamin Franklin Bache;* Jefferey A. Smith, *Franklin and Bache: Envisioning the Enlightened Republic* (Oxford: Oxford University Press, 1990), pt. 2; Arthur Sheer, "Inventing the Patriot President: Bache's *Aurora* and John Adams," *Pennsylvania Magazine of History and Biography* 119 (1995): 369–399.

118. Edward C. Carter II, "A 'Wild Irishman' under Every Federalist Bed: Naturalization in Philadelphia, 1789–1806," *Proceedings of the American Philosophical Society* 133 (1989): 178–189.

119. Quoted in Smith, *Freedom's Fetters*, 9.

120. Smith, *Freedom's Fetters;* Leonard Levy, "Liberty and the First Amendment, 1790–1800," *American Historical Review* 68 (1962–63): 23–37.

121. Smith, *Freedom's Fetters*, 21. See also Richard N. Rosenfield, *American* Aurora: *A Democratic-Republican Newspaper Returns: The Suppressed History of Our Nation's Beginnings and the Heroic Newspaper That Tried to Report It* (New York: St. Martin's, 1997).

122. Stephen G. Kurtz, "The Presidency of John Adams," in *Essays on the Early Republic, 1789–1815,* ed. Leonard W. Levy and Carl Siracusa (Hinsdale, Ill.: Dryden Press, 1974), 109–137, quotation on 123.

123. Kurtz, "Presidency of John Adams," 116.

124. Keller, *Rural Politics,* 25–28; Elkins and McKitrick, *Age of Federalism,* 696–697.

125. For the Fries Rebellion, see Keller, *Rural Politics;* Elkins and McKitrick, *Age of Federalism,* 696–700; Paul Douglas Newman, "Fries Rebellion and American Political Culture, 1798–1800," *Pennsylvania Magazine of History and Biography* 119 (1995): 37–73.

126. This argument is Newman's in "Fries Rebellion."

127. Quoted in ibid., 61.

128. Elkins and McKitrick, *Age of Federalism,* 700.

129. Biographical information on Duane is taken from Kim T. Phillips, *William Duane, Revolutionary Editor* (New York: Garland, 1989), chaps. 1–2; Henry Simpson, *The Lives of Eminent Philadelphians, Now Deceased* (Philadelphia, 1859), 318–320.

130. For the conflicts in England during the 1790s, see Thompson, *Making of the English Working Class;* Goodwin, *Friends of Liberty;* Durey, *Transatlantic Radicals,* chaps. 1–3.

131. For the Federalists' campaign against Bache, see Smith, *Freedom's Fetters,* 188–220.

132. For the Federalist campaign against Duane, see ibid., 277–306.

133. Sharp, *American Politics in the Early Republic,* chaps. 11–12.

134. For early Washington, D.C., see James Sterling Young, *The Washington Community, 1800–1828* (New York: Harcourt, Brace and World, 1966); and Kenneth R. Bowling, *The Creation of Washington D.C.* (Fairfax, Va.: George Mason University Press, 1991).

Chapter 2. The Radicals Emerge: "The European Condition of Society" and the Promise of Democracy

1. I feel the need here to honestly acknowledge the limitations of my sources. The names of the Philadelphia Democrats listed in this chapter appear consistently in the *Aurora* between 1800 and 1812. These men chaired or attended meetings that the *Aurora* endorsed, were candidates the *Aurora* supported, and were often included in denunciations by Duane's and Leib's opponents. They left few letters, and I have

been able to discover little about them, save for Leiper, who was locally somewhat prominent. They remained supporters of Duane and Leib in the midst of vitriolic political conflict. Indeed, during this conflict enemies of the Philadelphia Democrats had no difficulty explaining the ideas of the city radicals, and it seems reasonable to me that those associated with these ideas possessed at least the same understanding of them as those who denounced them. Where I can cite these lesser Philadelphia Democrats, I have. With regard to Duane and Leib, these men chose propinquity. Given the stark, ideological divisions in Jeffersonian Philadelphia and Pennsylvania, I think it makes sense to view this choice as at least approaching conviction.

2. Jeffersonians used this phrase to describe the 1790s and particularly the presidency of John Adams. Though its usage was rhetorical, it was rhetoric they believed. The phrase appeared in newspapers and casual private correspondence. For examples see *Aurora,* June 24, 1802; and Andrew Gregg to Joseph Heister, August 9, 1805, Miscellaneous Collection, HSP. Gregg and Heister would become bitter enemies of the Philadelphia Democrats.

3. *Aurora,* April 13, 1803.

4. *Aurora,* September 29, 1803.

5. Leib's speech was published in the *Aurora* on May 17, 1804.

6. *Aurora,* November 2, 1801.

7. *Aurora,* August 1, 1801.

8. *Aurora,* September 7, 1803.

9. *Aurora,* August 1, 1801.

10. *Aurora,* September 7, 1803.

11. Thomas Paine, *Common Sense* (New York: Penguin, 1982), 78.

12. *Aurora,* August 22, 1803. Emphasis is in the original unless otherwise noted.

13. Ibid.

14. Ibid.

15. *Aurora,* August 18, 1802.

16. *Aurora,* June 10, 1803.

17. *Aurora,* June 17, 1805, and January 23, 1804.

18. *Aurora,* May 27, 1805.

19. *Aurora,* April 15, 1803.

20. *Aurora,* August 20, 1802.

21. *Aurora,* October 20, 1803.

22. *Aurora,* March 1, 1802.

23. *Aurora,* October 1, 1802.

24. *Aurora,* June 20, 1803.

25. For early defenses of judicial review, see Maeva Marcus, "Judicial Review in the Early Republic," in *Launching the "Extended Republic": The Federalist Era,* ed. Ronald Hoffman and Peter J. Albert (Charlottesville: University Press of Virginia, 1996), 25–53. The clearest early defense of judicial review is Alexander Hamilton's *Federalist* No. 78 in Hamilton, Madison, and Jay, *Federalist Papers,* 464–472.

26. The strange career of popular sovereignty and its antidemocratic implications in both England and America is a principal theme in Wood, *Creation of the American Republic;* Morgan, *Inventing the People.*

27. On the Addison case and the theory of dangerous tendency, see Peter Charles Hoffer and N.E.H. Hull, *Impeachment in America, 1635–1805* (New Haven, Conn.: Yale University Press, 1984), especially chap. 10. See also Richard E. Ellis, *The Jeffersonian Crisis: Courts and Politics in the Young Republic* (New York: Norton, 1971), especially chap. 11. For radical Pennsylvania Jeffersonian attitudes toward the judiciary in this period, see James Hedly Peeling, "Governor McKean and the Pennsylvania Jacobins (1799–1808)," *Pennsylvania Magazine of History and Biography* 54 (1930): 320–354; and Elizabeth K. Henderson, "The Attack on the Judiciary in Pennsylvania, 1800–1810," *Pennsylvania Magazine of History and Biography* 61 (1937): 113–136.

28. On the Chase impeachment, see Hoffer and Hull, *Impeachment in America,* chap. 11; Ellis, *Jeffersonian Crisis,* chaps. 11–13.

29. *Aurora,* May 24, 1803.

30. Ibid.

31. Ibid. For the attitudes of the Maryland framers, see Hoffman, "The 'Disaffected' in the Revolutionary South."

32. *Aurora,* May 27, 1803.

33. On this sentiment generally, see Charles M. Cook, *The American Codification Movement: A Study of Antebellum Legal Reform* (New York: Greenwood Press, 1981), esp. 3–45.

34. *Aurora,* March 31, 1803.

35. *Aurora,* October 31, 1801, reprinted from the *National Intelligencer.*

36. *Aurora,* March 3 and January 25, 1804.

37. Ibid.

38. *Aurora,* February 22, 1804, reprinted from the *Boston Chronicle.*

39. *Aurora,* May 11, 1803, December 19, 22, and 28, 1804.

40. *Aurora,* May 13, 1803. The *Aurora* also often criticized trial by jury. It did not oppose juries, but rather what it viewed as their easy manipulation by undemocratic judges. See *Aurora,* November 26, 1805.

41. Morton J. Horwitz, *The Transformation of American Law, 1780–1860* (Cambridge, Mass.: Harvard University Press, 1977); R. Kent Newmyer, *Supreme Court Justice Joseph Story: Statesman of the Old Republic* (Chapel Hill: University of North Carolina Press, 1985); and Newmyer, "Harvard Law School, New England Legal Culture, and the Antebellum Origins of American Jurisprudence," in *The Constitution and American Life,* ed. David Thelen (Ithaca, N.Y.: Cornell University Press, 1988), 154–175.

42. For the Pennsylvania Supreme Court's selective interpretation of the common law and the hostilities to its actions, see James F. Dinsmore, "Courts and Western Pennsylvania Lands: The Origins of the Attack on Pennsylvania's Courts,

1790–1810" (Ph.D. diss., Temple University, 1990), especially chap. 3. For the changing social structure of landownership, see Harper, *Transformation of Western Pennsylvania.*

43. William Findlay should not be confused with William Findley, the westerner who debated Robert Morris and participated in the Whiskey Rebellion.

44. In particular, Lemon, *Best Poor Man's Country.* On the ethic of the competence, see Daniel Vickers, "Competency and Competition: Economic Culture in Early America," *William and Mary Quarterly* 47 (1990): 3–27.

45. Carville Earle and Ronald Hoffman, "Staple Crops and Urban Development in the Eighteenth-Century South," *Perspectives in American History* 10 (1976): 7–78.

46. For yeomen's aspirations, see James A. Henretta, "Families and Farms: *Mentalite* in Pre-industrial America," *William and Mary Quarterly* 35 (1978): 3–32; and Alan Kulikoff, "The American Revolution, Capitalism, and the Formation of the Yeoman Classes," in *Beyond the American Revolution,*:80–119.

47. For the social structure and economic culture of southeastern Pennsylvania, see Lucy Simler, "Tenancy in Colonial Pennsylvania: The Case of Chester County," *William and Mary Quarterly* 43 (1986): 542–569; Simler, "Landless Worker,"163–199; and Lucy Simler and Paul G. E. Clemens, "The 'Best Poor Man's Country' in 1783: The Population of Rural Society in Late-Eighteenth-Century Southeastern Pennsylvania," *Proceedings of the American Philosophical Society* 133 (1989): 234–261.

48. Simler, "Tenancy in Colonial Pennsylvania."

49. Lemon, *Best Poor Man's Country,* 227.

50. Ibid. Simler corroborated Lemon's 1972 observation in her "James Lemon's Best Poor Man's Country Revisited: Chester County Pennsylvania in the Early Republic" (paper presented at the Philadelphia Center for Early American Studies, March 1, 1996).

51. Durey, *Transatlantic Radicals;* Wilson, *United Irishmen, United States.*

52. For Snyder, see "Autobiographical Notes by Simon Snyder," *Pennsylvania Magazine of History and Biography* 4 (1880): 248–249; and the *Dictionary of American Biography.*

53. Binns suggested as much. For his arrival in Northumberland and his reactions, see John Binns, *Recollections of the Life of John Binns, Twenty Nine Years in Europe and Fifty Three in the United States — Written by Himself with Anecdotes, Political, Historical, and Miscellaneous* (Philadelphia, 1854).

54. For an example, see *Argus,* January 7, 1804.

55. Dinsmore, "Courts and Western Pennsylvania Lands."

56. For frustrations with the legal system, see Ellis, *Jeffersonian Crisis,* chap. 11.

57. For Jeffersonian domination of Northumberland, see *Argus,* September 2, 23, and October 14, 1803. Jeffersonian domination of this region was greatly assisted by the events surrounding the Fries Rebellion.

58. *Argus,* May 20 and July 8, 1803.

59. *Argus*, May 20, 1803.

60. *Argus*, July 22, 29, August 5, and 12, 1803.

61. *Argus*, August 5, 1803.

Chapter 3. The Quid Challenge: Political Economy, Politics, and the Fault Lines of Conflict

1. *Evening Post*, May 26, 1804. The *Philadelphia Evening Post*, later renamed the *Freeman's Journal*, was the Quids' newspaper. I will discuss its beginnings later in this chapter.

2. Ibid.

3. Michael Leib to Matthew Carey, October 11, 1802, Lee and Febiger Collection, HSP.

4. Sanford W. Higginbotham, *The Keystone in the Democratic Arch: Pennsylvania Politics, 1800–1816* (Harrisburg: Pennsylvania Historical and Museum Commission, 1952), 58.

5. William Jones bill of sale, September 3, 1805; Jones to James Madison, n.d., William Jones Papers, Uselma Clark Smith Collection, both in HSP.

6. William Jones to Thomas Jefferson, February 12, 1803; Jones to John Randolph, March 19, 1803, William Jones Papers, Uselma Clark Smith Collection, both in HSP.

7. David Hackett Fisher, *The Revolution of American Conservatism: The Federalist Party in the Era of Jeffersonian Democracy* (New York: Harper and Row, 1965), 187.

8. J. Lithgow to Matthew Carey, September 8, 1804, Lee and Febiger Collection, case 1, box 38, HSP.

9. *Freeman's Journal*, July 10, 1804. The founding of the *Freeman's Journal* is discussed later in this chapter.

10. Matthew Carey to Tench Coxe, May 11, July 23, September 11, 1804, February 6, and 25, 1805; Matthew Carey, David Jackson, and Tench Coxe to William Duane, October 30, 1804, Tench Coxe Papers, Princeton University microfilm, reel 77.

11. *Freeman's Journal*, August 25, 1805.

12. James Hopkins to Alexander J. Dallas, May 28, 1803, Alexander J. Dallas Papers, George Mifflin Dallas Collection, HSP.

13. Ibid. Barton and Ellicott were Lancaster County Prothonotary and Secretary of the Land Office, respectively.

14. William Barton to Matthew Carey, January 13, February 12, and May 25, 1803, Lee and Febiger Collection, HSP.

15. Henderson, "Attack on the Judiciary in Pennsylvania." McKean's vetoes were printed in the *Aurora* on December 14, 1802, and March 24, 1803.

16. Hoffer and Hull, *Impeachment in America*, chap. 11; Ellis, *Jeffersonian Crisis*, chaps. 11–13.

17. *Aurora,* March 7, 1803.

18. Isaac Worrell (?) to Tench Coxe, June 15, 1804, Tench Coxe Papers, Princeton University microfilm, reel 77.

19. Isaac Worrell (?) to Tench Coxe, August 22, 1804, Tench Coxe Papers, Princeton University microfilm, reel 77.

20. *Freeman's Journal,* May 16 and 19, 1804. All citations are made to the *Freeman's Journal.* The paper was called the *Evening Post* between February 20 and June 12, 1804. It was the *Freeman's Journal* from June 13, 1804, until it went out of business in 1808.

21. *Freeman's Journal,* May 18, 1804.

22. Examples of early attacks on Duane and Leib are *Freeman's Journal,* May 25, June 16, 20, 21, 22, 23, July 3, 7, 10, 11, 19, 25, 28, August 15, 18, 19, 21, 22, 23, 24, 25, September 1, 5, 8, 10, 12, 14, 17, 28, 29, October 1, 2, 3, 5, 6, 8, 1804. These were campaign months before a particularly acrimonious but ultimately unsuccessful effort to prevent Leib's reelection to the U.S. Congress. The election occurred on October 10.

23. For the *Aurora's* influence, see Durey, "Tom Paine's Apostles: Radical Emigres and the Triumph of Jeffersonian Republicanism," *William and Mary Quarterly* 44 (1987): 661–688.

24. *Freeman's Journal,* September 8, 1804.

25. *Freeman's Journal,* February 22, 1804.

26. Ibid.

27. *Freeman's Journal,* March 7, 1804.

28. Ibid.

29. *Freeman's Journal,* February 28, 1804.

30. *Freeman's Journal,* May 28, 1804.

31. Ibid.

32. *Freeman's Journal,* February 20, 1804.

33. *Freeman's Journal,* June 21, 1804.

34. *Freeman's Journal,* February 21, 1804.

35. Ibid.

36. *Freeman's Journal,* February 25, 1804.

37. *Freeman's Journal,* March 17, 1804.

38. Thomas Jefferson, *Notes on the State of Virginia* (New York: Harper Torchbooks, 1964), 157–158; McCoy, *Elusive Republic;* Banning, *Jeffersonian Persuasion.*

39. McCoy, *Last of the Fathers.*

40. In addition to the works cited earlier, see Risjord, *Old Republicans;* and Shalhope, *John Taylor of Caroline.* Jefferson and Madison saw the virtue of certain manufactures, but as presidents they remained convinced that manufacturing should be largely limited to household production. Both men, especially Madison, altered their views after the War of 1812. See McCoy, *Last of the Fathers;* and McCoy, "An Unfinished Revolution: The Quest for Economic Independence in the Early

Republic," in *The American Revolution: Its Character and Limits*, ed. Jack P. Greene (New York: New York University Press, 1987), 131–148.

41. *Aurora*, September 7, 1802.

42. For examples, see *Aurora*, November 10, December 26, 1803; January 26, 1804; February 14, November 9, and December 4, 1805.

43. *Aurora*, July 9, 1802.

44. *Aurora*, June 10, 1803. See also *Aurora*, July 14, 1802.

45. *Aurora*, January 6, 1802.

46. *Aurora*, May 1 and September 21, 1801.

47. *Argus*, March 18, April 29, and August 5, 1803.

48. *Argus*, November 30, 1804.

49. On the ubiquitous support for internal improvement in the nation generally, see John Lauritz Larson, *Internal Improvement: National Public Works and the Promise of Popular Government in the Early United States* (Chapel Hill: University of North Carolina Press, 2001).

50. *Argus*, October 20 and 26, 1804.

51. *Freeman's Journal*, May 22, 1804.

52. *Freeman's Journal*, March 1, 1804.

53. *Aurora*, January 29, 1801.

54. Ibid.

55. Schultz, *Republic of Labor;* Phillips, *William Duane.*

56. My understanding of these issues has been assisted by the work of Michael Merrill and Sean Wilentz. See Merrill, "Putting 'Capitalism' in Its Place: A Review of Recent Literature," *William and Mary Quarterly* 52 (1995): 315–326; Merrill, "The Anti-capitalist Origins of the United States," *Ferdinand Braudel Review* 13 (1990): 465–497; Merrill and Wilentz, "The Key of Liberty: William Manning and Plebeian Democracy, 1747–1814," in *Beyond the American Revolution*, 246–282; and their introduction to *The Key of Liberty: The Life and Democratic Writings of William Manning "A Laborer," 1747–1814* (Cambridge, Mass.: Harvard University Press, 1993).

57. Brewer, *Sinews of Power;* Dickson, *Financial Revolution in England;* Plumb, *Growth of Political Stability in England.*

58. *Aurora*, November 5, 1801.

59. *Aurora*, February 18, 1801.

60. *Aurora*, January 11, 1805.

61. M. St. Clair Clarke and D. H. Hall, comps., *Legislative and Documentary History of the Bank of the United States Including the Original Bank of North America* (Washington, D.C.: Gales and Seaton, 1832), 316–317.

62. Ibid., 346.

63. On the Bank of Philadelphia, see *Aurora*, December 20, 21, 1803, January 7, 9, 12, 16, 23, and 24, 1804. I must confess that I was unable to discover whether the Bank of Philadelphia did conduct its business in a manner substantially different

from the other three banks in the city. I would discourage anyone who would take the *Aurora*'s insistence as proof. What the paper's comments do reveal, however, is the way that it hoped the Bank of Philadelphia would function, and thus the clientele whom it hoped the Bank would serve. Whether the Bank of Philadelphia did or not, the *Aurora* wanted it to serve the needs of small shopkeepers and urban workers. The sort of loan policies that would have helped them would also have assisted small rural holders seeking to make improvements in their property. For those still suspicious, one can always fall back on Quentin Skinner's useful point about Lord Bolingbroke. Even assuming that Bolingbroke was purely cynical, something Skinner himself does not believe, the fact that he used the language of country opposition shows how central those values and ideals were to the rural gentry he hoped to convince. At the very least, the *Aurora*'s comments suggest that its urban laboring readers took political economy very seriously and could best be approached with the language of democratized economic development. I do, however, believe that the Philadelphia Democrats, like the Quids and the Snyderites, were in the main sincere. See Quentin Skinner, "The Principles and Practice of Opposition: The Case of Bolingbroke versus Walpole," in *Historical Perspectives: Studies in English Thought and Society in Honour of J. H. Plumb,* ed. Neil McKenrick (London: Europa Publications, 1974), 93–128.

64. *Argus,* May 20, 1803. The complexities, strengths, and limits of the Snyderites' thought will be treated in chapter 5.

65. Thomas McKean to Thomas Jefferson, February 7, 1803, Thomas McKean Papers, vol. 3, 67, HSP.

66. McKean to Jefferson, January 8, 1804, and McKean to Uriah Tracy, January 4, 1804, Thomas McKean Papers, vol. 3, 82–83, HSP.

67. George Mifflin Dallas, *The Life and Writings of Alexander J. Dallas* (Philadelphia, 1879), 117.

68. ? to Alexander J. Dallas, February 17, 1804, Alexander J. Dallas Papers, George Mifflin Dallas Collection, HSP.

69. *Freeman's Journal,* October 2, 1804.

70. *Freeman's Journal,* October 5, 1804.

71. *Freeman's Journal,* June 18, 1805.

72. The dates are given in note 22.

73. *Freeman's Journal,* March 19, 1804.

74. Ibid.

75. Ibid.

76. Joseph Nicholson to William Jones, April 24, 1804, William Jones Papers, Uselma Clark Smith Collection, HSP.

77. *Freeman's Journal,* October 5, 1805.

78. Higginbotham, *Keystone in the Democratic Arch,* 70–72.

79. Ibid., 71–72.

80. *Aurora,* October 11, 1804.

Chapter 4. The Crucible of Conflict: 1805

1. William Jones to Joseph Nicholson, October 20, 1804, William Jones Papers, Uselma Clark Smith Collection, HSP.

2. Alexander J. Dallas to Albert Gallatin, quoted in Henry Adams, *The Life of Albert Gallatin* (Philadelphia, 1879), 326.

3. John Vaughan to Tench Coxe, November 13, 1804, Tench Coxe Papers, Princeton University microfilm, reel 77; Thomas Laws to George Logan, March 18, 1805, Logan Papers, vol. 5, 63, HSP.

4. ? to Tench Coxe, July 20, 1804, and Samuel Morse to Tench Coxe, September 23, 1804, Tench Coxe Papers, Princeton University microfilm, reel 77. The Georgians were probably influenced by the *Aurora*'s denunciation of the Yazoo settlement. See also the reprint in the *Freeman's Journal* of the New York City *Commercial Advertizer*. The *Advertizer* was edited by the Federalist Noah Webster. For the Yazoo affair, see C. Peter Magrath, *Yazoo: Law and Politics in the New Republic, the Case of* Flether v. Peck (Providence, R.I.: Brown University Press, 1966).

5. *Aurora*, November 19, 1804.

6. *Argus*, March 18, 1803.

7. For the wages of Philadelphia journeymen cordwainers and tailors, see Smith, *The "Lower Sort*,*"* 116, 121.

8. *Argus*, April 8, 1803.

9. *Argus*, October 21, 1803.

10. *Argus*, January 13 and October 12, 1804.

11. On this theme, see John M. Murrin, "Escaping Perfidious Albion: Federalism, Fear of Aristocracy, and the Democratization of Corruption in Post-Revolutionary America," in *Virtue, Corruption, and Self-Interest: Political Values in the Eighteenth Century*, ed. Richard K. Mathews (Bethlehem, Pa.: Lehigh University Press, 1994), 103–147.

12. Hoffer and Hull, *Impeachment in America*, 220–227.

13. *Freeman's Journal*, March 24 and April 19, 1804.

14. *Freeman's Journal*, April 3, 5, and 6, 1804.

15. *Freeman's Journal*, April 5, 1804.

16. *Freeman's Journal*, April 18, 1804.

17. The *Aurora* printed how each senator voted and underscored the names of the Jeffersonians who voted for acquittal. See *Aurora*, January 30, 1805.

18. William Barton to Jared Ingersoll, January 28, 1805, Alexander J. Dallas Papers, George Mifflin Dallas Collection, HSP.

19. James Hopkins to Alexander J. Dallas, January 7, 1805, Alexander J. Dallas Papers, George Mifflin Dallas Collection, HSP.

20. *Aurora*, August 21, 1805.

21. The first of many such calls appeared in the paper on that date.

22. *Aurora*, August 21, 1805.

23. Ibid.

24. Ibid.

25. *Aurora*, March 1, August 26, and September 30, 1805.

26. For further examples of support for one, some, or all of these positions, see *Aurora*, March 28, 30, and July 17, 1805.

27. *Argus*, September 16, 1803.

28. *Argus*, March 22, April 12 and May 10, 1805.

29. John Kean to Alexander J. Dallas, March 20, 1805, Alexander J. Dallas Papers, George Mifflin Dallas Collection, HSP.

30. Alexander J. Dallas to Albert Gallatin, January 16, 1805, quoted in Adams, *Life of Albert Gallatin*, 327–328. James Cheetham was a New York City newspaper editor and initially an ally of the Philadelphia Democrats. During Jefferson's second term he denounced the embargo and attacked Duane. See Twomey, *Jacobins and Jeffersonians*.

31. Dallas to Gallatin, April 4, 1805, quoted in Adams, *Life of Albert Gallatin*, 330.

32. *Freeman's Journal*, June 11, 1804.

33. *Freeman's Journal*, June 18 and 20, 1805.

34. *Freeman's Journal*, June 3, 1805, reprint from *Greensburg Farmer's Register; Freeman's Journal*, June 14, 1805.

35. Hugh Henry Brackenridge, *Modern Chivalry*, ed. and intro. Claude M. Newlin (New York: American Book Company, 1937), 335. All subsequent references are to this edition.

36. Ibid., 340.

37. Ibid., 369.

38. Ibid., 418.

39. Ibid., 449.

40. Ibid., 450, 463.

41. *Freeman's Journal*, August 30, 1805.

42. *Freeman's Journal*, August 19, 1805.

43. *Freeman's Journal*, June 5, 1805.

44. *Freeman's Journal*, June 14 and 28, 1805.

45. *Freeman's Journal*, June 19, July 4, 10, 11, and 31, 1805.

46. *Freeman's Journal*, June 3, 10, 1805.

47. The complicated intermediate ground taken by the Quids can be contrasted with the positions of staunch Federalists such as Maryland's James McHenry, secretary of war under Washington and Adams. He remained a Federalist until his death in 1816 and in 1803 wrote to Lafayette, "Were you to come among us, you would find yourself in many points of view, as it were, in a new world. Most of your old friends in private life, friends tremblingly alive to whatever is likely to affect their popularity. The people too changed, that is because more democratical. Great and lesser demagogues in every state and district and the prejudices and violence of party

leaving little or no room for moderation or social intercourse between men of oppo-site politics. . . . We cannot tell what further changes such democratical opinions may produce in the public mind, in the government itself. When the people are made to believe that they are everything, and have the right to have everything fashioned to their own way of thinking, they are in a sure road of alternatively ruling their dema-gogues and being ruled by them." Quoted in Charles Beard, *Economic Origins of Jeffersonian Democracy* (New York: Free Press, 1915), 49–50.

48. Of course this momentous change was a development larger than any one group in any particular place. For the rise of institutionalized popular politics in the eighteenth century, see Pauline Maier, *From Resistance to Revolution: Colonial Radi-cals and the Development of American Opposition to Britain, 1765–1776* (New York: Norton, 1971); Brewer, *Party Ideology and Popular Politics*, especially parts 3 and 4.

49. *Freeman's Journal*, June 19, 1805.

50. Ibid.

51. *Freeman's Journal*, June 4, 28, and August 20, 1805.

52. *Freeman's Journal*, June 17, 1805.

53. *Freeman's Journal*, June 11, 12, and July 5, 1805.

54. It is also reprinted in George Mifflin Dallas, *Life and Writings of Alexander James Dallas* (Philadelphia, 1871), 211–233. All subsequent references are to this edition.

55. Ibid., 211.

56. Ibid., 212.

57. Ibid., 217, 220.

58. Ibid., 221, 225.

59. Ibid., 222, 224.

60. Ibid., 232–233.

61. Ibid., 233.

62. *Freeman's Journal*, June 15, 1805.

63. *Freeman's Journal*, June 3, 5, 6, 10, July 25, August 17 and 22, 1805. There were probably meetings in other counties of which I am not aware.

64. *Freeman's Journal*, June 13, 1805. For the Philadelphia Democrats' control of the original Philadelphia Tammany Society, see *Aurora*, May 15, 1806.

65. *Freeman's Journal*, July 2, 1805.

66. *Freeman's Journal*, June 5 and 7, 1805.

67. *Freeman's Journal*, June 11, July 1, 29, August 9, 10, 15, 19, and 31, 1805.

68. *Freeman's Journal*, June 17 and September 3, 1805.

69. *Freeman's Journal*, June 19, 1805.

70. *Freeman's Journal*, July 6, 1805; *Aurora*, June 3, 1805; Higginbotham, *Key-stone in the Democratic Arch*, 85–86.

71. On this theme, see James Henretta, "The Slow Triumph of Liberal Individu-alism: Law and Politics in New York, 1780–1860," in *American Chameleon: Individ-ualism in Trans-national Context*, ed. Richard O. Curry and Lawrence B. Goodheard

(Kent, Ohio: Kent State University Press, 1991), 87–106; Henretta, "The 'Market' in the Early Republic," *Journal of the Early Republic* 18 (1998): 289–304; Tony Freyer, *Producers versus Capitalists: Constitutional Conflict in Antebellum America* (Charlottesville: University Press of Virginia, 1994); and Robert H. Wiebe, *The Opening of American Society from the Adoption of the Constitution to the Eve of Disunion* (New York: Vintage, 1984), esp. 194–290.

72. *Freeman's Journal,* June 25, 1805.

73. *Argus,* October 19, 1804.

74. *Argus,* October 19, 1804.

75. *Argus,* February 8, 1805.

76. *Argus,* December 28, 1804, January 4, 25, and February 1, 1805.

77. Nathanial B. Boileau to Alexander J. Dallas, March 25, 1805, Alexander J. Dallas Papers, George Mifflin Dallas Collection, HSP.

78. *Argus,* March 22, April 12, and May 10, 1805.

79. *Argus,* May 31, 1805. Boileau represented Montgomery County.

80. *Argus,* June 28 and July 12, 1805.

81. *Argus,* June 14, 1805.

82. *Argus,* June 21, 1805.

83. *Argus,* May 31, 1805. Simon Snyder was one of those members.

84. *Argus,* July 5 and August, 2, 1805.

85. *Argus,* August 16, 1805.

86. *Argus,* September 12 and 20, 1805.

87. *Argus,* August 16, 1805.

88. *Argus,* September 13, 1805.

89. *Argus,* September 6, 1805.

90. Ibid.

91. *Argus,* September 13, 1805.

92. Ibid.

93. *Argus,* September 20, 1805.

94. *Argus,* September 27, 1805.

95. *Aurora,* March 30, 1805.

96. *Aurora,* March 15, 1805.

97. *Aurora,* April, 5 1805.

98. *Aurora,* May 7, 1805.

99. *Aurora,* May 10, 1805.

100. For the development of this orthodoxy, see Wood, *Creation of the American Republic.*

101. *Aurora,* May 10, 1805.

102. On Parliament's theories about sovereignty and their relation to the American colonies, see Morgan, *Inventing the People;* and Edmund S. Morgan and Helen Morgan, *The Stamp Act Crisis: Prologue to Revolution* (Chapel Hill: University of North Carolina Press, 1953).

103. *Aurora,* June 6, 1805.

104. *Aurora,* June 7, 1805.

105. Andrew Gregg to Joseph Heister, August 9, 1805, Society Miscellaneous Collection, HSP.

106. *Freeman's Journal,* June 3, 1805.

107. *Harrisburg Dauphin Guardian,* June 15, 1805; *Freeman's Journal,* September 5, 1805.

108. ? to Alexander J. Dallas, August 29, 1805, Alexander J. Dallas Papers, George Mifflin Dallas Collection, HSP; *Freeman's Journal,* September 5 and 6, 1805.

109. *Aurora,* September 28, 1805.

110. *Freeman's Journal,* August 3, 1805.

111. Albert Gallatin to Jean Badolet, quoted in Adams, *Life of Albert Gallatin,* 331.

112. George Logan to John Dickinson, November 11, 1805, Logan Papers, vol. 5, 68; Deborah Logan to Algernon Sydney Logan, October 18, 1805, microfilm roll 7, HSP.

113. William Barton to Alexander J. Dallas, November 19, 1805, Alexander J. Dallas Papers, George Mifflin Dallas Collection, HSP.

114. Salinger, "Artisans, Journeymen"; Smith, *The "Lower Sort": Philadelphia's Laboring People, 1750–1800;* Wilentz, *Chants Democratic;* Schultz, *Republic of Labor;* Cynthia Shelton, "The Role of Labor in Early Industrialization: Philadelphia, 1787–1837," in *New Perspectives on the Early Republic: Essays from the* Journal of the Early Republic, *1981–1991,* ed. Ralph D. Gray and Michael Morrison (Urbana: University Press of Illinois, 1994), 214–243; Louis Arky, "The Mechanics Union of Trade Associations and the Formation of the Philadelphia Workingmen's Movement," *Pennsylvania Magazine of History and Biography* 76 (1952): 142–176.

115. *Aurora,* November 28, 1805; Schultz, *Republic of Labor.*

116. Fisher, *Revolution of American Conservatism,* 339–340, 349; Keller, "Diversity and Democracy," 157.

117. Commons, *Documentary History,* 3:67.

118. *Freeman's Journal,* August 20, 1805. The *Aurora* denounced Levy for his Quid politics on August 19, 1805.

119. For these economic developments, see chapter 1.

120. Commons, *Documentary History,* 3:77, 86–87, 99.

121. Ibid., 86–87, 100–101.

122. Ibid., 105, 106.

123. Ibid., 121, 123–124; *Aurora,* November 28, 1805.

124. Commons, *Documentary History,* 3:137.

125. Ibid., 68, 71, 138.

126. Ibid., 173, 203.

127. Ibid., 138–139.

128. Ibid., 3:180.

129. For Franklin's warehouse plan, see *Aurora*, January 15, 1806. On the differences between the defense and the defendants, see Christopher L. Tomlins, *Law, Labor, and Ideology in the Early American Republic* (Cambridge: Cambridge University Press, 1993), 128–139.

130. As evidenced by the remarks of the defense cited earlier and the correspondence between Rodney and Thomas McKean, February 20, and 25, 1814, Thomas McKean Papers, vol. 4, 35–36, HSP.

131. Commons, *Documentary History*, 3:188–189.

132. Ibid., 222.

133. Ibid., 223.

134. Ibid., 223–224.

135. Ibid., 224, 232.

136. Ibid., 232–233.

137. Ibid., 226.

138. Ibid., 232–233. On Levy's closing remarks, see Wythe Holt, "Labor Conspiracy Cases in the United States, 1805–1842: Bias and Legitimation in Common Law Adjudication," *Osgoode Hall Law Journal* 22 (1984): 621–625.

139. Commons, *Documentary History*, 3:171.

140. Quoted in Cook, *American Codification Movement*, 40.

141. Higginbotham, *Keystone in the Democratic Arch*, 100.

Chapter 5. "Perpetual Motion — Perpetual Change — A Boundless Ocean without a Shore": The Final Meaning of Democracy in Pennsylvania

1. *Aurora*, February 18, 1807.

2. *Aurora*, March 7, 1807.

3. Despite its name.

4. *Democratic Press*, March 30, 1807.

5. *Democratic Press*, May 15, 1807.

6. *Aurora*, January 29, 1807.

7. For a description of the charges, see Higginbotham, *Keystone in the Democratic Arch*, 126–127.

8. *Aurora*, February 7, 1807.

9. *Aurora*, March 27, April 3, 7, 21, and May 12, 1807; *Democratic Press*, April 6, 8, and 17, 1807.

10. *Aurora*, April 11, 1807.

11. Examples are *Democratic Press*, April 13 and May 1, 1807.

12. For examples, see *Democratic Press*, May 20 and 22, 1807.

13. *Democratic Press*, May 20, 1807.

14. *Democratic Press*, May 22, 1807.

15. Ibid.

16. *Democratic Press*, April 17, 1807.

17. Ibid.

18. Ibid.

19. Ibid.

20. *Democratic Press*, March 30, April 17, July 18, and December 14, 1807.

21. *Aurora*, June 3, 1807.

22. *Democratic Press*, June 5, 1807.

23. *Aurora*, July 27, 1809.

24. *Democratic Press*, August 10, 11, 12, and 15, 1807.

25. *Aurora*, August 19, September 11, 1807.

26. *Democratic Press*, August 18, 19, 20, and 21, 1807.

27. *Aurora*, September 29, 1807.

28. *Democratic Press*, August 26, 28, and September 25, 1807.

29. *Aurora*, September 3, 23, and 25, 1807.

30. Those interested in the accusations should see, in addition to the earlier citations, *Democratic Press*, September 4, 8, 11, 19, 22, 23, 24, 25, 30, October 2, 3, 5, 6, 7, 9, 10, 12, 13, 19, and 20, 1807.

31. *Aurora*, September 28, 29, October 5, 7, 9, and 12, 1807.

32. *Democratic Press*, September 9, 1807.

33. Good examples are *Democratic Press*, September 15 and 21, 1807.

34. *Democratic Press*, June 8, 1808, and January 11, 1809.

35. *Democratic Press*, September 18, 1807.

36. *Democratic Press*, September 25 and 27, 1807; *Aurora*, October 3, 1807.

37. *Democratic Press*, October 5, 1807. Other examples of the attack on Duane and Leib appeared in the paper on October 1, 6, 12, and 13, 1807.

38. *Democratic Press*, October 16, 17, 21, and 28, 1807; *Aurora*, October 20, 1807.

39. *Democratic Press*, April 20, May 14, 17, and July 5, 1808.

40. *Democratic Press*, December 10, 1807, and January 28, 1808.

41. Alexander J. Dallas to Caesar A. Rodney, February 6, 1809, Caesar A. Rodney Papers, Library of Congress.

42. For the background to the War of 1812 and Jeffersonian policy, see McCoy, *Elusive Republic*, chap. 9; Marshall Smelser, *The Democratic Republic, 1801–1815* (Prospect Heights, Ill.: Waveland, 1968), chaps. 7–11; Stagg, *Mr. Madison's War*, especially chaps. 1–2; Roger H. Brown, *The Republic in Peril: 1812* (New York: Norton, 1964); Donald R. Hickey, *The War of 1812: A Forgotten Conflict* (Urbana: University Press of Illinois, 1989), chap. 1.

43. Andrew Gregg to Alexander J. Dallas, November 16, 1807, Alexander J. Dallas Papers, George Mifflin Dallas Collection; William Jones to Albert Gallatin, August 10, 1808, Andrew Gregg to William Jones, William Jones notes on a town meeting, n.d., in William Jones Papers, Uselma Clark Smith Collection; Andrew

Gregg to James Hamilton, February 15, 1808, James Hamilton Papers; Andrew
Gregg to J. Potter, December 18, 1807, Society Miscellaneous Collection; Manuel
Eyre to ?, February 18, 1809, Claude W. Unger Collection; all in HSP.

44. John Dickinson to Thomas McKean, October 2, 1805, Thomas McKean
Papers, vol. 3, 106, HSP.

45. The speech can be found in the *Aurora,* December 5, 1805.

46. Joseph B. McKean to Samuel Bryan, February 2, 1805, Society Collection, HSP.

47. Joseph B. McKean to James Hamilton, March 9, 1806, James Hamilton
Papers, HSP. Higginbotham, *Keystone in the Democratic Arch,* 107–108.

48. Thomas McKean to William Tilghman, February 25, 1806; and Tilghman to
McKean, February 28, 1806, Thomas McKean Papers, vol. 3, 105–106, both in HSP.

49. Joseph Hopkinson to ?, May 22, 1808, Dreer Collection — American Lawyers, HSP.

50. For Ross, see Fisher, *Revolution of American Conservatism,* 344–345. For Federalist sensibility generally, see Kevin M. Gannon, "Escaping 'Mr. Jefferson's Plan
of Destruction': New England Federalists and the Idea of a Northern Confeder-
acy, 1803–1804," *Journal of the Early Republic* 21 (2001): 413–443; Steven Watts,
"Ministers, Misanthropes, and Mandarins: The Federalists and the Culture of Cap-
italism, 1790–1820," in *Federalists Reconsidered,* ed. Doron Ben-Atar and Barbara
Oberg (Charlottesville: University Press of Virginia, 1998), 157–175; William C.
Dowling, *Literary Federalism in the Age of Jefferson: Joseph Dennie and* The Port
Folio, *1801–1811* (Charleston: University of South Carolina Press, 1999); Linda K.
Kerber, *Federalists in Dissent: Imagery and Ideology in Jeffersonian America* (Ithaca,
N.Y.: Cornell University Press, 1970); James M. Banner, *To the Hartford Conven-
tion: The Federalists and the Origins of Party Politics in Massachusetts, 1789–1815*
(New York: Knopf, 1970); Fisher, *Revolution of American Conservatism.*

51. Charles Harr to William Tilghman, February 1, 1808; Tilghman to Harr, February 3, 1808, William Tilghman Papers; Harr to Tilghman, March 21, 1808, Society Collection, all in HSP.

52. Charles Harr to William Tilghman, March 16, 1808; New York Committee
of Correspondence to William Tilghman, July 11, 1808, William Tilghman Papers,
both in HSP.

53. Jasper Yeats to William Tilghman, April 8, 1808, William Tilghman Papers,
HSP.

54. McCoy, *Last of the Fathers;* John R. Nelson, *Liberty and Property: Political
Economy and Policymaking in the New Nation, 1789–1812* (Baltimore: Johns Hop-
kins University Press, 1987); Richard K. Matthews, *If Men Were Angels: James
Madison and the Heartless Empire of Reason* (Lawrence: University Press of
Kansas, 1995).

55. *Democratic Press,* August 3, 4, 1808.

56. *Democratic Press,* August 15, September 28, 1808.

57. *Democratic Press,* October 12, November 7, December 30, 1808.

58. See Charles Jared Ingersoll to Rufus King, December 3 and 6, 1808, Charles Jared Ingersoll Collection, HSP.

59. *Democratic Press,* June 8, 10, 15, 1807; Thomas Craig to Charles Jared Ingersoll, n.d. 1809, Charles Jared Ingersoll Collection, HSP.

60. John Binns to Charles Jared Ingersoll, May 31, June 9, 14, 19, July 11, and 13, 1813, Charles Jared Ingersoll Collection, HSP; James Roger Sharp, *The Jacksonians versus the Banks: Politics in the States after the Panic of 1837* (New York: Columbia University Press, 1970), 289.

61. William Petrekin to Tench Coxe, January 15, 1808, Tench Coxe Papers, Princeton University microfilm, reel 81. This reel is misidentified at the beginning as the year 1807.

62. John Binns to Tench Coxe, November 15, 1808; February 9, October 15, 1809; June 30, 1810, Tench Coxe Papers, Princeton University microfilm, reels 82–83; Jacob Cooke, *Tench Coxe and the Early Republic* (Chapel Hill: University of North Carolina Press, 1978).

63. *Aurora,* July 27, 1808.

64. *Democratic Press,* May 30, June 13, August 4, 1809; *Aurora,* July 31, 1809. For evidence that these men were initially Philadelphia Democrats, see *Aurora,* May 15, 1806.

65. William Duane to Caesar A. Rodney, January 28, 1807, Gratz Collection, case 8, box 9, HSP.

66. *Democratic Press,* May 31, 1809. Binns printed the announcement on June 2, 3, 8, 10, 12, 14, 15, 21, 27, and August 8, 1809.

67. *Democratic Press,* November 30, 1807, and January 7, 1812.

68. *Democratic Press,* February 15 and 26, 1808.

69. *Democratic Press,* January 7 and 21, 1812.

70. *Democratic Press,* February 19, December 9, 1808, and January 11, 1812.

71. *Democratic Press,* January 21, 1812.

72. *Democratic Press,* April 6, June 22, August 14, 1807, and January 15, 1808.

73. *Democratic Press,* December 28, 1807.

74. *Democratic Press,* Resolution of N. B. Boileau, January 29, 1808.

75. *Democratic Press,* June 1, 22, December 30, 1807, January 12, and 19, 1808. The Snyderites were in the vanguard of the American protectionist movement, which was one reason they attracted Matthew Carey and Tench Coxe. The first explicitly protective tariff was not enacted in the United States until 1816, and it provided a basic impost rate of 20 percent. See Sidney Ratner, *The Tariff in American History* (New York: Van Nostrand, 1972), 12–14.

76. *Democratic Press,* January 4, 1808.

77. *Democratic Press,* May 13, 27, 1807, June 9, 1808.

78. *Democratic Press,* June 3, 1807.

79. Some examples of this line of argument and further defenses of domestic manufacturing appeared in the *Democratic Press,* April 8, May 13, June 13, 15, 21,

26, July 1, 8, 16, 21, 27, 30, December 26, 1807, January 18, 1808, and January 16, 1811. These are by no means the only days that the paper discussed these matters.

80. *Democratic Press*, December 7, 1810, December 6, 1811; *Aurora*, December 11, 1811.

81. *Democratic Press*, February 2, 1808.

82. The full title of Duane's pamphlet was *Politics for American Farmers; Being a Series of Tracts Exhibiting the Blessings of Free Government, As It Is Administered in the United States, Compared with the Boasted Stupendous Fabric of British Monarchy*. It is reprinted in *Pamphlets on American History*, vol. 2 (n.p., n.d.). The essays appeared in the *Aurora*, January 1, 7, 8, 9, 12, 15, 19, 20, 21, 28, February 2, 4, 9, 10, 20, March 4, 5, 7 16, 28, and April 11, 1807. *Politics for Mechanics* appeared on January 29, February 3, 5, 7, and March 27, 1807. The pamphlets were reprinted widely in other Jeffersonian newspapers, though not in the *Democratic Press*.

83. For commitment to internal improvements, manufactures, fear of Britain, and support for mechanics and farmers, see *Aurora*, January 10, 16, 28, February 17, April 2, May 1, June 17, 27, 1807, January 14, 17, July 16, 1808. These are but a sample of the paper's discussion of these issues.

84. *Aurora*, January 22, 1807.

85. *Aurora*, February 16, 1807.

86. Ibid.

87. *Aurora*, July 24, 1807.

88. *Aurora*, January 3, 1807.

89. *Aurora*, January 10, July 25, 27, November 17, 1807.

90. *Aurora*, December 21, 1807.

91. *Aurora*, December 29, 1809. For more on this plan see *Aurora*, November 17, December 19, 1807, January 12 and February 2, 1808. For Michael Leib's comments on these matters, see *Aurora*, February 19, 1808. Leib, speaking in the state legislature, also argued for an amendment to the U.S. Constitution requiring the election of federal judges. Leib insisted that support for the amendment would prove his fellow legislators' commitment to democracy.

92. *Aurora*, December 29, 1809.

93. *Aurora*, February 14, 1809.

94. *Aurora*, September 26, 1809.

95. For the *Aurora*'s efforts to keep alive the Philadelphia Democrat agenda of 1805, see, in addition to the dates cited previously, December 19, 1808, January 22, 31, February 1, April 19, November 14, 1810.

96. The best discussion of Olmsted is Higginbotham, *Keystone in the Democratic Arch*, chap. 8.

97. For the Snyderites' support of Clinton, see *Democratic Press*, March 16, April 2, 6, 9, 18, May 12, 13, 19, July 14, 18, 1808. For Clinton's politics and political economy, see Young, *Democratic Republicans of New York*.

98. The Olmsted affair can be followed in the *Democratic Press,* March 1, 3, 4, 16, 29, 30, April 15, 17, 18, 21, 25, 27, 28, 29, May 5, 9, 10, 11, 1809. The state legislature backed Snyder completely. See *Aurora,* January 22, 1810.

99. For the Olmsted affair from the Philadelphia Democrats' perspective, see *Aurora,* March 2, 3, 18, 20, 22, 28, April 6, 11, 17, May 15, 1809.

100. Dallas's policies as secretary of the Treasury and the crucial role the Quids played in the formation of National Republican thought are discussed later in this chapter.

101. The Simon Easy editorials appeared in the *Democratic Press,* August 19, 25, 27, 31, September 3, 7, 1807.

102. Simon Snyder to Nathanial B. Boileau, August 31, 1808, Simon Snyder Correspondence, HSP; *Democratic Press,* December 20, 1808.

103. That phrase appeared in the *Democratic Press,* January 30, 1808.

104. *Democratic Press,* December 15, 1809.

105. The Quids' growing nationalism will be discussed later in this chapter.

106. Samuel D. Ingham to Thomas Rogers, December 27, 1816, Dreer Collection, HSP. One can get a sense of the Findlayites from the following letters: Ingham to Rogers, January 17, 1817, Dreer Collection; Christian Hutter to Rogers, February 16, 1817, Dreer Collection; Hutter to Rogers, January 25, 1818, Dreer Collection; James Hopkins to Lewis Coryell, October 8, 1818, Coryell Papers, vol. 1, 50; Samuel Preston to Coryell, September 10, 1822, Coryell Papers, vol. 1, 88; Preston to Coryell, September 24, 1822, Coryell Papers, vol. 1, 91; White and Hazard Company to Coryell, November 22, 1822, Coryell Papers, vol. 1, 92; Preston to Coryell, September 14, 1823, Coryell Papers, vol. 1, 100; Jacob Wagener to Coryell, February 15, 1824, Coryell Papers, vol. 1, 110; R. Fisher to Coryell, December 25, 1824, Coryell Papers, vol. 1, 118; Hutter to Rogers, January 22, 1825, Dreer Collection; Ingham to James Buchanan, James Buchanan Papers, roll 1; William Findlay to Coryell, March 18, 1824, Society Collection; Findlay to Coryell, Coryell Papers, vol. 1, 114; and Preston to Coryell, Coryell Papers, vol. 1, 113; all in HSP.

107. *Aurora,* February 7, 1810.

108. John Steele to Michael Leib, March 15, 1811, Society Collection, HSP.

109. Snyder's veto was reprinted in the *Democratic Press,* October 29, 1818.

110. Simon Snyder to John Binns, August 30, 1819, Society Collection, HSP.

111. Binns, *Recollections of the Life of John Binns,* 232–234.

112. See the comments about Leiper in the *Freeman's Journal,* June 18, 1805. For Leiper's involvement in the rechartering of the national bank, see Alexander J. Dallas to the Initial Subscribers of the Second Bank of the United States, April 25, 1816, Uselma Clark Smith Collection, HSP. For Leiper's alliance with the Snyderites, see *Democratic Press,* June 8, 1819.

113. John Taylor to Thomas Leiper, February 1, 1820, Kane Family Letters, HSP.

114. Undated Petition of Thomas Leiper, Society Miscellaneous Collection, HSP.

115. On this theme of unquestioned commitment to developmental policies in Pennsylvania after 1815, see Larson, *Internal Improvement*, 80–91.

116. Richard Rush to Alexander J. Dallas, July 5, 1814, Lewis Biddle Collection; Rush to Dallas, October 5, 1814, Alexander J. Dallas Papers, George Mifflin Dallas Collection, both in HSP.

117. Charles Jared Ingersoll to Alexander J. Dallas, September 30, 1814; Ingersoll to Dallas, December 31, 1815, Charles Jared Ingersoll Collection, box 4, file 2, both in HSP.

118. Alexander J. Dallas to William Jones, September 30, 1814, William Jones Papers, Uselma Clark Smith Collection, HSP. For Madison's similar thinking regarding the constitutionality of the second Bank of the United States, see James H. Read, *Power versus Liberty: Madison, Hamilton, Wilson, and Jefferson* (Charlottesville: University Press of Virginia, 2000).

119. Alexander J. Dallas to William Jones, September 30, 1814, William Jones Papers, Uselma Clark Smith Collection, HSP.

120. A good discussion of the policies and political economy of the National Republicans is Charles Sellers, *The Market Revolution: Jacksonian America, 1815–1846* (Oxford: Oxford University Press, 1991), chaps. 2–3. For a discussion of the psychological impulses that influenced the National Republicans, see Stephen Watts, *The Republic Reborn: War and the Making of Liberal America, 1790–1820* (Baltimore: Johns Hopkins University Press, 1987).

121. One can see Carey's influence as both a writer and a policy consultant in the following letters: Bird, Hopkins, and Whiting to Matthew Carey, April 17, 1811, Lee and Febiger Collection; Richard Rush to Matthew Carey, February 8, 1817, Lee and Febiger Collection; Jonathan Roberts to Carey, December 9, 1816, Matthew Carey Papers, Edward Carey Gardiner Collection; Walter Franklin to Carey, October 25, 1819, Matthew Carey Correspondence, Edward Carey Gardiner Collection, vol. 1, no.71; William Paterson to Carey, May 15, 1819, Matthew Carey Papers, Edward Carey Gardiner Collection; Richard Powall to Carey, December 11, 1819, Matthew Carey Papers, Edward Carey Gardiner Collection; and Josiah Randall to Carey, January 31, 1820, Matthew Carey Papers, Edward Carey Gardiner Collection; all in HSP. See also Edward C. Carder II, "The Birth of a Political Economist: Matthew Carey and the Recharter Fight of 1810–1811," *Pennsylvania History* 33 (1966): 271–288.

122. List's essays are reprinted in Margaret E. Hirst, *Life of Friedrich List and Selections from His Writings* (London, 1909). His letters on political economy were addressed to Charles Jared Ingersoll, vice president of Cary's Pennsylvania Society for the Promotion of Manufactures. Though they would come to disagree about who should implement the policies (Snyderites became Jacksonians, and Quids moved toward National Republicanism and eventually the Whig Party), they broadly agreed about the nation's future. For List, see also Joseph Dorfman, *The Economic Mind in American Civilization, 1606–1865* (New York: Viking, 1946), 2:575–584.

123. John C. Calhoun to Charles Jared Ingersoll, April 10, 1816, December 14, 1817, Charles Jared Ingersoll Collection, HSP; Henry Clay to William Jones, October 16, 1816, December 17, 1816, January 2, 8, 12, 1817, March 7, 1817, and August 2, 1817, William Jones Papers, Uselma Clark Smith Collection, HSP.

124. *Democratic Press,* January 16, 1816.

125. Most recently by Sellers in *Market Revolution,* chap. 3.

126. Murray N. Rothbard, *The Panic of 1819: Reactions and Policies* (New York: Columbia University Press, 1962), chap. 1.

127. For a good discussion of this economic climate, see Sellers, *Market Revolution,* chap. 4.

128. William Jones to Alexander J. Dallas, February 27, 1816, Alexander J. Dallas Papers, George Mifflin Dallas Collection, HSP.

129. Bray Hammond, *Banks and Politics in America from the Revolution to the Civil War* (Princeton, N.J.: Princeton University Press, 1957), 251–285, esp. 254.

130. On the panic of 1819, see Rothbard, *Panic of 1819;* Hammond, *Banks and Politics in America,* chap. 10; Sellers, *Market Revolution,* chaps. 4–5; Samuel Rezneck, *Business Depressions and Financial Panics: Essays in American Business and Economic History* (New York: Greenwood Press, 1968), chap. 3; and David J. Lehman, "Explaining Hard Times: Political Economy and the Panic of 1819 in Philadelphia" (Ph.D. diss., UCLA, 1992).

131. Sellers, *Market Revolution,* chap. 5; *Democratic Press,* August 20, 1819.

132. For early opposition to the Bank of the United States, see *Aurora,* January 29, 1807.

133. For these positions, see Phillips, *William Duane,* 473–475.

134. For Duane's stance in the legislature, see Rothbard, *Panic of 1819,* chaps. 3–5.

135. The *Democratic Press* denounced Simpson, who used the pseudonym Brutus, on May 6, 9, 11, 12, 16, 21, 22, 23, 25, 27, 29, November 20, 1818, 26, 1819, January 14 and 19, 1820.

136. Findlay and his supporters earned their sobriquet by keeping appointments all in the family.

137. *Democratic Press,* December 4, 1818; January 20 and December 1, 1820.

138. *Democratic Press,* May 24, 1819.

139. *Democratic Press,* July 26, 1819.

140. *Democratic Press,* August 20, 1819.

141. *Democratic Press,* April 18 and 22, 1820.

142. The essays by Carey's organization appeared in the *Democratic Press,* April 23, 24, May 3, 7, 15, 20, 25, and 26, 1819.

143. *Democratic Press,* May 31, 1819.

144. Rothbard, *Panic of 1819,* chap. 3.

145. Philip S. Foner, *History of the American Labor Movement in the United States: From Colonial Times to the Founding of the American Federation of Labor* (New York: International Publishers, 1947), 565.

146. For the connection of Simpson and Thackera to the Philadelphia Democrats, see *Aurora,* May 15, 1806; *Democratic Press,* October 23, 1820. For evidence that the Philadelphia Democrats were Pennsylvania's first Jacksonians, and indeed the first Jackson supporters in the North, see Kim T. Phillips, "Democrats of the Old School in the Era of Good Feelings," *Pennsylvania Magazine of History and Biography* 95 (1971): 363–382; and Phillips, "William Duane, Philadelphia's Democrats, and the Origins of Modern Politics," *Pennsylvania Magazine of History and Biography* 101 (1977): 365–387.

147. For a fine narrative of these events, see Philip Shriver Klein, *Pennsylvania Politics, 1817–1832: A Game without Rules* (Harrisburg: Pennsylvania Historical and Museum Commission, 1940).

148. The letter is confusing and is possibly the result of a faulty memory. The corrupt bargain was first alleged in 1825, and Crawford had been disabled by a stroke in 1824. The letter is used here to show that future leading Jacksonians such as Ingersoll did not include Jackson in their calculations in 1824 and were not part of the movement that delivered Pennsylvania to him.

149. Charles Jared Ingersoll to Richard Rush, February 1823, Charles Jared Ingersoll Collection; Ingersoll to S. B. Davis, December 11, 1830, Charles Jared Ingersoll Collection; Samuel D. Ingham to ?, November 8, 1824, Dreer Collection; Thomas Rogers to Lewis Coryell, Lewis Coryell Papers, vol. 1, 112; Samuel Preston to Coryell, Lewis Coryell Papers, vol. 1, 94; all in HSP.

150. William Darlington to Lewis Coryell, February 18, 1824, Lewis Coryell Papers, vol. 1, 109, HSP.

151. For Simpson's *Columbia Observer,* see Klein, *Pennsylvania Politics,* 60, 121.

152. For the Pennsylvania Jackson campaign of 1823–24, see M. J. Heale, *The Presidential Quest: Candidates and Images in American Political Culture, 1787–1852* (New York: Longman, 1982), 48–61; and Heale, *The Making of American Politics, 1750–1850* (New York: Longman, 1977), 140–142.

153. George Mifflin Dallas to Samuel D. Ingham, February 6, 1825, George Mifflin Dallas Collection, HSP.

154. Samuel D. Ingham to Isaac Barnard, February 7, 1826, Towshend-Lemaistre Collection under Barnard; and Samuel McKean to Ingham, March 10, 1827, Gratz Collection, case 1, box 39, both in HSP.

155. Jackson himself sided with original Jacksonians like Simpson. He accepted the Family Jacksonians only once it was clear that he could not win in Pennsylvania unless he followed their direction in that state. See Klein, *Pennsylvania Politics,* 169.

156. George Mifflin Dallas to Samuel D. Ingham, May 26, 1826, George Mifflin Dallas Collection, HSP.

157. George Mifflin Dallas to Samuel D. Ingham, February 16, 1825, George Mifflin Dallas Collection, HSP.

158. George Mifflin Dallas to Samuel D. Ingham, June 14, 1825, George Mifflin Dallas Collection, HSP.

159. Marvin Meyers, *The Jacksonian Persuasion: Politics and Belief* (Palo Alto, Calif.: Stanford University Press, 1957); Peter Temin, *The Jacksonian Economy* (New York: Norton, 1969); and Daniel Feller, *The Jacksonian Promise: America, 1815–1840* (Baltimore: Johns Hopkins University Press, 1995), esp. 118–168.

160. Quoted in Klein, *Pennsylvania Politics,* 169.

161. George Mifflin Dallas to Samuel D. Ingham, July 8, 1829; and George Mifflin Dallas to Samuel D. Ingham, December 1830, George Mifflin Dallas Collection, both in HSP.

162. Quoted in William A. Sullivan, *The Industrial Worker in Pennsylvania, 1800–1840* (Harrisburg: Pennsylvania Historical and Museum Commission, 1955), 163.

163. See Arky, "Mechanics Union of Trade Associations"; Laurie, *Working People of Philadelphia, 1800–1850,* chap. 5; and Schultz, *Republic of Labor,* chap. 7 and epilogue. For Simpson's participation in labor politics, see Edward Pessen, "The Ideology of Stephen Simpson, Upperclass Champion of the Early Philadelphia Workingmen's Movement," *Pennsylvania History* 22 (1955): 328–340.

164. Benjamin Chew Jr. to William Tilghman, November 7, 1824, William Tilghman Papers, HSP.

165. On Jackson and the anticapitalist strains in national Jacksonian politics, see Arthur M. Schlesinger Jr., *The Age of Jackson* (New York: Little, Brown, 1945); Sellers, *Market Revolution,* chaps. 9–10; Harry L. Watson, *Liberty and Power: The Politics of Jacksonian America* (New York: Hill and Wang, 1990); John Ashworth, *"Agrarians" and "Aristocrats": Party Political Ideology in the United States, 1837–1846* (Cambridge: Cambridge University Press, 1983); and Sharp, *The Jacksonians versus the Banks.*

166. For an excellent and concise statement of the anticapitalist Jacksonian impulse, see Richard B. Latner, "Preserving 'The Natural Equality of Rank and Influence': Liberalism, Republicanism, and Equality of Condition in Jacksonian Politics," in *The Culture of the Market: Historical Essays,* ed. Thomas L. Haskell and Richard F. Teichgraeber III (Cambridge: Cambridge University Press, 1993), 189–230.

167. The frustration of Pennsylvania Jacksonians over Ingham's growing isolation is clear in George Mifflin Dallas to Samuel D. Ingham, May 29, 1830; Dallas to Ingham, January 30, 1831; Dallas to Ingham, April 5, 1831; Dallas to Ingham, April 21, 1831; and Dallas to Ingham, May 8, 1831, George Mifflin Dallas Collection, all in HSP. Ingham's obituary appeared June 6, 1860, in the Philadelphia *American Gazette.* It is preserved in the Conarroe Collection, vol. 5, HSP.

168. Jonathan Roberts to Nicholas Biddle, March 7, 1836, Gratz Collection, U.S. Senators, case 2, box 2, HSP.

169. On the distinctions in states' rights theory, see George Mifflin Dallas to Samuel D. Ingham, March 15 and April 3, 1830, George Mifflin Dallas Collection, HSP. See also Richard E. Ellis, *The Union at Risk: Jacksonian Democracy, States' Rights, and the Nullification Crisis* (Oxford: Oxford University Press, 1987).

170. For the development of the second party system in Pennsylvania, see Richard P. McCormick, *The Second American Party System: Party Formation in the Jacksonian Era* (Chapel Hill: University of North Carolina Press, 1966), 134–147.

171. John Binns to John Seargent, January 17, 1834, Society Miscellaneous Collection, HSP.

172. Binns's coffin handbill is reproduced in Sean Wilentz, ed., *Major Problems in the Early Republic, 1787–1848* (Lexington, Mass.: Heath, 1992), 350. Binns produced this broadside in 1828 for the John Quincy Adams campaign. For the Whigs generally, see Daniel Walker Howe, *The Political Culture of the American Whigs* (Chicago: University of Chicago Press, 1979); and Michael F. Holt, *The Rise and Fall of the American Whig Party: Jacksonian Politics and the Onset of the Civil War* (Oxford: Oxford University Press, 1999).

173. Henry Clay to Jacob Strattan, September 13, 1842, William Jones Papers, Uselma Clark Smith Collection, HSP.

174. For challenges from within the party, see notes 165 and 166. For challenges from without, in addition to works cited previously, see Wilentz, *Chants Democratic;* Laurie, *Working People of Philadelphia, 1800–1850.*

175. David Brion Davis, "Some Themes of Counter-subversion: An Analysis of Anti-Masonic, Anti-Catholic, and Anti-Mormon Literature," *Mississippi Valley Historical Review* 47 (1960–61): 205–224; Mary P. Ryan, *Cradle of the Middle Class: The Family in Oneida County, New York, 1790–1865* (Cambridge: Cambridge University Press, 1981); Paul Johnson, *A Shopkeeper's Millennium: Society and Revivals in Rochester, New York, 1815–1837* (New York: Hill and Wang, 1978); Ronald G. Walters, *American Reformers, 1815–1860* (New York: Hill and Wang, 1978); Dale T. Knobel, *Paddy and the Republic: Ethnicity and Nationalism in Antebellum America* (Middletown, Conn.: Wesleyan University Press, 1986); and Knobel, *America for Americans: The Nativist Movement in the United States* (London: Prentice Hall, 1996).

176. Eric Foner, *Free Soil, Free Labor, Free Men: The Ideology of the Republican Party before the Civil War* (Oxford: Oxford University Press, 1971).

177. See Sharp, *The Jacksonians versus the Banks,* to view this process at work.

178. John Quincy Adams to Charles Jared Ingersoll, August 22, 1832, Charles Jared Ingersoll Correspondence, HSP.

Conclusion. History and Historiography

1. William Duane to Thomas Jefferson, October 19, 1824, *Proceedings of the Massachusetts Historical Society* 20 (1906–7), 382.

2. *The Political Writings of Thomas Jefferson* (New York: Bobbs-Merrill, 1955), 74–75.

3. For a more extensive discussion of this comparison of political economies, see Shankman, "'A New Thing on Earth.'"

4. Wood, *Radicalism of the American Revolution*, 316.

5. "Hamilton on the Louisiana Purchase: A Newly Identified Editorial from the New York *Evening Post*," *William and Mary Quarterly* 12 (1955): 268–281.

6. On this theme, see John M. Murrin, "The Jeffersonian Triumph and American Exceptionalism," *Journal of the Early Republic* 20 (2000): 1–25; Joyce Appleby, *Inheriting the Revolution: The First Generation of Americans* (Cambridge, Mass.: Harvard University Press, 2002); Wood, *Radicalism of the American Revolution*, esp. 325–369.

7. Carey's pamphlet is reprinted in Walter Hugins, ed., *The Reform Impulse, 1825–1850* (New York: Harper and Row, 1972), 79–83. The above quotation is from 79–80; all subsequent references are to this edition.

8. Ibid., 80.

9. Ibid., 82–83.

10. See Appleby, *Inheriting the Revolution*.

11. Arky, "Mechanics Union of Trade Associations"; Pessen, "Ideology of Stephen Simpson"; Wilentz, *Chants Democratic*.

12. David Montgomery, *Beyond Equality: Labor and the Radical Republicans, 1862–1872* (New York: Vintage, 1967); Montgomery, *Citizen Worker: The Experience of Workers in the United States with Democracy and the Free Market during the Nineteenth Century* (Cambridge: Cambridge University Press, 1993); Eric Foner, *Reconstruction: America's Unfinished Revolution, 1863–1877* (New York: Harper and Row, 1988), 460–511; Leon Fink, *Workingmen's Democracy: The Knights of Labor and American Politics* (Urbana: University Press of Illinois, 1983); Lawrence Goodwyn, *The Populist Moment: A Short History of the Agrarian Revolt in America* (Oxford: Oxford University Press, 1978).

13. Joyce Appleby, "The Vexed Story of Capitalism Told by American Historians," *Journal of the Early Republic* 21 (2001): 1–18, quotation on 18.

14. Pocock, *Machiavellian Moment;* Murrin, "Great Inversion"; Banning, *Jeffersonian Persuasion;* Plumb, *Growth of Political Stability in England;* Kramnick, *Bolingbroke and His Circle;* Dickinson, *Bolingbroke*.

15. Watts, *Republic Reborn*.

16. Joyce Appleby, *Capitalism and a New Social Order: The Republican Vision of the 1790s* (New York: New York University Press, 1984); Appleby, *Liberalism and Republicanism in the Historical Imagination* (Cambridge, Mass.: Harvard University Press, 1992).

17. A view most famously propounded by Louis Hartz, *The Liberal Tradition in America* (New York: Harcourt Brace Jovanovich, 1955).

18. Richard Ashcraft, "Revolutionary Politics and Locke's Two Treatises of Government: Radicalism and Lockean Political Theory," *Political Theory* 8 (1980): 429–486; Emma Rothschild, *Economic Sentiments: Adam Smith, Condorcet, and the Enlightenment* (Cambridge, Mass.: Harvard University Press, 2001).

19. Lance Banning, "Jeffersonian Ideology Revisited: Liberal and Classical Ideas in the New American Republic," *William and Mary Quarterly* 43 (1986): 3–19;

Joyce Appleby, "Republicanism in Old and New Contexts," *William and Mary Quarterly* 43 (1986): 20–34.

20. James T. Kloppenberg, "The Virtues of Liberalism: Christianity, Republicanism, and Ethics in Early American Political Discourse," *Journal of American History* 74 (1987): 9–33; John M. Murrin, "Fundamental Values, the Founding Fathers, and the Constitution," in *To Form a More Perfect Union: The Critical Ideas of the Constitution*, ed. Herman Belz, Ronald Hoffman, and Peter J. Albert (Charlottesville: University Press of Virginia, 1992), 1–37; Murrin, "Escaping Perfidious Albion"; Isaac Kramnick, "The Discourse of Politics in 1787: The Constitution and Its Critics on Individualism, Community, and the State," in *To Form a More Perfect Union*, 166–216.

21. To a certain extent they were different from the Virginians, particularly the most stringent ideologues such as John Taylor and John Randolph, because the conditions of the Middle Atlantic region made them so, something John Ashworth noted some time ago. See John Ashworth, "The Jeffersonians: Classical Republicans or Liberal Capitalists?" *Journal of American Studies* 18 (1984): 425–435.

22. Appleby, *Capitalism and a New Social Order*, 9.

23. The inability to foresee and the anachronistic search by historians for concerns about capitalism are recurring themes in Appleby's argument that a political economy intended to expand autonomy and independence carried within it the seeds of its own destruction. For recent remarks in this vein, see Joyce Appleby, "Vexed Story of Capitalism," 14.

24. Virtually all the participants in the original debate welcomed this development, and many of them contributed to the efforts at synthesis.

25. Henretta, "Families and Farms"; Henretta, "Slow Triumph of Liberal Individualism"; Henretta, "The 'Market' in the Early Republic," 289–304; Vickers, "Competency and Competition"; Freyer, *Producers versus Capitalists*.

26. Hobbs-Pruitt, "Self-Sufficiency and the Agricultural Economy"; Rothenberg, *From Market Places to Market Economy;* Lemon, *Best Poor Man's Country;* Simler, "Tenancy in Colonial Pennsylvania"; Simler, "Landless Worker"; Simler and Clemens, "The 'Best Poor Man's Country' in 1783."

27. Merrill, "Putting 'Capitalism' in Its Place"; Merrill, "The Anti-capitalist Origins of the United States"; Merrill and Wilentz, "The Key of Liberty"; and introduction to *The Key of Liberty: The Life and Democratic Writings of William Manning "A Laborer," 1747–1814* (Cambridge, Mass.: Harvard University Press, 1993).

28. This devotion to the market cannot be doubted with publication of Larson's *Internal Improvement*.

29. Robert Heilbronner, *The Nature and Logic of Capitalism* (New York: Norton, 1985). See also Ellen Meiksins Wood, *The Pristine Culture of Capitalism: A Historical Essay on Old Regimes and Modern States* (London: Verso, 1991); and Maurice Dobb, *Studies in the Development of Capitalism* (London: Routledge, 1946). Dobb

of course was a significant twentieth-century Marxist, and Wood is a neo-Marxist. Heilbronner is not a Marxist. But all benefited from the tradition of Marxist thought and from Karl Marx's *Capital: A Critical Analysis of Capitalist Production*, esp. vol. 1, pt. 8.

30. Wood, "Interest and Disinterestedness"; Gordon S. Wood, "The Enemy Is Us: Democratic Capitalism in the Early Republic," *Journal of the Early Republic* 16 (1996): 293–308; Wood, "Inventing American Capitalism," *New York Review of Books* 41 (1994): 44–49; Wood, *Radicalism of the American Revolution;* Appleby, *Inheriting the Revolution.*

31. See Barbara Clark Smith, "The Adequate Revolution," and Michael Zuckerman, "Rhetoric, Reality, and the Revolution: The Genteel Radicalism of Gordon Wood," in "Forum: How Revolutionary Was the Revolution? A Discussion of Gordon S. Wood's *The Radicalism of the American Revolution*," *William and Mary Quarterly* 51 (1994): 684–692, 693–702.

Index

Adams, Abigail, 65
Adams, John, 63, 66
  constitutional thought of, 13, 23
  and election of 1800, 71
  and Fries Rebellion, 68–69
  and the XYZ affair, 65
Adams, John Quincy, 85, 215, 224
Agrarian law, 6, 8, 193, 232
Alexandria, Virginia, 162
Alien and Sedition Acts, 40, 66, 70, 84
Allegheny County, Pennsylvania, 57,
  153
American Revolution, 240
  consequences of, 18, 24, 42
  and Pennsylvania, 23
  Philadelphia Democrats' views of,
    76–77, 79
  and the Whiskey Rebellion, 57
American System, 207, 223, 227–228
Ames, Fisher, 12, 32–33, 36, 228
Anti-Federalist Party, 23–24, 56
Anti-Masons, 220
Appleby, Joyce, 233, 238–240, 243
  capitalism discussed by, 236–237
  and republicanism-liberalism debate,
    234–235
Arbitration
  endorsed by the Philadelphia
    Democrats, 88
  endorsed by the Snyderites, 94
  and the $100 Act, 127

opposed by the Quids, 99, 112, 121
philosophical differences provoked
  by, 128
Articles of Confederation, 28, 34
  and agrarian law, 193
  and the Alien and Sedition Acts, 67
  and arbitration, 88, 99, 172
  and *Commonwealth v. Pullis*, 161, 165
  decline of, 187, 217
  and democracy, 72, 80, 81–84, 87,
    156–157, 194
  denounces Hugh Henry
    Brackenridge, 131
  denounces Thomas McKean, 121
  and impeachment of Samuel Chase,
    85–86
  and John Binns, 173
  opposes Alexander Hamilton, 44
  opposes Federalist Party, 48, 71
  opposes Jay Treaty, 61
  opposes Society for Establishing
    Useful Manufactures, 43
  and origins of tyranny, 75–79
  and political economy, 110, 114, 119,
    192
  and the Snyderites, 174, 177–178,
    202
  supports constitutional convention,
    134–135
  and Thomas Passmore, 101
  William Duane's arrival at, 69–70

287